CONTENTS

Roch the wind in the clear day's daw-in',
Blaws the cloods heelster gowdy ow'r the bay,
But there's mair nor a roch wind blawin'
Through the great glen o' the warld the day.
It's a thocht that will gar oot rottans –
A' they rogues that gang gallus fresh and gay –
Tak' the road an' seek ither loanins
For their ill ploys tae sport an' play.

Nae mair will the bonnie callants
Mairch tae war, when oor braggarts crousely craw,
Nor wee weans frae pit-heid an' clachan
Mourn the ships sailin' doon the Broomielaw.
Broken families in lands we've herriet
Will curse Scotland the Brave nae mair, nae mair;
Black an' white, ane til ither mairriet
Mak' the vile barracks o' their maisters bare.

O come all ye at hame wi' freedom,
Never heed whit the hoodies croak for doom;
In your hoose a' the bairns o' Adam
Can find breid, barley bree an' painted room.
When Maclean meets wi's freens in Springburn
A' the roses an' geans will turn tae bloom,
And a black boy frae yont Nyanga
Dings the fell gallows o' the burghers doon.

Hamish Henderson
The Freedom Come All Ye
[Reproduced by permission]

THE BAIRNS O' ADAM

The story of the STUC

Keith Aitken

Polygon
Edinburgh

In memory of my father

First published by
Polygon
22 George Square
Edinburgh
EH8 9LF

Set in Meridien by
Palimpsest Book Production Limited,
Polmont, Stirlingshire

Printed and bound in Great Britain by
Cromwell Press, Broughton Gifford,
Melksham, Wiltshire

ISBN 0 7486 6200 6

A CIP record is available for this title

GLOSSARY

AUTHOR'S NOTE

One of the labour movement's less endearing traditions is to generate acronyms (and adopt other people's) in huge abundance, and to alter them every few years like the cyphers of a secret service computer. Wherever possible in the text, I have avoided their use and sought alternatives which, I hope, provide limpidity at occasional cost to accuracy. For example, I have usually referred to 'the engineers' rather than to the AUEW, AEU, AEEU or any of the other alphabetical compounds by which their union has been known down the years. It has not always proved practical to avoid these formulations, however, although I have generally used the title in full at least once before falling back on initials. The following glossary constitutes a quick guide to the principle ingredients in the alphabet soup.

ACAS	Advisory, Conciliation & Arbitration Service
AEEU	Amalgamated Electrical and Engineering Union
AEU	Amalgamated Engineering Union
AUEW	Amalgamated Union of Engineering Workers
BS(C)	British Steel (Corporation)
BSP	British Socialist Party
CBI	Confederation of British Industry
CLWC	Clyde Labour Withholding Committee
CND	Campaign for Nuclear Disarmament
CPGB	Communist Party of Great Britain
CPRS	Central Policy Review Staff
CSA	Campaign for a Scottish Assembly
CSEU	Confederation of Shipbuilding & Engineering Unions (*aka* the Confed)
CWC	Clyde Workers Committee
DEA	Department of Economic Affairs
EEC, EU	Euriopean Economic Community, European Union
EEF	Engineering Employers' Federation
EIS	Educational Institute of Scotland
GFTU	General Federation of Trades Unions
HIDB	Highland & Islands Development Board
IBM	International Business Machines
ICFTU	International Confederation of Free Trade Unions
ILP	Independent Labour Party
IMF	International Monetary Fund

LEC	Local Enterprise Company
LiS	Locate in Scotland
LRC	Labour Representation Committee
MFGB	Miners' Federation of Great Britain
NATO	North Atlantic Treaty Organisation
NCB	National Coal Board
NEC	(Labour Party) National Executive Committee
NGA	National Graphical Association
NHS	National Health Service
NMM	National Minority Movement
NUM	National Union of Mineworkers
NUS	National Union of Seamen
NUSM	National Union of Scottish Mineworkers
MUWM	National Unemployed Workers' Movement
OECD	Organisation of Economic Co-operation & Development
OMS	Organisation for the Maintenance of Supplies
OPEC	Organisation of Petroleum Exporting Countries
PR	Proportional Representation
PSBR	Public Sector Borrowing Requirement
SCDI	Scottish Council Development & Industry
SCPS	Society of Civil & Public Servants
SCWT	Scottish Council for Women's Trades
SDA	Scottish Development Agency
SDC	Scottish Development Council
SDF	Social Democratic Federation
SDP	Social Democratic Party
SEC	Scottish Economic Committee
SE(P)C	Scottish Economic (Planning) Council
SET	Selective Employment Tax
S/HIE	Scottish/Highlands & Islands Enterprise
SHRA	Scottish Home Rule Association
SLP	Scottish Labour Party
SNP	Scottish National Party
SOGAT	Society of Graphical & Allied Trades
SSEB	South of Scotland Electricity Board
STB	Scottish Tourist Board
STO	Supply and Transport Organisation
STUC	Scottish Trades Union Congress
SWPEC	Scottish Workers' Parliamentary Elections Committee
SWRC	Scottish Workers' Representation Committee
TINA	There Is No Alternative
TINALEA	This Is Not A Legally Enforceable Agreement
TGWU	Transport & General Workers' Union
TUC	Trades Union Congress
UCATT	Union of Construction, Allied Trades & Technicians
UCS	Upper Clyde Shipbuilders
UDM	Union of Democratic Mineworkers
UMS	United Mineworkers of Scotland
VAT	Value Added Tax

FOREWORD

When considering how best to celebrate the centenary of the Scottish Trades Union Congress, the STUC General Council was keen both to celebrate one hundred years of achievement in the industrial, social and economic life of Scotland, and to reflect our wider role in Scottish civic and public affairs.

Since its inception, a fundamental plank of STUC policy has been to improve the quality of life of all its members and of the Scottish people. The STUC's fight for full employment, better working and living conditions, free education, better housing and social services, along with peace in the world and international understanding have all aimed at improving the conditions within which the culture of our people develops. This holistic approach to trade unionism is at the heart of our philosophy and has conditioned our approach to involvement in all aspects of Scotland's society.

Of equal importance to us in celebrating our centenary, however, was the need to look to the future – a future embracing a directly elected and powerful Scottish Parliament with gender equality. This radical concept for democratic and representative equality was first pioneered by the STUC and has been vigorously campaigned for as an integral part of our campaigning work as a member of the Scottish Constitutional Convention. We intend to play our part in shaping the future in which the Scottish economy grows, develops and brings more people into secure and adequately paid employment and a future in which the STUC and Scottish trade unions contribute to the development of democratic trade unionism throughout the United Kingdom.

These twin themes of celebrating our history and looking to the future underpin all our activities during our centenary year. As the millennium approaches and we begin our second century it seemed an appropriate time to look at both the past and present situation of the trade union movement in Scotland. We were determined that we should not have a hagiography; rather we sought an informed yet independent biographer as chronicler of the STUC story.

I was therefore delighted when Keith Aitken expressed enthusiasm for the project. He has the virtue of having served his time as a member of that now dying breed – the industrial correspondent – and is widely respected as a journalist and broadcaster. So we put our archives into Keith's hands and let him get on with it unhindered. The result is a lively and readable history which takes us up to the present day. The conclusions are those of the author and not necessarily those of the STUC, but it is none the worse a book for that.

Campbell Christie
General Secretary, Scottish Trades Union Congress

INTRODUCTION

Occasions which simultaneously involve trade unionists, journalists and alcohol have a way of deteriorating inexorably into barbed banter. In December 1987 I was coming to the end of a three-year spell as Labour Correspondent of the *Scotsman*, and was preparing to leave the paper's Fleet Street office to come home to Edinburgh as Industrial Editor. One of my last social engagements in London was to attend the annual Christmas press reception given by the TUC in the general secretary's rooms at Congress House. Midway through a pleasantly raucous evening, I found myself cornered by the amiable bulk of Norman Willis. 'I hear you're going back to Scotland,' he said, in tones of mock amazement. 'What the hell do you want to go back to Scotland for?' Before I could reply, a colleague from a London paper chipped in: 'Because they've still got a labour movement up there, Norm.'

Willis, a most likeable man and rather an under-rated TUC general secretary, responded with digital brevity. But there was an element of truth in the crack, and one which I was often asked about by sincerely perplexed English colleagues. Why was it, in a period when the TUC could no longer get past the policeman on the gates of Downing Street, that the STUC still seemed to command a privileged prominence in the public life of Scotland? Why did every deputation which came south include, if it did not begin with, the STUC? Why, after eight years of Margaret Thatcher, and with the 'enterprise culture' at its gaudy height, did Scots still turn instinctively to organised labour as their vehicle of choice for conveying almost every conceivable type of grievance? Why were they so preoccupied with the melancholy imagery of industrial decline as a totem of national injustice? What was it about the Scots? What was it

1

about the STUC? Writing this book was an attempt to find some answers.

What emerged was a story which intersected with most of the developments that have shaped Scotland over the past century, which is perhaps one answer of sorts in itself. Sometimes the intersection was a glancing one. I hope I have resisted the temptation, all too beguiling for the intrigued chronicler, to put his subject in the goalmouth when it was actually watching from the stand. More often than might have been expected, though, the STUC was indeed to be found somewhere in the thick of the action and not always in circumstances which bore any too obvious a relevance to its nominal purpose of representing the interests of people at work. Diffidence has never been a conspicuous STUC failing.

Almost anywhere you care to look in the last hundred years of Scotland's history you can find the STUC's fingerprints. One of the arguments to be found in this book is that the STUC has been, almost from its inception, much more significant politically than it has been industrially: that it has often played a motive part in influencing public policy, but relatively rarely in affecting the outcome of industrial issues. This is not a popular argument with trade unionists. I stand by it none the less, though with the important provision that it requires a broader definition of politics than the familiar burlesque of the parties and their leaders. It is as a voice in public debate that the STUC has excelled over the past hundred years, a distinctive voice, sometimes a courageous one, and one that stubbornly refuses to be ignored. It was Campbell Christie's boast during the bleak years of the 1980s that the labour movement traditions which the STUC embodies were woven into the fabric of Scottish society. He could not have meant that Scottish trade unionism had been any less afflicted than English by the legislative onslaught of Margaret Thatcher, by the debilitating growth in unemployment, or by the employer ascendancy which ensued. Rather, I take him to have meant that Scots continued to expect their trade union movement to be involved in the public life of the nation, and continued to listen with some respect to what it had to say. The late Conservative minister, Sir Alex Fletcher, once complained that a stranger venturing north of the border for the first time would swiftly conclude that the spokesman for Scotland was called the STUC. The STUC, of course, bristled with pride. That is what I mean by politics.

I was therefore attracted by the idea of setting the STUC's story in a broad context: of recounting a century of history from the perspective of the STUC, rather than a century of STUC history. The advantage of this approach was that it helped turn the disparate activities of a busy organisation into a tale, rather than a bundle of minutes. The disadvantage was that detail sometimes had to give way to narrative, and a lot of difficult decisions needed to be made about what to omit. I have tried hard to ensure that selection has not meant distortion. In that sense, I suppose the book is primarily a work of journalism. Certainly, it is the work of a journalist, rather than of a historian.

We had better be clear what else the book is, and what it is not. First, it is an authorised history, but not an indentured one. It was written at the suggestion, and with the co-operation, of the STUC, and I hope that they will judge it a worthy contribution to their centenary celebrations. But, as was agreed and maintained from the outset, they have exercised no control whatsoever over its form, its content, or its conclusions, with some of which I expect them to disagree. They neither saw, nor asked to see, the manuscript ahead of its submission to the publishers. I record that fact stubbornly, though with gratitude. I was honoured that they should have approached me to undertake the task. That they so readily accepted my insistence on complete editorial licence, particularly given my sometimes critical coverage of their affairs as a journalist, stands greatly to their credit. It follows, of course, that the responsibility for everything the book has got wrong is mine and mine alone.

Second, this is not a work of scholarship. Many excellent studies of the Scottish labour movement by distinguished authorities are already in publication, and reading them has been one of the great pleasures of writing this volume. In particular, I must acknowledge my debt to Angela Tuckett's painstaking account of the STUC's first 80 years, which provided a consistently useful framework for my own researches. A list of the principal texts consulted appears at the back of this book, and the serious student is respectfully directed to them. The present work does not aspire to rival their learning. It sets out with the much humbler objective of trying to tell a good story in as interesting a way as it can. It owes that mission to the distinct preference of both the STUC and the author. From our earliest discussions, the STUC made it clear that they hoped the book would be an accessible and readable history, rather than an exhaustive or erudite one. My publishers readily agreed. And so did I.

First and foremost, then, I must express sincere thanks to the officers, staff and affiliates of the Scottish Trades Union Congress for the help, encouragement and trust they extended to me during the preparation of this book. They answered many awkward questions, and asked very few back. My personal honours list begins with Audrey Canning, the STUC librarian, whose prodigious knowledge is matched by generosity on equivalent scale. I took ruthless advantage of both, and can honestly say that without Audrey's wise advice, and her uncomplaining readiness to track down information for me, this book would have taken twice as long to complete or, more probably, never have been completed at all. Audrey, thank you. Emphatic thanks are likewise due to Mary Picken, the STUC officer most closely involved with the project from inception to completion, whose confidence and enthusiasm about the book were always at their greatest when my own were flagging. A mutual taste for malicious gossip and draught ale was a bonus. Archie Fairley, co-ordinator of the STUC's centenary celebrations, was an energetic arrival on the scene towards the end of the project, lending fresh momentum when I needed it most. Campbell Christie, Bill Speirs, Richard Leonard, Ronnie McDonald and Grahame Smith chipped in many useful suggestions while tactfully refraining from pressing me on whether I had taken them up: as they can now see, I usually did. Along with distinguished former staffers like Jim Craigen and Doug Harrison, they helped guide me through that mistiest of times, the recent past. My fellow conscripts on the STUC Centenary Committee were touchingly content to take my word for it that everything was going just fine. Without exception, the staff at Middleton House treated me with great kindness and good humour – but then, they always have. A communal word of thanks, too, to the numerous and necessarily anonymous trade unionists, journalists, politicians and others who provided me with information along the way. As a result of some of it, the sex lives of several individuals who feature in the text are now an open book to me. Happily, it is not this book.

When the project was first under discussion, Arnold Kemp, then editor of the *Herald*, very generously offered free run of his paper's excellent picture archive. No less handsomely, his successor, George McKechnie, honoured the undertaking when told of it many months later, and most of the photographs which enhance this volume are the splendid consequence. My thanks to them both. Thanks too to Jim Seaton, editor of the *Scotsman* and one of my oldest friends in the business, for continuing to extend the courtesy of the North Bridge cuttings library to me after I had resigned to go freelance, an act of treachery which he shows no sign of forgiving. The library staff there, like the library staff on every newspaper, perform daily acts of unsung heroism without which the ignorance of journalists would be cruelly exposed. I gladly record my belated thanks for that, and my more timely gratitude for their unfailing helpfulness while I was researching this book.

The title comes, of course, from Hamish Henderson's inspirational anthem, *The Freedom Come All Ye*. I am grateful to him for granting me permission both to pinch the line, and to reproduce the lyric. He was probably right to forbid me to anglicise 'o'' into 'of' in my title. Marion Sinclair at Polygon was a model of gently supportive tolerance, exuding a patient calm about the project which I appreciated all the more for its being entirely unjustified. Lastly, I owe perhaps the biggest debt of all to the three formidable women in my life – wife Chris, daughter Cara, and mother May – for putting up with two years of grumpy preoccupation during those fragments of my time to which they are usually entitled to lay claim. Chris read the manuscript with a perceptive eye, undertook all manner of practical chores at which she knew I would be useless, and above all supplied her infallible sense, support and love, without which I would never accomplish anything.

CHAPTER ONE

WHYS AND WHEREFORES

We might start by debunking a minor myth. It is sometimes recounted in STUC circles, with understandable pride, that the first general secretary was a woman; and that so ahead of its time was this innovation, and such an exceptional woman was she, that she eventually demitted office because of her altruistic perception that the new organisation would be taken more seriously with a man at its helm.

This story is true in every sense except the strictly literal. Margaret Harding Irwin was indeed a quite remarkable woman: shrewd, determined and visionary. Until her resignation in 1900, she was secretary to the parliamentary committee (as the general council was called before 1923). She did step down, in part at least, because of a belief, to which she held doggedly true from the first, that for the STUC to be led by a woman in its formative years 'might be somewhat prejudicial to its interests' (as she told the first meeting of the parliamentary committee). Legend is also fully justified in according her foremost credit for the organisational zeal which turned an ill-sorted collection of variously disgruntled trade groups into the makings of a coherent trades union congress. No less importantly, it is also true that women played, certainly for the time, a disproportionately significant part in the founding of the Scottish Trades Union Congress; and that concern for the rights of women at work was, from the outset, an STUC pre-occupation. So it remains.

All that is really wrong with the story is that Margaret Irwin was not the first holder of the secretary's post. That honour fell, albeit briefly, to a factory inspector, Andrew Ballantyne, who represented, oddly enough, the National Federal Council for Scotland for Women's Trades. He had, like Irwin (who represented the Glasgow Council for Women's Trades) played a prominent part in the provisional committee formed in 1896 to prepare the ground for the establishment, a year later, of the STUC. But of his performance as general secretary history records little, beyond the fact that his employers, the Home Office, got to hear of his election and immediately ordered him to desist. Ballantyne protested that he could see nothing in civil service regulations to debar him from the post, but to no avail. Less than two months after taking office, Ballantyne resigned. He would return fleetingly, and unhappily, to the STUC story eight years later, when his appointment as manager of the Glasgow Public Houses Trust signally failed to endear him either to the movement's formidable temperance wing or to those who knew Glasgow publicans for notoriously illiberal employers. Meanwhile Irwin, who had previously declined an invitation to chair the parliamentary committee, agreed reluctantly to take Ballantyne's place as secretary, while insisting with characteristic firmness that her appointment must remain interim.

It is hard, fairness to the untested Ballantyne notwithstanding, to regard these circumstances as anything other than a stroke of great good fortune for the fledgling congress. Irwin, despite her vaguely middle-class origins (born in 1857, she was the daughter of a Broughty Ferry ship's captain), possessed an unrivalled knowledge of Scottish industrial organisation. It derived from her tenure as secretary to the Scottish Council for Women's Trades and to the Women's Protective and Provident League, a pioneering quasi-union for women formed in England in 1874. In an age when acquaintance tended to be local, her contacts throughout the Scottish unions were an invaluable aid to the provisional committee. But, from the sketchy accounts available, it is plain that Irwin's contribution was a great deal more than the merely logistical. What emerges is the compelling impression of a woman possessed of iron principles and a like will to pursue them. Her work in promoting union federation ran in parallel with an enduring commitment to the suffragist cause, and she skilfully piloted a suffrage motion through the first STUC congress. She was for several years secretary of the Glasgow and West of Scotland Association for Women's Suffrage, and continued to serve on its executive until 1907 – long after her formal association with the STUC had ended. She saw the two causes as tightly intertwined, and made frequent speeches to trade union meetings about the extent to which the exploitation of unorganised female labour was being used to drive down male earnings. The remedy she prescribed was for women to join unions, and for unions to make strenuous effort to recruit women. Margaret Irwin was, in summation, exactly what was needed to bring purposeful cohesion to the fractious diversity of early trade unionism. At the end of the STUC's first year, the president, John Keir, closed the 1898 Aberdeen congress with a handsome tribute to Irwin, of whom 'more than any man or woman in the country, [is] due the position of the Scottish trades unionists assembled there as a Congress.' With that contemporary judgement ringing in the ears, it is right to follow the convention of beginning the STUC story with Margaret Harding Irwin.

More important than the question of who, though, is the question of why. The STUC did not pioneer uncharted territory. The TUC had been established for almost thirty years by the time the STUC came into existence, and while the TUC's London base undoubtedly lent it a remoteness to Scottish trade unionists, it was not foreign to them. It had held its annual congress in Glasgow as recently as 1892 and in Dundee in 1889, and would meet in Edinburgh – its sixth congress in Scotland – a mere six months before the STUC's founding congress of 1897. Its publications circulated widely in Scotland. In fact, the first ever national (meaning British) conference of trade unions had been convened at the behest of Glasgow Trades Council in 1864, four years before a similar initiative by Manchester Trades Council gave birth to the TUC. Nor was Scotland the first territorial breakaway from the TUC. The Irish had gone their own way in 1894, dissatisfied at the level of interest shown in matters Hibernian by the TUC.

Though there were at that time dozens of purely Scottish trade unions, many Scots workers already belonged to unions constituted, to varying degrees, on a UK basis. The Amalgamated Society of Engineers, ancestor of today's AEEU, had been centrally organised under an elected national leadership since 1851. Even the Scottish miners, ever renowned for their feisty independence of mind, had been steadily drawn into a national body that had begun as far back as 1841 (as the grandly-titled Miners' Association of Great Britain and Ireland) and had gained momentum from 1889 as the Miners' Federation of Great Britain, forerunner of the National Union of Mineworkers. This duality would, and does, lead to a certain constitutional tangle in the lines of authority and loyalty to which Scottish trade unionists are attached. It also would, and does, lead to periodic asperity between Glasgow and London, though relations now proceed placidly enough – most of the time – on a working understanding that nobody really wants to make an issue of the matter. Things were not always quite so congenial.

The primary cause of the 1897 split (though neither the STUC nor the TUC acknowledged it in those terms) was an issue too easily dismissed now as arcane and archaic: the status of trades councils. To understand why this was important to Scots trade unionists then, and why it is still held important now, we need to look at the structure of industry in the last decades of the nineteenth century, and at the maturing politics of socialism. What becomes clear is that the trades councils were less a *casus belli* in their own right than the totem for a whole range of factors which played differently in Scotland from elsewhere. These differences, rather than the trades councils themselves, are what remain pertinent today.

After more than a century of convergence, the economic interests of Scotland and England began to differentiate – diverge would be too strong a verb – in the last quarter of the nineteenth century. The structure of industrial ownership, and of the labour market, had started to change quite rapidly, and would do so at still greater pace in the decades ahead. Victorian prosperity had run into a decade-long recession from around 1875, aggravated north of the border by the collapse of the City of Glasgow Bank which took many Scottish businesses with it. The downturn impacted particularly on the heavy industries of which Scotland, even then, had a disproportionate share. As would always prove the case, depression stunted trade union development. But, from the mid-1880s onwards, the impetus of rearmament and recovery brought a rapid revival in the fortune of the shipyards and of their allied industries. In Scotland, there was a burgeoning demand for unskilled and semi-skilled labour, much of which was drawn into a trade union movement hitherto dominated by the rather staid, conservative would be another word, craft associations. At the same time, the great family dynasties which were to dominate Scottish industry well into the twentieth century – the Stephens, Finlays, Tennants, Colvilles, Lithgows, Murrays and their like –

were drawing closer to each other, and to similar dynasties in the south.

These linkages, often achieved through judicious marriages or interlocking directorships, were conceived primarily as a means of defending vulnerable markets rather than of strategic rationalisation. There was little conscious attempt to replicate the sophisticated corporate amalgamations being actively promoted by the banks in the emergent industrial economies of the US and continental Europe, a failure that would, after the First World War, cost Scotland dear. It was a forgivable complacency, though ultimately a telling one. Trade was booming, powered by the shipbuilding might of the Clyde and the opportunities of empire. Only later did the want of innovative mass production methods and transnational marketing techniques become apparent.

Nevertheless, the linkages did produce a growing tendency to merger, and therefore to more centralised industrial ownership. Employers also began to join forces to combat growing workforce truculence. A winter of conflict in 1895–96 over pay in the engineering trades, during the course of which more than 7,000 workers on the Clyde were locked out, culminated in the formation of an engineering employers' federation covering Clydeside, Belfast and the Northern England shipyards. It made consequent sense for the craft unions to follow this pattern and to join up into national unions capable of addressing nationally-constituted employers. They were also rather devoted to the idea of protecting the dignity and differentials of their trades against the incursions of mechanisation and the swelling army of lesser-skilled and less expensive labour that stood ranged behind it. Jealousies between crafts, but more particularly between the skilled and the semi- or unskilled, became a potent source of dissension within the fledgling labour movement. It was a tension enthusiastically encouraged by employers, who from the early days of industrialisation, had recognised the advantages of dividing labour into ever more intricate tiers of demarcation. This both discouraged employee solidarity and provided a way of holding on to the best skilled workers. New production processes accentuated the sub-division, as Adam Smith had foretold more than a century earlier. The recourse of a ready pool of unskilled labour, largely non-unionised, also suited the employers' purposes admirably.

These industrial differentials began to be mirrored in a new urban class structure. The unskilled, semi-skilled, craftsmen, artisans, foremen, clerks and the rest stood apart from each other, and not just in the workplace. They were also distinguished by dress, speech, manner, housing and by what we would now call lifestyle. An austere work ethic, sponsored by a stern Kirk which also dispensed such poor relief as was available, translated these rankings into a moral scale, running from respectable to disreputable. The influx of unskilled Irish labour, affiliated to a quite different Church, did nothing to encourage proletarian cohesion.

Such distinctions remain visible in Scotland's social geography today. In the latter half of the nineteenth century, they were stark. The urban peasantry of the heavy industries were as different from the douce craftsmen as yokels from the gentry. Scotland had a lot of them, too. Immigration from Ireland began as early as the late eighteenth century. By 1892, a third of Scottish trade union members, twice the proportion in England, worked in heavy industry. They lived in cramped, insanitary, jerry-built tenement housing; had limited use for the learning the 1872 Education Act offered them; spoke in accents made loud and harsh by the need to prevail against noisy machinery; ate terribly, drank voraciously, bred copiously, died young and were conveniently replaced by fresh inflows from the glens and from Ireland. The 1841 Census reveals the impressive statistic that the average Scot was then imbibing six times the annual spirits intake of his English counterpart. Life expectancy in Glasgow by the late nineteenth century was 30 years, 16 below the UK average. As late as the eve of the First World War, nearly two-thirds of the city's population lived in homes with two or fewer rooms, and almost fifteen per cent of children died before their first birthday.

The trades councils afforded a tribune for the least advantaged workers, and in Scotland they seem to have shown particular and early enthusiasm for extending trade unionism to unskilled labour. Accordingly, they began to become an irritant to some of the national craft unions. Included among the least advantaged were women, to whom the trades councils offered a welcome denied by many craft unions. Margaret Irwin was, inevitably, a prominent voice in arguing that the distinctive nature of women's work in Scotland lent force to the case for a Scottish focus to trade unionism. In 1892–93, when the Royal Commission on Labour produced the first systematic account of working conditions in Scotland, Irwin served as a member of a sub-commission inquiring into women's employment, particularly homeworking. But while concern for women's issues has been a distinctive and abiding trait from the STUC's earliest days, it would be wrong to ascribe too potent a role in the founding to prototype feminism. At the 1897 congress, Irwin was one of only two women among the 73 delegates, even though four delegates represented organisations of women workers.

It would also be wrong to see the trades councils solely as the rallying point for the *sans culottes* of the labour movement. By no means all the craft unions engaged in national mergers: 30 of the 45 unions which affiliated to the STUC in its inaugural year organised only in Scotland, and some more locally still. By the same token, there is persuasive evidence that the 'new unionism,' the more socialist-inclined agitation conventionally correlated with organisation of unskilled labour, had its followers in the craft unions too. It is too easily forgotten that the expansion of heavy industry created new crafts – and new craft unions – as well as employing the unskilled in unprecedented numbers. In all, there were something over 100 Scottish unions in existence at the time. In an age when travel was still a tortuous business, the trades council provided a much more convenient forum of association than any London-based federation could have done, and also one in which the smaller unions could punch their weight. The councils came, therefore, to assume rather greater significance in Scotland than elsewhere, though they were an important focus for union activity throughout Victorian Britain.

An argument is still sometimes heard among Scots trade unionists over whether the break with the TUC arose out of a wish more effectively to represent purely Scottish concerns, or whether it was because the TUC had decided to exclude the grassroots voice articulated through the trades councils. The answer is probably a bit of both, in the sense that the two motivations were inseparable. Prior to the foundation of the STUC, the trades councils were really the only tribune for expressing a trade union view on Scottish issues. They were also the only practical collective recourse for the smaller Scottish unions, which could not afford to send delegates to London. Indeed, many of the Scottish trades councils had never bothered attending, or affiliating to, the TUC. Lastly, at a time when pay and conditions were still mostly bargained locally, and were therefore more sharply differentiated between districts than between Scotland and England, the trades councils were more natural co-ordinating units for activism than they would later become. From 1885, their numbers grew rapidly. In half a dozen years, new councils formed in Dundee, Port Glasgow, Govan, Motherwell, Greenock, Arbroath, Falkirk, Kirkcaldy and Paisley. By 1903, Glasgow Trades Council alone registered more than 250 delegates, representing almost as many organisations.

One necessary piece of context to bear in mind when considering these factors, though, is the extent to which trade unionism remained at the time a decidedly minority pursuit among the Scottish workforce. The Scottish press, which would be heartily hostile to the STUC for many years, rarely passed up the opportunity to reassure readers that the leaders of the Scottish movement were unrepresentative of Scottish labour both numerically and – or so it was asserted – politically. Delegates to the STUC's founding congress represented just 40,871 members, though a year later affiliations had risen above 100,000. But it was the eve of the First World War before trade unionism anywhere in Britain began to take on the mantle of a mass movement: the 1896 TUC in Edinburgh recorded just over a million affiliated members. In Scotland, geographical remoteness and population dispersal worked as further obstacles to collective organisation, and it would be the 1930s before levels of union membership caught up with those of England. Sidney and Beatrice Webb calculated that in 1892 two-thirds of Scottish trade unionists worked in or around Glasgow, though the Webbs are not always an unimpeachable source.

The other necessary context is politics. Once again, we should be wary of gilded legend. To see the national unions as complacent drones of a gradualist bourgeois politics, and the trades councils as radical hornets, is not wholly wrong, but it is a hefty simplification. Certainly, social ambition was not unknown among skilled craftsmen. Their unions were often better noted for exclusivity than for fraternal solidarity towards comrades in adversity, and their horizons were somewhat narrowly defined in consequence. The earlier brands of radical thought, like Chartism, had left relatively little mark on industrial Scotland despite the venerable tradition of the urban mob, though some of Chartism's moral heritage would be preserved in the early trade union movement.

But in the middle years of the nineteenth century, industrial action passed largely out of fashion as a tactic for advancing the cause of labour, and it would remain a bone of tactical contention among trade union leaders well into the twentieth century.

Radicalism, in mid-Victorian Scotland, was more likely to be found among the middle classes than the workers, in the east of the country than the west, and in rural rather than urban grievance. Land reform, particularly in the 1880s, awoke the Highland radical instinct, to the unlikely extent of provoking riots on Skye in 1882. The moment was ripe. A Liberal Party flying apart over the Third Reform Bill and Irish Home Rule was uncommonly susceptible to persuasion. A newly-formed Crofters' Party, fired by the rhetoric of a visiting US radical, Henry George, seized four Highland seats and won the ever-romantic heart of the Liberal left. An embattled Gladstone, already facing the departure of many right-wingers in protest at Irish Home Rule, settled swiftly; the 1886 Crofters' Holdings Act established heritable secure tenure and a rents tribunal. The Crofters' Party rejoined the Liberals in 1892, encouraged by the departure in high dudgeon of several eminent lairds for the Tories.

It is possible that the tide of migrants coming into the cities to take up unskilled jobs brought some of the rural radical instinct with them, though it would have been confronted with a set of issues quite different from those it was used to addressing. Certainly, the trades councils had taken an early and keen interest in politics beyond the workplace, and particularly in issues of parliamentary reform. From the 1860s, both the Glasgow and Edinburgh councils were prominent in that cause, which gradually broadened out to embrace questions like the laws governing master–servant relations and the criminalisation of picketing. Home rule, interestingly enough, was then seen as rather a fey, literary preoccupation, most common among Tories; only in the closing years of the century did it begin to attract radical support. Overall, though, there is persuasive evidence that even those most directly involved in forging Scottish socialism were much less influenced by Marx than by Carlyle, Burns and, perhaps above all, the Bible. Keir Hardie, it is easily forgotten, was for a time as interested in promoting temperance as in advancing the cause of workers' rights, and harboured to the end of his days an odd streak of nostalgic, pastoral moralism which led him once to assert that socialism was 'not a system of economics.' His co-founder of the Independent Labour Party, Bruce Glasier, was later to write that he doubted whether Hardie had ever read Marx. Among early trade unionists in Scotland, even in the mills and the mines, socialism or anything much resembling it was far from universal.

None the less, by the 1880s, a fundamental debate about tactics and doctrine had begun to rage within the working class movement. Trade unionism did not arrange itself any more neatly on either side of the argument then than it would now. As Tony Crosland remarked in *The Future of Socialism*, many ingredients went into the making of British socialism. Their numerous permutations have often made for curdled politics.

The main focus for debate was whether the interests of the industrial working class, and of trade unionists, should continue to be pursued in the context of the Liberal Party or by means of independent representation. Several trade unionists had become MPs since the extensions of the franchise in 1868 and 1884. One such was Alexander McDonald, leader of the Lanarkshire miners and later of the miners' National Association, though he represented an English constituency, North Staffordshire. At its extremes, the debate ranged between those who thought that the proper concern of trades unions was confined to industry and that political activity should amount to little more than lobbying political parties on an issue-by-issue basis; and those who held that society needed fundamental change rather than gradual reform, and were beginning to become attached to an explorative Marxian agenda. Neither camp was notably united. Among the radicals, some favoured independent parliamentary representation while others saw little gain in a parliamentary approach and argued instead for a more syndicalist strategy, based on prodigies of education, organisation and industrial disruption. Though the Liberal Party had, under and after Gladstone, moved steadily leftwards from its earlier dalliance with the *laissez-faire* notions of Cobden and Bright's Manchester school, its enduring status as a party of capital marched ever less in step with the growth of working class activism. The hope that the two sides of industry could resolve their differences in gentlemanly fashion grew increasingly forlorn. Writing his memoirs half a century later, the sometime Liberal leader, Viscount Samuel, recalled

Keir Hardie's 1892 election as Independent Labour MP in West Ham as a turning point after which 'it was easy to foresee that this movement might grow and spread.'

Hardie was the first politician of national moment to rise to prominence through Scottish trade unionism. His crusading sense of injustice is sometimes traced to a boyhood dismissal for poor timekeeping from a Lanarkshire bakery, but it was in the coalfields of Lanarkshire and Ayrshire that he honed a taste and talent for agitation. His activities swiftly curtailed his mining career (and those of his four brothers: the coal-owners were taking no chances) and he was blacklisted throughout the industry. He turned to radical journalism and was adopted by the Ayrshire miners as their secretary, in which capacity he devotedly created as much trouble as he could contrive. He conceived his parliamentary ambitions early, but was rejected as a candidate by the Liberal Party. Next, he was to stand as an independent Labour candidate in a mid-Lanark by-election, to disappointing effect. That no doubt helped foment his conviction that the working class movement needed its own political vehicle. In 1887 he stunned the Swansea TUC congress with a devastating attack on Henry Broadhurst, secretary to the TUC parliamentary committee, in which he accused Broadhurst, and by extension the craft unions, of class collaboration and much else besides. The following year, with the support of a number of leading lights from the trades councils, he formed the Scottish Parliamentary Labour Party, more often known simply as the Scottish Labour Party, and equipped it with an ambitious programme which included abolishing the House of Lords and all hereditary office, widespread nationalisation, free education for all, and some fearsome constraints on the sale of liquor. It was far from an instant success, but it did provide a stimulus for socialists to pursue their arguments all the more forcibly in the trades councils, some of which had begun to sponsor candidates in municipal and parliamentary elections. The radical agenda became increasingly evident in the activities of the Scottish trades councils; Glasgow, for example, mounted an impressive demonstration against the House of Lords in 1884, and ostentatiously boycotted Victoria's jubilee celebrations in 1887 as a protest against poverty. Shrewdly, in turn, the new political force took the lead in promoting industrial causes, like shorter hours for railwaymen and miners, that were dear to the hearts of the trades councils. Eventually, in March 1892, socialists from the councils were to form their own party, the inelegantly-named Scottish United Trades Council Independent Labour Party. It was subsumed, a year later, into the Independent Labour Party which had been formed, at Hardie's prime instigation, in Bradford. In 1895 the SLP also merged with the ILP.

The tensions of this turbulent period were fast growing intolerable for the TUC. Its annual congress was becoming more of a battleground with each year that passed. The 1894 gathering reached inspired heights of acrimony, as substantive business fell victim to vituperative political in-fighting. Resolved to avoid a repeat performance, the TUC instructed its parliamentary committee to draw up changes to standing orders ahead of the following year's congress in Cardiff. There followed one of those perverse combinations of vindictiveness, lack of forethought and sheer ineptitude that so often provide history with its turning points. Had the committee confined itself to recasting the standing orders so as merely to proscribe the most conspicuous socialist troublemakers, the resentment – in Scotland, as elsewhere – might very well have proved containable. But it went beyond its brief, and came up with proposals that were, not just in retrospect, bound to generate uproar. First, the new rules excluded not only socialists but all trades council delegates. That in itself was probably catalyst enough to create the backlash that followed, but there was more. The revised standing orders were not to be presented for approval at the Cardiff congress, but brought into force ahead of it. They introduced new block vote procedures, whereby unions were allocated a share of the vote determined by affiliated membership rather than delegation numbers. The effect, which has endured, was to ensure that a very small number of national union leaderships held sway over policy-making. It was not the finest hour of TUC democracy.

A stark chronology of what ensued in Scotland conveys a sense of grim resolve. At the Cardiff congress, Scottish delegates featured prominently in an attempt spearheaded by the London Trades Council to overturn the amended standing orders, but the new-style card vote defeated the motion by a margin of almost two to one. Ironically, given what was to follow, it was a Scot who was put up by the craft unions to propose the reforms. John Burns – erstwhile dockers' leader, pioneer of the 'new trade unionism,' once known as 'The Man with the Red Flag' –

was already embarked on an ideological journey that eventually saw him end up a Liberal Cabinet minister and little regarded for it by the socialists he had left behind him. As William Diack would regretfully recall nearly half a century later in his charming memoir of Aberdeen trades unionism, this was a man who was 'never ashamed to tell the world that his mother at one time scrubbed floors in the east end of Aberdeen.'

There was talk of London Trades Council calling a national trades council conference in protest, but it came to nothing and defiance in England soon began to ebb. In Scotland, by contrast, a chilly resolve swiftly hardened. The week after Cardiff, Aberdeen called a conference of the Scottish trades councils to discuss the rule changes. Diack, who attended the relevant meeting of the Aberdeen executive, once more takes up the story: 'I do not think the members of the Aberdeen Trades Council were unduly perturbed over the decision of the congress. We may have thought that Mr Burns and his friends were a trifle narrow in their views, but we did not sit down and "holler" over the new decree of Cardiff. Not a bit of it.' For all their stoicism, though, the invitation was duly agreed and the conference took place that September in Dundee. Wholly unbeguiled by the prospect of the following year's TUC being held in Edinburgh, the councils attending voted both to keep up the pressure for readmission and to participate in the London Trades Council's protest conference. They were not, Diack remembers, 'disposed to take the Cardiff ukase lying down.' London, however, had by now thought better of its petulance, and decided instead merely to press for slightly less restrictive rules for affiliation to the TUC.

Undeflected, the Scots held a second trades council conference of their own the following April, in Falkirk. This time, 13 councils supported the initiative, compared with the six who had attended in Aberdeen. Now the talk was openly of a Scotland-wide federation of labour, with doubt focused mainly on whether it should consist only of the trades councils or, as the unanimously-approved motion eventually decided, become 'a trade union conference for Scotland.' A provisional committee, with Irwin as its secretary, was formed and by the time the TUC met in Edinburgh in September 1896, the committee had a federal scheme ready for consideration. It was a pragmatic blueprint, concerned mostly to construct mechanisms for resolving inter-union disputes and promoting co-operation. Crucially, though, it also proposed that membership would extend beyond Scottish-based organisations: unions headquartered in England would be entitled to affiliate their Scottish members to the new federation. In that thoughtful codicil lay much of the future strength of the STUC.

The provisional committee's aim had been to devise a scheme modest enough to secure widespread acceptance, but the meeting which convened in Edinburgh to consider it decided to venture further, and to hold an annual Scottish Trades Union Congress. An enlarged provisional committee set to work afresh, and on 25 March 1897 the founding congress of the STUC met in Glasgow's Berkeley Hall.

Once more, some context is required. If the TUC's motivation for casting out the trades councils had been primarily political, the reasons for the Scottish response were less thoroughly so. The radical impetus was certainly part of the driving force behind events in Scotland, but only part. A number of purely practical considerations pointed in the same direction. Without representation through the trades councils, the TUC was beyond the reach and the purse of most of the Scottish unions. The decision for a Scotland-wide structure was less a choice between rival centres, than between a new centre or none at all. In earlier times, the trades councils themselves might have served as an adequate focus for the smaller unions, but the employers had begun to set up their own federations to co-ordinate employment policy and combat a growing incidence of industrial unrest. A response in like kind made obvious sense. Inter-union bickering had become an increasingly pressing problem in a number of recent Scottish disputes, notably those involving the miners and the ironworkers; some tribunal for resolving these rivalries was a pressing need. By the same token, though, the imperative of solidarity was one of the few considerations arguing against the establishment of a Scotland-wide trades union centre to rival the TUC. The new STUC would have to take care to complement rather than to divide loyalties.

Contemporary accounts of the discussions leading up to the Berkeley Hall congress show a clear understanding of the dangers of schism. Hardie (though later attracted to the idea, never fully realised, of a trades federation) was among those who argued forcibly against the suggestion of an alternative British TUC based on the trades councils. He was undoubtedly right to do so; not only would the rivalry have been ruthlessly exploited by employers, but it would also have set large union against small and strong against weak. The need to avoid such division unquestionably prompted the defining realisation that the new STUC would have to find some way of accommodating unions based furth of Scotland. Lastly, there was (though it should not be overstated) a whiff of nationalism in the air. At the Falkirk meeting, John Mallinson of the Edinburgh Trades Council talked of the 'Saxon' domination of the TUC; while at the Berkeley Hall itself the STUC's first president, Duncan McPherson of the tinplate workers, offered the oft-quoted justification for the new congress that 'there are many questions which affect Scotland particularly to which our English fellow trade unionists cannot be expected to devote the necessary time and attention they deserve.' He leavened this observation with the diplomatic reflection that the STUC, far from setting itself up in opposition to the TUC, was really just lightening the TUC's burden by sparing it the chore of involving itself in matters Caledonian. It was a kindly thought, though not one, it may be surmised, which was anywhere taken too seriously, least of all in London. It did, however, establish a style of courteous but stubborn resolve in which the STUC would, in the coming century, often perform to virtuoso standard.

The Berkeley Hall congress was a distinctly workmanlike gathering, perhaps in conscious contrast to the mayhem of recent TUCs (to which mayhem some of the Scots there gathered had diligently contributed). 'To have passed eight resolutions and dealt with a quarrel between two trade unions would in general be counted a good morning's work,' remarked the *Scotsman* after the second day's proceedings. 'But on resuming after luncheon yesterday the Scottish Trade Unions [sic] Congress were so dissatisfied with their performance that they proceeded to pass a resolution restricting the length of time allowed for speeches to ten minutes for the proposer and five minutes for subsequent speakers . . . when so ordered, the proceedings of a Congress of the kind become a sort of liturgy of labour, in which someone advances a proposition and the people say "Amen" . . . the usual Collectivist resolution was passed without much demur.'

Diack recalls a certain disappointment at the level of inaugural affiliation, and at the initial reluctance of some older unions to associate themselves with the new body. Little of that, though, is apparent in the minutes. Congress addressed itself to a succession of deeply practical issues: how to beef up industrial accident inquiries; whether the labour department of the Board of Trade should establish separate Scottish representation; tenancy law; jury entitlements; factory inspectorates; a score of industrial matters large and small. Margaret Irwin successfully proposed a motion calling for women's suffrage which, she acknowledged, she had favoured as 'more a pious opinion than a living faith' prior to her involvement with the labour movement. Typically, she seems to have couched her argument astutely, in terms calculated to defuse any male unease it might have aroused. There was humour – to laughter, she admitted that she would 'rather organise ten men's unions that one women's union' – but also a shrewd appeal to both principle and pragmatism. Women ought, as of right, to take up any work suitable for them, she said; what was wrong was that they should take men's work at half male earnings. Congress was duly won over.

Some of the motions adopted a political tone of markedly stronger timbre than might have been countenanced by the TUC. One briskly declared that workers would never gain full value for their labour (nor strikes ever become redundant) until the land, mines, machinery and industrial capital were owned by the state for the people. This was opposed, noted the *Scotsman* joyfully, by a member of the Musicians Union concerned to prevent his fiddle becoming the property of the state. The gathering also culminated in the election of a parliamentary committee on which ILP members held no fewer than eight out of the fourteen seats. But, reading accounts of proceedings now, one is more readily struck by the dignity of the occasion, and by the high moral tone adopted by many of those present. A case in point was McPherson himself, who included in his presidential address an appeal to temperance and morality that must have had Keir Hardie, present as a guest on the platform with his wife, nodding in saintly endorsement.

Not everyone was quite so impressed. The *Scotsman*, going through one of its high libertarian interludes, grudgingly accounted the congress relatively businesslike and moderate, but deplored the tone of collectivism (ever since a bitter strike by production staff in the 1870s, the *Scotsman* had been non-union, and it would later be the only British daily to publish right through the General

Strike). Having earlier applauded the TUC's disaffiliation of the trades councils as a clipping of socialist wings, the paper now thought Duncan McPherson's speech uninspiring and inconsequential, and likened trade unionists in general to barrel organs, ever playing the same tunes. The *Glasgow Herald* thought the STUC a pleasant contrast with the rancorous incoherence of the TUC, but was likewise dismayed by its collectivism.

Nor was the TUC thrilled by the development. Since the STUC was not setting out to poach affiliations from it, outright resistance was inappropriate: those Scottish unions which had been affiliated to the TUC prior to 1897 generally remained so. On the other hand, the emergent politics of the new organisation – evident in the role played in its formation by ILP leaders like Hardie, George Carson (who would succeed Irwin as secretary), and Robert Smillie of the miners (who chaired the parliamentary committee in its first year) – were plainly different from those prevalent in the still Liberal-inclined TUC. Actually the ILP, with its powerful emphasis on working class unity, was a potent force in ensuring that the formation of the STUC did not develop into schism. The TUC response, then as sometimes still, might best be described as watchful forbearance. If there was no retaliation, neither was there much of a welcome. The second STUC congress, in Aberdeen, had benefit of a telegram from the TUC wishing it all the best. But a motion later that year at the TUC congress in Bristol, proposing fraternal contacts with the STUC and Irish TUC, was heavily defeated, not least because of fears that the Welsh might be poised to follow the same route (they never did, though they did raise the idea with an unimpressed TUC in 1987). There was to be no formal recognition of the STUC from the TUC until the end of the First World War, and persistently touchy relations ever after. Even now, it is not uncommon to hear TUC grandees express the view, privately of course, that the STUC is really just an overblown trades council.

It was not just within the labour movement that the new congress had trouble getting itself taken seriously. Government, while exercised enough to dislodge the unhappy Ballantyne, took some persuading that the new upstart was worthy of its time. The STUC actually secured its first formal meeting with government after just seven months, in October 1897, when a deputation saw the Secretary for Scotland and the Lord Advocate to argue that fatal accident inquiries in Scotland should carry the same weight in investigating workplace fatalities as did English coroners' courts. But the Secretary for Scotland was in those days a junior post. The Scottish Office was only twelve years in existence, and it would be nearly thirty years before its chief minister attained full Secretary of State rank. Smillie and Peter Ross of Govan Trades Council also took themselves to London in the course of the year to lobby for the establishment of a separate Scottish labour branch within the Board of Trade. They managed to beard the President of the Board of Trade, Lord Balfour, who told them squarely that he did not want to cede this responsibility to the Secretary for Scotland, and that the Secretary for Scotland did not want it. The minister with the most important industrial powers, the Home Secretary, bluntly spurned an approach from the parliamentary committee, observing with elegant imperial hauteur that no useful purpose would be served by engaging in discussion with 'a separate deputation of persons resident in Scotland.' He would relent a year later, in November 1898, and see Irwin and Smillie in London, but to little gain for the STUC. The 1898 congress in Aberdeen railed, bitterly but impotently, against what delegates variously described as 'a deliberate affront to the organised trades of Scotland' and 'a violation of ordinary courtesy.' It would be many years before the STUC could begin to expect ministerial access as of right, and it soon came to wonder whether trying to arrange such meetings, though initially identified as a prime function, was not a wasteful diversion of time and resources from industrial objectives. Nor was the TUC, which did have regular meetings with ministers, remotely helpful in gaining its Scottish colleagues a hearing. Indeed, Irwin complained to the parliamentary committee that TUC deputations had, perhaps unsurprisingly, signally failed to raise Scottish policy decisions with ministers.

The new congress certainly had its hands full enough with industrial matters, even if the limitations of its relevance to them were also swiftly evident. Unrest was growing in a number of industries. In the summer of 1897, the recently-federated engineering employers responded to localised strikes in London by launching a nationwide lock-out, almost certainly with the prime objective of undermining moves toward a more unified union structure within the industry. The lockout ended in union defeat after seven months. It would cast a very long shadow within the trades union movement. At one level, it encouraged those who favoured the parliamentary route to change, by raising doubts about the ability of workers to mount effective industrial action against determined employers. That case, at its most apprehensive, was to be heard in John Keir's presidential address to the 1898 congress in Aberdeen, when he declared: 'A strike should only be resorted to after every other means of adjustment has failed, and I am confident that this opinion is largely shared by the trades unionists of the present day, whom I believe regard strikes as a misspent force of trades unionism.' But the lockout equally hardened the radicals' conviction that nothing short of a wholesale overthrow of the capitalist system could deliver industrial justice. One delegate dismissively described Parliament as 'one of the biggest fads in this country.' Yet the experience also raised acute questions about the effectiveness of the STUC and its London counterpart, both of which retained the principal objective of lobbying Parliament for legislative reform and lacked the capacity to offer much more than rhetorical support to workers in dispute.

These arguments permeated every debate at Aberdeen, and defied simple resolution. If the engineers, one of the biggest and richest of all the unions, could be crushed beneath concerted employer malevolence, smaller unions need hardly expect to do better. The swelling ranks of the unemployed offered employers every temptation to try to drive down wages, and to divide and rule. What was needed was to move forward from the fragmented agitation that had marked most union endeavour hitherto. As John Keir put it: 'It must now be perfectly apparent to all that if the workers of this country are going to hold their own with the ever-increasing combinations of the employers in all and every branch of industry, they must, and that without delay, awake to the necessity of meeting federation with federation.' Unity, in other words, was strength, but what form should it take?

The parliamentary committee had a proposal to table, distilled from a special TUC conference the previous month, for a mutual fund to subsidise strike pay. It was moved, with a conspicuous lack of enthusiasm, by Bob Smillie, who said little to deflect the impression that it was a poor compromise in the face of rampant union rivalry. The proposal failed even to find a seconder. Instead, on Hardie's encouragement, delegates endorsed a vision which the ILP had been promoting for some time for a trades federation capable of providing mutual financial support in dispute, though they thought better of setting strike pay (as some advocated) at the level of the weekly wage. The parliamentary committee was charged with pursuing this idea, known as the 'Clarion Scheme,' with the TUC, and did so, but little came of it. Many of the bigger unions remained suspicious and, though a General Federation of Trades Unions was formed the following winter, it failed to develop into either an effective mutual support network or, as some had hoped, a federal parliament for the British labour movement.

The STUC, though, was growing steadily into its own aspiration to become the parliament of the movement in Scotland. Already, by its second congress, it was gazing around expansively at all manner of social and political issues which surrounded it, and presuming to take a view of them. The two most contentious resolutions passed at Aberdeen had only tangential connection with workplace adversity. They concerned education, whereby delegates voted in favour of compulsory free schooling of children to the age of 14 and free dinners for them into the bargain. The *Scotsman* was outraged, fulminating that such notions, 'permeated with socialism,' ran counter to the self-respect of working men who had no wish to see the state subsume their role as parents. 'The Aberdeen resolution is but a half-hearted, halting, stupid proposal,' ran a sulphurous leader in the issue of 24 April, 1898. 'The Aberdeen Congressionists represent neither the principles nor the common-sense of working men, but only the greeds and the jealousies of the ignorant and discontented, and the fads of a few political sciolists.'

Robust stuff. What was seen in the offing was something which Liberal opinion plainly knew, even then, held within it the potential to transform the landscape of British society; the politicisation of labour. It would take a long time to take form. But the STUC – new, self-confident, and avowedly political from the start – consciously epitomised the distant threat. The best that Liberal commentators like the *Scotsman* could hope for was that the as yet modest affiliation roll of the STUC would keep the danger marginalised. 'A Scottish Trade Union Congress has been sitting, and talking, and resolving at Aberdeen without attracting or deserving very much attention from the general public,' began the *Scotsman* leader optimistically. 'It has, however, provided the country with some fresh reasons for believing that these Congresses do not truly represent the opinions and the solid common-sense of the great body of the men for whom they profess to speak. The organisers and orators are often clever men; almost always restless, pushing ambitious; sometimes self-seeking; sometimes mere windbags. As a rule they are not fair specimens of the industrious, shrewd, well-informed, reasonable and prudent class of workmen . . . they represent the comparatively few workmen of extreme opinions whose heads are filled with class prejudices and political delusions, and who imagine that the interests of other classes of the community are hostile to the interests of the working class.'

The STUC had undergone an awkward birth and, in several respects, a frustrating first twelve months. Yet now, just a year after its inaugural congress and with politics a growing preoccupation in its ranks, it was already starting to hear the harsh but satisfying sound of an Establishment becoming distinctly rattled.

CHAPTER TWO

TO THE AID OF THE PARTY

The STUC is sometimes described, to its public denial and private delight, as the political wing of the Labour Party in Scotland. It was a joke which found particular resonance in the 1980s and 1990s, when Labour struggled determinedly to solve the riddle of electability, while the STUC led a fulfilling existence as genial paterfamilias to Scottish protest against the new Conservatism. Quite often, the STUC has cut a policy path which Labour's Scottish high command would later cautiously tread: for example, on gender balance, proportional representation and a role for civic politics in a devolved Scotland. Indeed, the home rule cause itself was adopted (or rather, re-adopted) by the STUC in 1968, fully six years before the Labour Party, alarmed by a suddenly resurgent SNP, formally took the point. It has not, then or later, always made for congenial relationships: Willie Ross, Labour's forbidding Scottish Secretary in the Wilson governments, used to grumble irritably about the 'Scottish Trades Union Congrouse.'

Considering these matters for a previous book, I suggested that the STUC, of the Thatcher years in particular, had grown more muscular politically than industrially; that it was highly adept at appearing greater than the dwindling sum of its parts, and was essentially a protest vehicle. This was intended quite admiringly, though it was not an entirely popular analysis with the STUC hierarchy. It still seems to me to hold good. Where it was perhaps misleading was in the implication that this taste for political adventurism was a recent development.

As we have seen in the previous chapter, the STUC was forced in its very first year to confront the limitations of its influence in affecting the outcome of industrial conflict. The parameters of that influence would shift back and forth throughout the ensuing century, though they would always remain constrictive in relation to the STUC's ambitions to bring about change. Looking back from today's vantage point, it is hard to escape the conclusion that the STUC's greatest achievements have generally arisen from the political rather than the industrial side of its activities, though there is naturally room for an argument about definitions. What is certain is that politics were a preoccupation of the STUC from its very earliest days. They played a significant part in its founding, and would loom much larger as the organisation matured through its first decade. In those days, it must be acknowledged, the mission of advancing the lot of working people did not much trouble itself with distinguishing between the proper respective realms of politics and trade unionism.

Some commentators have been tempted to make quite grand claims for the part played by the STUC in the formation of what became the Labour Party. It is a question which repays a cautious approach. Certainly, in their formative years, the two wings of the labour movement had many prominent personnel in common. Certainly, the STUC set out fairly directly from its inception to help create a dedicated political vehicle for the labour cause; indeed, as we shall see, there were some who felt the STUC had served its purpose once the Labour Party was solidly in being. Certainly, too, the STUC held the ring for some of the defining discussions which shaped the party that was to emerge, and the Scots who took part in that process would bear powerful influence in the party for many years to come.

All of that adds up to a motive and creditable part played in the birth of the Labour Party. It does not quite add up to the conclusion that without the STUC there would have been no Labour Party. The impetus of history, much of it predating the STUC, insists otherwise. The London TUC, for one thing, had set up a Labour Electoral Association fully ten years before the STUC was founded, and thirteen years before the STUC convened the Scottish Workers' Parliamentary Elections Committee (SWPEC), its prototype Labour Party. Room must also be found for the inconvenient fact that, particularly prior to 1906, but also for a while thereafter, socialism in Scotland did rather badly at the polls.

As we have already seen, Keir Hardie and the ILP were to the fore in STUC counsels from the Berkeley Hall onwards.

They were not the only voices audible, however. The more rigorously Marxist (though largely middle class) Social Democratic Federation, committed to a concept of perpetual class struggle for which Hardie had absolutely no enthusiasm, had been active in Scotland since 1884. As late as 1909 it was claiming, somewhat questionably, 40 Scottish branches. In its early days it had brought into activism some of those who would later rise to eminence in the ILP: Bruce Glasier, for one; for another, the flamboyant gentleman-adventurer Robert Cunninghame-Graham, who ultimately achieved the unique hat-trick of being the founding-president of three political parties – the Scottish Labour Party in 1888 (he was a Liberal MP at the time), the National Party of Scotland in 1928, and the Scottish National Party in 1934. Though based in London, the SDF had a Scot as its leader, Henry Hyndman, and counted the supremely charismatic Govan polemicist, John Maclean, as a member. It did much to establish the hallowed tradition among British Marxist groups of splintering into shards at regular intervals. The Socialist Labour Party, a rather austere syndicalist faction which split from the SDF in Scotland in 1903, included such luminaries as James Connolly – later to face a British firing squad in Dublin Castle for his part in the Easter Rising – and the future Labour MPs Neil Maclean, John Muir and David Kirkwood. It was greatly drawn to French and US thinking which saw industry as the catalyst for political change, advocating political strikes and state ownership of industry under worker management. The SLP also specialised in withering contempt for the 'collaborationist' tendencies of the ILP. Eight years later, Victor Grayson's British Socialist Party would also split off from the SDF, in unironic pursuit of 'socialist unity.' Life in the SDF was rarely dull.

More to the immediate point, the SDF was a force alongside the ILP in the Scottish Trades Union Congress. It was particularly strong in Aberdeen, but had activists elsewhere too. They included a stalwart of the STUC's early years, the fiery Edinburgh compositor, Robert Allan. Allan, a ubiquity in Congress debates, was to become the first secretary of the SWPEC. Some 18 years later, he would follow George Carson into the post of STUC secretary, just as Carson had followed Allan as SWPEC secretary in 1902. They were to prove a durable, and at times formidable, double act.

There were other political elements also on the scene: William Morris's Socialist League, another repository for SDF dissidents;

the Webbs' Fabian Society (in one among many endearing misjudgements, the Webbs opposed the formation of the Labour Party, only recanting and joining the ILP in 1912); the Co-operative movement which, by the turn of the century, had an enviable mass membership of more than 250,000 in 200 Scottish societies. There were still some in the STUC, particularly among the craft unions, who held loyal to the Liberal or Lib–Lab ideal. The most significant of these were the miners who, with the notable exception of Robert Smillie, took until 1908 to switch their affiliation to Labour.

There were also some senior STUC figures who were distinctly uneasy about the headlong rush into party politics. They included Margaret Irwin, who warned the 1898 Congress in Aberdeen about the risks inherent in unions delegating authority to 'outside parties.' There is some evidence that this reserve may have helped accelerate Irwin's departure from the general secretaryship; what is certain is that the tide of opinion, and of events, was running against her point of view. On a motion from Allan, powerfully backed by Smillie, the Aberdeen Congress supported the estab-lishment of 'a party distinct from the two great political parties,' and agreed that unions should be asked to contribute financially to its creation and support. By the autumn of that year, ahead of parallel endeavours in the TUC, the STUC parliamentary committee under Smillie's chairmanship was embarking on the steps needed to put the decision into force.

It would prove an intricate and challenging project, and would take longer than most of those involved had hoped. The frag-mentation of the socialist cause at the time was probably less of a drawback than today's perspective makes it seem, and certainly less than it would soon become. The plurality of groups, though not without its pettinesses, reflected young ideas still being worked out as much as it reflected fractiousness. In that respect, the interplay of debate was to some extent a necessary and a constructive process. The ILP in particular was a good deal better at flights of covenanting rhetoric than at formulating cogent and detailed policy. This characteristic gained it breadth of appeal, at some cost to doctrinal momentum. The ideas, and particularly the Marxist ideas, being developed by its rivals lost something in translation into the gusty declamation of a Hardie, a Glasier or even a Ramsay MacDonald, but they did lend some policy substance to the prodigies of moralistic grievance. All the same, the challenge of channelling all this energy into a purposeful and practicable political machine, and of connecting it up to a naturally disputatious trade union movement, was daunting.

What is nowhere evident is any trace of self-doubt in the minds of those who took on the task that the STUC, though barely a year old, was the instrument with which to perform this operation. This is all the more remarkable given that both the ILP and the SDF were to differing degrees, and despite the preponderance of Scots in their leaderships, based in England – the SDF in London and the ILP in Yorkshire; or that the much more mature TUC had yet to hazard the same ambitious project in any very concerted fashion. The STUC has rarely been found lacking in self-confidence, and so it seems to have been from its infancy. Even Margaret Irwin's dogged reservations mostly concerned the wisdom, rather than the feasibility, of the mission.

In October 1898, midway between the Aberdeen and Dundee congresses, Irwin dutifully arranged a special meeting of the parliamentary committee to hear a presentation from Hardie and Glasier. The upshot was that the ILP leaders were invited to table a paper on the options for labour representation. This they did, proposing a special conference to expedite a decision. The parliamentary committee, meeting the following month, was not immediately persuaded. It decided first to test the water with a preliminary meeting, to which the Scottish Co-operative Society and the SDF would also be invited. This time it was the Co-operative Society, where the Lib–Lab tradition ran deep, which seemed least certain how to proceed, and the meeting proved difficult to arrange. Eventually, the following February, the parliamentary committee, on Carson's prompting, decided to force the pace by by-passing the Co-ops and meeting the ILP and SDF leaderships to decide whether to call a conference. The more cautious elements on the parliamentary committee insisted, however, that the meeting should be exploratory rather than executive. It took place on 4 March 1899, and agreed in principle that a conference should be held.

But unease persisted about the speed at which to proceed. The political leaderships – including Carson – wanted a conference arranged urgently, in time to coincide with the April STUC congress in Dundee. They proposed as much at the 4 March meeting. The STUC delegation, though, was divided. Margaret Irwin argued that the support of the Co-ops was worth waiting for, since it could deliver working-class votes in constituencies that Labour candidates could not hope otherwise to carry. Eventually Smillie, whose skills in the chair seem to have been formidable, came up with a compromise: the parliamentary committee would bring a motion before the Dundee congress, seeking approval for a conference later in the year. This was sufficient both to carry the meeting and to isolate Irwin. The other principal STUC doubter, John Mallinson of Edinburgh Trades Council, was persuaded to draft the congress motion (successfully moved, come April, by Carson and Allan), and by the time delegates gathered in Dundee, Mallinson had been nominated against Irwin for the secretary's post. Typically, she endorsed his candidacy, protesting as always her unwillingness to occupy the position on anything more than a temporary basis. In the event, despite the backing of several parliamentary committee members, Mallinson withdrew from the contest. It was, none the less, the beginning of the end for Margaret Irwin's secretaryship. Dundee was to be her last congress in the post.

When she stepped down the following year at Edinburgh, she attributed her decision wholly to 'the increasing claims of other work.' Certainly, she had no shortage of other commitments. But she had also spent a growing proportion of her STUC time on the losing side of policy arguments. She had enthused about conciliation boards, and condemned the strike tactic as 'uncivilised,' during a period of mounting confrontation between workers and managements. She had battled for the concept of equal franchise for women, at a time when the STUC was more concerned to see the property qualification scrapped. She had borne, somewhat unjustly, the brunt of criticism directed at the parliamentary committee for its perceived lack of zeal about the campaign for an eight-hour working day. She was caught in the middle of periodic asperity between the STUC and the Scottish Council for Women's Trades. It is also easy to believe that her middle-class articulacy and encyclopaedic knowledge of Scottish industry grated on some of those who were none too attuned to the notion of women holding senior positions, despite her evident attempts at tact. She had never been a member of a trade union, and her withdrawal from the upper ranks of the STUC (she continued to turn up, off and on, as a congress delegate) seems to have diminished not at all her enthusiasm for campaigning.

She remained secretary of the SCWT into the 1930s, long after it had ended its affiliation to STUC, and continued to turn out scrupulously-researched and precisely-written pamphlets on the conditions of working women. She was awarded the CBE in 1927, and died in her 83rd year in January 1940.

Meanwhile, on the political front, matters still dragged. A committee headed by Carson and Allan was formed to organise the special conference. A second committee worked in parallel to organise a concurrent trades council conference on the campaign for an eight-hour working day. But it took until the first weekend of the new century for the gathering finally to take place. By then, dissent was subsiding. Hardie had bluntly warned the Dundee congress that the 'missing word' in the labour cause was combination – the lack of a dedicated political capability was weakening and dividing the movement. Proper promotion of the labour interest in Parliament, he said, was being impeded by 'the want of an intelligent conception of the need for labour representation.' The measure of this failure was that a city the size of Dundee still lacked a single socialist elected to the town council. Hardie acknowledged the fears of some that withdrawal from big-party politics would leave the labour movement marginalised. But the alternative was to trust to parties whose aims were diametrically opposed to its own, since on every issue affecting the interests of the workers there was 'absolutely no difference from a socialist point of view between the front bench Liberal and the front bench Tory.' Neither, as he pointed out, did the labour cause have support anywhere in the Scottish daily press.

Ever on cue, the *Scotsman*'s leader-writer chipped in: 'Fortunately, the working classes of this country are not such fools as many of those who profess to speak for them at these congresses, and the opinion in which they hold their self-constituted representatives is probably the explanation of their unwillingness to elect them to positions of responsibility and trust . . . Labour candidates, though abundant in quantity, are evidently not of a quality which commends itself to those whose suffrages they seek. According to Mr Keir Hardie, this shows lack of intelligence on the part of the electorate. In truth, the electors are more intelligent than he knows.'

The *Scotsman* judged the socialism increasingly preached by trade unionists to be 'a singular jumble of ideas that have been partially assimilated.' But it did find room graciously to compliment the STUC on 'an energy worthy of more fitting application.'

South of the border, meanwhile, events were by now fast moving towards the same destination. In September of 1899, the TUC Congress resolved to convene a conference 'of all the co-operative, socialistic, trade union and other working class organisations' to agree 'ways and means for securing the return of an increased number of Labour members in the next Parliament.' A special joint committee of awesome diversity was appointed to tackle this project. The TUC parliamentary committee contributed four delegates – two supporters of independent labour representation and two Liberals (the TUC's talent for compromise was even then impressive). The ILP sent Keir Hardie and Ramsay MacDonald. The SDF also sent two delegates; as did the Fabians, one of them George Bernard Shaw. Against all portent, the committee proved efficient and effective. Within a very few weeks it had hammered out the parameters for the conference, and on 27 February 1900, 129 delegates from 65 trade unions and three socialist groupings met at the Memorial Hall in London's Farringdon Street to establish the Labour Representation Committee. It is this gathering which history usually credits with the foundation of the British Labour Party.

But the STUC, whether by chance or design, had got there first. By October 1899 the two sub-committees were finally ready to issue invitations to the special conference. On 2 January 1900, 226 delegates gathered in Edinburgh as the Scottish Labour Representation Conference. It was both a bigger and a wider meeting than the one which would muster the following month in Farringdon Street. The co-operative movement was in the event substantially represented, as were – inevitably – the Scottish trades councils, 16 of which sent delegates. Like the ensuing London meeting, the conference elected a representative committee, the Scottish Workers Parliamentary Elections Committee. It comprised four STUC delegates (led by Allan, who became secretary to the committee), four co-op representatives, and two each from the ILP and SDF. Unlike the London meeting, the Scottish conference also roughed out a policy agenda for the new body, which included the eight-hour day, pensions, disablement benefits, tax reform, full employment and a statutory minimum wage.

The conference cemented George Carson's reputation. Having chaired the sub-committee which set it up he – deservedly – gained much of the credit for the undoubted success of the conference. He also acted as conference secretary. In his report of its proceedings he explained, a little ponderously perhaps, the essence of the case which the STUC saw for the creation of a party to advance labour's cause: 'The parliamentary committee of the Scottish Trades Union Congress have remitted to them from the trades congress from time to time a large number of important instructions, most of them dealing with industrial legislation. In trying to have these instructions carried out, the PC have occasion to wait upon Ministers of various Departments as well as upon Members of Parliament to impress upon them the need for these matters being looked into and at the same time to urge them to give effect to the clearly expressed wishes of the organised working classes on these important points. While some small concessions have been granted, no doubt due to these representations, still it may be said in this connection that the results were out of all proportion to the time, energy and money spent by the PC in bringing them about, and there was the added disadvantage that they were conceded as favours rather than recognised as rights . . .'

Put more succinctly, the STUC had been unable on its own account to achieve the influence over public policy which its founders had intended and its membership expected. As had happened in the dignified uprising over the TUC's treatment of the trades councils, the STUC's role in the foundation of the Labour Party brought ideology and practicality into happy concurrence.

George Carson, leader of the tinplaters, followed Margaret Irwin into the STUC secretaryship after the Edinburgh congress in 1900, and would hold the post for the next 18 years. From 1902, he was simultaneously secretary of the SWPEC (and of Glasgow Trades Council). There is no denying the commitment of this bearded, twinkling man to his many beliefs, though there is persuasive evidence that he rather lacked the exceptional qualities needed to do so many onerous jobs at once, and well. What his appointment did mean was that, at leadership level at least, the union between the political and industrial wings of the movement was consolidated. But it would be some years before the assent of the membership, as voters, could be so readily delivered.

The Edinburgh congress endorsed the creation of the SWPEC with a resolve no doubt heightened by indignation at the (Tory) town council's decision to deny delegates the customary civic reception, on the grounds that the STUC had become a political organisation. Bob Smillie affected to be glad at the slight, since the congress was not gathered for recreation. The *Scotsman*, rather more convincingly, regretted that the age had passed when Smillie might have challenged the Lord Provost to a duel in the Queen's Park. Refreshed instead by the hospitality of Edinburgh Trades Council, delegates went on to debate how the project of political representation might be put on a firmer financial footing.

A motion was approved calling for MPs to be paid a salary, and for the public purse to meet candidates' election costs. But the debate had an oddly despondent air about it. The Edinburgh baker, Thomas Wilson, who was that year's STUC president, supported the idea but fretted that funding would encourage the candidacy of professional scallywags 'who, with oily tongues and elastic consciences, would reduce the cajoling of the working man to a fine art.' Mallinson, who had been put up to move the resolution, was not much more enthusiastic. He said that payment might 'perhaps' increase the number of labour representatives, adding gloomily that he was 'inclined to believe that once the workers were intelligent enough to elect the right men to Parliament, they would be intelligent enough to make a slight pecuniary sacrifice to keep them there.' Still, the motion was passed with only two of the 110 delegates dissenting. A proposal that Scottish trade unionists be recommended to contribute a penny a quarter to the cause of labour representation provoked much greater opposition, though it too was eventually agreed. John Keir of Aberdeen, moving, argued that fourpence a year was modest enough call on a worker's loyalty to the party dedicated to advance his aspirations. But there was also substantial support for an amendment, declining to specify a sum and contending that donations should be left to individual conscience rather than congress decree. Smillie was among those who favoured the purely voluntary route, significantly admitting that many of his miners remained committed to the Liberal or even the Tory cause and might thus conclude that the STUC was trying to get its hands on their money to put its own leaders into Parliament.

Neither debate rang with confidence that the new political movement, launched with such panache just three months earlier, was poised on the threshold of political success. There was a great deal of complaint about the culpable inability of working-class voters to recognise where their interests lay. It does not, in retrospect, impress as a terribly noble or attractive line of argument. On the other hand, the pessimism was to prove prescient. At the 'Khaki election' five months later, the Unionist alliance took a majority of Scottish seats at the expense of a demoralised Liberal Party, and the increasingly senile Marquis of Salisbury was returned to Downing Street with an overall majority of 134. The ILP, despite affiliating an inflated 13,000-strong membership to the SWPEC, found it lacked the funds to contest the election. The STUC, still less than united in its enthusiasm for the new labour politics, did little to help. On 23 June 1900, the parliamentary committee considered a letter from Hardie 'suggesting that in view of the nearness of a general election, a joint meeting of the parliamentary committee and the workers election committee should be held; or, if it were not possible, that a deputation might be appointed to meet with the workers election committee to discuss future action.' The parliamentary committee, however, took the matter no further. No-one seems to have noticed the irony in the next item on that day's agenda being a report from Carson of yet another refusal by ministers to receive an STUC deputation. Eventually, on 22 September with the election campaign now underway, the parliamentary committee did hold a joint meeting with the SWPEC. Carson's crisp copperplate minutes the occasion as follows: 'After a somewhat lengthy discussion, it was found that no joint working arrangement could be come to, and the meeting separated.'

Nor was the SWPEC's first serious assault on Westminster an unqualified success. Bob Smillie was put up in September 1901 as an independent miners' candidate at the North-east Lanark by-election, part funded by the STUC. Three parliamentary committee members were seconded to his campaign, commendably undeterred by a report that electioneering in Bellshill was hazardous 'owing to the rowdyism prevailing.' No less ominous was a report from one of the three, Thomas Wilson, that 'what organisation existed in the constituency was of the slimmest character.' Smillie came a respectable third. But the main effect of his candidacy was to erode the Liberal vote and let in a Unionist.

The stark truth was that the fledgling movement in Scotland, despite the collaboration between its wings, lacked organisational structure, political cohesion, and anything approximating to mass support. In Glasgow, a loose coalition of socialist groups, with the trades council to the fore, had established a bridgehead (the 'Socialist Stalwarts') in municipal politics from as early as 1889, and built modestly on it thereafter. Elsewhere, progress was minimal and unity strained. The SWPEC may have come into existence first, but it was the Labour Representation Committee in England which proved far the more effective political vehicle. In Scotland there were too many divisions in working class loyalties. The Irish community was an endemically troublesome impediment to common cause. A deep loathing had sprung up between the ILP and the priests which neither side was much inclined to try to heal, so diluting the support which the movement might have expected from unskilled and semi-skilled labour. The craft unions, meanwhile, remained largely thirled to the Liberal cause. The consequence was to weaken both the trade unions in Scotland and their capacity to mobilise electoral support behind Labour candidates. For all the ambition and bravado of its formation, the STUC had really not come all that far as a grassroots movement since Beatrice Webb confided to her diary, after the 1892 TUC in Glasgow, that 'the Scottish nature does not lend itself to combination.' The STUC of the early 1900s was, in the *Scotsman*'s cruel but perceptive judgement, 'a big phrase with a puny reality behind it.'

In the first decade of the new century, the harsh truth of that assessment began to be borne ever more forcibly on the STUC. A precocious infancy gave way, rather swiftly, to a troubled adolescence. On a growing number of fronts, the objectives of the STUC were being frustrated. A new influx of immigrant labour, this time from Poland, was being used to undercut wages in industries like gas supply, steelmaking and coal-mining, and to break strikes. Smillie put their numbers in the Lanarkshire coalfield alone at 3–4,000. The STUC and its affiliates could fulminate about that, but little more. There were strikes and lockouts taking place in almost every industry, but to little gain except hardship for the strikers and a growing incidence of inter-union strife: in 1902, for example, the STUC expelled one of its grandest affiliates, the Association of Ironmoulders of Scotland, for blacklegging during a strike by Brassmoulders at J&G Weir of Cathcart, and so had to deprive itself of a prestigious and politically-influential chairman for the year, the Ironmoulders' general secretary, Baillie James Jack MP. Worse still, 1901 brought the infamous Taff Vale case, in which the Railway Servants were successfully sued for what we now know as secondary picketing. Though the case eventually resulted in a 1906 law granting the unions immunities which held until the Thatcher legislation of the 1980s, there was a period in which it seemed open to question whether effective strike action could lawfully be called. All of that lent force to the case for both political representation and trade union unity, while simultaneously reducing the prospects of either. Instead, Carson and the general council found themselves struggling to contain a swelling tide of inter-union conflicts and demarcation disputes. The aftermath of one such saw Smillie lead all but the West Lothian miners out of the 1902 Congress at Falkirk because West Lothian had broken a strike at Polkemmet. William Muirhead of the Central Ironmoulders, who had taken Jack's place in the chair, told Congress: 'Absolute unity is the lost chord of our endeavour and, having struck it once in the morning of our movement, we seem never to be able to strike that great chord again.' Eloquent words, but not exactly pulsing with hope.

A trade union movement unable to deliver industrial unity has little chance of delivering political dynamism. The STUC began to find that its impotence made it easy to ignore at a time when it badly needed to be heard. Ministers refused to meet its deputations, or even to acknowledge its existence. The TUC in London saw ever less need to act as broker for the breakaway. In August 1900, Carson solemnly read the parliamentary committee a letter from his TUC opposite number, Sam Woods, which 'pointed out that his committee regretted the existence of sectional congresses, which they said divided the forces of Labour, weakened their influence and made them an easy prey to the capitalistic classes, and that the time had come when they should cease to exist.' All of this was taking place against the unhelpful backdrop, as we shall see, of a Boer War about which the STUC felt a disquiet that jarred with wartime popular patriotism; and of a gathering recession, which reinforced the determination of employers to drive down wage costs. Carson, in these early years of his secretaryship, was also proving a somewhat feckless leader, easily distracted from the urgent but daunting task, and sometimes giving the impression that he could achieve more through his trades council than his STUC activities. The parliamentary committee was increasingly short of funds, and of direction, its energies sapped by the need to grapple with a ceaseless tide of disputes among unions, and with an outbreak of acrimony between unions and Co-operative Society employers. Since the SWPEC was now dominated by a leading co-operator, Henry Murphy, these disputes can have done little to foster harmonious purpose between the industrial and political wings of the movement.

There was also a more serious disjuncture. Since their launch within days of each other in 1900, the SWPEC and the LRC had not enjoyed harmonious relations. Almost from the outset, the LRC, under the secretaryship of Ramsay MacDonald, saw the existence of a separate Scottish grouping as an irritant, one that needed to be absorbed if possible and neutered if not. There were periodic attempts by London either to take over the Scottish body, bag and baggage, or else to turn it into a regional satellite without policy-making powers. Though it is customary these days to view suspiciously anything of which MacDonald was in favour, the motives behind this were not merely predatory. To MacDonald and others – possibly including Hardie – the challenge of creating a national Labour Party was demanding enough without the complication of a separate party forming in Scotland. MacDonald's pragmatism, for which history reviles him, also had its positive side. He was arguably the most far-seeing strategist of the Labour Party's formative years, the necessary catalyst to transform Hardie's inspirational brand of righteous protest into a potential to govern. MacDonald perceived from an early stage that the state needed not to wither – as Marx had prescribed – but to grow strong and benevolent. It was a creed which would serve Labour well for most of the twentieth century, and it laid a powerful premium on unity. A different Labour Party in Scotland was not the way to unity.

Besides, any objective observer would have been hard-pressed to see much of a future for the SWPEC. In the harsh industrial climate of the early 1900s, few British-based unions were inclined to pay more in affiliation fees than they had to, and therefore their Scottish members were generally counted in to a single affiliation to the LRC. In the wake of Taff Vale, British unions had turned to the LRC in ever greater numbers, giving it a strength which contrasted all the more starkly with the waning prospects of the SWPEC. In 1902, the SWPEC attempted to relaunch itself with a more focused organisational structure and a new name – the Scottish Workers' Representation Committee (SWRC) – but to little avail. There was, and is, a perfectly respectable case for arguing that the distinctive characteristics of Scottish politics demand a distinctive Labour approach. Scottish politics were certainly different from those of England in the early years of the century; but not, to the SWRC's misfortune, in a way that lent appeal to Labour representation. The principal difference was a much more radical Liberal Party, which (prompted partly by a Kirk with a growing social conscience) had taken an increasing interest in the grievances of the working classes. Scottish Liberals vigorously endorsed issues like shorter working hours, or extending the responsibilities of employers towards their workforces. Still more shrewdly, they backed home rule for Ireland, thus keeping most of the Catholic vote on board. And where the Liberals controlled local government, notably in Glasgow, they proved impressive social reformers, pioneering public ownership of the municipal utilities. The Glasgow 'Stalwarts,' by now mainly ILP, fought back by focusing on the most intractable municipal issue, the city's appalling housing problem. It began to pay dividends, particularly after ILP figures like John Wheatley and Tom Johnston drew compelling analogies between the rapacity of city slum landlords and that of the Highland and Irish aristocracy. George Carson became increasingly caught up in this most emotive issue in his role as secretary to Glasgow Trades Council, ultimately provoking a rather pointed motion from Edinburgh at the 1905 STUC congress in Hawick calling for the parliamentary committee to be reconstituted to ensure that other areas besides Clydeside could play a full part in its counsels: at that stage nine of its 11 members lived on Clydeside. But there were also those, at the same time, who were starting to wonder whether the STUC would do better to limit its political ambitions to the municipal context, and leave parliamentary politics to others. For all that, the Hawick congress ended in delegates presenting the gift of £150, plus a rousing chorus of *For He's a Jolly Good Fellow*, to James Keir Hardie in recognition of his contribution to Labour politics.

In fact, Hardie knew something which no-one else in the hall did. Two years earlier, MacDonald had negotiated a secret pact with the Liberal chief whip, Herbert Gladstone, to co-operate with the Liberals in the next general election in the interests of ending two decades of virtually unbroken Tory rule. In agreed constituencies the two parties would not oppose each other, an *entente* made easier to reach by the existence at that time of twin-member constituencies. In the event, the faltering government of Arthur Balfour collapsed under the weight of its own inadequacies in December 1905, allowing the Liberal leader, Campbell-Bannerman, to form ahead of the election an interim Cabinet that was balanced enough to ensure that the deal with MacDonald could carry through into Labour support for the new government. The outcome was the Liberal landslide of January 1906, when Tory seats – including Balfour's – tumbled across the breadth of the land. It was a watershed for British politics in several respects. It broke the grip of privilege on parliamentary office: many of the new MPs were not the sons of landed gentry, but were lawyers, teachers, journalists. It also conferred a colossal majority on the new government, setting the scene for eventual conflict with a House of Lords still dominated by Tory aristocrats. Campbell-Bannerman's Liberals had 129 more seats than all the other parties combined, and on most votes could command a majority of 357. Above all, the election saw no fewer than 53 Labour members returned, 24 of them Lib–Labs allied to the Liberal Party, but 29 affiliated to the LRC. Some socialists feared that MacDonald, now the MP for Leicester, had sold his party's soul in tying its fortunes so tightly to the Liberals. But it is highly unlikely that the LRC could have made the breakthrough into parliamentary politics without the pact. More astute observers saw the influx of Labour MPs as the beginning of the end for the Liberals as a party of government.

It was also the beginning of the end for the SWRC. The MacDonald–Gladstone pact did not apply in Scotland, and the nine Labour candidates who stood had Liberal opponents. None the less, two were elected: Alexander Wilkie in Dundee and George Barnes in Glasgow. Both were well-known general secretaries of UK-based unions: Wilkie of the shipwrights, Barnes of the engineers. And both had stood under the banner, not of the SWRC, but of the LRC. The SWRC had fielded five of the nine candidates and all had done poorly, in part because they had stood mainly in mining seats and the miners still held loyal to the Liberals (as late as 1912, four years after the miners had affiliated to Labour, a Labour candidate was humiliated in mining Midlothian, gathering only enough votes to allow the Tory to squeak home ahead of the Liberal). In 1907, the SWRC became the Labour Party (Scottish section), later the Scottish Council of the Labour Party.

But 1906 was a turning point in other respects too. It was the year in which one recession ran, after the briefest of respites, into another and much more enduring economic downturn. Unemployment began to rise rapidly. Britain's imperial dominance of world trade, and the complacency it had encouraged in investment and modernisation, faced increasingly powerful challenge from continental Europe and from the US. Manufacturers sought to offset tougher international competition by raising domestic prices, embarking on belated mechanisation programmes. and driving down wage costs. Scottish industry, being disproportionately dependent on international trade, felt the squeeze disproportionately acutely. By 1908, unemployment in the Clyde shipbuilding trades was running at close to 25 per cent, more than three times the UK average. One consequence was to usher in a period of mounting industrial conflict that reached its peak in the immediate pre-war years. Glasgow Labour History Workshop has calculated the number of strikes during 1912 in west-central Scotland alone at 70. Among them was a national strike for a minimum wage by a million miners, at that time the biggest stoppage ever mounted in Britain. The employers fought back with a ruthlessness that government at first did little to discourage, and later actively reinforced. Blackleg labour was increasingly used to break strikes, as were lockouts, evictions and blacklisting. For the STUC and its affiliates, the advent of a more politically congenial government was to prove, in many respects, a sorry disappointment.

The STUC had early intimation that its own relations with Westminster were not destined to be rapidly transformed by the change of government. It nominated Bob Smillie to serve on a Royal Commission, set up by the Tories but continued by the Liberals, to look into the operation of the Poor Law and the growing problem of unemployment. The nomination was rejected, and a consequent request for a meeting with

Campbell-Bannerman refused. When Wilkie raised the issue in the Commons, he was brusquely told that the Commission was full, that the London TUC had a seat on it, and that Scots did not lack for Parliamentary influence. The new government also turned Smillie down for a place on an inquiry into the truck legislation, moving him to inform the 1906 congress in Greenock that the new government's treatment of Scottish organised labour was 'little short of a scandal.'

Other grievances swiftly gathered against the Campbell-Bannerman government. It might have put right the Taff Vale ruling, but its industrial legislation was seen by many Scots trade unionists to be reluctant, tentative and inadequately informed by any real understanding of the conditions workers faced in the factories, mines and shipyards. As the tide of industrial unrest rose, the government sanctioned ever more repressive measures against the agitators. At first police, and later troops, were used against pickets, some of whom were jailed and others beaten up. As early as 1906, the feeling was already growing that the new administration would be little different from the old in needing to be pushed every inch of the way to yield any significant advance in the lot of working people. The Greenock Congress compiled a shopping list, destined greatly to lengthen in the years ahead, of measures which delegates expected the new Labour MPs to press the government to implement. Yet the suspicion was developing in some minds that some of these MPs were growing closer to the government than to the activists whose cause they were meant to be promoting. Conversely, but simultaneously, the first whispers began to be heard of the view that the unions, having brought their movement to the maturity of Parliamentary representation, might do best to fade gracefully from the scene. Both arguments probably reflected nothing more measured than frustration at the pounding organised labour was taking in workplace disputes, but they would recur frequently over the coming years of industrial conflict. For the moment, they were confronted squarely by that year's STUC president, the Glasgow carpenter John Howden, who urged the Labour Party to 'realise the impossibility of permanently benefiting our class by merely tinkering with palliative proposals.' He condemned both the guerrilla syndicalism being promoted by the Socialist Labour Party and the 'befogged' view that Parliamentary pressure was in itself sufficient to achieve labour emancipation.

The syndicalist route was gaining in appeal, however. The effectiveness of official union structures in the face of growing lay-offs and wage-cuts was open to ever increasing scepticism, and the continued fractiousness between rival trades left unions fighting each other as well as the employers. Increasingly, industrial action was spontaneous and localised in character. This was particularly evident in sectors like transport and engineering, where union leadership was centralised and often remote. Aggrieved workers were not always prepared to postpone a response to workplace provocation while they awaited authorisation from the union executive. It was to leave a lasting legacy in the strength of the shop stewards' movement in Scotland. Come the Great War, this would find notoriety in the enduring legend of the Clyde Workers' Committee. In the shorter term it raised questions not just about the worth of national unions, but about the purpose of the STUC.

The 1908 congress came within a whisker of giving up on the STUC's aspirations to be an effective national force for change. A resolution moved by David Palmer of Aberdeen Trades Council, a parliamentary committee member and subsequently STUC president, called for the STUC to end its 'effete, expensive and obsolete' devotion to political lobbying, and reduce its activities to overseeing a structure of autonomous local organisations. The motion was actually carried, though by a narrow enough margin to allow its implications to be fudged. In large part, it reflected resentments elsewhere in Scotland at the Glasgow domination of STUC activities under Carson's leadership. But the strength of support it attracted also indicated widespread concern that national trade unionism was proving woefully irrelevant to the pressures workers were having to endure on the shopfloor.

Yet other forces current at the time continued to work for unity rather than fragmentation, and union amalgamations remained a prevalent trend. Recession was driving smaller employers out of business, or into the maws of bigger corporate predators, and a more centralised employment structure encouraged union cohesion. The number of purely Scottish unions dwindled rapidly. Between 1898 and 1911, the STUC's affiliated membership virtually doubled from 76,274 to 140,705. But the number of affiliated unions fell from 45 to 44, and the number that were Scottish-based from 30 to 22. This helped bring some respite to the STUC from the endless grind of inter-union disputes, but it also raised fresh doubts about the purpose of a distinctively Scottish trades union centre. Activists in the new amalgamated unions found purpose in working together at local level – through the trades councils – to overcome the cumbersome procedures of dealing with centralised union leaderships. They saw less gain in devoting much of their time or attention to the STUC. George Carson's own preoccupation with Glasgow Trades Council (he remained its secretary until 1912, after which time the STUC secretaryship was made a full-time post) was scarcely likely to encourage activists to trade local involvements for engagement in the national body.

There was also an increasingly heady whiff of ideology in the air. The weekly newspaper *Forward* was founded in 1906, edited with much panache by a young man who, a generation later, would become arguably the greatest Scottish Secretary of them all: Tom Johnston. Labour papers had come and gone before *Forward*, and would continue to do so in the years ahead. But few ever matched it in its ability to inspire the disparate forces of the labour movement, particularly in its Clydeside heartland. For half a century, it provided a powerful platform for Scottish socialism, reporting labour affairs with a rich mixture of dogged thoroughness and stylish agitation. Early on, Johnston himself contributed a celebrated series of abrasive essays on the aristocracy, gleefully defiling the reputations of noble families one at a time. A book of these essays, which their author later recalled as 'historically one-sided and unjust and quite unnecessarily wounding,' sold a remarkable 120,000 copies.

Though as Johnston would admit in his memoirs, the founders of *Forward* were mostly of Fabian inclination, the paper swiftly became a notable outlet for ILP views. ILP membership, not coincidentally, grew by 60 per cent between 1904 and 1908. One notable recruit was John Wheatley, the Waterford-born miner-turned-journalist, who had risen to eminence in the Irish community in the West of Scotland by arguing, to the dismay of his Church and the Liberal Party, that socialism and Catholicism were compatible. Wheatley founded the Catholic Socialist Society in 1907, and joined the ILP a year later. With the Liberal government failing to live up to its rhetoric in advancing Irish Home Rule, Wheatley and those around him fought a long, bitter, but gradually fruitful campaign to break the long-standing Liberal loyalties of the Catholic vote. Ninety years on, Labour's unshakeable hold on the politics of west-central Scotland continues to owe much to the fealty of the Catholic electorate. Meanwhile, Glasgow had also become the focus for an increasingly radical faction within the SDF, which was starting to win wider appeal through the hugely popular Marxist lectures of John Maclean. At last, the Scottish working classes were beginning to politicise.

Forward's other lasting impact on Scottish trade unionism was its enthusiastic marrying of the Scottish home rule cause to the socialist agenda. It is, then, poignant to bear in mind Johnston's confession years later that this advocacy was not entirely unconnected with the fledgling paper's frequent recourse to loans from the wealthy tanner, and nationalist stalwart, Roland Muirhead.

In 1908, the Scottish labour movement's growing disenchantment with the Liberal government gained a helpfully serviceable demon. Winston Churchill, having crossed the Commons floor from Tory to Liberal (he would retrace his steps in 1924) was found a seat in Dundee to contest. He won, with the Labour candidate, endorsed by the STUC, trailing third. It was the start of a long animosity. First as President of the Board of Trade and then, from 1910, as Home Secretary, Churchill held the two key governmental posts which the STUC aspired to influence. They found him stubbornly unresponsive. Repeatedly, he refused to meet STUC or Scottish Labour Party deputations. It was not until the eve of war that the STUC finally managed a meeting with the Home Secretary, and by then Churchill had been replaced in the post by Reginald McKenna. Churchill, meanwhile, insisted that he heard as much as he needed of labour viewpoints from the equivalent London-based bodies. With tact never high among his attributes, he further enraged the STUC by refusing one deputation on the grounds, first, that all the important unions in the STUC were also TUC affiliates, and secondly that the TUC spoke for British labour, not merely for the workers of England and Wales. Meeting, appropriately enough, in Dundee, the 1911 congress took the trouble of passing a motion expressly to inform him that the STUC and not the TUC was the body empowered to represent the union movement in Scotland. By then, Churchill had earned himself much broader labour enmity by sending troops to police a colliery lock-out at Tonypandy, and then refusing an inquiry into the ensuing mayhem in which two Welsh miners were killed. The Dundee congress was able to offer fellow-feeling about Churchill, as well as condolence and support, to a visiting delegation from the South Wales coalfield. Churchill, characteristically enough, remained undaunted, and in the closing years of peacetime would devote ever greater resources to marshalling police, special constables and soldiers – even, on one occasion, two gunboats to invigilate a dispute at Leith – against striking workers. In part, he was motivated by the strengthening of links between troublesome trade unionists in Britain and seditious Ireland. Yet his heavy-handedness was to have the enduring effect, at a pivotal moment in history, of instilling profound mistrust among the organised working classes for the forces of state authority. The consequences of that would prove profound, and the warnings were there for all to see. Barely four months before the outbreak of the First World War, the STUC congress at Kirkcaldy rang with furious condemnations of the military, and demands for action to bring the armed services under the control of the working class.

But the Liberal government had in any event begun to lose its way before that. Campbell-Bannerman, in failing health, had handed on the premiership in 1908 to a man long measured for the job, Herbert Asquith, who sat for East Fife. David Lloyd George replaced Asquith as Chancellor of the Exchequer, providing (with Churchill, though in other respects they were very far from political soulmates) a potent source of dissent, particularly over economic policy. Lloyd George, who had entered Parliament as a Radical, introduced a raft of social reforms as Chancellor which, arguably more than the Attlee measures 40 years later, laid the foundations of the welfare state: the old age pension (for which Asquith deserved, though rarely gains, much of the credit), unemployment insurance, employment exchanges and National Insurance among them. History remembers Lloyd George for funding these innovations by raising taxes on the wealthy and, in the process, provoking a constitutional crisis by pitting the Commons against the Lords after the latter threatened to reject his 1909 People's Budget. But Lloyd George's radicalism, coupled with a cavalier disregard for party discipline, also deepened the divisions within the government between those who clung to the classical Liberal faith in free trade and small government, and those who saw in the rising tides of industrial militancy and of suffragism the need for fundamental social change. Asquith, wearied by the ceaseless agonies of the Irish question and by the gathering crisis in Europe, proved increasingly incapable of holding his party together under these stresses, despite its Commons majority. The two general elections of 1910, called to resolve the constitutional impasse, saw the Liberal majority collapse. Now, the balance of power lay with the 40-strong Labour contingent and with 70 distinctly volatile Irish Nationalists. Lloyd George and Churchill cut an increasing dash by arguing that the country needed to prepare for war.

The old Liberal coalition was unravelling and Labour's time was fast at hand. Yet Scotland still had little to contribute, in parliamentary terms at least. The elections of 1910 saw just one more Labour MP, Willie Adamson of the miners (later to become the first Labour Scottish Secretary), elected to join Wilkie and Barnes. For all its industrial militancy, Scottish labour remained incapable of mobilising effectively behind the new political force it had done so much to help create. But the Victorian age was at last ending. War was coming, and would change everything in its wake. And, in its midst, Scottish labour militancy would find a notoriety that legend would never be allowed to forget.

CHAPTER THREE

GREAT AND SECRET DANGERS

> When a strike passes from the constitutional to the anarchic phase,
> it gathers to itself all manner of undesirable elements . . . it is
> against such a development that we must now be armed . . . this
> strike movement holds great and secret dangers.
>
> *Scotsman,* 1 February 1919

The opening day of the 1900 STUC congress in Edinburgh had to
compete for space in the columns of the Scottish newspapers with
dispatches on what was judged to be a bigger story – the siege of
Mafeking. The *Scotsman* of that day reported that Lord Roberts's
forces were making good progress in the eastern Free State in
keeping the Boers away from the British flank, but that things
were looking grimmer at Mafeking. 'Mafeking possesses water,
and the food and ammunition will last to the middle of May, but
the food only on a scale to keep body and soul together,' the paper
reported. The people there were 'very, very weary of it all . . .
and yet the town continues to take its troubles in a light-hearted
manner. Sowans porridge, made by a Scotsman from oatbran
husks, had proved "an immense boon to the community". As
for the fighting, everything was satisfactory . . . .'

Against such a backdrop, the STUC could not hope to look
much better than mildly irrelevant. Yet relevance was the least
of its concerns. Then, as later, issues of war had the capacity to
divide socialists as could nothing else. Ramsay MacDonald, always
a good reference source for students of dilemmas, admitted as
much in an article in the *Socialist Review* in October 1914, two
months after the outbreak of the First World War: 'The position
of the Socialist during war is a difficult one,' he wrote. 'With very

few exceptions, the British Socialist movement condemned this war . . . . But when a war is actually upon us, when our friends are dying in the trenches and being mown down on the battlefields; when Europe is in the melting pot and our own country is not quite safe from attack, a set of problems different from those which faced us at the outbreak of the war have to be dealt with.' Perhaps, but there were many in the movement who would continue to feel, as the pacifist slogan once put it, that a bayonet was a weapon with a worker on each end.

Exactly that dichotomy had confronted the young STUC with the outbreak of the Boer War. The powerful instinct of most socialists was to oppose the war as unjust, imperialist and unnecessary. They were fortified in this position by the disruptive effect which the conflict had both on trade and on the political climate at home. The government had found, as governments do, that war was a terribly handy pretext for postponing costly policy decisions, and was using it to resist demands for better pensions provision. The Edinburgh congress railed against the 'popularising or glorifying of war' yet could not quite overcome the inconvenient fact that the war *was* popular, and that those who questioned its conduct ran the risk of being held up to patriotic scorn for their treachery.

The previous month, the *Scotsman* had carried a fascinating account of an anti-war meeting at the City Hall in Glasgow which turned into a minor riot. Speakers included Keir Hardie and David Lloyd George – it is hard not to wish to have been there. 'The audience,' reported the *Scotsman*, 'was of the working-class type and, judging from the ready sale of Socialist publications, was largely composed of sympathisers with the Independent Labour Party. Evidently, it was not entirely so, for the appearance of Mr Keir Hardie passing through the body of the hall elicited cheers and groans in fairly equal proportions . . . .' Worse was to come, for despite a ticket-only admission policy, the hall had been infiltrated by pro-war demonstrators, and speakers were hissed and heckled. Bailie John Ferguson in the chair, having stoutly warned the hecklers that they would be ejected 'with that amount of violence which was necessary,' went on to insist that the speakers 'were as true to the interests of Glasgow and of Scotland as any man in Scotland, but they loved justice above nationality.' All the same, Lloyd George, despite 'his faculty of humouring his audience,' was prevented from speaking for quarter of an hour by a contingent singing *Rule Britannia* at the back of the hall. Meanwhile, outside in Candleriggs, 2,000 pro-war demonstrators were facing the police across barricades and banging tin trays against the walls of the hall to drown out the speakers: 'When Mr Keir Hardie appeared with a number of his friends at the door of the hall they were surrounded, hooted and jostled . . . one young man had a swollen and bleeding face . . . a cab was sent for and in it Mr Keir Hardie and his friends made their escape . . . the *Labour Leader* office in Queen's Arcade was visited by one of the numerous bands of noisy demonstrators, and the windows were broken . . . .'

Given such divisions in popular sentiment, the STUC was understandably cautious about venturing too robust a stance. The minutes book suggests that the parliamentary committee spent much of the period finding other things to talk about. The 1900 congress, likewise, opened with bitter debate about whether to discuss the war at all or whether to avoid such 'political' matters in favour of concentrating on affairs of trade. It did not, in the event, go to quite those lengths of self-censorship, though Edinburgh Trades Council was persuaded to sublimate its powerful anti-war impulses within a heroically indistinct motion on the evils of imperialism. A firmer stand was taken against conscription, but only after Margaret Irwin had mildly pointed out that this contingency, however inflammatory, was not actually in serious prospect.

On the eve of the First World War, such issues had become magnified to a scale that could not be so easily overlooked. As we have seen, the labour movement approached that grand tragedy in a mood of open antagonism towards a British establishment in whose defence its members would shortly be required to sacrifice their lives. Almost a decade of industrial strife could not be shrugged lightly aside, and while the electoral support for socialism remained patchy, the influence of the ILP, SDF and others in the workplace had grown steadily more powerful. If that was an ominous circumstance for the employers or the government to contemplate, it was no more comfortable for the leaderships of the major unions or of the STUC.

The last day of April 1914 found the eighteenth STUC congress at Kirkcaldy locked in a furious debate over the readiness of Glasgow Trades Council, under Emanuel Shinwell's hotspur influence, to embrace and affiliate new 'breakaway' bodies created out of disenchantment with the stolid ways of the established unions. In particular, a schism in the health insurance sector was to engage the parliamentary committee for many months. Condemning the trades council's activities, Bob Smillie made a poignant admission. There was, he acknowledged, 'a greater tendency to rebellion than ever in the trade union movement in the case of a few discontented members who are not in a position to rise with sufficient rapidity into official positions because of the leaders not dying out quickly enough.' It was, as Smillie must have known, not merely a matter of ambition thwarted. The impatience was fuelled by frustrations of much greater substance. Yet, Smillie's words serve well as a prelude to the edgy years of conflict and defiance that lay ahead. Those who had worked in the early days to give the Scottish labour movement a coherent voice and to make that voice heard were still, by and large, in command of its high counsels. Events were to yield ample evidence of how much mood and matters had changed since those times, and to leave the movement's ageing leaders, time and again, looking slow of wit, clumsy of foot, and irresolute before a rising tide of dissension and discontent.

The tensions of warfare on an unprecedented scale, and of the unsettled peace that followed, were to raise the mighty totem of Red Clydeside. Historians ever since have debated how much of the legend is a myth, and how much the hot-bloodedness that ensued was premeditated, ideologically focused, or merely exaggerated. It is a debate that will persist for as long as Scots take an interest in their heritage, and resolving it definitively is beyond the ambitions of this book. But a number of factors in the equation need to be borne in mind. First, the protests that brought the tanks to Glasgow in February 1919 were no impulsive emulation of the drama of St Petersburg, but were a link in a chain of events that stretched back to the earliest years of the century. As we have already seen, the use of the military to combat industrial unrest was not a new recourse for government. Nor, by 1919, were imprisonment or exile exceptional sanctions for proletarian troublemakers. Second, government fears that the workers were taking their cue from beyond these shores had already been nurtured in the context, not of Russia, but of Ireland, and had been further deepened by four years of nervous speculation about the commitment of the organised Scottish working class to victory on the battlefields of Europe.

Third, while Scotland may have captured the reputation, it was not alone in its discontent. Fourth, it is important in considering what happened to distinguish between opposition to the war itself and opposition to the domestic legislation which it provoked – even if the government of the day did not always so distinguish. Lastly, those who would detect a unity of revolutionary purpose must overcome the compelling evidence that unity of any sort was little apparent within the labour movement across the period in question: growth, certainly; politicisation, and emboldened impatience, undoubtedly; but little consensus about either means or ends.

What is none the less beyond dispute is that the mood in the workshops and yards of west-central Scotland dismayed and unnerved the very highest ranks of British imperial power. Equally clear is that for much of the period in question, the leadership of the trade union movement in Scotland was almost as unnerved. It had watched with apprehension the growing popularity of syndicalist groupings like the Socialist Labour Party and of John Maclean's Marxist lectures. As events unfolded, it reacted more than it led. It struggled, often honestly and more often ineffectually, to understand, address and channel the resentments of the rank and file. In so doing, and in generally failing, its authority would be forever qualified, even as the mass movement its greying elders had dreamed of mobilising finally began to take form. The most lasting effect of 'Red Clydeside' for the STUC lies in the tradition, which endures, of a shop stewards' movement that national leaderships disregard at their peril.

The 1914 congress took place against the twin backgrounds of gathering war and of industrial tensions which had moderated only marginally from their height at the time of the great miners' dispute two years earlier. The issue of the *Scotsman* which reported the opening day of congress also carried reports of demonstrations in Wales for a minimum wage in the pits, accompanied by a strike in Abertillery over the coal-owners' refusal to allow posters for the demonstrations to be displayed on the premises; a wage cut of 2.5 per cent imposed on the Durham miners; a wage freeze imposed on Scottish furnacemen; a 3d wage cut for Scottish shaleminers; a wage strike by Scottish basketmakers; a wage strike by Kirkcaldy linoleum workers; a wage strike by Dalkeith joiners; and a wage strike by Aberdeen ship painters. A strike by gas engineers in Warrington was reported settled. Alongside this, by now daily, column on trade disputes, the paper also reported a rally in Glasgow organised by the Socialist Labour Party, the Industrial Workers of Great Britain and the *Daily Herald* League. The theme was international workers' solidarity, and the principal speaker was Jim Larkin, James Connolly's romantic co-agitator, who launched an embittered attack on the leaderships of both the Labour Party and the trade unions for 'deliberately misleading the working class movement.' The *Scotsman* reported: 'Mr Larkin said he was, and had always been, a rebel. That meant to be something out of the ordinary, or, as Mr [George Bernard] Shaw said, to be a super-woman or a super-man. He supported the cause of internationalism. In the mouths of some that meant let Bob Smillie, Ramsay MacDonald, Bill this or that flourish, but did not mean let Labour flourish . . . .' As a snap-shot of the moment, those few square inches of newsprint serve well.

Inside the hall, the same tensions were evident. The congress of 1914 was a fractious, volatile affair. The previous year's gathering had listened calmly to a declaration by that year's president, Alex Turner, that 'war is an enemy of the workers,' but as the real prospect of it drew closer, wide divergences of opinion had begun to open up. Bob Smillie and Keir Hardie were against British participation from the outset. Page Arnot, who spent time with both men at this period, believed that Hardie's despair at a war 'which threatened to wreck his whole life's effort for working-class independence, socialism and peace' contributed to his death less than a year later. Smillie, who was by now president of the Miners' Federation of Great Britain, found that few of his colleagues on the executives of either the MFGB or the Scottish Miners' Federation shared his anti-war views. More galling still, when war came his members hastened to the recruitment offices: a quarter of Scotland's miners had signed up by 1915, and the country was facing a serious coal shortage in consequence. James O'Connor Kessack, the dockworkers' leader and parliamentary committee member (later killed in action), favoured international meetings between trade union movements to agree common action in the event of war, echoing the (vain) call of the Second International for a general strike in all affected countries to prevent the war taking place. Others in the STUC leadership, including both Carson and Allan, inclined from an early stage towards the view that, however deplorable war might be, once the nation was under threat it was everyone's duty to defend it. The movement was no more united at UK level. Ramsay MacDonald, for example, joined the Union of Democratic Control, formed in 1914 to lobby for a peace initiative, while Hardie would have nothing to do with it. The Carson and Allan viewpoint noted that German workers had signally failed to observe the International's strictures and strike in protest at their government's aggression. Allan later explained his position thus: 'I am an internationalist, because I believe in nationalism. Therefore the [German] outrage on Belgium and the invasion of France were to me a violation of international principles.' That was also the view among most socialist MPs and, almost certainly, most rank-and-file workers. By December 1914, a quarter of the workforce in the West of Scotland had enlisted.

In those last months of peace, though, it was the legitimacy of the armed forces in relation to industrial disputes which still most preoccupied the delegates. The presidential address of Robert Climie from Ayrshire Trades Council included a section headed 'Army versus the People,' which drew a pointed parallel between the gunboats at Leith and the much more brutal deployment of troops in Ireland. A motion from the miners, seeking the strengthening of the Parliamentary Labour Party so that the armed forces could be brought under working-class control, was passed unanimously. O'Connor Kessack also piloted through a motion deploring the importation of police and troops into strikes, declaring that 'Mr Churchill, the plutocrat, now in charge of the navy' had been preparing a 'huge army' of troops to break a threatened strike by railwaymen. To applause, he gave warning that such an approach, should it continue, would oblige the unions to 'organise forces to meet the forces opposed to them.' Three months before the outbreak of war, the image of the military as an instrument of class oppression was sharply defined and deeply resented.

Even disregarding the shadow of war, the 1914 congress conveys the impression of a movement in a state of uneasy transition from the practices and personalities of its foundation into something altogether more political and abrasive. Kessack and Shinwell conducted what the *Scotsman* tactfully called a 'heated scene' on the congress floor over the Glasgow Trades Council row. There were motions demanding coal nationalisation and a State medical service. The days when temperance and socialism walked hand in hand were also plainly receding, and a call for prohibition gathered just 12 votes. The congress was the first to receive fraternal greetings from a full-time Scottish Organiser of the Labour Party – Ben Shaw, appointed on Ramsay MacDonald's initiative to do something about Labour's electoral weakness in Scotland. And, little noticed at the time, the congress also gave its backing for the first time to the establishment of a Scottish parliament.

Thirteen weeks later, on 4 August, Britain went to war. The King and Queen were cheered down the Mall to Buckingham Palace, and Lord Kitchener was appointed Secretary for War. As it happened, the STUC parliamentary committee was due to be in London on that fateful Tuesday for a series of ministerial meetings. The visit was cancelled (David Palmer, having failed to receive his telegram in time, went anyway). In the Commons, Radical MPs tabled a motion asserting 'that no sufficient reason exists in the present circumstances for Great Britain intervening in the war, and most strongly [urging] His Majesty's Government to continue negotiations with Germany with a view to maintaining our neutrality.' Nearby, the executive of the Labour Party was adopting a resolution which ascribed the outbreak of hostilities to 'foreign ministers pursuing diplomatic policies for the purpose of maintaining a balance of power.' The British Foreign Secretary, Sir Edward Grey, was specifically indicted for having 'committed without the knowledge of our people the honour of the country to supporting France in the event of any war in which she was seriously involved, and [having given] definite assurance of support before the House of Commons had any chance of considering the matter.' But the motion stopped just short of advocating neutrality. It recalled that the Labour movement had 'opposed the policy which has produced the war' and declared that the movement's duty now was 'to secure peace at the earliest possible moment *on such conditions as will provide the best opportunities for the re-establishment of amicable feelings between the workers of Europe*' (emphasis added). Meanwhile, socialist organisations should concentrate their energies on measures 'to mitigate the destitution which will inevitably overtake our working people whilst the state of war lasts.'

They did not have long to wait. The impact of war on Scottish industrial life was swift and profound. The Clyde's engineering, munitions, and warship capacity were of pre-eminent strategic importance to the government. By the same token, peacetime projects – for example, in the civil construction field – were placed in indefinite abeyance. The immense disruption which ensued had traumatic consequences. In those industries with little to contribute to the war effort, there was a rapid run-down, and widespread unemployment. At the same time, sweatshop industries faced manpower shortages as workers left for the forces or for better-paid posts in the rapidly expanding war-related sectors. In these sectors, however, the forced rise in output brought an influx of unskilled labour, much of it from furth of Scotland. That both undermined the position of skilled labour and brought fresh pressure to bear on Clydeside's already woeful housing provision. Landlords were able to exploit the sudden demand for housing by lofting rents, adding to an already soaring increase in living costs as food came into short supply because of both transportation constraints and widespread hoarding. Inflation, in those early months of war, approached 50 per cent.

In west-central Scotland, it was as if the heat had suddenly been turned up under a long-simmering cauldron. Both workers and government were acutely aware how central Clydeside's contribution to the war effort was, and the potential leverage which that importance afforded. The government alternated, as it was to do throughout the war, between cajoling and coercion. The workers looked to their unions for leadership in the great adversity that was upon them, and found it lacking. At UK level, most unions had accepted the need for government direction of production, and the dilution of skills which it implied. They were prepared to suspend peacetime aspirations in return for an input to the strategic planning process and a promise that conditions would return to normal once the war – generally expected to be of very brief duration – was over. It is easy now to portray this stance as craven and misguided, yet the union leaders were far from alone in those early days in believing that the war would last months rather than years. They therefore calculated that, for a minimal sacrifice, they could significantly advance the influence of trade unionism within the counsels of the state, possibly winning a permanent right to be consulted in governmental policy-making. It proved a mistaken view but it was, at the time, a tenable one.

Almost at once, however, a rash of disputes broke out in the engineering plants of Clydeside. There was open talk of a general strike of engineering workers. It was not the first time such talk had been heard. Similar threats in the past had helped Clydeside engineers resist the diminished status which mechanisation had brought elsewhere in the country. Familiarity may partly explain the employers' resistance to the shopfloor demands which now erupted for pay rises and for preservation of the status of skilled workers. What also became swiftly apparent was that the agitators did not enjoy anything like the full backing of their national unions. The employers, with government encouragement, stood firm. The shop stewards accordingly decided that they would have to instigate and implement their own strategies. It was a decision that was to have far-reaching repercussions.

This might have been exactly the sort of circumstance in which the STUC could have played an important mediating role. But it was not to be. Allan, as we have already seen, held the honest belief that the priority for the unions as for the country lay in seeing the war won. Deputising now much of the time for an increasingly frail George Carson – who, in any event, shared his view of the war – he was deeply conscious that other senior socialists saw the matter quite differently. His instinct, therefore, was to try to avoid outright discussion of the rights and wrongs of the war. Again, it would be wrong to be lured by hindsight into too severe a view of this stance. There were great risks inherent in opening up to public view the deep divisions which existed within the movement on the issue. It was, after all, a period in which the more zealous breed of patriot was engaged in bestowing white feathers and worse on men who failed to enlist – the topic could not have been more sensitive. The ILP too had instructed members to avoid raising questions about the principle of the war, and those of its leading lights who were instinctively anti-war generally stopped short of saying so. James Maxton, for example, took to the columns of *Forward* in October 1914 to urge socialists not to become 'swallowed up in a war or peace propaganda, but [to] continue to conduct the business of socialist manufacturing.' Accordingly, the approach of people like Allan and Carson was to focus instead on reaching practical decisions about helping unions respond to dilution of skilled labour and other incursions on workplace rights. At the first parliamentary committee meeting of the war, on 22 August 1914, Allan raised the issue of how best to respond to the unemployment which would inevitably be an early feature of the conflict. A special meeting of the committee on 5 September called on the government to subsidise local authorities to create work, and asked unions both to monitor the growth in lay-offs and to keep the STUC in touch with the inroads rising benefit payments were making on their funds. That same meeting was to confront for the first time a frustration that would recur throughout the conflict: the STUC's inability to gain representation on key wartime committees.

Initially, this strategy of sticking doggedly to practicalities won majority support on the parliamentary committee. But it soon came under mounting challenge, principally from Glasgow Trades Council which was facing severe pressure from the shop stewards. At that same special meeting, barely a month after war was declared, Kessack and Alex Turner tried unsuccessfully to initiate a parliamentary committee debate on the issue of the war. Two weeks later, Turner (Kessack had by now enlisted) tried again for a 'pronouncement on the war to the trades unionists of Scotland.' Uninformatively, the minute book merely records that: 'After considerable discussion the subject was allowed to drop.' We do know, however, that the nature of the discussion was such that Turner afterwards submitted his resignation, withdrawing it only on receiving an apology at the next meeting from one of his protagonists, WG Hunter of the Glasgow Bakers, for remarks made in the heat of debate. Meeting again on Boxing Day 1914, the committee decided by five votes to two (with Allan one of the dissenters) that it would be best in the circumstances to cancel the 1915 congress – the only time in a century that the STUC congress has not taken place.

Events outside were not showing the same restraint. Early in 1915, two related protests paralysed Clydeside. In February, 10,000 engineering workers in 26 factories came out on strike for a wage increase of 2d an hour. Shortly afterwards, the first in a series of rent strikes began, with women (particularly servicemen's wives) taking a leading role through the Glasgow Women's Housing Association, supported by the shop stewards, the ILP, and Glasgow Trades Council. Both campaigns scored qualified successes: the engineers did ultimately gain a pay rise, and the government was forced to introduce in December 1915 a Rents Restriction Act, limiting the increases private landlords could impose. But their significance stretched far beyond the immediate issues they addressed. The engineers' dispute was refused authorisation by the district committee of their union, the Amalgamated Society of Engineers, in line with the union's national undertakings to government. With workforce backing, the stewards formed the Clyde Labour Withholding Committee (an awkward title devised to avoid a sedition charge under the Defence of the Realm Act), which duly became the more broadly-based Clyde Workers Committee. The CWC swiftly took on an agenda, and an eminence, that extended beyond the immediate concerns of the factory craftsmen: helping organise, for example, the rent strikes. Yet, contrary to the more fanciful retrospection, it remained a vehicle for pursuing grievance, rather than revolution. Much of the action it co-ordinated was directed against two pieces of emergency industrial legislation: Lloyd George's Munitions Act of June 1915, which began as a measure to boost armaments production through 'dilution' of skilled labour by drafting in unskilled workers, particularly women, to undertake tasks previously restricted to craftsmen, and was later amended to become what amounted to industrial conscription; and the introduction in August 1915 of a system of 'leaving certificates,' which provided that workers could leave jobs only with their employer's permission. The CWC mounted a succession of strikes against both provisions, and added its voice to the calls growing in the movement throughout the country for Labour nationally to withdraw from participating in the government's war-time administrative machinery.

The pressure on the STUC to lift its game was becoming unbearable. The parliamentary committee resisted demands from Glasgow Trades Council to organise a mass meeting on the hardships facing working people, relenting only sufficiently to send committee members to similar meetings organised by others, and to publish advisory literature for affiliates. Instead, it pursued its traditional peacetime approach of seeking meetings with ministers and relentlessly requested representation on war-time emergency committees. These efforts came, almost without exception, to nothing. Allan was even refused a place on the Scottish advisory committee of the Prince of Wales National Relief Fund. Trades council delegates (though not Turner, who had by now followed Kessack into the forces) stepped up the pressure for congress to be held as usual to discuss the mounting mayhem wrought by the wartime provisions. The metalworkers and other unions took up the call.

Eventually, on 29 May, the parliamentary committee buckled sufficiently to sanction a one-day conference on 'certain questions relating to present conditions.' The conference, held in Glasgow on 3 July, addressed a tightly-defined agenda. David Gilmour of the miners, that year's president, warned the 200 delegates that no place would be given to those who tried to raise 'very dangerous topics regarding the war.' Instead, discussion would be confined to 'questions on which Scottish trade unionists could unite.' These turned out to consist of ideas for controlling rises in the cost of living, improving war pensions and benefits, and preparing for peacetime. Though a strong supporter of the war, Gilmour could not resist a glancing reference to the Clyde engineers' 'moderate and reasonable' pay claim, but otherwise controversy was kept on a tight leash. Speakers stressed time and again their wish to avoid causing the government embarrassment. A motion was adopted urging the government and the Labour Party either to peg prices by statute or to adopt full state control of supplies. Another called for administration of War Relief to be centralised, with appropriate worker representation, while a third suggested that strategic industries be retained under public control after the war ended to ensure employment for returning servicemen. The long-standing commitment to an eight-hour working day was reaffirmed. Only as the day neared its end did the realities of what was happening on the Clyde threaten to intrude, as delegates tried to initiate debate on female labour and on nationalisation of the munitions industry. Overall, the practical impact of the conference was negligible.

Clydeside was far the most important industrial centre of the war effort, but it was not alone in reacting against wartime deprivations. Much of Bob Smillie's attention over this period was engaged in resolving a bitter strike by the Welsh miners, over both wages and tough new measures to curb absenteeism. It was finally settled at the outset of September, when a deal was brokered by ministers, including David Lloyd George and Labour's Arthur Henderson. Coal output had fallen by more than 28 million tonnes since the outbreak of war.

A few days later, the TUC – which had not cancelled its congress – met in Bristol. It did not shrink from discussing the merits of the war, but neither did it need to. A motion describing the Allied action as 'completely justified' was approved almost unanimously amid much patriotic rhetoric. David Gilmour, representing the MFGB, won a cheer by tearing up a dissident leaflet which persons unknown had left on delegates' seats during the lunchbreak and which, he said, was aimed at 'whitewashing the Germans.' Another motion, passed with only two delegates dissenting, congratulated the Parliamentary Labour Party on playing a full part in the national recruitment programme, though not before Ernest Bevin, representing the Bristol Dock Workers' Union, had pointed out that German soldiers had suffered the same sorts of brutality at Russian hands as British troops had from the Germans. Delegates reacted with concern to an allegation from Lloyd George that some unions had failed to honour undertakings to government to maintain output. Ramsay MacDonald, there to convey fraternal greetings, told them: 'We have never said that you should shirk your duties. We have never said that you should forget at this moment that the nation demands the best you can give it.' Once the war was over, he said, it would be time to consider the future role of trade unionism: for the moment, thoughts must be with the trenches. Delegates did vote unanimously against the principle of conscription, in line with past policy. But the overall tone of the congress was to endorse the government's message that the war would be as much won in the workshops as the trenches. 'It could be wished,' remarked the *Scotsman* with its mind no doubt focused closer to home, 'that there were signs that it has been as thoroughly learned by the rank and file of the labour movement as by the great majority of their leaders.' As if in answer, the TUC decided a couple of months later to cancel plans to hold its 1916 Congress in Glasgow.

Also in September 1915, in a nursing home in Glasgow, Keir Hardie died of pneumonia. In an affectionate obituary, the *Scotsman* commented: 'As a platform speaker, Mr Hardie was resourceful and effective, and the rashness of some of his statements was no doubt the result of a desire to drive home his point at all costs rather than of a desire to mislead.' He was 59.

Meanwhile, the government decided to embark on one last attempt at calming the Clyde by persuasion. In the afterglow of the Rents Restriction Act, Lloyd George, the munitions minister, travelled to Glasgow on 23 December 1915, accompanied by some distinctly nervous Whitehall officials. Frances Stevenson, then his mistress and later his wife, confided to her diary just how seriously the government was by now taking the unrest on Clydeside: 'D[avid] says that the men up there are ripe for revolution, that they are completely out of hand . . . D is convinced that there is German money up there.' His first port of call was Beardmore's Forge in Parkhead which, with David Kirkwood as shop stewards' convener, had become a notable focus for the protests. Around 100 police were in attendance. Kirkwood asked his stewards to give the minister a 'patient hearing,' adding pointedly that 'every word he says will be carefully weighed. We regard him with suspicion because every act with which his name is associated has the taint of slavery about it.' Lloyd George, unabashed, made a patriotic appeal for acceptance of dilution, and pointed out that the Munitions Act had been drafted and administered in consultation with union leaders like the ASE secretary, James Brownlie. Kirkwood replied that the problem lay less with dilution than with the lack of worker participation in management, and added of Brownlie: 'We repudiate this man – he is no leader of ours. Brownlie has been told the same to his face.'

The next day, Christmas Eve, Lloyd George met the CWC leadership, and was again warned that dilution would be acceptable only if carried out under worker control. No-one seems to have thought it odd that he saw no need to meet the STUC. Instead, on Christmas Day, he addressed a now infamous public meeting chaired by Arthur Henderson at Glasgow's St Andrew's Hall. A heavily censored account of the meeting appeared in the Scottish press, ominously prefaced: 'The Press Association is authorised to publish the following report.' It consisted, almost entirely, of Lloyd George's scripted speech, in which he explained the basis for dilution: 'Our proposal is that the light work, which requires neither strength nor skill, that can be acquired by short training, should be performed by women, so that the skilled men should be taken away to man the national gun and projectile factories. If we fail to obtain your adhesion to this programme we are faced with one of two alternatives. We can go to the trenches and say to the British soldiers, we are sorry that we cannot get the necessary guns to enable you to win through in 1916 – the trade union regulations stand in the way . . . the other alternative is that we should send to the Kaiser telling him frankly that we cannot go on . . . the highly skilled workmen of this country, whose patriotism has been manifested by the readiness with which they have given their sons to fight the country's battles, I do not believe that they will give me this answer . . . you cannot haggle with an earthquake.' The censored report mentioned 'some singing of the "Red Flag" by the Syndicalists present,' but insisted that the reception was 'on the whole, good humoured,' and that it ended with Lloyd George holding a discussion 'of a highly satisfactory character' on dilution with the ASE district committee.

In fact, the St Andrew's Hall meeting – which had drawn a crowd of 3,000 – had been highly charged, contemptuous, and peppered with constant interruptions. 'A more unruly audience surely never gathered in Glasgow,' recalled Tom Johnston in his memoirs. The experience convinced Lloyd George that the time had come for the government to take the gloves off in its dealings with Clydeside. The meeting itself provided the first pretext for the new hard-line approach. On 1 January 1916, *Forward* published an unabridged account of events at St Andrew's Hall by its reporter, Tom Hutchison. Hutchison's version omitted Lloyd George's references to matters of military sensitivity, but otherwise reported the speech and the audience's interjections verbatim, including such gems as the minister's self-pitying lament for the burdens of office and the riposte from a member of the audience that at least the money was good. More to the point, it revealed that the meeting had ended in disorder, with John Muir of the CWC standing on a chair amid the melée, demanding a right of reply. Memorably, the *Forward* report began: 'The best paid munitions worker in Britain, Mr Lloyd George (almost £100 per week), visited the Clyde last weekend in search of adventure. He got it.'

Before New Year's Day was out, the police had begun raids on newsagents which sold the paper, on the homes of known subscribers and on the printers. The *Forward* offices were, in Johnston's words, full of 'high ranking police and military officers smelling through wastepaper baskets and old correspondence files in an endeavour somehow or other to find evidence *post facto* for an amazing and petulant and wholly illegal act of press suppression.' In the event, the over-reaction backfired. Labour MPs protested mightily in the Commons, and only a few weeks passed before Lloyd George invited Johnston to London, addressed him as 'my dear young man,' and assured him that the whole affair had been a comedy of errors. *Forward* was back in business.

But the CWC was not. The days of its wartime defiance – arguably, of 'Red Clydeside' itself – were at an end. Its paper, the *Worker*, was suppressed, as was John Maclean's *Vanguard*. The government moved swiftly. By the spring of 1916 most of the CWC leading lights were either forcibly exiled from Clydeside or in jail, after government attempts to enforce individual dilution agreements on a plant-by-plant basis were met with a series of strikes. The CWC chairman, Willie Gallacher, was arrested and charged with sedition, as were two other office-bearers, John Muir and Walter Bell. Kirkwood and several other leading Clydeside shop stewards were arrested and deported, some to Edinburgh, others to England or Wales. Forty workers from Beardmore Forge were prosecuted under the Munitions Act for unlawfully striking. Protesting against the arrests at a meeting on Glasgow Green, James Maxton of the ILP (a prominent Scottish spokesman for Fenner Brockway's anti-conscription movement) and James MacDougall of the British Socialist Party were also arrested and charged with sedition. By the time they had been sentenced to 12 months each, they were able to join Maclean, Muir, Gallacher and Arthur Woodburn of the ILP in Edinburgh's grim Calton Prison: 'my ancestral home,' Maxton called it.

On 4 January, Lloyd George introduced a new clause to the Munitions Act enforcing dilution through a structure of area committees. He was obliged to spend much of the Commons debate defending his visit to the Clyde and the seizure of *Forward*. Visibly discomfited, he attributed his reception in Glasgow to divisions within the Scottish trade unions: 'There was suspicion of trade union leaders, and they were suspicious of each other. There were syndicalists and socialists, who had a contempt for each other. It was almost impossible to make a bargain with them.' He also insisted that *Forward* had been suppressed for inciting workers to break the law, rather than for disclosing the hostile response to his oratory. It was not a pretext that sat altogether comfortably with his later avuncular treatment of Johnston. Even the mainstream press felt emboldened to report that he lacked his usual command of the

House. But the clause was approved, and next day Prime Minister Asquith followed through with a still more contentious measure – compulsory military service for single men.

Conscription had long been the line that the labour movement, north and south of the border, had been unwilling to see crossed, and both the unions and the Labour Party had thrown their weight behind Lord Derby's programme to persuade single men voluntarily to register their readiness to enlist. The STUC too had offered to help foster voluntary recruitment, though it was rather taken aback when the TUC suggested it take over responsibility for the Derby scheme in Scotland. But the scheme failed to meet its quota, and when compulsory conscription finally came, the movement had grown hesitant about venturing too forthright an opposition to it. A number of individual unions declared themselves hostile, while others embarked on hasty consultation exercises with their members. Some of these, like the boilermakers, were staggered when the consultation showed the membership to be broadly in favour of conscription. The Joint Labour Board, comprising the TUC, the General Federation of Trade Unions, and the Parliamentary Labour Party, agreed that the Commons vote should be left to the individual consciences of Labour MPs. The Triple Alliance of railwaymen, transport workers and miners – formed in 1913 amid the pre-war industrial strife, and now reconstituted under Smillie's chairmanship – immediately pledged to resist. The railwaymen raised the cry, swiftly adopted by others, that the price for conscription of men should be conscription of private wealth – prompting the *Scotsman* to wonder, in a sourly sarcastic leader, whether the unions were sincerely willing 'to barter away the precious liberties of the working classes for a mess of pottage.' The left-wing *Daily News*, by contrast, argued somewhat ingeniously that those single men who had been unwilling to attest under the Derby scheme were unlikely to make suitably patriotic soldiers, while the *Daily Chronicle* said the scheme had not been given sufficient time to do its work. By July, Lloyd George was able to observe, with more than his usual hubris, that the labour problem had been 'solved.'

Difficult though it was, the conscription issue finally forced the STUC off the sidelines. The parliamentary committee, with Allan to the fore, had been stolidly resisting calls for some months, particularly from Glasgow Trades Council, for a special conference on the prospect of conscription. Since the STUC supported the Derby scheme, Allan reasoned none too logically, there was no need to discuss any other. On 4 December, Ben Shaw led a Labour Party deputation to reinforce demands for a conscription conference. By six votes to two, the parliamentary committee again resisted, this time on the grounds that 'the present time was not suitable to hold a conference.' Whether it sounded any more impressive then than it does now is hard to say.

On the night the Bill was introduced, Glasgow Trades Council passed, by 90 votes to three, a stoutly-worded resolution which declared conscription to be 'dangerous to national stability and opposed to the principles of freedom,' and which demanded that the STUC set up machinery actively to combat the legislation. Next day, the Scottish Labour MPs decided at a special meeting that they too would oppose conscription. At last the parliamentary committee shifted. At a special meeting on 8 January, lobbied again by a Labour deputation, it agreed to hold a joint conference on conscription with the Party on 15 January. This time, the decision was unanimous, after what the minutes denote – possibly euphemistically – as 'a friendly discussion between the PC and the deputation.'

The conference, held in Glasgow's Central Halls, was a turbulent occasion and, though it culminated in a clear statement of 'emphatic condemnation' for the Bill, it also mapped vividly the chasms that existed within the movement over attitudes to the war. Bob Smillie moved the substantive motion, which demanded the Bill's withdrawal and also warned the government 'against any attempt to bring about industrial compulsion in this country,' which many trade unionists feared was the next item on the government's agenda. Kitchener, Smillie said, had secured the numbers of recruits he had previously said he needed, and they included thousands of trade unionists. But Peter McLuskey of the bottlemakers moved an amendment urging Labour to support the Bill in the interests of victory, provided certain safeguards were met. The unions, he argued, were not above compulsion themselves in recruiting members and should not oppose the legislation unless they had something better to put in its place. The amendment fell in favour of the motion, but then Palmer and Allan moved another. Their amendment called for a ballot of affiliated bodies on the conscription issue. Allan seconded it in emotional terms. Opinion, he suggested, had shifted among union members in favour of conscription over the preceding 18 months and a ballot was likely to confirm as much. As a Social Democrat he believed that it was the duty of citizens, and socialists, to defend the state against aggression, and he would therefore support conscription. The amendment fell, but not before it had brought two old comrades to loggerheads. Smillie, summing up against the amendment, remarked that Allan had shifted his views a long way in the years he had known him. Allan replied that this was 'the meanest and most contemptible thing he had ever heard.' That evening John Muir of the CWC also spoke against conscription at an ILP rally in Edinburgh, reporting a mood of pessimism on the Clyde that there could ever now be a return to pre-war conditions.

Allan's speech had damaged his standing within the STUC, of which he was already effectively acting secretary and would shortly become president. In February, the metalworkers demanded a further conference on conscription as the clamp-down on the Clyde began to bite. The parliamentary committee refused. When the STUC met at the Scottish Co-Operative Wholesale Society Hall in Glasgow on 27 April for its first full congress of the war, Emanuel Shinwell rose with a bitterly-worded motion condemning the decision. It was defeated, but only by 58 votes to 47. This time, there could be no avoiding the issue of the war. Gilmour, in his presidential address, outlined what was emerging as the STUC's preferred approach to the matter: to use the sacrifices undergone by trade unionists as a lever to pressure for future reform. The parliamentary committee, he conceded, had differed in their views of 'many aspects of the war,' but they were united on the need to protect and advance the interests of the working classes. Workers had been widely vilified for agitating for wage rises, yet in no single industry had wages risen in real terms. Board of Trade figures showed that living costs had risen by 45 per cent since 1914, and wages by less than 25 per cent. Similarly, he pointed out that many of those now subject to conscription still lacked the vote, and were entitled to expect that position to be remedied urgently once peace returned. Much of the rest of the congress was pitched in similar terms. There were motions reaffirming the commitment to a minimum wage, demanding STUC representation on public bodies, seeking huge public investment in better housing provision, and urging the Labour Party to press for the establishment of a Right to

Work to meet the anticipated unemployment of demobilised men. The sentences passed against Maclean and the Clydeside stewards were roundly condemned. And, perhaps with the recent Easter Rising in Dublin fresh in their minds, Glasgow Trades Council reprised their 1914 motion demanding home rule for Scotland. The miners opposed the motion, but it was passed overwhelmingly.

By 1916, public perceptions of the war had changed. It was no longer a topic for spirited debate, but a long nightmare whose horrors mounted relentlessly, numbing and appalling the British people. The reality of what had been happening on the Somme, at Mons and in Churchill's disastrous Gallipoli adventure had borne down on national consciousness. A grief-stricken nation faced deepening food shortages and escalating inflation. Asquith's conduct of the war was growing unpopular, and the press had begun to publish unprecedented gossip about the Prime Minister's drinking habits. He commanded an increasingly divided and intrigue-ridden government, and his evident revulsion at the mounting toll of casualties allowed him to be portrayed as lacking sufficient stomach to prosecute the conflict to victory, a view reinforced by his strong reservations about conscription. He was wounded by the Easter Rebellion, having devoted so much effort to the Irish question; and by two personal setbacks, the marriage to a rival of his long-time confidante, Venetia Stanley, and the death on the Somme of his son Raymond. As the year closed, he was associated – somewhat unjustly – with a leaked Cabinet memo which proposed opening negotiations with the Germans to end the slaughter of British servicemen. Faced with an ultimatum from Lloyd George, he resigned and Lloyd George succeeded to the premiership, forming a government dominated by Conservatives but in which the Labour Party remained involved.

The changing public mood was reflected in an increasingly directionless, demoralised and embittered labour movement as the war entered its closing stages. Acts of workplace and individual defiance continued, with numerous factories striking against the imposition of dilution procedures and many prominent socialists, particularly from the ILP, braving the wrath of the law and of public opinion to resist the draft. But any sense that industrial discontent could turn into concerted mass action for fundamental social change had gone. The ILP increasingly broadened its focus away from the workplace to wider social welfare issues, succeeding not merely in stemming the loss of support it had suffered in the early years of the war, but in tripling its Scottish membership between 1916 and 1918. The shop stewards' movement, while continuing to spread its influence as the voice of shopfloor grievance, was too preoccupied with the case-load of disputes and victimisation cases from the factories to think much of more general protest. The rapid growth of the general unions – reflecting the influx of unskilled workers – brought a new rash of inter-union turf wars: the supremacy within the movement of the old 'labour aristocracy' was ending.

Yet something of the thrawn spirit of Clydeside endured. In March 1917, an uprising in the textile factories of Petrograd turned swiftly to popular revolt. The Tsar abdicated, giving way to the establishment of the first Workers and Soldiers Soviet, and of a provisional government under Alexander Kerensky. The immediate reaction from the TUC and the Labour Party, though couched in sympathetic terms for the oppression Russian workers had suffered under the Romanovs, was to urge the leaders of the revolutionary government not to weaken their commitment to the war against Germany. The response from the STUC, on the opening day of its April 1917 Congress in Falkirk, was more straightforward. Delegates endorsed a motion from the parliamentary committee which warmly congratulated the Russian workers on their victory and expressed the hope that their example 'will be followed by the peoples of all lands.' But the first concrete opportunity to pursue that hope found the parliamentary committee somewhat less resolute.

The Russian provisional government, having decided to remain a combatant against Germany for the time being, prevailed on the Socialist International to convene a conference in Stockholm to seek a socialist formula for peace. In the mainstream labour movement, and in government, this move created great apprehension that the Russians were looking, as they were, for an early exit from the war. The presence of German representatives in Stockholm further disquieted many. Somewhat presumptuously, the Sailors and Firemen's Union refused to convey Henderson and MacDonald to Stockholm, which they were to attend with the government's blessing: indeed Henderson, a member of Lloyd George's War Cabinet, went with the specific mission of trying to talk Russia out of pursuing a separate peace. The STUC parliamentary committee expressed unanimous disapproval of the seamen's embargo, but when in June a national Workers and Soldiers Council, on the soviet model, was established at a Leeds rally chaired by Bob Smillie, the parliamentary committee pointedly withheld its endorsement from plans to form an embryonic soviet in Glasgow. This was eventually established at a conference in Glasgow on 11 August. But after long discussion, the parliamentary committee decided by six votes to three not to attend. In the event, the council swiftly faded.

The 1917 congress reinforced the impression of a parliamentary committee struggling to keep pace with the events erupting around it. It had spent the preceding year toiling away on the same sort of endeavours that had so often failed to gain it ground in the past – seeking meetings with ministers, demanding representation on national bodies. Not that it didn't try. There had been constant lobbying, for example, on behalf of those deported or imprisoned for their trade union agitation. In June the parliamentary committee endorsed the campaign to free John Maclean. In August it offered help to the ASE to combat blacklisting of Clyde deportees. Yet these efforts, while sincere, were ineffectual and ultimately farcical. Allan had led a series of negotiations aimed at getting deported stewards returned to Clydeside, and in the light of his report back the parliamentary committee duly passed a motion announcing that the stewards were now willing, if allowed home, to submit to the discipline of their unions. Then Allan visited Kirkwood in Edinburgh, who told him, courteously but firmly, that he had no intention of giving any such undertaking.

Despite being both president and *de facto* secretary, Allan did not approach the 1917 congress from a·position of unalloyed strength. He was a war supporter among many objectors, an old-order figure before the new, and his presidential address trod a delicate path. It regretted the absence of peace talks but warned against the movement being dragged into 'a quagmire of pacifist impossiblism.' On Allan's prompting, congress heard a presentation from the Director of National Service, one Neville Chamberlain, who had been sent north by a wary government to smooth the path for a further round of dilution and conscription measures. But delegates voted strongly against the principles of both military and industrial conscription, for conscription of wealth, and in favour of peace negotiations. The congress also put down markers on several issues that would assume rather greater importance after the armistice: extending the franchise, strengthening the labour movement, and restoring union rights. It demanded that strategic industries like coal and rail which had been brought under state control in wartime (the pits had come under governmental authority as late as February 1917, and only after Lloyd George had guaranteed the coalowners' profits) be fully nationalised once peace returned, with workers on their boards. Lastly, congress passed its by now ritual demand for a shorter working week.

It is hard in retrospect not to feel some sympathy for Robert Allan. He had been a doughty fighter for the movement from the earliest days of the STUC. He was decent and diligent, if rather less methodical than the secretary's post demanded, and had selflessly shouldered much of the unenviable wartime workload which George Carson was unable to bear. Carson had remained unwilling formally to renounce the secretaryship and, indeed, when he was finally persuaded to retire ahead of the 1918 congress, retained a place for a further year on the parliamentary committee as 'consultant to the Secretary,' possibly reflecting the STUC's sentimental wish to keep a touchstone with its founding generation. Yet, by the time Allan succeeded officially to the job he had so conscientiously understudied, his stock within the movement was running low. The issues thrown up by war had both divided socialists ideologically, and deepened the gulf between the movement's elders and a younger, brasher generation schooled in grassroots activism. Though Allan was the only nominee to succeed Carson at the 1918 congress, the succession was messy, with many delegates feeling that the matter had been sprung upon them by the parliamentary committee. Allan's tenure was to be brief, embattled and unhappy: and was to end in scandal and tragedy.

The March revolution in Russia, driven as much by war-weariness as revolutionary fervour, had replaced the Tsar with a provisional government dominated by well-meaning but undynamic liberals. It was faced, from the outset, with a powerful alternative structure focused upon the populist Petrograd Soviet, and sought vainly to accommodate the rival by sharing powers. Any prospects of this relationship proving durable evaporated after April, when Lenin took command at Petrograd. Though his Bolsheviks remained a minority force within the emerging state (contributing just 105 out of 822 delegates to the first All-Russian Congress of Soviets in June 1917), their superior organisation and increasingly rigorous ideological discipline made further upheaval inevitable. Desperately, the government switched tack from appeasement to suppression as unrest grew. On the night of 6–7 November 1917 (24–25 October on the old Russian calendar), the Bolsheviks staged a successful coup.

The harshness of this new force – which grew more brutal the following year when an attempted rising against Lenin was followed by the murder of the Romanovs and of numerous other enemies of Bolshevism – unsettled British socialists. Henderson, having been persuaded of the merits of the Stockholm initiative, had won over the Labour conference to it in August 1917, and departed the government in consequence. MacDonald, similarly, had described the Kerensky revolution as 'a sort of spring-tide of joy.' But the revolutionary Marxism of Lenin was an altogether different phenomenon, and MacDonald in particular was concerned from an early stage to distance the ILP at home, and the Second International abroad, from the stringencies of communism. 'Violent means and a socialist object do not go together,' he wrote in the *Venturer* in 1921. More immediately, Lenin had seized power on a promise to the Russian people to bring an early end to the war and, on 3 March 1918, the Treaty of Brest Litovsk agreed terms with the Germans, conceding them the Ukraine. This, more than anything, confirmed mainstream British socialism in its reservations about the new powers in Moscow.

Given the conjecture which has been spun around the political origins of Clydeside militancy both during and after the war, it is important to be clear that attitudes to Russia were not greatly different within the Scottish labour movement. Undoubtedly, some were inspired by the triumph of Marxism in Moscow. Willie Gallacher, in particular, was moved by visiting the new Soviet state to talk longingly of a Petrograd on the Clyde. In January 1918, John Maclean – whose fearless anti-war stance had impressed Lenin – was appointed Russian Soviet consul in Scotland. Lloyd George certainly saw the resurgent post-war militancy on Clydeside as a product of spreading Bolshevism, though his intuition about the forces underlying Scottish industrial grievance scarcely had an impressive track record. When the Communist Party of Great Britain was formed in 1920, a disproportionate number of Scots were to be found in its senior ranks, much as they had been when the Labour Party came into being a generation earlier. But they were drawn mostly from the ranks of the SLP and BSP, and Maclean – arguably, the only true revolutionary of the Red Clydesiders – was not among them, having insisted on a separate Scottish party. The Communist Party would play a significant role in Scottish industrial politics into the 1980s, but it was never to be a serious rival to Labour for the loyalty of Scottish trade unionists. Indeed, in Scotland the bigger political phenomenon of the period following the October Revolution was the accelerated growth of the ILP, as the closing stages of the war diminished public resistance to its anti-war sentiments of old. According to its own – admittedly questionable – figures, ILP membership in Scotland rose from 5,656 to 8,904 between June and September 1918.

The STUC was no more united than any other part of the movement in its view of the Bolsheviks, but Hugh Lyon of the Scottish Horse and Motormen undoubtedly spoke for many when he declared in his presidential address to the 1918 congress: 'We have watched with fear and anxiety the fate of a great people tremble in the balance. Those who authorised the demobilisation of Russia were either simple fools or German tools.' That September, the parliamentary committee endorsed a motion originating from Bristol Trades Council which condemned Allied military intervention in Russia and Siberia. But in the version of the motion in the minutes book, Allan's pen has drawn a firm line through a reference to 'the anti-Socialist Kerensky.'

By now, in any event, the STUC had more urgent domestic questions to consider. The entry of the Americans into the war had made victory a question of when rather than whether, and the challenges of peace were foremost in the minds of the delegates at Ayr in April 1918. There were ambitious calls for the Socialist International to be developed to fulfil the sort of mediatory peace-keeping role already being planned for the League of Nations. Shinwell and Smillie also stirred up a lively debate with a successful motion seeking a statement of war aims from the government that would commit Britain to a less imperialist role in the post-war world. But the greater concern, properly enough, was for the circumstances that would prevail in Scottish workplaces once the war effort had subsided and the troops returned home.

It had long been plain that peace would bring as much industrial dislocation as had war. Memories of the aftermath of the Boer War, a much lesser conflagration, left little room to doubt the trauma that lay ahead. There was no mood for trusting vague ministerial assurances that the workers would be looked after once victory was secure. The munitions workforces, swollen with unskilled labour, would be run down. Thousands of servicemen would come home in search of jobs and homes. Industries which had been brought under state control would be returned to profit-hungry private owners. New technologies forged in the heat of war would be put to use streamlining production methods. Less readily foreseen, but in the event no less serious, captured German shipping would be sold off at bargain prices, to the lasting injury of the Clyde yards, and the distilleries would suffer grievously from the onset in 1920 of prohibition in the US.

The STUC, like the rest of the movement, had formulated over the years a battery of policies to meet the advent of peace: full-scale nationalisation of strategic industries like coal, shipping and the railways; massive public investment in housing; radical reform of benefits provision (the previous August, the parliamentary committee had politely but firmly rejected an appeal from Harry Lauder for contributions to a £1 million fund for disabled servicemen, 'our position being that the State should provide for the disabled.') In the course of the war's final year, the parliamentary committee found a decisiveness it had previously often lacked in addressing the questions raised by the approach of peace. It proposed local committees to overcome food shortages. It opposed government measures to deprive conscientious objectors of citizenship rights. It campaigned for repeal of the increasingly harsh censorship laws, protesting at the seizure of the Socialist Labour Party press. It demanded a resumption of parliamentary elections. And it lobbied hard for trade union officials now to be exempted from the draft, particularly after Allan had stunned the June meeting by announcing that he had been called up.

But the key measure addressed the problem of surplus labour and capacity much more directly. The working week would have to be reduced. It was this objective that was to dominate the immediate post-war period: and its pursuit that was to secure forever Clydeside's unwonted reputation for incipient insurrection. Yet, there is little evidence that it was consciously selected as a vehicle for revolution. At most, the decision to focus both STUC and Labour Party endeavour on this single aim may have reflected a belief that it was, if pursued single-mindedly enough, an attainable reform. The simpler explanation is that the issue was seen to be highly important. At each of its wartime congresses, the STUC had passed motions demanding an eight-hour working day. The reality was that the war effort had pushed the working week for many closer to 60 hours. Therefore, the strength of grassroots support for a shorter week was not in question. For Scots trade unionists, the issue commanded natural, rather than calculated, priority.

Meeting on 12 January 1918, the parliamentary committee had called a joint conference with Labour and the co-operative movement (which had now decided to adopt a more overtly political role) 'to consider the labour organisation in Scotland with a view to more clearly defining the same as a Scottish movement.' There were a number of motives behind this initiative. One was that the STUC had been pressing its right to an automatic presence on all Labour Party bodies as the designated representative of Scottish trade unionists, and had come up against opposition from the party's southern command. Allan was instructed to write to the party's general secretary suggesting that since Labour had lately become committed to 'Home Rule all round,' it might lead by example by affording a proper place in its structures to the STUC. There was also a need – eventually resolved by agreement – to prevent co-operators standing against Labour Party candidates at elections. But the conference was dominated by the working hours issue, on which the STUC had been tirelessly lobbying ministers. Out of it came a special meeting of senior officials, which drafted a movement-wide 'Forty Hours' policy to the effect that, on demobilisation, the working week should be defined as five days of eight hours each.

Yet, a month later, that long-cherished policy was to run into difficulties that starkly illustrated both the uncompromising mood fermenting among grassroots activists, and the degree to which the leaderships of the unions and of the STUC had drifted out of touch with their members. When the parliamentary committee moved its now incantatory 40 hours motion in Ayr, Emanuel Shinwell stormed the rostrum with a different proposition. His amendment, moved on behalf of Glasgow Trades Council and with the backing of the sailors and firemen (also, more importantly, of the CWC stewards), demanded that 'the first act of reconstruction after the war should be a reduction of the hours of labour to six per day.' Remarkably, Shinwell's amendment was carried, by 77 votes to 51. The STUC was now formally committed to a working week of not 40 hours, but 30. Yet Labour's Scottish Advisory Committee, with which the STUC had agreed to mount joint action on the working week, remained pledged to 40 hours. Something would have to give.

If the parliamentary committee recognised the challenge which this posed to the STUC's authority, its minutes convey little immediate sense of crisis. Possibly the significance of the Shinwell assault was less apparent than hindsight makes it. After all, his was not the only variant circulating on the official stance of 40 hours – several unions (some with officials on the parliamentary committee) were engaged in negotiations towards 48 or 44 hours. The most important trade of all, the engineering workers, had been pursuing a pre-war claim for 48 hours, and were now abruptly offered 47, provided they put the offer to immediate and binding national ballot. There seems little doubt that the objective underlying this move by the employers was to defuse the Clydeside agitation for 30 hours. In the event, it had the opposite effect, since the modest concession turned out to have been offered at the cost of a valued meal break and without thought to compensation for those on piecework.

In June, the senior officials who had devised the joint policy in January were quietly reconvened, and the commitment to 40 hours was reaffirmed. But the decision was not publicised, and when it emerged months later there was some dispute on the parliamentary committee as to whether STUC policy could be so casually redefined. Otherwise, in those crucial few months, the STUC leadership seems to have opted for a strategy of keeping its head down on the issue. On 12 October 1918, Neil Beaton of the shopworkers reported routinely to the committee that he had taken an opportunity to raise the case for a shorter week with the Minister of Labour, but the matter seems merely to have been noted. Only on 16 November, after the Armistice had been declared, did the committee rouse itself. It decided to call a special conference for 27 and 28 December on the problems of demobilisation. Two weeks later, sensing 'unmistakable signs' that the government was about to hand strategic industries back to private ownership, the committee suggested that both the Labour Party and the unions put their executive committees into continuous session in readiness for conflict. On 20 December, the committee decided after preliminary contacts with Churchill (who was now munitions minister) also to place before the special conference the issue of lay-offs in the munitions factories, which had begun to take place.

One more contributory factor to the frustrations of the moment, too often overlooked, needs to be mentioned here. In November, a snap general election was called. The outcome was victory for the Lloyd George coalition, but for Labour – and particularly in Scotland – the long-awaited breakthrough was missed by a tantalisingly close margin. Labour and co-operative candidates (excluding those standing beneath the coalition banner) secured almost a quarter of the Scottish vote even though they contested only 42 of the 71 seats. But they returned just six MPs in Scotland, and 57 across the UK as a whole. For every victory like Neil Maclean's in Govan, the ILP scored a string of near misses – Maxton in Bridgeton, Wheatley in Shettleston. In the medium-term, the prospects were encouraging. But, more immediately, it was industrial activism that held the greatest promise.

Events had by now taken on a momentum which was beyond the control of the STUC. The special conference formally confirmed the objective of a 40-hour week, and sought vainly to recapture the mood of the workers by charging the parliamentary committee to draw up plans for industrial action in pursuit of the claim. When the committee met on 11 January 1919 to discuss how to proceed on this instruction, however, William Shaw from Glasgow Trades Council reported that he had also attended a meeting called by the CWC shop stewards – an 'unofficial conference of the engineering and shipbuilding trades,' as the minutes describe it – and that the mood there had been both impatient and uncompromising. The parliamentary committee seems finally to have recognised the urgency of the position. At a special meeting a week later, on the morning of 18 January, it agreed to call an emergency conference on 1 February of union district committees, Glasgow Trades Council and the Clyde Engineering Trades Federation; and to recommend that union executives order a strike from 10 February if the 40 hours claim had not been met by the employers.

But this belated fast footwork was not fast enough. Earlier that week, the shop stewards had called a special conference, supported by Glasgow Trades Council, to decide on action in pursuit of 30 hours. This conference met on the afternoon of 18 January, immediately following the parliamentary committee meeting, and drew shop stewards from all over Scotland. The parliamentary committee, after much deliberation, had agreed to accept an invitation to attend, and a four-strong delegation turned up with a motion encompassing that morning's decisions for 40 hours and a 10 February deadline. The motion met a mixed response. Despite opposition from some of the Clyde stewards, the conference settled on 40 hours rather than 30. But it brought the deadline for a strike forward to 27 January, with no regard to whether the action was approved by union executives or not. A joint strike committee was formed, with Shaw as its joint secretary. To his intense discomfort, Hugh Lyon – as STUC president – was invited to join both the strike committee and the sub-committee drafting its manifesto, *A Call to Arms of the Workers*.

Three days later, the parliamentary committee was back in emergency session. On Shaw's casting vote, it was decided that Lyon, whose instinct was to resign simultaneously from the parliamentary committee and the strike committee, should remain on both. The effect of this decision was both to endorse reluctantly the 27 January strike, and to acknowledge implicitly that the stewards, not the STUC, were now in control of events. Thus bounced, the best the parliamentary committee could do was to press ahead with its 1 February conference and try to get the strike declared, *post factum*, official.

For once, Allan was moved to reflect candidly on the dilemma in the minutes book. He wrote: 'Thus far, and not as a deliberate action on the part of the PC, we seemed to be committed to a General Strike on 27 January 1919 . . . the opinion was freely expressed that we had been rushed into precipitate action, but on the whole the committee felt it was difficult to avoid such a result, as undoubtedly if a movement for 30 hours had once been launched it would seriously have jeopardised the position of the 40 Hours Movement and caused no end of dissension. On the other hand, the co-operation of the PC with a non-official movement was seriously questioned by other members . . . .'

If the STUC had been left trailing ruefully behind events, the government was determined not to be. The dispute now moved rapidly to its famous climax. On Tuesday, 27 January, 40,000 Glasgow workers downed tools. The following day, 30,000 more had joined them, with others poised to follow. The strike was rapidly gaining support in other Scottish cities like Edinburgh, where the Waverley Market was forcibly occupied. There were simultaneous stoppages by London transport workers and municipal employees in Belfast. But it was Glasgow that captured the moment. The government decided on a two-pronged response. It made a show of edging towards conciliation, offering an industrial conference to consider the claim for shorter hours. But, at the same time, it fell prey to the fears of the Secretary for Scotland, Robert Munro, that the strike was the pretext for a Bolshevik rising, and ordered a detachment of troops into Glasgow. When an estimated 20,000 demonstrators gathered in George Square on Friday, 31 January to hear news of the government's latest position, a police baton-charge turned the meeting into a near-riot. The official version of events held that the charge was ordered after rioters raided a beer lorry for bottles to throw and tried to blockade the trams. The strike committee's *Strike Bulletin*, in contrast, insisted that the crowd had been waiting peaceably for the strike leaders to emerge from the City Chambers: 'The bludgeon attack . . . was deliberately ordered by the officers, and was unprovoked. The attack was sheer brutality by the police to satisfy the lust of the masters for broken skulls.' In any event, the Riot Act was duly read (or rather recited: the document was torn from the Sheriff's hand as he tried to read it outside the main door of the City Chambers, and he delivered the text from memory). Both Kirkwood and Gallacher were first bludgeoned, and then arrested, though they were allowed, on Neil Maclean's request, to address the crowd from the City Chambers and appeal for calm before being taken into custody. In all, a dozen strike leaders were arrested, including Shinwell, chairman of the strike committee, who had been smuggled out of the square but was detained at his house in Govan the following morning. By then, the military presence in Glasgow had escalated to 12,000 troops, 100 troop lorries and six tanks, and the city was under virtual martial law.

Was a revolution seriously in prospect? The political establishment of the time certainly chose to believe so. Shinwell was jailed for five months for inciting the trouble (he was released just in time to greet the assorted dignitaries of the TUC when they finally brought their congress to the St Andrew's Hall in September). Gallacher and Muir were sentenced to three months each. The *Scotsman*, in some of the least measured reporting of its distinguished history, headlined its account of the conflict 'Failure of Terrorism' and began it with the words: 'Methods of terrorism were attempted yesterday by the strikers in Glasgow . . . .' That was just the news story. The leader column took the authorities to task for 'excessive consideration' in allowing the injured Kirkwood and Gallacher to speak, and declared: 'If the necessity has not yet arisen for military intervention, it may arise at any moment, and the authorities will be judged culpably negligent if they do not take measures now to secure for the citizens the protection which armed military force can alone ensure.' Yet even the *Scotsman* was forced to conclude, in a rather calmer leader a couple of days later, that 'there is reason to believe that even on the Clyde the supporters of syndicalism and the advocates of revolution are comparatively few in number.' There were numerous local engineering union branches – in Renfrew and Yoker, at Stephen & Sons in Linthouse, and even at the Alexandria naval munitions plant – which roundly condemned the violence. So, in much stronger terms, did the ASE executive, which called for a return to work. Certainly, revolution was never on the ILP agenda, publicly or privately. Even Gallacher was to recall in his memoirs that while the workers were ready for a rising, 'the leadership had never thought of it.'

And what of the STUC? To its credit, it stuck by the strike committee of which it had latterly become the reluctant partner. On Saturday, 1 February – the day after the George Square disturbances – its special conference went ahead as planned, with 185 delegates attending Glasgow's Co-Operative Hall. By an overwhelming majority, they approved a motion which 'protests in the strongest possible language against the authorities and the police for their brutal attack on the people . . . holds them criminally responsible for what took place, and demands the immediate release of Councillor Shinwell, William Gallacher and David Kirkwood.' The motion went on both to endorse the parliamentary committee's support for the strike committee, and to urge union executives to give the strike their full official backing, with the aim of securing legislation for a 40-hour week. An amendment condemning the parliamentary committee for supporting an unofficial strike was rejected by 92 votes to 22, while an addendum, urging that the strike be called off in favour of official union pressure on the government and the employers, was defeated by 77 votes to 24. The STUC's role in the affair may never have been dynamic, but neither was it finally dishonourable.

In the event, the strike began almost immediately to subside, and there was a steady return to work. The government did eventually set up an industrial conference, but it was ultimately left to individual unions to secure the best working hours agreements that they could. Come the 1919 STUC congress at Perth, delegates approved a motion which urged every union to seek 'a substantial reduction' in hours. But an amendment from Glasgow Trades Council calling for a uniform 40-hour week was defeated.

Whatever it was that Red Clydeside amounted to, or might have amounted to, the disturbance in George Square wrote its coda. Within three years, several of the leading agitators had become Members of Parliament. For the STUC, too, there was a clear sense of changing times. At the 1919 congress, George Carson, who had been a delegate all those years ago at the Berkeley Hall, finally retired. At that same congress, Robert Allan proposed – on behalf of the majority on the parliamentary committee – that the STUC adopt the system of block voting used by the TUC: the very issue on which the STUC had been founded back in 1897. The motion was defeated by a margin of two to one. Some principles were still too important to discard. Yet, the realisation had finally borne home that there could be no return to the 'normality' that had preceded the Great War. The future, not the past, was what needed attention.

It would be a future in which Robert Allan would play little part. The wartime rise in membership had generated grand plans in many unions to demonstrate their new maturity by investing in suitably elegant bricks and mortar. Allan was a particular enthusiast for this fad, and had taken personal charge of a parliamentary committee scheme to found a Scottish Labour Institute in Glasgow. The problem was that, as post-war conflict and unemployment steadily eroded resources, Allan's ambitions on the real estate front grew ever more expansive. Finally, the parliamentary committee learned in March 1922 that he had contracted the STUC to meet instalments on a property deal that it could not remotely afford, and that legal action was now pending. Six weeks ahead of the 1922 congress, he was suspended, so debarring him from seeking renomination. Yet, he was to be spared the humiliation of dismissal, at the cost of a bizarre personal misfortune. A few days after his suspension, he lost both legs in an accident at Carlisle railway station. The affair of the Labour Institute was hushed up (it was settled out of court, expensively, three years later), and the congress marked his departure with expressions of kindly sympathy. It was the end of Robert Allan, and of the first age of the STUC.

Whys and wherefores: delegates to the first STUC congress, 1897. Margaret Irwin, seated third from left. (All pictures the *Herald* unless otherwise stated.)

To the aid of the party: Labour's first MPs take tea on the Commons terrace. They include Alexander Wilkie (extreme left), George Barnes (fourth from left) and Keir Hardie (pointing).

Great and secret dangers: a tank in the Trongate bears testament to government fears of an uprising in Glasgow in 1919.

Great and secret dangers: the George Square leaders stand trial. From left, Emanuel Shinwell, Willie Gallacher, George Edbury, David Brennan, David Kirkwood and James Murray.

Hard times: William Elger.

Hard times: George Middleton.

The new Jerusalem: Clement Attlee speaking in Larkhall before a
banner dedicated to Bob Smillie.

The new Jerusalem: Harold Wilson and Abe Moffat welcome the Chinese miners' leader, Chin Chih-Fu, to the 1955 Scottish miners' gala.

Friend and foe: George Brown and Barbara Castle en voyage to STUC congresses in Rothesay.

Of devolution and discontent: Vic Feather, Jimmy Jack and the UCS shop stewards march through Glasgow.

Of devolution and discontent: Jimmy Reid welcomes Harold Wilson to UCS.

CHAPTER FOUR

SHOWDOWN

Allan's successor was from a very different mould from those that had gone before. William Elger did not emerge from long services to struggle on the parliamentary committee. He seemed to emerge almost from nowhere. He was never an elected member of the parliamentary committee, nor of its successor, the general council. The STUC, having been piloted through its first quarter century by its founding generation, suddenly had a general secretary who had been six years old at the time of the Berkeley Hall Congress.

No less startling was the manner of Elger's emergence. He first surfaced at a special congress in January 1921, called to consider a sweeping reorganisation package, which included reconstituting the parliamentary committee as a general council and upgrading its secretaryship to the post of general secretary on a salary of £300 a year. The task of proposing the motion on the general secretaryship fell to Elger, a young clerk in a paper mill who was attending his first congress having just been elected president of Edinburgh Trades Council. Less than 18 months later, Elger himself had the job and the salary. He had been appointed over the heads of several long-serving and better-known applicants, including David Marshall of the dockworkers who had acted as interim secretary after Allan's abrupt departure. Elger would remain in the post from his appointment just after the STUC's twenty-fifth birthday until his death just short of its fiftieth.

What was behind this swift and soaring ascent? Contemporary sources pay respectful tribute to Elger's shrewdness, industry and competence, but rarely find cause to mention his idealism. The researcher uncovers few passages of inspirational Elger rhetoric. Critics, both contemporary and retrospective, charge him with holding the TUC in excessive thrall, with appearing ever anxious to follow its lead, take its counsel and copy its procedures. Yet he guided the STUC through several crises which threatened its survival as an independent trade union centre, and he moved it steadily into the mainstream of Scottish public life. He held command of the STUC for nearly a quarter of its existence: even so, the remarkable thing is how many of the standard texts afford him only cursory mention. Nowhere at all does one find William Elger described as colourful, though an admiring STUC obituary of him by Joseph Duncan, veteran leader of the Scottish farm servants, does describe him as 'in every way as loveable as he was big and fine.' He is therefore peculiarly difficult to get right.

But he was undoubtedly significant. Not only was he in charge of the STUC through some of its most turbulent years, but many of the organisation's enduring characteristics – both strengths and weaknesses – can be traced to his personal influence. Under his stewardship, it changed rapidly from being an annual gathering with a committee that did a bit of intervening lobbying, into a professionally-run, full-time presence in Scottish affairs, turning out papers and pamphlets on every topic of the day. Elger was, first and foremost, not an agitator nor a campaigner, but an administrator. It seems to have been an early passion, and one that never left him. He was an Englishman, born in London of Austrian descent, who had come to Edinburgh looking for work at age 14 when his father died. Having found it in a paper mill, he joined the National Union of Clerks in 1912 and almost immediately set about trying to reorganise it into a federation of quasi-autonomous guilds. The impression forms of an able and determined man, but not a particularly warm one. A film director looking to cast the role might think instinctively of Robert Stack or Kevin Costner. His years in office were marked by a constant churn of organisational initiatives, not all of which came to fruit, and a positive deluge of forms and questionnaires, not all of which the affiliates troubled to return. But some of his logistical inno- vations have continued to serve the STUC well. He developed, too, the ambassadorial role which has since become a central part of the general secretary's remit, and became a ubiquitous presence on public bodies. Without William Elger, the STUC might or might not have survived the stresses of the inter-war years: but it would certainly have been a very different organisation from the one now embarking on its second century.

Elger's rise rode several powerful imperatives of the times. Robert Allan's failed attempt at the 1919 congress to wish the block vote on the STUC reflected widespread recognition that organisational change was long overdue, and equally widespread disagreement about the form it should take. Carson and Allan had both been doughty fighters but, however diligent their intentions, their administrative talents had been on a distinctly modest scale. The demands on the STUC had been growing exponentially, yet its structures had evolved very little from the energetic amateurism of its founding years. Allan's investment misfortunes were not the only development of the early 1920s to point to an urgent need for professionalism at the top. Wartime had brought a rapid influx of members, but growth intensified the stresses and rivalries within the movement, and strained its capacity to look after its new legions. The onset of mass unemployment added further pressures, both financial and political, and despite Elger's perpetual membership drive, affiliations peaked in 1926 at just over 329,000, a level they would not recover until 1938. The STUC's meagre resources – income in 1923 totalled just £1,139 – could no longer be so haphazardly managed.

More urgently still, the movement had failed to achieve unity, or even co-ordination, in a series of set-piece confrontations with state and employers. The Triple Alliance, that supposedly invincible pact between the country's most powerful groups of workers, had fallen into disrepair. Increasingly, too, the politics of socialism were becoming factionalised and acrimonious. Particularly significant, from the STUC's point of view, was the growth of the Communist Party and of its trade union wing, the National Minority Movement, which, from 1924, was to badger unsuccessfully but persistently for a more centralised structure to organised labour, in which a separate TUC in Scotland had no very obvious place. The labour movement entered the 1920s faced with powerful and implacable enemies, and rarely looking the equal of the challenges it faced. The melodrama in George Square had already demonstrated just how high the stakes had risen. But another confrontation, later in 1919, was to convey an arguably more telling lesson about the fundamental weakness of the movement, and the might of the forces now ranged against it. In the autumn, the railwaymen decided to strike over pay. It was one in a succession of strikes which took the number of workings days lost through industrial action across Britain that year to almost 35 million, more than three times the 1918 total. The miners had been out – though they were enticed back to work by the establishment of Mr Justice Sankey's Royal Commission on the Coal Industry – as had the engineers. The railwaymen's dispute too was settled reasonably quickly. Its significance lay in the portents it sounded for what lay ahead.

First, the strike should have triggered – but did not – sympathetic action from the other two elements in the Triple Alliance, the miners and the transport workers. The reasons for the inertia remain open to dispute. One version holds the TUC parliamentary committee responsible, in that it failed to act swiftly enough to mobilise support. Another version blames the railwaymen's leader, Jimmy Thomas (later a Labour Cabinet Minister) for not troubling to activate the Alliance. Either way, the clear signal was conveyed that brave promises of solidarity in strife might prove easier to declare than to deliver. That message was forcefully underlined 18 months later, when the miners were locked out, and the executive of the Triple Alliance decided, at the eleventh hour, not to support them.

Secondly, the rail strike, though relatively uneventful in itself, brought into sharp relief the full measure of the government's preparedness to crush any sign of industrial insurgency. In February 1919, in the immediate aftermath of George Square, the Cabinet had formed an Industrial Unrest Committee to co-ordinate the official response to stoppages in major industries. The rail dispute was its first big test, and the general view in Whitehall was that the speed at which arrangements were put in place to counter the effects of the strike had been impressive. In October, the government decided to set the committee on a permanent, and more ambitious, footing. The Supply and Transport Committee (STC), also known as the National Emergency Committee, was formed with the explicit remit of maintaining essential services during strikes. It was backed up by a civil service network, the Supply and Transport Organisation (STO), and reinforced the following March by the appointment of 11 regional commissioners ready to take rapid charge of STO operations in their areas in the event of trouble. Also in 1919, the Police Act was passed, outlawing trade unionism and industrial action in the constabulary. In October 1920, these measures were consolidated in the Emergency Powers Act, which enabled the government to declare a state of emergency and take over the running of essential services should they be disrupted by strikes. That Act was used for the first time when troops were deployed during the miners' lock-out of 1921. The Leader of the Commons, and future Conservative Prime Minister, Andrew Bonar Law declared: 'Both miners and railwaymen are servants not of employers but of the state . . . a strike would be against the state and the state must win and must use all its power for that purpose, otherwise it would be the end of government in this country.' The state, drawing on the lessons of wartime contingency planning, was now fully geared up to meet any challenge – real, potential or merely imagined – that organised labour might contrive to pose.

Organised labour had little choice but to try to remarshall its forces in like order. Trade unionists, too, had learned from wartime experiences, and a frequent cry during this period was of the need for some form of 'general staff', a strategic command structure to lead the workers' battalions into battle. The TUC acted first, at a special congress in December 1920, where it decided to reconstitute its parliamentary committee into a general council. The logic was that the old concept of a parliamentary committee, charged with lobbying for legislative reform, had been superseded by the development of a Labour Party with growing parliamentary strength. Borrowing from the lessons of military discipline, a general council could channel the attentions of affiliated unions much more coherently into achieving industrial ends. This deepening distinction between political and industrial militancy was not one universally accepted by trade unionists, then or later. The TUC also brought the Women's Trade Union League into full membership, a testament both to the expansion of female labour during the war (though an estimated 600,000 women had lost their jobs within months of the war ending), and to the effectiveness of action staged by various organisations of women trade unionists during the war years.

The driving force behind these reforms was the longing for unity, though it would be wrong to suppose that the strengthening of official trade union structures was viewed with unalloyed dismay by ministers. For the moment, anything which strengthened the hand of the unions' national leaderships over upstart local activists was welcome to a still jittery government. Even Winston Churchill, no friend of organised labour, had argued in Cabinet that official trade unionism was the only form of workers' organisation with which the government could deal, and that its 'curse' was that there was not enough of it to keep local officials in line. 'With a powerful trade union, either peace or war can be made,' Churchill said. Therefore, the immediate post-war period saw the government increasingly co-opting union officials on to public bodies, and growing numbers of employers seeing advantage in recognising major unions. For exactly the same reasons, many grassroots activists were profoundly suspicious of any reforms which would strengthen the power of national union leaderships.

For the STUC, the imperatives were much the same, but the calculations rather more complex. For one thing, grassroot and shopfloor prerogatives were, proportionately at least, a much bigger consideration in Scotland, and were much more powerfully represented in STUC decision-making through the trades councils. The TUC's block vote structure translated fairly easily into a general council but, as Robert Allan had found, the STUC was not ready to discard that badge of its heritage. Besides, the more closely the STUC followed the TUC's lead, the less clear was its case for remaining independent at a time when the usefulness of that independence was coming into question. Therefore, a balance had to be struck between the Scottish way of doing things and the TUC's example of how they could be done better. On that much, Scottish trade unionists were largely agreed. Just where the right balance lay, however, was a much more contentious question and one that was to preoccupy the STUC through the early 1920s and beyond. The appointment of William Elger, an evangelist for the TUC approach, was an answer of sorts, but never a final one.

So Elger was the product, rather than the instigator, of the prevailing resolve. The convergence with TUC methods, and with the TUC itself, had begun before he erupted onto the scene. When the TUC finally brought its congress to Glasgow in September 1919, the STUC's president William Shaw (who was also secretary of Glasgow Trades Council) wrote its minutes. The two parliamentary committees met twice in joint session during the week, and a number of proposals for closer co-operation were discussed, though to no very palpable effect. The STUC, familiarly, argued for a standing invitation to serve on national and international bodies, while the TUC, equally familiarly, raised the prospect of the STUC subsiding into a regional offshoot of its own structure. But the tone of the discussions seems to have been constructive and amicable, and to have reflected a common acceptance that change was necessary. The old wounds between the two organisations had begun to heal.

In the wake of the railwaymen's strike, pressure mounted within the STUC for reform. A special conference of officials, held just after the strike was settled, agreed a motion from the indefatigable Shinwell along the general staff lines – suggesting a central body within the STUC which would be responsible for organising joint action in support of any major dispute. But the parliamentary committee was deeply divided on this idea, particularly when Glasgow Trades Council followed up by proposing a general strike in protest at the British embargo on trade with Soviet Russia, which was threatening to develop into open support for a Polish military invasion. Increasingly, the parliamentary committee inclined towards the TUC route to reform, though racked with doubts about what a general council might achieve in terms of solidarity that the mighty Triple Alliance had been unable to deliver.

That concern gained wider currency after 'Black Friday,' in April 1921, when Thomas had to tell the miners that their railway partners in the Triple Alliance would not be supporting them in the nationwide lock-out which followed the government's abrupt decision to hand full control of the pits back to the coal-owners. The pretext for the climb-down was that the miners had rejected the opportunity of a temporary settlement, based on local deals, and proposed by their secretary, Frank Hodges. But that rationalisation could not disguise the scale of the retreat. It was clear that government had decided, not for the last time, to attempt a definitive showdown with the miners. The miners' federation, particularly in Scotland, had certainly exhibited an escalating taste for politicisation: in the preceding few months it had not only declared a policy of active resistance against any government moves towards war with Russia, but had affiliated for good measure to the Scottish Home Rule Association and had backed home rule for India. There had been a two-week national stoppage the previous autumn, the Datum Line Strike (named after a production bonus threshold). In March 1921, unemployment rose for the first time beyond a million, and would stay there into the Second World War. Britain's imperial domination of international trade was crumbling, and the post-war shake-up in the world economic order was placing key sectors, particularly the heavy industries on which the Scottish economy was founded, under awesome pressure. Circumstances were ripe for confrontation.

But the miners had reckoned without both the vacillation of the Triple Alliance and, more significantly, the preparedness of the government for conflict. Every agency of the state was marshalled against them. A legally dubious decision was taken to deny them unemployment benefit, even though they were locked out rather than striking. Large contingents of police and troops appeared instantly in the coalfields, and were used more proactively than ever before, intervening in some districts to stop union officials from different pits from meeting, and more generally mounting guard to enable managers to keep pits operating. There were, inevitably, some ugly scenes, and many arrests. The government had learned the value of publicity, and successfully focused public attention on the union's decision to withdraw health and safety cover. Its efforts reached rare heights of inventiveness in Scotland, where for a while press coverage of the dispute was dominated by the fate of two pit ponies said to have been drowned at Leven because the dispute had prevented pumping of the pit. An animal welfare group issued summonses against local union activists, and the matter got as far as protests to the Prime Minister in the Commons before it finally emerged that the fault for not bringing the ponies to safety had actually lain with management. On 1 July, the miners, demoralised and defeated, agreed to return to work after 14 weeks of action.

It was just after the Triple Alliance's retreat from supporting the miners that the 1921 STUC met in Aberdeen for what was to prove a turbulent congress. Delegates grappled intently with the enormity of the challenge which now faced them. Feelings were running high, but there was also a flavour of the wake in some of the speeches. The more defiant voices argued that the scale of the government's contingency planning to see off a general strike needed to be matched by equal levels of preparedness on labour's part to mount one. Yet there was little consensus about what precisely ought to, or could, be done. Some favoured a rebuilt Triple Alliance as the vanguard of resistance, while others thought too much power had been vested in the Alliance executive and that national leaders could no longer be trusted to fight true. Still others countered that there had been little evidence of willingness among grassroots members to give the miners the support denied by the leaderships, and counselled that the movement would do better to trim its ambitions to a more realistic assessment of its capabilities.

The prescriptions were not much more coherent than the diagnoses. There was condemnation of the Emergency Powers Act, which John Queen of Glasgow Trades Council described as a provocation to revolution. Yet the suggestion that Labour should withdraw from the Commons until the Act was repealed was – sensibly – resisted. What the congress did convey was both a sense of urgency, and a refusal to be crushed by the weight of governmental antagonism. Delegates approved a motion from Aberdeen Trades Council calling for, in essence, the creation of a parallel structure to the STO within the labour movement, a nationwide machinery to ensure union control of food supplies, transportation, publicity and 'other factors essential to [the] success' of a major dispute. The parliamentary committee, though charged with developing this idea, did nothing much about it. But the proposal did add impetus to the momentum for change. Also reinforced by the experiences of spring 1921 was the STUC's still-powerful enthusiasm for Scottish home rule, which had been buttressed by a close and enduring interest in events in Ireland. This quasi-nationalistic mood acted, for a while, as a counterweight to the logic of the STUC becoming more closely aligned to the TUC, even if there was little objective evidence to support claims from some quarters that an autonomous Scottish Triple Alliance would have done better by the miners.

It was against this background of dislocation and frustration that the STUC decided to rebuild the parliamentary committee as a general council, but it would be two more years before an agreed scheme was fully in place. The TUC's example could not translate directly into an STUC context, even if the broad principles were to be similar. The general council would be constituted on a basis of trade groups, so as to ensure representation for all the main sectors of industry. A system of sub-committees would be able to share common experiences, confront common challenges and promote co-operation – or amalgamation – between unions. In considering how best to implement the change, the STUC took copious advantage of its rapprochement with the TUC, and there were numerous consultations between the two parliamentary committees. For a time, it even looked possible that the TUC's long wish to reabsorb its Scottish comrades might gel from this new cosiness, and there were some in Scotland as well as south of the border who thought that option now made sense. But it was not to be. The principles which had led to the STUC being formed in the first place continued to hold sway with Scottish trade unionists, and from that it followed that the Scottish model would have to differ in several respects from the TUC's. Most importantly, it would have to accommodate the trades councils. Even so, their influence within STUC decision-making would be permanently diminished by the creation of a general council. Equally, the TUC trade groupings built naturally on the proportionality afforded by the block vote, which remained unacceptable in Scotland. Eventually, an STUC general council of 12 members was agreed, made up of delegates from 10 trade groups (the mining and quarrying sector, far the biggest, had two representatives, the rest one each), plus one representative of the trades councils. It was 1924 before the last pieces of the scheme were finally cemented into place, and by then the post-war impetus to create a military-style strategic command had subsided. But the model did, with minor adjustments, prove durable, and it did create a mechanism for better understanding and co-ordination of trade unionism's rich diversity in Scotland.

If trade unionism was making little headway against adversity in those early years of the 1920s, the picture politically was, initially at least, much more encouraging. Lloyd George's coalition, so long held together by the personal allegiances of its leaders, had reached the end of the road. The dream of perpetuating it in a new centre party, nurtured between Lloyd George, Churchill and FE Smith at the dinner table of the Other Club, had never really been shared by, or with, their respective parties. Liberals grew resentful of Lloyd George's conspiratorial friendships with the Tory *haut monde*, while Tories, now increasingly mistrustful of the Welsh Wizard, came to long for the restoration of their doctrinal distinctiveness. First Bonar Law detached himself from the coalition, and spoke out against it: then a little-known junior minister, Stanley Baldwin, organised a coup from the courtly portals of the Carlton Club. With infinite reluctance, and spitting venom at recalcitrants of both persuasions, Lloyd George went to the country.

At the general election of 15 November 1922, the Labour Party at last achieved its long-awaited electoral breakthrough, and Scotland, at last, played a full part in the advance. Labour overtook the Liberals to become the principal opposition to Andrew Bonar Law's short-lived 'government of the second eleven,' so called because the Tory elders who had been coalition ministers refused to serve in it. Scotland contributed 29 of the 138 Labour MPs, capitalising both on the 1918 extension of the franchise and on the success, particularly after Irish partition in 1921, of activists like Wheatley in weaning the Catholic vote away from the Liberals (a task made easier by Labour's waning enthusiasm for temperance, since publicans played almost as important a part as priests in organising the Catholic vote!). Labour won a shade under a third of the Scottish popular vote, compared with a quarter for the Tories and just over a fifth for the Liberals. Wheatley, who took the Shettleston seat, was just one of several Clydeside untouchables suddenly translated to Westminster. There was also Maxton in Bridgeton, Kirkwood in Clydebank, Johnston in West Stirlingshire, Shinwell in Linlithgow, George Buchanan in Gorbals, Campbell Stephen in Camlachie, Rosslyn Mitchell in Paisley. No less gratifyingly for the movement in Scotland, Churchill lost abstemious Dundee to a prohibition Socialist, Edwin Scrymgeour. As the new MPs left St Enoch Station for Westminster, a crowd sang the 23rd Psalm and the Red Flag.

But the mood of celebration was tempered by the implications for organised labour of a return to Tory government for the first time since 1905. At first, it seemed that the Tories' tenure might be of short duration. Bonar Law, suffering from terminal cancer, lasted in post just six months. Baldwin, who had been Chancellor, succeeded him. By then they had already courted electoral unpopularity by agreeing an expensive schedule for repayment of war debt to the US: shortly afterwards, Baldwin went to the country to secure electoral consent for a commitment, inherited from Bonar Law, to protectionist tariffs. He lost, and Ramsay MacDonald (though commanding just 191 MPs, 67 fewer than the Tories) formed Britain's first Labour government.

It was, and not just in retrospect, a most anti-climactic triumph. MacDonald, knowing that the Liberals held the balance of power and the will to use it, decided not to risk a socialist programme at home. This timidity both soured relations with his two principal ministers, Arthur Henderson and Philip Snowden, and stirred the antipathy of the Left, particularly after the Lloyd George anti-strike apparatus was used against Ernest Bevin's transport workers. MacDonald concentrated instead on diplomacy (he was simultaneously Foreign Secretary and Prime Minister), succeeding in fashioning a new alliance with the French. But he also concluded a commercial treaty – and thus formal recognition – with the Soviet government in Russia. This ran against public mood, and when he fought clumsily shy of prosecuting the Communist editor of *Workers' Weekly*, JR Campbell, for incitement to sedition, the Liberals and Tories united against him, forcing a vote of confidence which he lost. His fate was sealed when the ensuing election was dominated by anti-Communist sentiment, aggravated by publication of the forged Zinoviev letter, which purported to show that MacDonald had agreed the Russian treaty under Communist influence. The first Labour government had lasted less than a year. Baldwin was back in office, and this time with the most formidable Tory grandees alongside him in Cabinet, including Churchill who had retraced his steps across the floor of the Commons and was now Chancellor. That, it swiftly became clear, was bad news for organised labour.

It had also become evident that the newly swollen Labour ranks at Westminster would be a fractious force. In particular, Labour's partnership with the Scottish-dominated ILP – which had sponsored 40 of the 43 Labour candidates in Scotland in 1922 – gave rise to mounting friction as the 1920s progressed, though the ILP itself also grew increasingly riven by factional acrimony. Within weeks of their arrival at Westminster, the Clydesiders had helped secure the election of Ramsay MacDonald – 'their chief man,' as Beatrice Webb was later ironically to recall – as party leader, and had then set about making gleeful nuisances of themselves. In June 1923, Maxton accused Tory MPs of murder because they had supported cutbacks in funding hospital places for children. Challenged by the Speaker to withdraw the remark, he refused and was vociferously supported by Wheatley, Stephen and Buchanan in the ensuing procedural exchanges. All four were suspended, to the mortification and lasting fury of MacDonald. Johnston was also soon in ill odour with the leader for exposing a financial scandal in Sudan in which Asquith's son was embarrassingly implicated. By the time MacDonald came to form his minority government in 1924, he was already rising in the demonology of the Left, even though just two years had passed since he had been chosen, on Shinwell's nomination, as the Left candidate for party leader. Among the Clydesiders, only the gifted Wheatley – as housing minister – gained significant preferment in MacDonald's first administration. In the years to come, the ILP under Maxton's leadership would become a focus for anti-MacDonald resentments, and in 1932 it disaffiliated from the Labour Party.

The political maelstrom of the times exercised a powerful, and in some respects debilitating, influence on the STUC. It was not just in organisational terms that the STUC in this period drew closer to London. Ideologically, too, its agenda became less distinctively Scottish from the early years of Elger's secretaryship onwards. After 1923 it more or less stopped discussing Scottish home rule for the best part of a decade, though it remained nominally in favour and individual leading lights – such as Charles Gallie of the railway clerks – continued to be prominent in the home rule movement. But such issues were seen increasingly to lie beyond the proper concerns of the STUC. The Westminster road to socialism, now mapped, seemed clear. The task before the STUC was to equip the Scottish trades union movement for that road, rather than to dabble much itself in political argument.

Indeed, the ILP in Scotland became an increasingly passionate advocate of the home rule cause during the 1920s, even organising in 1923 a prototype of the Bannockburn rallies that were later to become a regular item in the SNP's calendar. There were two home rule Bills introduced by Scottish Labour MPs in this period. The first, tabled by George Buchanan in 1924, was a fairly modest, proto-federalist measure drafted by Labour's Scottish council. Despite uneasy assent from MacDonald and energetic advocacy from the Clydesiders, it was talked out by the Tories. The second Bill, in 1927, was rather different. Drafted by the Scottish Home Rule Association and moved by James Barr, it sought to give Scotland the status of an independent dominion, parallel to the Irish Free State, with virtually all governmental functions transferring from Whitehall to a Scottish parliament, and the Scottish MPs withdrawing from Westminster. The potency of its proposals cost it the support of all but a handful of Labour MPs and, incidentally, of the STUC: both Elger and Joseph Duncan of the farmworkers voiced public concerns. Duncan, from then on, became a prominent opponent of home rule having previously been a supporter and, when the STUC next debated the issue in 1931, he declared that the interests of Scottish and English workers were now identical – a point he would underline a year later by merging the Scottish union he had created twenty years previously with the TGWU. On that occasion, the STUC again backed home rule, but with enough big unions like the railwaymen opposed for the policy to move to the margins of STUC ambition. Support in the Labour Party had also by now dwindled to a core of Scots and a few older radicals. Most of the party furth of Scotland held no enthusiasm whatever for the idea. The issue served to emphasise the somewhat ambiguous autonomy afforded to Labour's Scottish council by the redrawn party constitution of 1918. The ambiguity, to an extent, remains.

An early indicator of the new mood within the STUC came at the 1921 congress in Aberdeen, which unanimously endorsed a motion from the Scottish miners demanding a UK wages board. Though the miners were still home rule supporters (having been won over to the cause in 1918), Peter Chambers, proposing, prefaced the times that lay ahead by arguing forcibly that socialism, like capitalism, should know no national boundaries and should 'look to the day when the workers of all countries would become one great industrial organisation.'

This eye to the bigger stage was becoming evident too in relation to union organisation. With the blessing of the STUC, the amalgamations process took on fresh impetus across the 1920s. Amalgamation by industry was, as we have seen, something to which the STUC had long been ready to give its backing, but as the pace of merger quickened, this endorsement – though never weakening – grew increasingly altruistic. By now the vast majority of Scottish trade unionists belonged to unions headquartered south of the border. There remained some feisty exceptions, like the Scottish Horse and Motormen's Association, but increasingly Scottish-based and craft-based unions were drawn into the big industry unions. There were two dynamics driving the process. First, as had happened in the early years of the century, deteriorating economic circumstance was encouraging employers to band together to drive down wage costs. Second, it was assumed by many trade unionists that the Labour Party, having attained governmental maturity, would in due course deliver worker control of industry, for which industry-wide unions seemed the prudent preparation. There was thus both a defensive and an offensive logic to merger. The problem for the STUC was that the national bargaining and arbitration which flowed naturally from the process left it progressively marginalised as a motive force in influencing pay and conditions for Scottish trades unionists.

Another problem that was to dog the general council across the inter-war years had started to surface. In 1920, a Scottish former engineering shop steward, Wal Hannington, had formed the London Council of the Unemployed – drawing together various groupings of jobless ex-servicemen – and had begun to lobby the labour and trade union movement for recognition. By November 1921, similar committees had sprung up in sufficient industrial towns across the country, including several in Scotland, to form a nationwide federation, the National Unemployed Workers' Movement. The following October, they mounted the first of the famous hunger marches to London, led off by a 350-strong contingent from Scotland. The movement caught the public imagination, and crowds lined the streets to cheer the marchers on. Yet it was to prove a potent source of dissension within the labour movement generally, and the STUC in particular. Cautious indulgence turned to mounting suspicion, and finally to sullen, if uncomfortable, hostility. In the process, a wedge was to be driven between the STUC and the bodies which had been its primary pretext for coming into being; the trades councils. There would even be a short-lived Elger experiment, begun at the 1926 congress in Inverness, to set up a parallel structure of 'county and local trade union committees.' Echoes of that estrangement would continue to be heard for decades to come – arguably, to the present day.

The NUWM and its local offshoots presented two connected difficulties for the STUC leadership. First, the unemployed committees attracted the early attention of the Communist Party, which became a powerful presence within many of them. They thus became a target for the febrile anti-Communist mood, diligently nurtured by the right-wing press, that would result in the Zinoviev Letter lethally damaging the first Labour government. In truth, the NUWM's support ranged much wider than the CP, and included most of the Clydeside Labour MPs, as well as substantial numbers of non-Communist shop stewards, councillors and union officials. But none of that prevented the right-wing press from portraying the NUWM as a Communist front, marching to Moscow's drumbeat. MacDonald's well-matured distaste for

Communism, it must be borne in mind, was not universally shared at this time in either wing of the labour movement, and there were numerous local confrontations involving old comrades who found themselves on opposite sides of what many saw as a false boundary. In 1924, for example, Aitken Ferguson, a leading light in both the Minority Movement and in Glasgow Trades Council, contested a by-election in Kelvingrove as 'a Communist, and a trade unionist, standing as the official candidate of the Labour Party.' He had been endorsed by the constituency Labour Party, in defiance of national policy, and though the party nationally disowned his campaign, several Labour MPs spoke in his support. That year also saw Labour's Scottish conference draw close to passing a motion in favour of sanctioning Communist affiliation to the Labour Party.

Second, as the STUC began to edge away from the NUWM, many of the trades councils sprang to its defence, and argued that they should be entitled to consolidate the close informal relations which, in many areas, they had forged with local NUWM committees. The NUWM, after all, was often dominated at local level by ex-shop stewards who had been stalwarts of their trades councils before they lost their jobs. It was also a loyal presence in support of workers in dispute. None the less, a disquiet on the part of the STUC that trades councils were vulnerable to becoming vehicles for far-Left agitation and entryism took root at this time, and would endure long after the NUWM was the stuff of history.

On the other hand, the NUWM's political embarrassment factor needed to be weighed against the attractions of reversing the membership haemorrhage which mass unemployment was causing. The Lanarkshire miners alone reported a fall of nearly half – from 47,000 to 25,000 – in their affiliated membership in the two years to 1922. Not only was union membership still a minority pursuit for Scottish workers but, according to a 1924–25 general council survey, only around 60 per cent of Scottish union members were affiliated to the STUC. Elger was a perpetual enthusiast for membership drives, and took up in Scotland the lead set in this regard by the TUC. The trouble was that the obvious front-line forces for recruitment should have been the trades councils. Yet the commitment of the trades councils to the industrial context was increasingly open to debate. Not only was there suspicion at their links with Communist-tinged unemployed workers' committees, but many councils had become virtually indistinguishable from the local Labour parties set up under Labour's 1918 constitution. The general council survey found that most now operated jointly as trades and labour councils and, more worryingly, that many of them existed more powerfully in name than in substance. With Elger keen to confine the STUC to the industrial side of the labour equation, the trades councils seemed to be becoming drawn steadily into the political ambit. One of the defining changes which the post-war era had wrought in the movement was the importance now being attached to that distinction.

Still, the STUC's initial response to the rise of the NUWM was one of cautious encouragement and sympathy. In this it followed the lead of the TUC, which set up a joint advisory council with the NUWM in 1924. The STUC did not go that far, but it did eventually adopt, after due rephrasing, most of the policies for better treatment of the unemployed agreed between the NUWM and the TUC. In the closing months of Allan's secretaryship, it urged affiliates to campaign on the rights of the unemployed, threw its weight behind NUWM complaints at the inefficiency of labour exchanges, and noted with apparent approval the joint initiatives with unemployed groups being taken by many trades councils. Where it baulked, and would continue to baulk, was when the unemployed sought affiliation.

This call first surfaced at the 1922 congress in Edinburgh, where an NUWM delegation was warmly received, and Edinburgh Trades Council suggested, in the course of debate, that unemployed committees should be able to affiliate to trades councils on equal terms with union branches. The following year, in Dundee, the demand had hardened markedly. An NUWM delegation was again welcomed, and this time delegates heard a barn-storming address by Harry McShane, friend of Willie Gallacher and partner of John Maclean in the nomadic propagandist group, the Tramp Trust Unlimited, who had lately left the British Socialist Party for the CPGB. McShane acknowledged the labour movement's sympathy for the unemployed, but said they 'did not want any more sympathy and did not require it.' What they wanted was the right to affiliate both to trades councils and to the STUC, 'as a movement that had demonstrated its worth, not in words but in deeds . . . as good as any organisation represented here today.' Not only that, but they wanted a general strike in support of full maintenance benefit for the unemployed, and sought to win over the STUC to this by pointing out that the existence of an army of unemployed workers allowed wages to be driven down for those still in jobs. The congress listened with slightly dazed courtesy to this rhetorical *tour de force*, and then proceeded to show how little unanimity it could muster on the matter. William Shaw, for the standing orders committee, moved that the application for affiliation be remitted back to the general council rather than decided immediately. Intense debate ensued. Several speakers, including Neil Maclean, wanted the application agreed without delay. Others, including Elger, insisted that new affiliations could only be sanctioned if the application was circulated ahead of congress. Eventually, Shaw's proposal prevailed, on a vote of 83 to 36. What mattered was that the STUC had shown itself deeply divided on the issue. So it would remain.

The following year at Ayr the NUWM did not turn up, but another procedural tussle arose over whether to consider a written application for affiliation. Again, the vote went against, but this time by a narrower margin of 74 to 40. Over the next 12 months, attitudes on both sides of the debate toughened with the fall of MacDonald's first administration. An NUWM delegation was again in attendance for the 1925 congress in Dumfries, and again the affiliation question gave rise to embittered debate. Supporters argued that, with unemployment remorselessly rising, affiliation of unemployed trades unionists was a logical precaution for the STUC to take. Opponents, including the general council, objected somewhat meretriciously that this would amount to dual representation for such members (both through their unions and through the NUWM). Only after affiliation had been rejected was the NUWM allowed to address congress, and when it did its organiser, Fred Douglas, treated delegates to a detailed account of the extensive co-operation taking place with trades councils and local Labour parties across Scotland. When he had finished, the trades councils reopened the issue. Edinburgh moved that local unemployed committees be allowed to affiliate to trades councils, Glasgow that individual unemployed members be entitled to join appropriate trades council sections. Both calls were defeated, as was a demand from Glasgow for a joint NUWM–general council liaison committee, in line with the TUC example. Edinburgh did win a commitment to creation of a general council standing committee on unemployment. It was a modest victory, and it did nothing to bridge the widening gap between an STUC increasingly beguiled by the grand canvass of national industrial unions, and a tier of trades councils, in varying states of repair and insubordination, which growing numbers of grassroots members saw as the more worthy channels for their activism.

The stage was set for the greatest setpiece confrontation of all between organised labour and the British establishment. It was not planned as such, and neither was the labour movement – in Scotland, or anywhere else – in an ideal state of purpose, unity and preparedness. Yet, in another sense, the General Strike was the logical, even inevitable, culmination of more than a decade of tension, and in that sense both sides were ready for it. What is beyond doubt is that in its wake much would change forever.

The defeat of the miners in 1921 carried a powerful symbolism for more than just the labour movement. In its aftermath, employers enforced wage cuts in most of the big strategic industries. The movement was on its back foot, and a rapidly worsening economic climate encouraged the employers to press home the advantage. With the defeat of MacDonald's first government, and the election of a Conservative administration united, resolved and determined to apply rigorous remedies to the country's economic ills, matters moved swiftly to a head.

Once again, the miners were the catalyst. During the brief interlude of the MacDonald administration, they had won a year-long pay deal on broadly favourable terms, thanks largely to a committee of inquiry, the Buckmaster Committee, set up by Shinwell, to whom MacDonald had given responsibility for the mines. But the respite, like the government, had a distinct look of impermanence, despite a short-lived boom in demand for coal. The miners had a new secretary, Arthur J Cook of the Minority Movement, who had taken over when Hodges was co-opted into a minor governmental post, and he used the period of the agreement to rebuild unity and confidence in the coalfields. He also quietly began rebuilding the Triple Alliance into a Workers' Industrial Alliance, covering most of heavy industry and transport. Though never fully completed, it was a shrewd precaution. The return of Baldwin brought immediate signals from the coal owners that they would not be prepared to countenance a continuation of the Buckmaster terms beyond their scheduled expiry in June 1925. No less ominous was the monetary policy now undertaken by the movement's old adversary, Winston Churchill. In the spring of 1925, Churchill decided to heed the pleading of the Treasury, and defy the advice of John Maynard Keynes, and to peg sterling to the Gold Standard. The consequence, Keynes warned him on the eve of the announcement, would be a precipitous slump in demand for British exports, leading to 'unemployment and downward adjustment of wages and prolonged strikes in some of the heavy industries, at the end of which it would be found that these industries had undergone a permanent contraction.' So it proved.

The coal-owners, faced with the need to reduce costs by 10 per cent merely to counter-balance the rise in the value of sterling, gave notice on 1 July 1925 that they proposed unilaterally to cut wage rates in the pits and abandon the industry's minimum wage. They gave the miners until the end of the month to accept their terms, or face a national lock-out. But the miners stood firm, refusing even to negotiate while the owners' proposals remained on the table, and this time the movement stood with them.

On 10 July, the TUC general council backed the miners' stand, declaring that 'no self-respecting body of organised workers could negotiate on such terms.' A special TUC congress on the 24th saw several key unions reward Cook's bridge-building efforts by pledging support should the miners be locked out. On the 29th, the TUC met Baldwin to appeal for a subsidy to maintain earnings in the industry. Baldwin refused, and on the 30th another special congress empowered the TUC both to order unions out in support of the miners and to provide financial backing for a general strike. An embargo on all coal movements was ordered from midnight on the 31st. At 4 pm on Friday the 31st, the Cabinet buckled, and agreed a nine-month Treasury subsidy amounting to £23 million, or £750,000 a week, running to 1 May 1926. It was a famous victory for the movement after a long run of defeats, and even though wiser heads warned that it was little more than an armistice, the euphoria of 'Red Friday' worked a powerful effect on morale. But that, in turn, was to generate a fatal complacency. While the trades union movement celebrated, the government put the time it had bought to better use, and prepared for confrontation. This time, the government had not been ready to take on the miners: next time it would be. It was a circumstance which would find remarkable parallels 60 years later.

Part of the settlement of Red Friday was the establishment of a Royal Commission on reorganisation of the industry, chaired by Sir Herbert (later Viscount) Samuel, the well-meaning Liberal grandee of whom Lloyd George once engagingly remarked that when they circumcised him they threw away the wrong bit. Samuel and his Commission (which included Sir William Beveridge, later canonised as the architect of the modern welfare state) duly agonised away at the matter, as Samuel's memoirs show. Pay was not high, yet living costs were falling; the subsidy was unsustainable and unjustly favoured one industry above others; yet the pits undoubtedly needed investment and reorganisation. When the Commission reported in March 1926, it was with a virtuous compromise that was doomed to failure. Wages should be cut in the short-term, the Commission said, while discussions took place between owners and unions towards an agreed reorganisation of the industry, including nationalisation of coal royalties. To no-one's surprise, the miners rejected the first part of this formula, and the owners the second part. In the few weeks remaining before the subsidy ran out, an abortive attempt at negotiation took place, but without any serious prospect of success. The main achievement of the Commission, however unwitting its members, had been to help keep the unions' eye off the ball.

While the Commission had been sitting, the government had been busy. MacDonald's brief administration had not got around to dismantling the STO. It had not convened the STC during that period but the STO, being a civil service mechanism, had little need of ministerial supervision to keep itself functioning. Almost as soon as Baldwin returned, the STC began meeting on a regular basis and bringing its preparations rapidly up to speed. A week after Red Friday, the Cabinet authorised the establishment of a permanent headquarters in each part of the country to supervise emergency provision. In the early months of 1926, this activity became increasingly purposeful and focused. Police and troop movements were planned. A formidable propaganda campaign was laid in readiness. The STO regional commissioners were staffed and briefed. Detailed contingency plans were finalised to ensure the maintenance of essential services in every part of the country. In Scotland, more than 20 branches of the Organisation for the Maintenance of Supplies were formed under the overall presidency of the Earl of Stair and the secretaryship of Captain

AR Dunlop. Though the recruitment of volunteers in Scotland was reported to be slower than elsewhere in the country, several hundred were in place before the strike began, and in Glasgow some 2,000 had reportedly enlisted in a parallel organisation, the Roll of Voluntary Workers. By the end of the General Strike, the number of enrolled volunteers in Scotland was estimated at 25,000, many of them students granted exam deferments by their universities. Meanwhile ministers, Churchill in particular, made moralising speeches about the nation's peril, secure in the knowledge that everything was in place, tested and ready.

With the government openly spurring the mine-owners on, negotiations swiftly reached a deadlock that TUC intervention could do nothing to break. In mid-April, the mine-owners gave notice that existing contracts of employment would be terminated on 30 April – the day the subsidy expired – and new wage rates applied from the following day. The choice now was between conflict and capitulation. On 29 April, just 24 hours before the deadline for acceptance or lock-out, a special TUC conference of 200 union executives met at London's Farringdon Hall. It tried hard not to confront the awful reality of what lay ahead. On a motion from Jimmy Thomas, the railwaymen's leader, the conference resolved to continue in session into the following day, in the hope that the TUC's industrial committee could find a way of keeping the negotiations open beyond the now imminent deadline. There seems to have been, to the end, a fond belief that something would turn up to avert disaster, as it had nine months earlier. That morning, Friday 30 April, the employers tabled their final proposals, which included both a severe wage-cut (for Scottish faceworkers, the cut amounted to almost 20 per cent), and an increase in the length of the shift from seven to eight hours. The miners immediately rejected the package.

At last, the assembled union executives turned their minds to waging, rather than avoiding, a strike. They were presented by the TUC general council with an agreed list of trades which were to come out: transport, print, metals, heavy chemicals, engineering maintenance (but not engineering production) and construction (except for those building houses or hospitals). These front-line troops were to be supported by the best endeavours of the gas and electricity workers. There would be no disruption for the moment to provision of health services, food or sanitation. Authority to initiate, or terminate action would be vested by the unions concerned in the general council, and there would be no resumption of work without general agreement. A General Strike would begin at one minute to midnight on Monday 3 May. By 3,653,527 votes to 49,911, these arrangements were approved.

Once again, the government showed no inclination to await the dispositions of the TUC. On 30 April, the King signed the proclamation declaring a state of emergency, and the government issued a string of emergency regulations. Before the weekend was over, troops were in position in principal industrial towns and cities. In Scotland, local authorities were instructed to put into action the emergency arrangements that had been detailed to them in a series of circulars from the Scottish Office dating back several months. Midnight of Monday 3 May found an implacable state, ready and waiting.

And what of the STUC? Two of the delegates at Farringdon Hall were William Elger and Peter Webster of the Scottish Horse and Motormen, installed the previous week as STUC president. They sat in on the sessions of the TUC general council and conferred with the TUC general secretary, Walter Citrine, as the decision to strike took form. The result was conveyed by Elger to the STUC general council when it met on the eve of the strike, Monday 3 May, for what was to be a continuous session lasting right through the strike. Arrangements, Elger reported, had been made 'for the STUC applying the general plan of strike action in Scotland.' For the duration of the strike, the general council would accept the remit of ensuring that the TUC's decisions were implemented in Scotland as precisely and as thoroughly as possible. The STUC had fought off repeated attempts down the years to reduce it to a regional offshoot of the TUC, but at this greatest of all crises for the labour movement it was to behave, for the first time, in just that capacity.

There is no reason to doubt that Elger and Webster's motives in accepting this subordinate role were pragmatic and honourable. Indeed, while several aspects of the general council's conduct of the strike were to be hotly criticised at the 1927 congress, their agreement that crucial weekend to follow TUC direction was not directly challenged. A longer historical perspective affords no particular grounds to dispute that contemporary judgement. Given the immensity and readiness of the forces ranged against them, the strikers' only weapon was unity. Unity would scarcely have been served by the STUC standing on its dignity, even if the timetable of events had left space for such indulgence, which it assuredly did not. Yet delegation of strategic control did also carry some incidental advantages for Elger and the STUC general council.

One was that it created a precedent for the closer working relationship with the TUC which Elger hankered after. The previous year he had put in place an arrangement for the two general councils to exchange all their circulars, and the TUC had lately become involved alongside the STUC in trying to resolve a dispute over a wage cut in the Scottish shale-mining industry. More to the point, the STUC general council appears to have been content in the spring of 1926 to leave the mounting crisis in the coal industry, and any preparations for confrontation, to the TUC. The minutes book yields no evidence that it felt moved even to discuss the Samuel Report. To operate, once the strike came, as a remote agent of the TUC was to take that process of convergence a mighty step onward, yet the circumstances were plainly exceptional enough for most of the protests that might have been expected to be withheld.

More importantly, though, it also absolved the STUC of much of the responsibility for the strike's eventual failure, and particularly for the manner of its ending. This was no small gain for the moderate general council of a radically-inclined congress. Affiliates had watched the coming of the conflict with greater apprehension than unity. At the Inverness congress, earlier that month, a motion supporting the miners' battle and noting that its loss would damage every group of workers in the country was adopted unanimously. But thereafter divisions opened. Joseph Duncan, as outgoing president, poured derision on militants who aspired to rally the workers to the ramparts at the behest of a labour movement 'general staff'. He saw little prospect of the workers obeying such injunctions and, rather more presciently, pointed out that those hungry for a general strike had yet even to define the essential services that they would maintain through its duration. Somewhat optimistically, he placed his faith instead on the state as conciliator. Responding in an ensuing but allied debate, Peter Kerrigan of Glasgow Trades and Labour Council (which was by now affiliated to the Minority Movement), pointed to the increasing incidence of violence being perpetrated against socialists by right-wing and fascist groups, and called for the creation of a workers' defence corps. That motion fell, as did a further proposal from Kerrigan and fellow Communists to co-opt the support of the Scottish Co-Operative Wholesale Society 'in resisting the capitalist attack.' Poignantly, the general council instead persuaded congress to delete the reference to Co-op joint action, and replace it with an undertaking to keep in touch with the TUC. Communists were later to argue, with pride and some justification, that they had been pressing for preparations for many weeks before the dispute came to a head, and particularly after a dozen of their leaders, including several former Clydeside shop stewards, were jailed for sedition.

In the event, the logistics of the strike in Scotland ran remarkably effectively, given the lack of preparation beforehand, the still patchy extent of organisation (and of TUC, or even STUC, affiliation), and the remote command structure. The response from members of the front-line unions was swift and resolute, and co-ordinating bodies were put into place on the ground quickly and efficiently. The railwaymen, train drivers and even the moderate rail clerks were fairly solidly out; so were the miners – of course – the dockers, the bulk of the metalworkers and most of the printers. Those unions which were not affiliated to the TUC responded less certainly: the Scottish Typographical Association decided, at a hastily-convened executive, to join the strike, while the Scottish Horse and Motormen were markedly more diffident, not least because of persistently unclear instructions from the TUC as to which essential supplies it was permissible to transport. But, in general, most of what moved in the targeted industries in Scotland was moved by blackleg labour, and in many cases – particularly in the transport sectors – it took the government's supporters several days to muster more than a token service. These activities resulted in numerous angry clashes with pickets, punished by heavy-handed policing. By the third week in June more than 400 people in Scotland had been jailed for strike-related offences. By and large, however, the military build-up in Scotland, which included an ostentatious naval presence in the Clyde and the Forth, was little used.

Such failures of co-ordination as took place were attributable more to the hurried ambiguity of the TUC plans than to any shortcomings in implementation by the Scottish labour move-ment. For example, shipbuilding and most engineering had been excluded from the action by the TUC, yet little thought seems to have been given to how workers in these industries would get to work without buses and trams running. In any event, the Clyde engineering trades, given their history, took badly to being left out of the strike and many found excuses for not being at work. The STUC general council, in an unaccustomed moment of presumptuousness, appealed to the TUC to reconsider these exemptions, but was told to stand by the original decision. There are grounds to speculate that the TUC was nervous of letting the genie of 1919 back out of the bottle, and these are reinforced by the fact that on its first day in permanent session, the STUC general council – presumably either acting on, or interpreting, London's wishes – decided to block plans formulated by the trades council for a major city centre demonstration in Glasgow. Similarly, trades like building found the distinctions drawn between those who were meant to work as normal and those who were meant to strike to be ill-defined and contradictory. Journalists, too, had a confusing time of it: they were not affiliated to the TUC and were therefore not on strike, but they were under instruction not to replace the work of other trades or to co-operate with blackleg labour. It made for untidy union discipline.

It was journalism, in a different sense, that gave rise to the biggest single source of dissension between Glasgow and London. The issue was whether the STUC should produce its own strike journal, or merely distribute the TUC's *British Worker*. This might seem a banal cause of dispute until one remembers just how vital effective communication was amid the chaos of the strike. The STUC had moved swiftly to set up lines of physical communication, which generally worked well. Strike committees were formed in all the key centres, bringing together representatives of the unions that were on strike and of the local trades councils. The STUC general council, in unbroken session from 3 to 15 May, sat at the centre, receiving reports, issuing a daily bulletin and passing down decisions. Information was transmitted by a surprisingly sophisticated courier system, operating via relay stations along the major roads. Each strike committee was responsible for organising its section of the network, and a steady flow of material moved by every sort of vehicle, including bicycles. At Carlisle the STUC network connected up with the TUC's. But while this system proved an efficient way of communicating with strike organisers, it could not satisfy the need to speak also to non-activists and to the wider public.

By long pre-planning, the government had brought its own propaganda sheet swiftly into circulation, the *British Gazette*, edited by Winston Churchill. The TUC responded from 5 May with the *British Worker*, no less dedicated to putting a favourable gloss on events, though it was also concerned to encourage calm resolve and discourage spontaneous militancy. Neither publication circulated in Scotland, but the non-union *Scotsman* and its evening stablemate, the *Dispatch*, continued to publish in Edinburgh, and elsewhere in the country other papers managed to get out sporadic emergency issues. None of these was remotely sympathetic to the strike, and there was therefore pressure from Scottish strikers for a paper to put their side of the case.

But the TUC had decided that the *British Worker* was to be the only exception to the call-out of printworkers. There was some flexibility in this ruling; many local strike committees produced their own bulletins, Kirkcaldy's being sufficiently well-organised to include paid adverts from local shops. The general council issued an instruction that these bulletins were to be produced by duplicator only, and not printed. In any case, they scarcely met the need to counter state propaganda in like measure. At the outset of the strike, both *Forward* and the Minority Movement's Glasgow-based paper, the *Worker*, had offered to place their columns at the disposal of the general council, but were rebuffed on the grounds that 'no exceptions were to be made' to the print embargo. *Forward* ceased publication for the duration of the strike: the *Worker*, despite general council admonishment, did not. Pressure mounted on the general council, particularly after Glasgow newspapers combined to produce an emergency publication. Eventually, on 7 May, a TUC instruction reached Glasgow that strike newspapers were to be published in 'various centres.' The general council immediately arranged to use *Forward's* facilities to publish from Monday 10 May a paper called the *Scottish Worker*, which Duncan would edit. But, on the eve of publication, a fresh instruction arrived from the TUC that the paper was simply to be a Scottish edition of the *British Worker*, reprinting, unamended, proofs couriered from London. For once, the STUC general council demurred, predicting – accurately – that the logistics of this would prove impracticable. Eventually, on the Sunday evening, a compromise was reached with London, providing for the paper to be a mix of TUC and STUC copy. But the TUC copy turned out to take days rather than the projected hours to reach Carlisle, and so the six issues of the *Scottish Worker* that appeared contained purely Scottish material. In the course of its brief existence, circulation trebled to 75,000 copies a day.

By then, unknown to most of the labour movement, the end of the strike was at hand. At far off Lake Garda in northern Italy, a holidaying Lord Samuel learned of the stoppage and decided, with patrician concern, that his country needed him. He returned to London on 6 May, and contacted Jimmy Thomas, who readily agreed to set up meetings with the TUC general council. Baldwin, however, was less encouraging and told Samuel that there were to be no negotiations until the 'unconstitutional' strike was called off. The TUC, equally, was committed to the position that the strike could not be lifted without negotiation. Samuel himself, as his *Memoirs* show, deplored both the strike and the lack of any official measures to resolve it. He therefore agreed with Baldwin to act as an unauthorised intermediary. With Thomas's help, he held three days of secret talks with TUC representatives at the Mayfair home of the South African mining magnate, Sir Abe Bailey, during which Samuel formed the clear impression that the TUC was looking for a way out of the strike. Astonishingly the miners, while aware of the talks, were not included in the TUC negotiating team until the fourth day, Monday 10 May, by which time an outline formula was in place in the form of the 'Samuel Memorandum'.

The memorandum had two main elements. First, wages would not be cut without 'sufficient assurances' that the reorganisation proposed by the Samuel Report would actually take place and that the miners would have a say in it. Second, wages would be reviewed by a national wages board, comprising owners, miners and an independent element, and the board would seek to safeguard the welfare of the lowest-paid workers. Though the memorandum proposed a temporary extension of the coal subsidy, it did not represent any significant advance on the original commission proposals. When the miners' representatives, led by their secretary, Cook, and their president, Herbert Smith, were finally let in on the deal late on the Monday, they were appalled. Samuel, none the less, made some minor adjustments to his memorandum and sent it that evening to the TUC general council, which forwarded it to the miners with a note expressing the view that it now constituted 'a satisfactory basis for the reopening of negotiations.' Meeting that night, the miners' executive decided that it constituted nothing of the sort, and demanded radical amendment. What followed would always be seen by the miners, and by many of those still robustly supporting them in the strike, as a betrayal.

Early next morning Samuel sat down to draft a report to Baldwin. He noted the unmistakable signs of disparity between the TUC negotiating committee, which had received his ideas warmly, and the miners. But he also saw the miners' objections to be, for the moment, insurmountable. He would later recall: 'Before the typed copy was ready for signature, the situation was completely changed. I had a message that the TUC committee were on the point of separating themselves from the miners.' The tip-off, probably from Thomas, proved correct. That night, the TUC general council sent a deputation to meet the miners' executive. The miners once again made clear that the memorandum was unacceptable. The next morning, the general council met Baldwin and his Cabinet at Downing Street and announced that, on the basis of the Samuel Memorandum, the strike was being called off.

The immediate response among workers across the length of the country was one of confusion, giving way as details emerged to disbelieving dismay. There had been no significant weakening of the strike: indeed, ironically, on the morning it was called off it had been scaled up (on an instruction issued two days earlier) to include the 'second line' of shipbuilders and engineering workers. Morale was generally running high. When first word of the stand-down reached Scotland, it was presumed to betoken victory, and there were celebrations in some towns. The first news bulletins setting out the terms of the return to work were widely presumed to be a further example of government propaganda. Only gradually did the truth of the matter penetrate. In Montrose, a mass meeting of strikers was in progress as confirmation came. It was being addressed by the solitary socialist on the town council, Councillor Christopher Murray Grieve – the poet, Hugh MacDiarmid. Forty years later, when he came to write his autobiography, *The Company I've Kept*, the memory remained raw: 'We had the whole area sewn up. One of my most poignant memories is of how, when the news came through, I was in the act of addressing a packed meeting mainly of railwaymen. When I told them the terrible news most of them burst into tears – and I am not ashamed to say I did too.' Across Britain, the reaction was the same. Ernest Bevin predicted, entirely accurately: 'Thousands of members will be victimised as the result of this day's work.' Telegrams of protest began to deluge TUC headquarters.

The STUC general council had been afforded little idea of what was taking place. Only in retrospect does a message received the previous Sunday from EL Poulton, the shoemakers' general secretary, seem to hint at what was going on. Poulton had been put in charge of the TUC's publicity committee, and thus of the *British Worker*, and his relations with Glasgow had frosted markedly during the exchanges over a separate Scottish strike paper: agreement to a *Scottish Worker* had only been secured by Duncan and Elger appealing over Poulton's head to Arthur Pugh, the TUC chairman. Shortly after 6 pm on Sunday 9 May, Poulton telephoned Elger to complain that he had heard of demands emanating from Scotland for the strike to be extended. A TUC typescript of the conversation records him asking Elger: 'Will you see that all that stuff is kept out [of the *Scottish Worker*] and nothing provocative put in? The negotiating committee are sitting now and do not want a word said which will prevent them from continuing.' Whether Elger recognised what this meant is unclear. But there is no evidence that the STUC general council was prepared for the phone call from Poulton on the morning of 12 May instructing it to circulate, word for word, a message appearing in that day's *British Worker*: 'To resume negotiations General Council British Congress have terminated General Strike today. Trade Unionists before acting must wait instructions of own Executive Councils. Circulate information in your area.'

Somewhat mystified, the STUC general council complied. The statement left huge questions unanswered. What provision did the settlement make for those arrested? What assurances were there that strikers would not be victimised? What was the position of the miners? Both Elger and Duncan tried anxiously to contact Citrine but were informed that he was not available. All Duncan was told was that the statement in the *British Worker* represented a TUC general council instruction. Eventually, they wired Citrine, remarking with commendable restraint: 'Surprised no information from you since Monday.' Citrine's response was less than accommodating. It asked the STUC to find out details about any 'humiliating terms' employers were imposing on those returning to work, and to report back on their findings. For the next three days, an increasingly besieged general council continued dutifully to collect information from the outlying districts and to publish the *Scottish Worker*. Only on Saturday 15 May, the day the general council came out of continuous session, did it allow its frustrations to show. In the last ever issue of the *Scottish Worker*, it defended itself against allegations that it had suppressed news of the miners' refusal to accept the Samuel Memorandum: 'We desire to make it perfectly clear that the message we received from the TUC general council was published exactly as we received it. In the message supplied to us, there was no hint of any kind that the miners were not a consenting party.'

The miners would struggle on alone until November, returning to their pits defiant but beaten. Years of victimisation, recrimination and schism lay ahead of them. It was not until their campaign was near the point of collapse that the TUC stirred to consider a levy in their support – tempers were just too volatile in the wake of the May debacle to brook serious discussion of the matter. By then, the miners were in a sorry state. Local authorities, particularly in Scotland, had been forced by the length of the lock-out to reduce the scale of relief paid to colliery families, despite the continued readiness of the public to contribute to the Miners Relief Fund. Among the contributors were Russian trade unionists, forging an affectionate link that would continue to ring true decades later. Eventually, the fund exceeded £1.8 million, a remarkable figure for the day, though thin fare when set beside the numbers of men, women and children suffering in the pit villages.

But not even the final rout of the miners could draw a line beneath the General Strike of 1926. The government had no intention of leaving the unions in peace to lick their wounds. In its wake, ministers introduced the 1927 Trade Disputes and Trade Unions Act, a more draconian constraint on union activities even than Taff Vale. Peter Webster called it 'the most outstanding example of class legislation in our time.' The Act outlawed 'political' strikes, which were sweepingly defined as strikes called in sympathy with other workers, strikes called to apply political pressure on the government, and strikes which caused the public hardship. Limits were placed on the rights of all public employees to take industrial action. The civil service unions were forbidden from affiliating to either the TUC or the Labour Party, and the political levy in all unions was placed on a basis of contracting in rather than contracting out. The government was signalling its determination to ensure that never again could organised labour pose a threat to the stability of the British state.

In fact, a much heavier shackle was locking into place even as the legislation made its bitterly contested way through Parliament. By the end of 1926, unemployment had climbed beyond one and a quarter million, and a still steeper ascent lay ahead to a peak above three million. The paralytic fear of harsh idleness, more than the scourge of vindictive legislation, drove many trade unionists to shrink back from the failed valour of setpiece militancy, and to seek new ways to promote their cause. Some limped back from the great strike determined to forge a new and lasting peace with the employers through the comfortingly bureaucratic processes of Mondism. Others continued to seek new ways of waging class war against the injustices of the system that had triumphed in 1926. The differences between the two camps grew stark and bitter. Yet they had some elements in common beyond their mutual mistrust. Both approaches were essentially defensive, however visionary their rhetoric. Both made their respective cases by constant reference to the towering defeat of 1926.

The Welsh poet Idris Davies called the General Strike 'the great dream and the swift disaster.' In its bleak aftermath, the means and the will for defiance were sapped in equal measure from the organised working classes. 'It is all very well,' Ernest Bevin told Cook, 'for people to talk as if the working class of Great Britain are cracking their shins for a fight and a revolution, and we are holding them back. Are they? There are not many as fast as we are ourselves.' The movement was entering a period of decline and self-absorption that would last for almost a generation.

CHAPTER FIVE

HARD TIMES

The inside cover of the 1927 STUC Congress Report is taken up, poignantly enough, by an advertisement for James Henderson Ltd, a firm of Glasgow undertakers. Inside, the report solemnly minutes the STUC's post mortem at Galashiels on the General Strike. Peter Webster, in his opening address, tried to head off recrimination. 'Nothing has hindered trade union effort to a greater extent during the past six months than the sorry spectacle of those holding a position of authority in the movement being prepared to make use of any means of publicity, not for the purpose of uniting our forces, but for the purpose of discrediting some individual or section of the movement,' he declared. 'I think that the "shouldn't have been" and the "never again" cries should be left alone, and if the same attitude is taken up by those whose only contribution to the problem has been to shout "traitor" and "betrayal," and both parties recognise that our movement has to live and grow and endeavour to evolve new methods as a result of our experience, it would be a good thing for the movement . . . there was no failure, but a simple conception of duty which thrilled and inspired everybody concerned.'

It was bravely said, but it was no more successful than Webster presumably expected. Barely had he sat down than Aitken Ferguson launched the counter-attack, challenging the somewhat cursory account of the strike in the general council's report to congress, and focusing on the council's efforts during the nine days to curb the activities of the Minority Movement and silence its publications. He contrasted the disciplining of Communist agitators with the conduct of the national strike leadership, ending on an elaborately sarcastic note: 'If they had followed the magnificent lead of Mr JH Thomas and company, and run off the field of battle at the earliest possible moment, they would have been lauded.'

Elger responded with dogged patience: 'Whether we liked it or not, the general council assumed that during the time of a national strike there could be only one authority which might be right or wrong, but which had to be obeyed . . . for that reason, the general council took a very serious view of any section claiming to speak for the working class.' But others pursued the matter. James Campbell of the railwaymen complained that the general council had spent more time tinkering with the Scottish Horse and Motormen's system of food permits than ensuring the solidity of the strike, while others argued that it had been presumptuous of the general council in the first place to tell transport unions what they could and could not move. Peter Kerrigan of Glasgow Trades and Labour Council wanted the general council report remitted back on the grounds that it declined to venture any opinion on the conduct of the strike, despite the general council having been represented at the conference of executives which authorised the action. In the event, the report was adopted by 103 votes to 26, but argument over what had taken place the previous May continued unabated throughout the gathering.

In truth, the general council had itself grown unhappy about the relationship into which the strike had thrust it with its TUC counterpart. These concerns found expression in a protracted correspondence with Citrine over representation at a recalled national conference of executives, postponed until November for fear of the wrath of the miners and their allies, and over stewardship in Scotland of the campaign against the government's anti-union legislation. Citrine wanted a UK-wide campaign under the command of the TUC general council, but the STUC insisted on the right to conduct the campaign in Scotland under its own terms and authority, while sending a delegate to the national defence committee formed to fight the Bill. In the event, the measure passed into law, and was to remain on the statute book until its repeal by the Attlee government in 1946. Further disagreement arose over a proposal to invite Citrine to Galashiels, and the general council eventually decided merely to invite the TUC to be represented. The TUC, at last alert to the sensitivities in Glasgow, decided to send the elderly Bob Smillie, by now MP for Morpeth, whose credentials with the STUC were beyond reproach. It set a pattern for the next few years: the TUC recognised the prudence of having Scots represent it at the STUC. Only in 1932 did the convention begin of a fraternal address each year by the TUC chairman.

William Elger had a somewhat formal approach to minute-taking, and only tantalisingly discreet hints of the arguments that took place on the general council over this period are evident from the sparse official record. But the tensions which the strike had generated in relations with the TUC fell into sharp relief in debates both at Galashiels and at the following year's congress at Perth over the future of the STUC. Both debates leave posterity a vivid insight into the trauma which the strike had inflicted on the movement, and the profound political divisions it had exposed. The STUC's old talent for containing its disagreements had crumbled before the magnitude of defeat.

At Galashiels, the Manchester-based vehicle builders' union called forthrightly for the reduction of the STUC to the status of an advisory council of the TUC, in parallel to the Labour Party's Scottish council. Despite the chosen model, it was a proposition initiated by, and reflecting the post-strike resentments of, the Communists, which meant that its high embarrassment factor was unmatched by any serious risk of the motion being passed. Indeed, Joseph Duncan, who opposed the motion on the general council's behalf, grumbled feelingly that the CP-led Glasgow Trades Council, with a sixtieth of the congress delegates, seemed intent on taking up more than a sixth of the agenda. The Minority Movement, however, was not in the mood to be patronised. Charles Milne of the vehicle builders bluntly announced that while the STUC had done good work in the past, it had now 'outlived its usefulness.' His union, he said, had been drawn to this conclusion by the experience of the strike, during which the STUC general council 'were sitting like so many Micawbers waiting for something to turn up from the other side of the border. In view of the fact that the STUC proved that it could not act in a time of crisis, it should pack up . . . .' Seconding, Frank Stephenson of Glasgow Trades Council argued that the domination now of the scene by big southern-based unions made it inconceivable that the STUC could ever again act independently in a major dispute, and that its continued existence was perpetuating the survival of numerous small Scottish unions which would be better amalgamated into more powerful organisations. Aitken Ferguson (who, though then a dedicated centralist, would a decade later nudge Scottish Communists into a strongly pro-home rule position) claimed that the strike had found the STUC acting as a mere 'broadcasting centre' for the dispensations of the TUC. The response of the general council, while sufficient to carry the day with delegates, did not exactly brim with conviction. It acknowledged the closer relationship between the two congresses, but suggested that the subsidiary role of Labour's Scottish council stood as a salutary warning rather than a shining example. Much the same territory was covered, and with the same outcome, the following year at Perth. There, it was Edinburgh Trades Council which took the lead, arguing that labour needed to draw its forces together as the employers were doing, and that the process of amalgamation made the existence of a separate Scottish congress ever more incongruous. Once again, Duncan replied stolidly that the STUC found little that inspired in its experience of advisory councils.

These debates reflected a sense of dysfunction in the wake of May 1926 which was rife at all levels of the movement. Numerous unions were at odds with each other over incidents during and after the nine days of the strike, and in many of them the experience opened up internal divisions, some of which proved enduring. This was nowhere more evident than in the miners, whose wounds, being the deepest, took the longest to heal. Victimisation was widespread in Scotland after the strike, and the more militant union officials found themselves blacklisted throughout the coalfield. Many drifted south, notably to the Kent pits which, two generations later, retained both a reputation for militancy and a high proportion of Men of Kent with Scottish surnames. Among those who found work there was one Communist check-weigher from Acid Rig near Shotts, who was forced to make the arduous journey south with his young family, one of them a baby boy barely a year old. He would bring the family back in 1932, when he managed to get a job at Fallin. But the experience left its mark on the infant. In 1939, he too would join the Young Communist League, graduating to full membership of the party at age 18 in 1943 – the same year that he was sacked from Gateside Colliery for leading an unofficial strike. The family name was McGahey, and the baby was called Michael.

In Nottinghamshire, local coal-owners sought to destabilise

union militancy once and for all by setting up a company union, the Nottinghamshire and District Miners' Industrial Union, with the co-operation of a local union official and MP, George Spencer. Over the next decade, 'Spencerism' would be taken up by coal-owners across the country, and tame unions were set up in South Wales, Northumberland, Durham and – briefly – at Lochgelly in Fife. Numerous ructions ensued as the official union, led by the still unrepentant Cook, found itself vying for recognition against the Spencerist structures. 'Spencerist' remains a term of abuse in mining communities, where memories of perfidy are long: and the Nottinghamshire miners would remain an object of suspicion into the 1980s, when another great strike – which most of them refused to join – once more saw a more compliant breakaway union formed, the Union of Democratic Mineworkers.

Spencerism itself made only a fleeting appearance in Scotland, but the Scottish miners too fell prey to schism. In Scotland, unlike other parts of the British coalfield, sporadic efforts to bring the various county unions together under a single banner had faltered on local pride and political infighting. The trouble was at its most pronounced in Fife, where the general secretary was none other than William Adamson, Ramsay MacDonald's Scottish Secretary and a man little celebrated for either his radicalism or his fealty to democratic procedure. In 1923, Adamson's refusal to accept the results of a union election in which the Left had triumphed had provoked the formation of a rival Reform Union, headed by Philip Hodge. In the run-up to the General Strike, Smillie had pleaded in vain for the two bodies to re-unite, backed by a Minority Movement which was urging unity, and had made further attempts to create a single national union. But the proposed rules for the new body merely extended the dissension to other areas, notably the Lothians, Ayrshire, Dumbarton and Lanarkshire.

The hardships of the strike and the seven-month lockout did finally persuade the two rival Fife unions to bury their differences, but it also lent a fresh momentum to the Left. The first executive elections in the newly re-united Fife union saw Hodge and his left-wing followers sweep Adamson and his allies from office. When Lanarkshire voted, the leftward swing was still more dramatic, and went far enough to nominate a left-winger, John Bird, to challenge the venerable Smillie as Scottish president. The sitting Scottish executive, which had been in post since before the strike, tried to stall, quibbling about voting irregularities and repeatedly postponing the Scottish conference. Some of the besieged Scottish officials issued a much-publicised manifesto, widely seen as the foundation for a breakaway right-wing Scottish miners' union. Once again, Fife was the crucible, where left-wingers (among them, two brothers from Lumphinnans who would loom large in the Scottish miners in years ahead, Abe and Alex Moffat) moved to suspend Adamson for misrepresenting the views of his members. Adamson responded by forming a rival county union, shrewdly leaving his old colleagues the vast debts which had been run up during his secretaryship.

The split swiftly assumed Scotland-wide dimensions, and for the next seven years, some of hardest in the industry's tormented history, the Scottish miners were divided between two rival structures, the left-wing United Mineworkers of Scotland, and the right-led National Union of Scottish Mineworkers. It was a split which the coal owners exploited with ill-concealed glee, particularly after the national wage agreement was ended in November 1929. For five of those years, from 1929 to 1934, the acrimony also cost the STUC the affiliation of its biggest union, and the two mining seats on the general council were left vacant. When reaffiliation did take place, it was the NUSM which had emerged as the dominant grouping, and the UMS was excluded. It would be 1936 before the UMS would finally give up the struggle and dissolve itself, but even then bitterness remained. The Moffats, by now leading lights on the Left, were refused membership of the NUSM on the unconvincing grounds that they were not miners (they had both, in common with thousands of other union members, lost their jobs during the depression). Despite pressure from the Miners' Federation of Great Britain, the NUSM executive refused to budge from this somewhat puerile stance, and the coalowners helpfully saw to it that the Moffats were blacklisted across several coalfields. But there was to be a revenge. Just weeks before the UMS threw in its lot with the NUSM, Fife miners helped ensure that William Adamson lost his parliamentary seat at West Fife to the veteran Communist, Willie Gallacher. Three months later, Adamson died. In late 1939, the Moffats finally found jobs at a pit in Clackmannanshire which was outwith the coal-owners' trade association. Within a year, Abe Moffat had been elected by Fife to the Scottish executive.

Elsewhere in the movement, though, the Left was heavily outnumbered by those who felt that the lesson to draw from the strike was the need to find less bellicose means of settling industrial differences. That seemed to chime with the mood of a membership increasingly bowed down by economic stringency. The 1921 coal lock-out had taken the number of working days lost through strikes in Britain that year to a record 87 million, and the total for 1926 reached 162 million. Over the next quarter century the annual figure would only twice exceed five million, though the actual number of strikes held rose steadily from the early 1930s onwards, reflecting smaller disputes of briefer duration. There was ideology as well as hard circumstance behind the decline of setpiece industrial conflict. A brief motion at the 1927 STUC from the left-led woodworkers union, approved by delegates, deplored the 'propaganda of industrial peace,' and instructed affiliates to have nothing to do with it. In the event, the phenomenon turned out to be something much more substantial than mere propaganda.

That September's TUC congress in Edinburgh extended a sturdy olive branch to employers in the form of an offer in the presidential address by George Hicks of the building workers to embark on 'a common endeavour to improve the efficiency of industry.' The call was swiftly answered by Sir Alfred Mond, founder-chairman of Imperial Chemical Industries. He formed a consortium of eminent industrialists which, early in 1928, began the 'Mond–Turner Talks' with the TUC general council, chaired by the textile workers' leader, Ben Turner. By early July, after a series of twelve conferences, they had reached informal agreement on a broad-based platform of reconciliation, couched in terms of common economic purpose. There was agreed acceptance of the need to embrace new technology, best managerial practice, and a higher ratio of fixed capital to labour – in other words, rationalisation. The most specific consequence was the creation of a bi-partisan National Industrial Council, charged with settling disputes by conciliation and arbitration. The accord was, by and large, aspirational rather than practical in tone, and much of its virtuous intent was soon to be submerged in the chill of depression. Yet the Mond agreement, endorsed two months later at the TUC congress, was in many respects a watershed in British industrial relations, and it had in particular two far-reaching consequences.

The first was that it enmeshed the trade union movement firmly within the ambit of the British state. For the next half century, British trade unionism would assume the conceits of partnership in pursuit of greater economic and social wellbeing. There would, of course, continue to be disputes and confrontations, however hopeful the Mondists might have been that such vulgarities could be permanently replaced with civilised dialogue. But they would in future be presented as differences of means rather than ends. With the signing of the Mond–Turner agreement, any lingering expectation that the trade union movement might have harboured revolutionary intent was gone. Mondism ushered in the era in Britain of what would come to be called the corporate state, the idea that capital and labour should take their seats alongside government in plotting the national destiny. Trade unionists would be drawn ever more closely into the formulation and implementation of government policy, particularly when Labour was in power. They would serve on public bodies and would expect, up until the advent of Margaret Thatcher, to be consulted as of right in economic decision-making. It was much more than the pressure group role they had hitherto performed. That was the positive side of the agreement.

The negative side was that Mondism deepened the political divisions within the trade union movement beyond reconciliation. At the highest levels of the movement, there were few such divisions by this time. The only significant dissident on the TUC general council was Arthur Cook, though he too soon found the Mondists in the majority even on his own union executive. Cook called the Mond–Turner talks 'class collaboration', and saw traces of the same forces which had drawn the trade unions into Mussolini's fascist state in Italy, but he was heavily outnumbered among the major union leaders. At grassroots level, however, Mondism became the defining distinction between Left and Right. Many of the trades councils bitterly opposed it, as did the NUWM. Opposition was led by the Communist Party and the National Minority Movement, but other left-wingers joined in fighting it.

In June 1928, as the Mond–Turner talks entered their closing stages, a meeting took place in the Commons between Cook, James Maxton, Willie Gallacher, John Wheatley, George Buchanan, David Kirkwood and others, which culminated in publication of the 'Cook–Maxton Manifesto', calling on the working classes to mount unceasing war against Mondist capitalism. The manifesto, which also demanded closer relations between the Communist and Labour parties, was reinforced by a populist pamphlet, *Our Case for a Socialist Revival*, and by a series of public meetings addressed by Cook and Maxton. The meetings were well attended, yet even within the ILP there was no unanimity of view on Mondism, and Maxton – as ILP chairman – was taken to task by the party's national committee (with Shinwell prominent in delivering the rebuke) for publishing his material without authorisation. This attack was followed up by Ramsay MacDonald at the 1928 Labour Party conference, and further salt was rubbed into the wound when the Communist Party, following a new hard line adopted by the Comintern, condemned the manifesto as 'weak and sentimental.' Shortly afterwards, MacDonald, Snowden and several other prominent figures would leave the ILP, and it would remain split until Maxton finally led it out of the Labour Party in July 1932. Some have speculated that the anti-Mondism campaign was consciously conceived by Wheatley and Maxton to test the water for a parting of the ways with Labour.

The Mondists, in the meantime, struck back. The NUWM became a particular target for their malevolence, as the most voluble and popular facet of a Communist activism now formally held to be beyond the pale. In late 1928, Citrine wrote to all trades councils whose areas were to be crossed by a proposed NUWM hunger march instructing that no co-operation was to be given. Elger was likewise required by his general council to order trades councils to ensure that no-one connected in any way to the National Minority Movement was afforded membership. It was the start of a fitful and none too noble campaign by the right-wingers who now dominated the STUC general council to smear the NUWM with the taint of conspiracy. The campaign achieved little success, and was notable chiefly for creating a greater impression of remoteness than at any other time in STUC history between the congress and the grassroots workers whose interests had been a prime concern behind its creation. Aside from anything else, Minority Movement supporters remained active in the upper levels of many unions and could therefore not be eradicated from the STUC's own counsels even as it endeavoured to freeze them out of local activism. Unsurprisingly, there was a good deal of inconsistency in the response at local level. Some trades councils, like Edinburgh, continued to offer encouragement and assistance to the NUWM: in others, like Paisley, the votes sometimes went one way, sometimes another. Many councils simply found inventive ways of re-affiliating activists from proscribed organisations. It did little for the image, unity or discipline of the movement. The same inconsistency was evident in individual unions, and not just in Scotland. Ernest Bevin, for example, was an unenthusiastic but resigned convert to Mondism from its early days, and later would glory in the union movement having become, as he put it, 'an integral part of the state.' Yet Bevin's 1970s successor as TGWU general secretary, Jack Jones, recalls in his autobiography how, as a young shop steward in Liverpool, he joined a 1934 NUWM hunger march to London: 'My union branch endorsed the idea and I had the sympathy of fellow Labour Party members, although the main organisers of the march were members of the Communist Party.' When the march finally reached Westminster, Clement Attlee arranged for its leaders to see MacDonald.

The other troublesome factor about the NUWM was that it remained highly popular, despite the arrests with which a jumpy officialdom frequently favoured its rallies and marches. A demonstration in Glasgow in September 1931 drew more than 30,000 people, and 10,000 lobbied the City Chambers a few days later on an occasion that must have awakened uneasy memories of 1919 in many minds, particularly when it culminated in a mounted police charge. As the hardships of the early 1930s mounted, the STUC tried to counter the NUWM's popularity by organising special conferences on unemployment and by encouraging trades councils to set up a parallel structure of unemployed associations, to which end Elger dutifully distributed 'model rules' drawn up by the TUC. The experiment was a dismal failure: only four of the 63 Scottish councils complied, and those that did found the experience unrewarding. Aberdeen Trades Council, for example, reported to the general council in late 1936 that while it had managed to recruit 600 members to its unemployed association, the consequence was merely to create divisions among the Grampian jobless. It all served to add to the widespread impression that the official labour movement – unions and party – was more preoccupied with the rights of those in work than the suffering of those who lacked it. The NUWM was regarded by the unemployed themselves as the more sympathetic body, and the more effective in raising resistance to the increasingly harsh treatment of the unemployed by government. The additional problem for the STUC and the official movement was that the government in question was now a Labour administration.

Labour won the general election of 1929, affording one of those moments of short-lived hope in which the history of the movement abounds. It is sometimes speculated that Ramsay MacDonald's second administration might have been an altogether more effective and harmonious force than it proved had not Wall Street crashed within weeks of the poll, pitching much of the world into a depression of unprecedented savagery. But the evidence for that inference is thin. For one thing, the movement was, as we have seen, in neither united nor radical mood by the time Baldwin's government succumbed to the darkening economic circumstance. MacDonald's ministerial team held few places for the Left, and particularly not for the Clydesiders. Adamson was once again Scottish Secretary, with Tom Johnston his junior; the dour Edinburgh right-winger, Willie Graham, was President of the Board of Trade; and Shinwell, bizarrely, was made financial secretary at the War Office, though he later reverted to his old mining responsibilities. But for the wilder voices like Maxton there was no place, and the most gifted of the bunch, Wheatley, had already left the front bench under his own momentum. He would die a year after the election. So the government was, from the first, avowedly Mondist in outlook.

It was also, from the first, in a minority, having won just 287 of the 615 Commons seats, against 260 for the Tories and 59 for a Liberal Party briefly resurgent on the strength of the Keynes-inspired 'Yellow Book' on economic and industrial renewal. Scotland once again contributed above quota to Labour's performance, returning 36 Labour MPs, plus Neil Maclean (temporarily outwith the Labour whip) and the indomitable Scrymgeour still hoisting his prohibition banner in Dundee. For the first time, Labour had won a majority of the Scottish constituencies.

MacDonald had not the slightest sympathy with those on the Left who saw the economic tempest as an opportunity to overthrow a capitalist system in crisis. But, though it is often forgotten in consideration of what followed, the 27 months of Labour government did produce several significant measures to alleviate the suffering of a dole queue which swiftly lengthened by more than a million. Picking up on the theme, if not the scale, of the 'Yellow Book' vision (MacDonald shrewdly co-opted Keynes on to a new Economic Advisory Council), the government instituted a series of public works projects, costing more than £180 million, which created jobs in activities like slum clearance, land drainage and infrastructure improvement. Attempts were made to restore some measure of dignity to the mining industry, by establishing a statutory working day of seven-and-a-half hours. A number of stringencies in the welfare benefits regime were relaxed, and there were commendable initiatives in fields like rural medical provision and free milk for infants.

It was a more modest and ameliorative record of reform than many would have wished but, in the circumstances, not entirely shameful. The circumstances, however, continued to worsen. Unemployment rose to ever more unthinkable heights, and with it the budget deficit, giving rise in the summer of 1931 to a banking crisis and a run on the pound. The government's ensuing indecision is conventionally blamed on MacDonald, but there was little harmony in the cacophony of learned advice with which the ploughman's son from Lossiemouth was surrounded. An ill-sorted host of radical voices, running from the ILP to Lloyd George, demanded huge public spending on work creation, import controls and other like measures. Oswald Mosley advocated a managed currency, departing the government in characteristic dudgeon when his proposals were assailed by Snowden. Even Keynes publicly dithered about the gold standard. As each idea was considered and rejected, the economic straits grew more desperate. 'I have lifted the cup to my lips – and found it empty,' MacDonald would later write.

Thinking back, no doubt, to the secret ·pact that had ushered in the great reforming government of 1906, he began quiet negotiations with the Liberals, on whose Commons support the government relied. The possibility of Lloyd George joining the Cabinet was explored, though it has also been suggested that MacDonald was simultaneously involved in covert discussions with Baldwin, impelled by their mutual desire to put paid to the cantankerous Welshman once and for all. Still darker imputations of duplicity have been levelled, involving a colourful array of putative conspirators ranging from Montagu Norman at the Bank of England to King George V. The plainer truth is that

MacDonald was out of his depth, particularly after a brains trust of bankers and economists – the May Committee – recommended a 10 per cent cut in the dole payments on which two and a half million unemployed and their families now depended. The Tories, at all-party crisis talks in Downing Street, signalled their determination to force the government out of office (while cannily declining to support the dole cuts despite their persistent complaints about high public spending). MacDonald managed to push the cuts through Cabinet, in the face of resignation threats from nine of its members and the wholesale opposition of most of the rest of the movement, including the TUC and STUC. He concluded, however, that the game was up and, on 23 August 1931, submitted his resignation to the King, confiding to his family that he intended to retire. But his mind, as so often, was easily swayed. The King summoned him back and asked him, on grounds of patriotism, to continue in office at the head of an all-party coalition. Conservative voices too, notably that of Neville Chamberlain (shortly to become Chancellor), persuaded him that his presence was needed to bolster up what was left of international confidence in sterling. Whatever his other failings, MacDonald never lacked a sense of national duty, and this time he concluded that it over-rode his duty to a Labour Party in which anyway only Snowden and Thomas remained as significant loyalists to him. He commanded the resignations of his Labour ministers and formed instead a 'National' government, which included Baldwin as Leader of the Commons and Samuel as Home Secretary. Shortly thereafter, he went to the country in pursuit of a 'doctor's mandate', meaning the voters' sanction to do whatever was necessary. He got it, but at a terrible price for his old party and, in a deeper sense, for himself. The National Government won 554 of the 615 seats, but 469 of them went to Conservatives. Only 13 of the Government's Commons supporters were Labour, and just 52 Labour MPs sat on the opposition benches. Scotland succumbed to the landslide along with everywhere else. The government won 64 of the 71 Scottish seats, 48 of them going to Conservatives. Labour (a solitary government supporter aside) held just seven Scottish seats – fewer than half the number won by the Liberals – and four of these were 'unendorsed' ILPers. It was the worst electoral setback in Labour's history.

One aspect of MacDonald's remarkable naiveté was that he never did understand the acute bitterness which so many of his former colleagues bore him ever after. Another was his failure to anticipate that he had steered himself into leading what was, in all essentials, a Conservative government. The Tories, much more astutely, recognised that MacDonald's leadership bestowed a secular legitimacy on the government and its policies which unalloyed Conservative rule could not attain. He soldiered on for four years, an unhappy, weak and isolated figure, increasingly plagued by poor eyesight, encroaching senility and profound depression. On economic issues, he was frequently defeated in Cabinet, and many of the measures he himself had implemented between 1929 and 1931 were repealed. Even his old aptitude in foreign policy seemed to fail him, and he appeared paralysed by the spectacle of Hitler's rise in Germany – though, to be fair, few had any better idea of how to respond to that nightmare. The final humiliation came after he resigned the premiership in 1935, making room first for Baldwin and then for Chamberlain. MacDonald's old colleague Emanuel Shinwell – in whom the quality of mercy was ever a rationed commodity – took him on in the Seaham Harbour constituency and won. MacDonald died two years later.

The depression took, inevitably, a grim toll on the STUC. Membership had peaked in 1926 at close to 330,000, and would not recover that level until 1938. In the interim, it would fall by almost 100,000 to a trough of 230,478 in 1932. Affiliation income, likewise, fell by almost a third from its mid-1920s level, recovering only on the eve of war. Yet, thanks partly to Elger's fascination with organisational reform, the fabric of the movement in Scotland remained in better repair than might have been expected given the industrial and political havoc of the age. In some respects, it undoubtedly improved.

The 1924 congress at Ayr had conducted a protracted debate on future shape and strategy, which culminated in an instruction to the general council to conduct an exhaustive survey of the extent and the structure of union organisation in Scotland. The survey was, in large part, a recourse to keep at bay a contradictory and potentially divisive array of structural proposals then in circulation: industrial unionism, accelerated amalgamation, centralism, organising the unemployed, severing all ties with the Labour Party, and much more. The one common chord among all these discordant voices was that not enough was

known about the reach and the nature of the movement in
Scotland, and it was on this line of least resistance that the
general council shrewdly fixed. Elger took to it enthusiastically,
unleashing a tireless barrage of questionnaires and inquiries. The
results, though qualified by the disinclination of some bodies to
return their forms, were at once revealing and disquieting. Only
a third of the workforce was organised. A third of the unions
active in Scotland were still Scottish-based, but most of these
were tiny and affiliated fewer than 500 members each. Eighty
per cent of members were clustered in 16 per cent of unions. The
57 trades councils varied hugely from the perennially truculent
to the virtually moribund. Every seam of the structure betrayed
a lack of cohesion and co-ordination.

From these inferences, various initiatives would flow over the
next few years. One, as we have seen, was the unsubtle and
short-lived ploy of undermining the trades councils with county
union committees. Others were more constructive and enduring.
The survey had ascertained that around 40,000 women were
members of affiliated unions, and about 20,000 belonged to
non-affiliates: in total, below a fifth of women workers. It was an
area of obvious untapped potential for an STUC struggling both to
shore up its membership figures and to find new ideas about how
to meet the challenging age that lay ahead. The 1926 congress set
up a women's advisory committee to advance the role played by
women in the movement, and an inaugural annual conference
was held that September in the early aftermath of the General
Strike. The conference was open to unions with female members
(or 'affected by the organisation of women workers,' as the
general council's invitation rather archly put it), and 36 unions
attended. The early debate was conducted about, rather than by,
women trade unionists. At that first conference, just 22 of the
55 delegates were women, and it was 1933 before the general
council abandoned the policy of appointing a chairman and a
secretary (Elger) to guide the committee's deliberations. But the
numbers of women delegates attending rapidly grew, and in some
parts of the country women's trade unions groups – a sort of
unofficial women's trades councils – were formed, with active
STUC encouragement. In 1934, a Scottish committee of Labour,
co-op and trade union women was formed to promote combined
action on women's issues. They were modest beginnings, but they
were truly beginnings: the TUC did not get around to setting up a

women's advisory committee until 1930, one of the few instances during this period in which the STUC set the pace for its southern counterpart. It would be gratifying to think that Margaret Irwin, nearly seventy when the committee was formed, was somewhere looking on with satisfaction.

The committee proved energetic and innovative, and practical rather than ideological in its approach. It seems to have recognised from the outset the need to develop new ways of communicating with the women workers whom the conventional appeal of trade unionism had failed to impress. Rather than make speeches at them, it began to evolve new ways of persuading women aboard through one-to-one personal contacts by ordinary union members, always stressing bread-and-butter issues of particular concern to working women rather than the grander themes of trade unionism in general. These issues ranged from questions of childcare to the low wages and insecure employment which afflicted women. Weekend schools were organised from 1934 to train women members in the craft of trade unionism – negotiation, oratory, organisation. In 1932, two leading lights of the committee joined the general council, Bell Jobson (later to become the STUC's first woman president) and Agnes Gilroy. They were not the first women to reach the general council – the redoubtable Kate Maclean, for one, had served for three years just before the First World War – but their election reflected the importance which the committee had assumed within the organisation. The committee had become, and remains, an important platform for ensuring that the voice of women is heard and heeded in the counsels of the Scottish trade union movement. By 1948, the annual women's conference was attracting delegates from 50 unions, representing more than 132,000 women members.

As part of its approach to recruitment, the committee and its various offshoots forged links with organisations far removed from trade unionism – women's guilds, the YWCA, the British Women's Temperance Society, the women's section of the British Legion, the Scottish Girls' Friendly Society – and sought common ground on topics of general relevance to women. At one level, these contacts were only minimally successful, in that recruitment of women to union membership showed little immediate increase. But, at another level, the approach was to have far-reaching effects. From these associations gradually grew the distinctive

STUC practice of building and maintaining loose alliances with as wide as possible a range of civic bodies: churches, the voluntary sector, later the arts. Sixty years after the women's advisory committee first met, this shrewdly nurtured talent for making common cause would keep the STUC conspicuous and vibrant during the dark years of Thatcherism and beyond. The STUC owes a great deal to its women's committee.

It has less to be proud of in its record of establishing specific structures to draw the young into trade unionism. Perhaps this was because it took longer for that need to be recognised: the particular difficulties of recruiting women had been apparent from the first, whereas the inflow of youngsters, for example through apprenticeships, seemed part of the natural order. The depression changed all that. For one thing, the shortage of work impacted particularly on the young, increasing numbers of whom went straight from school to the unemployment queues. The army of young unemployed also constituted a temptation to hard-pressed employers as a source of cut-price labour, and this came to be seen in many quarters as a threat to the jobs of union members – particularly to work traditionally done by women. These objections strengthened rather than receded as the grip of recession at last began to slacken, in particular once rearmament gathered pace. Inter-union competition for the jobs that did start to become available took easy precedence over the virtuous mission of recruiting more youngsters to the movement. Almost three-quarters of affiliated unions, according to one of Elger's surveys in 1932, had adopted the policy of keeping in membership workers who lost their jobs, usually at little or no subscription charge. Getting those members back to work was, understandably, the priority. Besides, the improvement in economic circumstance had unleashed the inevitable rash of disputes, particularly on the Clyde, over pay and conditions. Lip-service could be paid to the importance of attracting the young, and was, but it took a long time to translate the words into action.

In 1933 a campaign was proclaimed to interest the young in trade unionism, though to no very evident effect, as may be judged by a call just two years later at the Montrose congress for just such a campaign to be started. The general council duly circulated affiliates, but again little seems to have been done.

The following year, the appeal to youth had become just one part of a much wider strategy for improving union organisation generally. The idea was floated of trade union fellowships for the young, which the trades councils were to organise. Charged with developing it, the general council decided to set up local union committees to discuss ways and means, but this leisurely process too became submerged in the rising tide of industrial disputes. In her presidential address to the 1937 congress at Inverness, Bell Jobson declared roundly that a period of industrial conflict was an ideal time to catch the interest of the young, and certainly more opportune than in the preceding decade when the movement had been on its back foot. But, by then, the young had taken matters into their own hands.

A few days before congress, apprentices at the Lobnitz shipyard in Renfrew had begun an unprecedented strike over pay differentials and conditions. Within a week, the protest had spread across Clydeside, to the east coast yards, and even briefly to Belfast. By then, well over 12,000 apprentices were out. The first of the four great Scottish apprentices' strikes – 1937, 1941, 1952 and 1960 – had begun. Each was to provide invaluable schooling for a coming generation of stewards and organisers. The 1960 strike, in particular, forged many of the men who, 11 years later, would provide the charismatic leadership for the campaign to save Upper Clyde Shipbuilders.

The apprentices had long epitomised the dilemma which young workers posed for the movement. Few doubted that they were exploited by the employers while learning their trades, and indeed some employers made a practice of sacking them the moment they completed their time and replacing them with more school-leavers on apprentice pay. By the same token, the suspicion was that apprentices were being used to supplant older craftsmen. This time, however, their seniors supported them, and on 16 April 1937 nearly 150,000 workers staged a one-day strike in sympathy. The STUC also lent fund-raising support. More important was the unity which the apprentices achieved among themselves, and the effectiveness of the organisation which they displayed across the four weeks of the dispute.

Meeting a year later in Girvan, the STUC Congress declared itself impressed, and a few months later, on 17 September 1938, a special conference was convened from which at last emerged the vestiges of a youth advisory committee. Eighty-four delegates attended from 29 unions. It would be stirring to infer that the STUC had quick-wittedly recognised in the dynamism of the apprentices' protest both the industrial potential and the organisational needs of young workers. In truth, the year between the strike and the Girvan Congress was given over to unedifying dither. Shortly before the strike, Elger had, somewhat predictably, issued a questionnaire on the general council's behalf. This addressed such crucial questions as whether or not it would be necessary to provide sports facilities to capture the interest of the young people, and if so whether these could be afforded. Together with more philosophical abstractions, like the proper definition of youth, and the rightful relationship of youth sections to both trades councils and unions, these no doubt captivating debates created a fine pretext for procrastination. Very little had been resolved by the time the special conference met. The conference decided against any positive encouragement to trades councils to form youth sections, settling instead for issuing a model constitution for any which decided to do so. The new youth advisory committee itself was given a predominantly fact-finding remit (there was, of course, to be a new questionnaire to inform its researches), and was explicitly forbidden any policy-making role. No doubt in consequence, the major manufacturing trades played, in those early years, little part in it. It was also severely chaperoned by the general council. The practice arose of appointing Elger's assistant as secretary to the committee, and so it would remain until after Elger's death. The last assistant on whom this chore fell was a sleek-featured man called Jimmy Jack who, just over a quarter century later, would himself become general secretary. Intriguingly enough, the timidity with which the youth committee had been constituted was roundly criticised at the 1939 Congress in Rothesay by a boisterous Communist from Glasgow Trades Council called George Middleton. Ten years later, Middleton would be the general secretary whom Jack would ultimately succeed. By then, however, the youth committee had been given its head, and become the forum in which many of the movement's later leading lights would serve their trade union apprenticeships. It remains a lively source of ideas and discussion, even if its activities cause the STUC's elders the odd sleepless night – most recently, when a campaign against working conditions at the McDonald's burger chain in the early 1990s attracted a libel writ.

The rightful relationship between the movement's political and trade union wings continued to be a source of tension through much of the 1930s. It was an argument which was political more than strategic, unsurprisingly given the turbulent politics of the times, and was driven in large measure by the efforts of a factionalised Left to develop its influence within the unions. As the decade progressed, heightening perceptions of the threat posed by fascism intensified the debate. For the STUC, the main effect was to generate still more bad blood between the general council and the trades councils. It was symptomatic of a more general political ferment.

The trauma of the 1931 general election, and of MacDonald's subsequent conduct, had a cathartic effect on Labour politics in Scotland, though the decay in the party's political fortunes had set in before then. In the preceding 12 months, four parliamentary by-elections in Scotland had borne striking testament to a rapid decline in popular esteem. Labour had struggled to hold three seats with previously commanding majorities – Shettleston (left vacant by Wheatley's death), St Rollox, and Rutherglen (fought by David Hardie, half-brother to Keir) – and had lost by a mile in the once-marginal East Renfrew. The by now open acrimony between Labour and the ILP was a potent factor, alongside the more general disfavour for MacDonald's efforts to grapple with the economic crisis. By contrast, the Conservatives had contrived to look energetic, constructive and united, and when the 1931 election disaster befell Labour it was as pronounced in the heartland seats of west-central Scotland as anywhere else. The following year, Maxton led the ILP out of the party, finally disgusted by Labour's commitment to gradual parliamentary change and its failure to share his vision of the 'revolutionary conception' with which economic hardship was imbuing the masses.

Almost at once, Labour's electoral performance began perceptibly to improve, though the reasons had less to do with the departure of the troublesome ILP than with the even-handed way in which recession bestows contempt on any government of the day. The new National Government added greatly to its own unpopularity with the introduction of the widely-despised Means Test, an insolence to the poor that dismayed many Conservatives as well as socialists. Bob Boothby, Tory MP for East Aberdeenshire, wrote in troubled terms to Baldwin in

January 1934: 'I don't share the views of some regarding the necessity for state 'planning' of industry . . . but I do jib at starving the unemployed . . . if something isn't done to mitigate the sufferings of the unemployed . . . I personally could not go on supporting the government.' His friend and fellow 'young progressive,' Harold Macmillan, was likewise appalled by what he later recalled as the 'shattering human indignity of working men in those times.' Such younger Tory elements found much in the Mondist ideal to attract them, and began to argue for greater state intervention to regenerate the economy and modernise industry. Twenty years later, their memories of those times would shape their stewardship of government.

For the moment, it added up to a powerful longing within the labour movement for unity, but two different forms of unity were on offer. For most senior figures in the movement, and on the STUC general council, the best prospect lay in exerting unprovocative influence by making common cause with those who shared the reformist concern to build something better out of the economic devastation: a unity of pragmatism. Elger in particular put repairing Scotland's battered economy at the head of the STUC's priorities, and sought representation on any public body that was set up to address that objective. It was not always an easy path to maintain. At the 1932 congress in Hawick the general council faced attack not merely for its lack of militancy in opposing the Means Test, but also for accepting two seats on the Scottish Council for Community Service During Unemployment, which the Left suspected of wanting to turn community centres into unpaid production units. These protests were led by the Falkirk baker, Charles Murdoch, yet another future general secretary of the STUC. In fact, events went some way to vindicate the general council, since the council agreed to incorporate a string of STUC safeguards in its remit (of which, in any case, it made little). A similar argument erupted over the Scottish Development Council. This was an industrialists' collective set up by the shipbuilder Sir James Lithgow in 1931. In 1936, it spawned a more broad-based offshoot, the Scottish Economic Committee, which became an influential voice in promoting a business case for diversification into lighter industries, for greater emphasis on marketing, design and training, and for the pursuit of what would later become known as inward investment. At that year's congress, the Left once again attacked the general council for accepting two seats.

The Scottish Development Council, it was suggested, bore the hidden agenda of making ready to mobilise industry for war, and besides Lithgow had been closing shipyards. Again, events vindicated participation. The council would be a key force in the post-war reconstruction of the Scottish economy after it was combined with another broad-based body to become the Scottish Council Development and Industry, of which the STUC remains a pillar.

The list of public bodies on which the STUC secured representation lengthened prodigiously across the 1930s. Scarcely a month went by without Elger reporting to the general council on the latest deliberations of the Joint Industrial Council for Local Government Service, the [Mondist] Board of Conciliation and Arbitration for Scotland, the Scottish Council of the Playing Fields Association, the Scottish Labour College board, the National Advisory Council for Juvenile Employment, the Clyde Navigation Trust, the National Council of Labour Colleges, the Glasgow Civic Press (publishers of *Forward*), the Queen's Institute of District Nursing, the board of Donaldson's Hospital for the Deaf. Elger himself, in addition to remaining an active officer in his own clerical union (he became its president in 1939), had been elected Labour councillor for Ruchill in 1931, and became a magistrate four years later. At the same time, the general council was itself generating a growing constellation of committees, all of which required to be staffed and serviced; and numerous liaison committees with bodies like the Labour Party, the Co-operative Movement and the trades councils. The STUC had transformed itself steadily from being a lobbying force on behalf of the Scottish trades union movement into an industrious and significant institution active at many levels of Scotland's public life. Thus were the foundations laid for the formidable role which the STUC would come to play in helping shape Scotland's destiny in the post-war years, and much of the credit for that lies with William Elger.

It seems that the strain began to tell on him, for in February 1937, the staffing committee reviewed the 'almost incalculable increase in the amount of work devolving on the congress staff,' and particularly on Elger. It remarked with satisfaction that, 'the work and influence of the congress had grown beyond all recognition compared with the period of the present secretary's predecessor,' but worried that the consequence for Elger was onerous since the amount of time he was having to spend serving on public bodies away from the STUC office in Glasgow's Elmbank Crescent meant that his more routine duties were consuming his evenings and weekends. 'Although the social life of trade union officers generally is very much restricted, it is almost totally absent from the life of the secretary of the congress,' the committee remarked admiringly. It was agreed both to share representative duties more evenly around the general council, and to increase subscriptions in order to increase full-time STUC staffing from two to three. The STUC's concern for women workers did not, however, extend in those days to an equal opportunities policy, for the committee concluded in reviewing Elger's workload that 'a male assistant is an urgent necessity,' though it did add that the office would shortly need 'additional typing assistance.'

The Left, meanwhile, was pursuing a different type of unity. After the fiasco of 1931, figures like Maxton and Fenner Brockway devoted increasing time to trying to re-group a fragmented Left around agreed principles of class struggle. Numerous pamphlets argued in particular for extra-parliamentary action through workers' councils. The Communist Party of Great Britain, now released from the Comintern's isolationist 1920s rubric, showed early interest, and more than 150 delegates from the CPGB and ILP, plus sundry trade unionists and Co-operators, attended a conference in Sheffield in December 1932, which culminated in the formation of a joint council of action. From this initiative, the CPGB conceived the United Front as an umbrella grouping of the Left to fight the twin menaces of unemployment and fascism. Both the Labour Party and the TUC, when approached, predictably decided to have nothing to do with it. The ILP liked the idea, though, and so did the recently-formed Socialist League, a left-wing ginger group within the Labour Party which counted Stafford Cripps and Aneurin Bevan among its members. There was to be some informal co-operation, notably in assistance to the NUWM. But the scheme foundered on the outright hostility of the mainstream labour movement, on a growing distaste for developments in Stalin's Russia, and on the (cogent) suspicion that the CPGB's ultimate objective was to absorb its partners. After the outbreak of the Spanish Civil War in June 1936, and the official labour movement's half-hearted support for the Spanish government, negotiations began afresh, encouraged by the growing numbers of middle- and upper-class members attracted to the Left as a foil to fascism. Again there were some notable joint initiatives, most famously the 'Battle of Cable Street' which stopped a march by Oswald Mosley's fascist Blackshirts through London's East End in October 1936. Three months later a 'Unity Manifesto' was published, to which Labour's national executive responded by outlawing the Socialist League. But the drive for a United Front was again stillborn, not least because the CPGB and the ILP supported different factions within the fatally-divided Spanish Left. All the same, fitful attempts to march in step would continue to be made.

One place where these contrasting drives for unity collided was in the trades councils. Though the Labour Party was still in some respects more left-wing in Scotland than in the rest of the UK, it was also if anything more resolute in its disdain for the Communists, largely because of its powerful need not to upset Catholic voters. Elger, who had strongly abstentionist instincts about politics in any event (tending to leave more political campaigning to the TUC to run), had already issued the instruction in 1928 that trades councils should refuse affiliation to anyone associated with the National Minority Movement. It had been little heeded. Now the Labour Party was growing increasingly concerned about the joint councils, and making its disquiet felt. This presented Elger with a dilemma. Though keen to maintain proper distance from the movement's political wing, he was undoubtedly sympathetic to these concerns: not least because of his belief in the separation of the political and industrial fronts. Equally, he knew the havoc that a wholesale witch-hunt would cause within the Scottish union movement. His first instinct, as always, was an inquiry, and the 1934 congress instructed the general council to prepare a report on the joint councils. Meanwhile, the general council issued a series of statements opposing any kind of United Front, including one in February 1935 which required all affiliated bodies to act within STUC policy, and another at the 1936 congress advising trades councils how to respond if approached to join any sort of political alliance. At the same gathering, the general council refused a request from Harry McShane of the NUWM for a meeting to discuss joint campaigning on unemployment issues. This decision produced an angry backlash from a significant minority in the hall, and pointed contrasts were drawn with the general council's readiness to consort with the likes of Sir James Lithgow. A few months later the biggest of all the hunger marches would count Alex Moffat and Peter Kerrigan among the leaders of its Scottish contingent.

Eventually, in early 1937, the general council's organisation committee did hold what the minutes firmly describe in more than one reference as a 'private and informal' discussion with Harry McShane and the NUWM Scottish Council. No account of the meeting was preserved, but it appears to have been fruitless. It had taken place on the persistent prompting of Aberdeen Trades Council, a body which had become and would remain more closely entwined within the civic life of its community than any other trades council in Scotland. Concerned at the divisions created between its own unemployed association and the local branch of the NUWM, the trades council had appealed to the STUC to press for a national rapprochement between the TUC and the NUWM. But, in February 1936, Elger wrote on behalf of the organisation committee that 'no scheme for organising more effectively unemployed persons appears at the moment to be practicable other than the scheme already approved by Congress, of unemployed associations under the auspices of trades councils.'

It took until October 1938 for the problem of the joint councils finally to be resolved. A conference attended by representatives of 24 councils agreed a formal separation of political and industrial functions. The decision was made easier by the fact that Labour's Scottish conference had ordered disjuncture five months earlier. Elger and Labour's Scottish secretary, Arthur Woodburn, had spent months negotiating a joint agreement on how to effect the separation. In some cases, the councils would be formally split into trades councils and local labour parties; in others, they would operate separate industrial and political sections. Elaborate conditions were agreed for the party to have jurisdiction over trade unionists active in the political context, and the STUC to be responsible when they were engaged in industrial activities. The general council recognised, wrote Elger to Woodburn in June 1938, 'the advantage of continued co-operation between us, and that the general council and your executive have each a responsibility of safeguarding the prestige of both our respective organisations.' It meant that future linkage between the two wings of the movement would take place at leadership, rather than grassroots, level. The party and the Scottish congress which had played such a big part in setting it up nearly four decades earlier had finally agreed to formal, if amicable, separation.

But by then, the eyes of the movement – as of the country – were

fixed on the international horizon. Clouds, deepening and darkening, gathered across the 1930s. For the labour movement, as for
the rest of the body politic, there was a unanimity of apprehension
but not of response. As the Conservatives fissured over whether to
appease or confront the growing menace of fascism, so too did the
Left divide over how best to prevent the warfare which seemed
to be drawing inexorably closer. Some placed their faith in the
League of Nations, though that faith grew progressively harder
to sustain; others in bilateral pacts and peace treaties; others still
in economic sanctions, international peace-keeping forces, global
socialist revolution or the worldwide general strike for peace so
fondly promoted before the First World War. History scorns the
Baldwin and Chamberlain governments, particularly the latter, for
their indecision and weakness in the face of the Nazi ascendancy,
yet it is often forgotten that the labour movement – though steadily
regaining electoral ground after 1935 – was no more resolute or
united. Memories of the 1914–18 carnage were fresh enough to
make avoidance of a new war in Europe the driving imperative
in many minds, however hateful the ideologies of fascism.

It would be foolish to pretend that the STUC was a central force
in this national debate, yet it did have a particular locus beyond
the common concern of the population at large. Rearmament, pro-
ceeding from the mid-1930s onwards, impacted particularly potently
on Scotland, which retained a powerful concentration of heavy
engineering industry. In the short-term, it conferred the significant
advantage of rapid employment growth in some of Scotland's most
deprived areas. By the latter half of the decade, rearmament was
sustaining a fifth of the work in the Clyde shipyards alone, as well
as stimulating huge demand for coal, steel, iron and munitions.
After a decade of unprecedentedly high unemployment, this was
not a gain to dismiss lightly. Yet it was also cause for disquiet. At
the international level, it signalled an evaporating confidence in the
capacity of diplomacy through the League to keep a peace in Europe.
At the Scottish level, it both revived the old spectre of dilution
and diverted funds away from the investment in newer industrial
capacity which, the STUC had become increasingly convinced, was
the way of the future for the Scottish economy. Fairly swiftly,
the STUC decided that rearmament, for all that it had shortened
Scotland's dole queues, was bad news.

Timing helped. Shortly before delegates gathered in St Andrews
for the 1936 congress, Mussolini invaded Abyssinia with what

many, not just in Britain, saw as British connivance. Baldwin's Foreign Secretary, Sir Samuel Hoare, had talked tough at the League about Britain's response to the Italian aggression, while simultaneously agreeing a pact with his French counterpart, Pierre Laval, that effectively sanctioned the partition of Abyssinia in Mussolini's favour. It severely undermined the authority of the League, which was left imposing ineffectual sanctions on Italy. Public condemnation of the manoeuvre cost Hoare his job, though that was of little consolation to the Abyssinians.

Neither did it soothe the disquiet of the STUC, which set the Abyssinia episode alongside the policy of rearmament and liked what it saw not at all. A general council statement issued immediately upon the invasion had warned the government against weakening the standing of the League. Now, in St Andrews, delegates reinforced that call and characterised the rearmament drive as a direct consequence of the government's unwillingness to pursue peace seriously through the League. A powerfully-worded motion expressed 'great alarm' at the government's decision to invest 'the vast sum of £300 million' in military renewal, predicting that the build-up would lead inexorably to war. The motion advocated the alternative of seeking security through a peace conference organised by the League, and argued that the government's willingness to go behind the League's back over Abyssinia, together with its condoning of German rearmament, 'show the National government as the enemy of peace and the friend of fascism.' Strong words, as were many of the accompanying speeches, notably that of James Young of the draughtsmen, who declared: 'The last armaments race did not prevent war and neither will a fresh one.' Several engineering delegates produced anecdotal evidence that dilution was already taking place within workforces swollen by rearmament. Another side of the STUC's unease was evident in an altogether quieter debate, which culminated in approval for a motion calling on the government to fund 'an authoritative Scottish body with suitable experience and knowledge, equipped with an expert staff' to draw up a programme for the 'orderly and planned development' of the Scottish economy.

A year later, at Inverness, the opposition to rearmament was focused still more closely in a motion which warned politicians and public that 'the present increased industrial activity and consequent decrease in unemployment, due mainly to the armaments programme, will, immediately this intensive programme concludes, be followed by an industrial depression even worse than that which followed the post-war collapse . . . the only way by which the disastrous social consequences of such a recurrence can be avoided is by promoting now a planned development of the industries and social services of the country.'

By then, though, the reality of war had moved closer to home. In July 1936, civil war broke out in Spain after the military, led by General Francisco Franco, staged an uprising against the socialist government with the increasingly overt backing of the fascist powers in Germany, Italy and Portugal. The initial response of the League of Nations, fearful of escalation, was a policy of non-intervention. This stance was endorsed by the National Council of Labour – the labour movement's central liaison body – which sanctioned no more partisan involvement than fund-raising. But the policy soon came under severe pressure both in Britain and abroad. Baldwin's National government, with Eden now at the Foreign Office, interpreted non-intervention rigorously, blocking all practical aid to the Spanish government and endeavouring to stem the flow of volunteers joining the International Brigade to fight Franco's forces. At the same time, it was becoming evident that the fascist powers were paying no heed whatever to non-intervention and were actively supporting Franco.

The consequence within the labour movement was once more to set the national leadership at odds with grassroots feeling, and particularly with the Left which saw no merit in non-intervention. The tensions were, as always, particularly acute in Scotland both because of the focus which the trades councils afforded the Left within STUC decision-making and because of the inevitable suspicion that the general council was acting merely as a satellite of the TUC. Besides, the International Brigade exercised a powerful appeal in Scotland, where many were drawn to the prospect of fighting a good cause as an alternative to life on the dole. All over Scotland, support groups were formed to channel aid to the Spanish government. For all these reasons, the STUC emerged from the affair with a slightly more creditable record than the TUC, though it took a while.

Two months after the war began, the general council wrote urging affiliates to give generously to the National Council's Spanish Workers Fund – which many were already doing – and to generate such 'local propaganda' as they could in support of the socialist cause in Spain. It was all too obviously a line that could not hold. Scarcely unaware of the tensions building up within the movement, the CPGB sought a meeting with the general council in January to invite the STUC to lead a 'united campaign' on a platform of generating aid for the Spanish government, opposing the British government's ban on the supply of arms and volunteers, demanding the withdrawal of Italian and German forces from Spain and supporting the dependants of British workers who had enlisted in the International Brigade. The approach caused, as it was no doubt intended to, fierce debate on the general council, culminating in a refusal to receive the CPGB deputation because such a campaign 'obviously involves fundamental questions of policy' which only affiliates could determine. A month later, the general council also decided not to attend a special conference organised by the Scottish Peace Congress.

Events once more took a hand. A week before the 1937 STUC congress met in Inverness, the Luftwaffe launched its infamous raid on Guernica, the first ever deliberate bombing of a civilian population. Horror at the carnage transformed the mood of delegates. An emergency motion deploring the slaughter was passed unanimously, but much more significant was a composite motion, passed with only two dissenting, on substantive policy towards the war. The majority belied the intensive procedural wrangling undergone to get the motion debated at all. The motion admired the 'heroic stand' of the Spanish government against fascist aggression, declared against the British government's non-intervention policy and promised support for International Brigade dependants: in other words, most of the points sought three months earlier by the CPGB. Critics of the motion, led by the theatre and cinema workers, wanted it referred back on the grounds that it countermanded the National Council of Labour's policy of non-intervention – which, to all purposes, it did. Replying, with gentle irony, for the general council, Robert Taylor of the Scottish Horse and Motormen observed that it was the government's policy which was being condemned, not that of the Labour Party which had 'not yet definitely declared itself one way or another.'

In the wake of that debate, the general council's neutrality became, if no less obstructive, at least conspicuously more reluctant. The National Council of Labour had widened the spread of its fund-raising, instigating a milk fund and a support fund for Basque children, and the general council urged affiliates to give generously. But the trades councils were badgering for ways to help the Spanish government more directly. Under pressure from the Edinburgh and Glasgow councils, a cross-movement meeting was convened by Elger in December 1937 which agreed in principle to place fund-raising in the hands of an 'authoritative Scottish body' while noting, in a classic Elger phrase, that 'certain administrative difficulties' needed to be sorted out first. Chief among these was the National Council. Elger had passed on the Inverness decision on support for International Brigade dependants to (now Sir) Walter Citrine, who ruled that aid could only go to Spanish workers or their dependants. Elger also issued a circular in January 1938 warning affiliates to have nothing to do with area joint committees, often Communist-run, raising relief funds for Spain. The trades councils, predictably, erupted, as did others and the row carried on to the Girvan congress in April. Successive delegates took to the floor to demand the withdrawal of the circular and to condemn what one described as 'Mr Citrine with his provincial outlook telling them . . . that they could not give money to the International Brigade.' Elger, just as predictably, replied that it was 'purely an administrative matter.'

The upshot was that the general council increasingly turned a blind eye as the movement got down to the business of providing much more direct aid for the socialist cause in Spain. There was a row between Elger and the Edinburgh and Glasgow Trades Councils a month after Girvan, when they organised a conference on arms for Spain and rearmament generally, and advertised Elger as a speaker without having asked him. After much acrimony, the general council agreed to endorse the conference on a vague assurance that any decision which flowed from it would accord with National Council policy. In fact, what flowed was an independent Scottish appeal which led, that October, to the Scottish labour movement sponsoring one of the first foodships to reach the beleaguered Spanish loyalists. The expedition was in defiance of British government policy, and the navy refused the ship protection (it had actively prevented an earlier ship from reaching Spain, and had arrested its master). When, two months later, an appeal for a second Scottish shipment was launched, it was the STUC general council which spearheaded the campaign. Also in December 1938, the general council agreed to be represented at a ceremony to welcome home the Glasgow contingent of the International Brigade – though, bizarrely enough, it would follow this up in April 1939 by refusing to endorse an appeal to raise funds for a national memorial to the Brigade's British battalion.

The experience of the Spanish Civil War served to harden opposition within the STUC to the appeasement policy which the National government, led since May 1937 by Neville Chamberlain, was adopting against the high tide of fascism. But there was little consensus as to the alternative. Some argued for outright military opposition, some for the formation of a 'peace bloc' through bilateral non-aggression pacts as promoted by the Soviet Union (a favoured option which would crumble to dust in August 1939 when the Soviets signed just such a pact with Berlin, so sanctioning the Nazi invasion of Poland and precipitating the war). Others merely longed for a change of government, and gazed bewildered at the quickening pace of events. As the omens mounted and darkened in spring 1939, Elger quietly began drafting a manifesto through which – in conscious contrast to 1914 – the STUC could shape the response of Scottish organised labour to the onset of war.

These arguments would no doubt have been talked through in depth at the April 1939 congress in Rothesay had not delegates disembarked the ferry to find the press waiting with startling news. Late the previous year, the TUC had reached agreement with Chamberlain for the establishment of a National Voluntary Service Scheme, on condition of a solemn undertaking by government that there would be no peacetime conscription. The STUC general council had endorsed the agreement in the teeth of opposition from the Left, as articulated by roughly half Scotland's trades councils. The STUC had nominated representatives to serve on the scheme's local committees, and Elger had joined the national committee as a TUC nominee. What delegates now learned from the reporters at Rothesay was that a statement would be made in the Commons later that day announcing the first stages of a programme of compulsory military service.

For once, political differences were cast aside. The general council felt every bit as betrayed as the Left, and immediately went into an emergency session that was to last, with only brief adjournments, for the duration of the congress. In London, the National Council of Labour was also in open-ended session but, such was the anger at Rothesay, that this time the general council was in no mood to await guidance from the metropolis. A motion, demanding that the government withdraw the scheme, was drafted and delegates were asked to endorse it without discussion so that it could be forwarded instantly to the Prime Minister and the Leader of the Opposition. Many delegates, however, complained that the motion did not go far enough and a decision was taken to defer further consideration until the following day, particularly after word was received that the National Council of Labour had adjourned its own consideration of the matter. The next day, the general council met in the unusual surroundings of the Paddle Steamer *Mercury* and agreed a statement, drafted by Elger.

The statement sounded slightly more robust than it actually was. It laid about the National government, declaring that it now constituted a danger both to world peace and to 'the democratic institutions of our people,' that it had violated its own promises on conscription at a time when the international threat demanded unity behind a strong and voluntary defence provision, and that every effort should be made to replace it with a Labour government committed to collective security and the preservation of democratic ideals and practices. But the statement was rather more cautious in relation to a specific response to the government's decision. It undertook that the general council would discuss with the National Council the best ways of combating compulsion, noting that union participation on the voluntary service committees might have to be reconsidered. In the ensuing debate, which was dominated by the Left, successive speakers called for a clear and immediate decision to withdraw from the voluntary scheme, while others spoke disparagingly of the National Council and its lack of distinctiveness from the policies of the National government. Middleton was prominent among these speakers, declaring that what the people wanted – and had been denied by government – was an alliance with the Soviet Union. But the statement was approved by a large majority.

For all the artifice in the statement, the general council went immediately to work in consolidating the opposition to conscription. Elger and William Quin, STUC president since Rothesay, began an urgent round of meetings with the National Council which culminated in their attending a TUC conference of union executives in London in mid-May. At the same time, the STUC general council resolved to mount a national campaign in Scotland against conscription, built around a mass petition, and to convene a special conference on 21 May. The contrast between the TUC and STUC conferences was, given the recent trend towards convergence, quite remarkable. The London one voted by a huge majority not to break with the national voluntary service scheme, and rejected a call for a general strike by a still larger margin. But the Scottish meeting instructed the general council, by a decisive majority, to withdraw from the voluntary scheme at both national and local levels, and also approved by a margin of more than two-to-one the principle of mounting combined industrial action against conscription, which the general council was to be ready to co-ordinate. It was a signal victory for those who believed that the Scottish movement was prepared to conduct itself more militantly than was prescribed by the leaders of the UK movement, on whose words the STUC general council paid such attendance. But the aftermath was also instructive. The general council ultimately had quietly to drop the national petition which, though moderate in tone, had only managed to muster around 4,000 signatures from the public. And when the general council came to consult affiliated unions on joint industrial action a few weeks later, well over a third declared themselves opposed to it. That plan too was discreetly abandoned.

It was to be the STUC's last significant gesture of defiance for more than half a decade. On 1 September 1939, Hitler invaded Poland. The world was once more at war. This time there was to be no seditious ambivalence from the Scottish trade union movement about justification. Meeting in special session at 11am on 5 September 1939, the general council swiftly cleared the decks of its routine business, and turned its attention to the declaration of war. A succession of forthcoming events was cancelled: the women's conference and a youth school scheduled for October, the youth conference due to take place in December. Elger was instructed to take no further steps meantime in organising the following year's congress (in the event it went ahead, at Aberdeen). All action on processing congress decisions was suspended and a five-strong emergency committee was formed. One of its first actions, when it met later that month, would be formally to abandon the campaign against conscription. Finally, Elger produced his draft manifesto. The general council went into recess until 5pm that day to consider it, and then authorised that it be issued to all affiliates and to the press. No dissent on that decision is minuted.

Even today, there is a disturbing thrill, a compelling sense of moment, in reading the manifesto. It ran to just eight paragraphs, and was elegantly and powerfully written, conceived to appeal to the broadest spread of opinion within the movement. It began: 'At this hour of tragedy the Scottish Trades Union Congress addresses this manifesto to the workers of Scotland.' The first three paragraphs described the basic purposes of trade unionism (including a long-term commitment to 'the more comprehensive purpose of abolishing capitalism'), and the threat which fascism posed to the democratic institutions which the unions had 'painfully, but persistently' laboured to build. The fourth, audaciously enough in the circumstances, set out the strictly-defined reasons why British unions had joined the international trade union movement in regarding Hitler's Germany as an aggressor nation: 'It was not so named by the trade unions in this country because the Hitler regime was against British imperialism: the unions are also against imperialism. It was not so named because that regime was against the British national government: the unions have had ample cause to doubt the value of that government to the British people. The Hitler regime was named aggressor by the trade union movement because wherever the swastika flies the free associations of the workers, their trade union and political organisations, have been crushed with a ferocious brutality.'

Then came the meat. This justification over-rode any consideration of solidarity with the German worker: 'ultimately only he can find his own solution. The general council are under no illusion that the war is a crusade of reform for the German people or that it will permanently remove the international antagonisms that have led up to it. But the general council can see no other course open to the people of the democracies than to resist to the utmost the aggressiveness of fascism . . . .'

The statement went on to argue that the experience of the last war had shown the need for a strong trade union movement to ensure that the rights and therefore the morale of workers were not trampled underfoot by emergency demands on the productive industries: 'In the pursuance of war, all the resources of the nation will require to be mobilised and mobilised efficiently. The collective security of the nation must not be impaired by any zeal to protect the individual rights of the owners of wealth . . . the mechanism of production must be kept running with due regard to the need for obtaining a full and willing co-operation of the workers themselves.' Finally, it gave warning that the workers of Scotland would not fight fascism just to see its precepts introduced at home:

'At a time of travail the nation cannot face both ways. It must not be weakened by denying those democratic qualities which are so essential in our national life. The people cannot successfully fight tyranny by losing freedom.'

It is, perhaps, the most significant document the STUC has ever issued. Its impact was profound. It gave a lead at a crucial time, where the lack of one had proved so dangerous a quarter of a century earlier. But it also set down the terms on which the compliance of the Scottish workforce could be delivered, and in so doing it drew in due course an answering bargain from government that brought fundamental change to the institutional and the economic structure of Scotland, the consequences of which persist to this day. The Red Clydesiders of 1915 may have won scant advance at the time for their defiance. But the common anxiety of the STUC and of the government to ensure that this time, with the issues much clearer and the dangers much greater, there would be no repeat of that dissension paid a lasting bounty not just to the movement itself but to Scotland.

The more immediate point about the rationale embodied in the manifesto was that it worked. Dissent about the justification for supporting this war was consigned to the margins of the movement, both in Scotland and beyond. The *Daily Worker*, later suppressed under emergency legislation, demonstrated the disarray on the Left by proclaiming on the day hostilities broke out that the war 'can and must be won.' Two weeks later, following an edict from the Comintern, the paper was just as stridently calling for the organised working-class movement to resist being drawn into a war between rival imperialisms. As it executed this U-turn, Harry Pollitt, the British Communist leader, issued a pamphlet in which he declared: 'To stand aside from this conflict, to contribute only revolutionary-sounding phrases while the fascist beast rides roughshod over Europe would be a betrayal of everything our forebears have fought to achieve.' The pamphlet cost Pollitt his position within the party hierarchy, yet it was indicative of the lack of a substantive and coherent anti-war movement even on the far Left. James Maxton, still heading a by now shrivelling ILP, exemplified the confusion all on his own, arguing bleakly throughout the war for peace terms to be sought but not at the cost of surrender. More importantly, though, the principal figures on the left wing of the Labour Party, who had kept open channels to the far Left, were solidly behind the war. They had, after all, spent several years attempting to persuade the party to adopt a more forthright policy against fascism. Jennie Lee wrote of the reaction of her husband, Aneurin Bevan, on hearing Chamberlain's declaration of war: 'We had discussed all this so often and so much. Now at last it had come. Our enemy Hitler had become the national enemy. All those who hated fascism would have their chance now. They would have their chance to fight back.'

When the STUC gathered in Aberdeen the following April, it approved the manifesto by a majority of three to one. The majority might well have been bigger but for the frustrations of the 'phoney war', which ended soon after with the fall of France. In his presidential address, Quin said: 'There are those amongst us who believe that if an immediate armistice were called and a peace conference summoned it would be possible to secure agreement between the belligerent powers. I fear they are unduly optimistic ... the more recent acts of aggression against Denmark and Norway must surely convince even the most ardent pacifist that peace is not possible while Hitler and his gang control the German Reich.' The following month, Chamberlain too was gone, replaced by a government which, though headed by the movement's old nemesis, Churchill, included a number of Labour ministers in senior positions. In a further manifesto published in the June 1940 issue of the *Scottish Congress Bulletin*, the general council celebrated Chamberlain's removal and called on the workers of Scotland to give 'every support to the new government' provided it stuck by the promise of its own Emergency Powers Act to place both services and property at the disposal of the state: an echo of the old cry for conscription of wealth. But the new manifesto defended the draconian powers (including control over wages and working conditions) which the Act bestowed on the government: 'The gravity of the war situation makes such powers inevitable. In accepting them the workers need surrender none of those rights fundamentally necessary to them. The powers which the state now assumes are not a step towards dictatorship, because dictatorship cannot exist while the free organisations of the workers prevail. Democracy is never more powerful than when it is resolutely determined to resist aggression.'

Clearly, a lot had changed since that distant Christmas Day when David Lloyd George could not make himself heard at the St Andrew's Hall in Glasgow.

CHAPTER SIX

THE NEW JERUSALEM

On 5 October 1946, William Elger collapsed during a meeting in Glasgow. It was a massive heart attack. He was rushed to Ruchill Hospital where a month later, on 6 November, he died. He was 55 years old.

The loss of a gifted, energetic and dedicated man in his mid-fifties is a sorrow in any circumstance, yet Elger's passing was, if only in retrospect, oddly symbolic of the position to which he had brought the organisation he had led for half its existence. His death was hastened, there seems little question, by over-work. His funeral, at Glasgow's Western Necropolis Crematorium, was attended not merely by trade unionists but by senior representatives of government, the employers' organisations, the armed forces and the broad panoply of Scottish civic life. It was a sad but eloquent testimony to the legacy he had left of an STUC transformed into a confident, polymathic ubiquity at the very core of Scottish public affairs. During Elger's tenure the organisation's affiliated membership had all but trebled from 226,822 to 606,448. Ironically, given the tireless effort he had devoted to recruitment, it is hard to attribute that increase any too directly to his leadership. Yet the equally exponential growth in the STUC's influence over that same period stands very much to Elger's personal credit. Under William Elger the STUC, to adapt Dean Acheson, had lost some of its distinctiveness but it had gained a role.

It was a role which wartime had greatly consolidated. The Labour movement reached an informal but resilient pact with government to rein back its pursuit of industrial advantage for the duration of the war in return for a degree of partnership in determining public policy. Nowhere was that partnership to prove more productive than in Scotland. This was a logical extension of the path which Elger had doggedly trodden throughout the 1930s, and also of the Mondist approach to industrial relations. But it took skill to deliver, persistence to maintain and imagination to exploit. Elger exerted all three, together with a measure of courage which it is easy to overlook in assessing his career. To take just one example, he came out in 1944 unambiguously in support of that old STUC demon, industrial conscription, insisting that 'the industrial worker has obligations in the war effort equal to those of the soldier.' By then, Elger held a number of posts in public bodies responsible for maintaining production, and was helping determine the quotas which the productive industries were set. It was important work, yet high office had never excused injudicious opinion in the STUC and his remained a bold stance to adopt. But faith in the leadership seems to have held firm among most of the STUC rank and file throughout the war, and indeed there was an oblique compliment paid from an unlikely quarter during one of the more troublesome debates at the 1941 congress in Dunoon, when some on the Left were voicing powerful reservations about the readiness of Labour to climb into government with the old enemy, Churchill. Glasgow Trades Council, concerned that such an alliance would undermine the interests of workers, said the real worry lay south of the border, where the TUC lacked the close affinity with its grassroots members that existed in the STUC.

Not all the normal run of workplace grievances that exercise unions were submerged by the war effort, and some were heightened. Disputes continued to break out here and there, including another apprentices' stoppage, in March 1941, over differentials and dilution. The strike, which lasted ten days, was eventually joined by more than 7,000 apprentices. It culminated in a formal inquiry by the Ministry of Labour, which later conceded some of the apprentices' demands in a national agreement. Yet there was little echo of the tendency during the First World War for union agitation to be cast as treason. Indeed, unions became resourceful at aligning their grievances with the war effort, and at capturing the sense of national community which prevailed through much of the 1939–45 conflict. Where employers did take advantage of war to try to steal a march on their workforces by imposing adverse conditions in the name of the national interest, they were harried for it with patriotic union rhetoric. Rarely had trade unionism seemed in better accord with the public mood. Joseph Westwood, Secretary of State for Scotland in the Attlee government, would write of the STUC in 1947: 'Their contribution to victory in the national ordeal from which we have so recently emerged has set the seal on their position as one of the great sources of national strength.'

Yet the contingencies of wartime did in themselves generate workplace differences. One, which arose early in the war, is of interest for the insight it gives into just how far the STUC women's committee had developed since the days when it was policed by male general council members. The issue was the terms under which women workers were being transferred to war work in the Midlands on poorer pay than they had been earning in Scotland. The general council had already intervened with the Scottish Secretary in 1941 to secure better allowances, but the matter was still rumbling on in October 1942 when the Ministry of Labour and National Service agreed after correspondence with the women's committee to receive a deputation. The general council appointed a deputation consisting of its own chairman, Charles Murdoch; Elger; and the chair and secretary of the women's committee. The women's committee was distinctly unimpressed at having been denied the opportunity to elect its own deputation, and roundly told Elger so. He responded, with more than his customary contrition, that 'the general council had always desired to have the closest harmony between the committee and the council and it was hoped that the decision made on this occasion would not disturb that harmony.' Unfortunately, the general council then compounded the felony by circularising a report of the ministerial meeting before it had briefed the women's committee. At its next meeting, the committee endorsed a proposal from its chair, Bell Jobson, that the time had come for a forthright discussion with the general council about the respective powers and functions of the two bodies. Two years later, the committee decided to change its own title to the Women's Advisory Council.

The trades councils were a source of rather greater anxiety for Elger and the general council, particularly while the CPGB, still an influential force in many of them, was in opposition to the war. In the immediate wake of the 1938 decision to de-merge the trades and labour councils, the general council had issued a memorandum, later approved by the 1939 congress, defining closely what it saw as the proper limits on the activities of the councils. It was concerned to spell out the view that they were there to perform an industrial rather than a political function. But Elger continued to worry about them, particularly as the shop stewards on Clydeside and beyond began to form ever tighter networks. The ghost of the CWC clearly haunted his nightmares. In April 1940 a national body, the Engineering and Allied Trades Shop Stewards National Council was set up to run alongside the officials-dominated Confederation of Shipbuilding and Engineering Unions (though the CSEU, more commonly known as the Confed, would itself become an important network for shop stewards). This prompted the STUC general council to write the following month to all the trades councils asking for formal assurances that they were abiding by the terms of the 1938 memorandum. It was followed up by approval, at the 1941 congress in Dunoon, of still tighter constraints on trades council activities, issued in the form of a handbook, which included a general council right to determine which external bodies were suitable for recognition. Elger remained nervous, and eventually tried twice – in 1943 and 1944 – to introduce a form of the block vote to curb the trades councils' voting power at congress. Both attempts failed, but the acrimony between the general council and the more left-wing trades councils was to endure long after Elger's death.

There is no doubt that some trade councils had become vehicles for the CPGB and other left-wing groupings. But there is also very little evidence that either they or the increasingly homogeneous shop stewards' movement posed any serious threat to the strategy of co-operation with the war effort. The Communist line against the war does not seem to have been universally popular even within the party. Mick McGahey would later recall receiving a fearsome rebuke from his father, a founder-member of the British party, for organising an unofficial strike in 1943. 'In the struggle against fascism, the blood of the working class in Europe is being spilled and you want the luxury of having an unofficial strike!' McGahey Snr had fulminated. In fact, in many workplaces the shopfloor authority of the shop stewards was an invaluable resource for the employers and the state in overcoming potential output blockages. In others, the stewards were active in exposing employer malpractice which was leading to waste, inefficiency and poor workforce morale. The Clyde ship-yard stewards, for example, conducted a lengthy and boisterous campaign against management inadequacy, which culminated in a symbolic 30-minute strike designed to capture the government's attention.

Other workplace issues which surfaced over the war years included time off for fire-watching duties, the composition and powers of joint production committees, raw material shortages, pay levels for the vast numbers of women drafted into the factories and the role of shop stewards in controlled factories. Yet, a common theme running through all of these issues was the declared will to maximise Scottish industry's contribution to the war effort, even if this tended to manifest itself in complaints that ran with the grain of normal union objectives. For example, much of the concern expressed in the movement about the joint production committees concerned their tendency to adopt a narrow focus of disciplining those who failed to pull their weight, rather than address wider issues of managerial failure and wasteful processes. Left-wingers like George Middleton were prone to argue that productivity was being hampered by the anxiety of big business to preserve profitability for when the war was over. But when a special conference of 800 shop stewards was convened in Glasgow in late 1941 to discuss issues of production, it gave an unqualified go-ahead for union participation in joint production committees. The STUC and its affiliates could justly claim to have kept their side of the bargain.

So too could the government. Under the influence of the TGWU's Ernest Bevin, co-opted into the War Cabinet, trade unions were involved ever more actively in the machinery of government. As the war progressed Elger in particular, but the STUC in general, added greatly to its portfolio of seats on public bodies. Elger chaired the Scottish Consultative Council on Factory Welfare, and served on the Scottish Housing Advisory Committee, the National Advisory Council for Scotland on Physical Training and Education, the National Production Advisory Council, the Scottish Regional Board for Industry, the National Advisory Council on Juvenile Unemployment. STUC representatives sat routinely on almost all the plethora of agencies generated by the war effort: all five Scottish local committees of the Ministry of Information, the food control committees set up in every town and burgh, the government's Scottish Youth Committee. War brought the quango culture to Scotland in a big way, and for more than three decades the STUC would expect and secure the right to serve at its heart.

Two important catalysts came together in the crucible of wartime to accelerate and intensify this process. One was the imperative for government, remembering only too well the bitterness of the First World War, to ensure that this time Scottish labour was kept fully supportive of, and involved in, the war effort. Churchill, who had succeeded Chamberlain to the premiership in May 1940, was scarcely a figure whom the Scottish labour movement regarded with instinctive warmth. Yet his own experience gave him ample cause to recognise the dangers inherent in allowing Scotland's industrial workers to grow disaffected about the purposes of the war. Elger plainly recognised these dangers just as acutely, for in December 1940 he personally invited to Scotland the man who now held Lloyd George's old post as munitions minister – Ernest Bevin. It was a shrewd initiative in two respects. First, it helped nip in the bud a nascent hostility among Scottish dockworkers, particularly in Glasgow, towards a registration scheme instituted under the government's emergency regulations. Bevin, as the dockworkers' great leader, could address these concerns better than anyone. Perhaps more important, though, was the symbolic contrast with Lloyd George's reception almost exactly 25 years earlier. Bevin spoke at huge meetings on successive nights in Edinburgh and Glasgow, receiving an inquisitive but cordial response from 5,600 union delegates.

The second catalyst was Tom Johnston, now appointed as Churchill's Secretary of State for Scotland. The student who approaches Johnston through the man's own memoirs needs little further help in grasping the magnitude of his achievements. Yet there is little doubt that Johnston wrought fundamental and lasting change in both the institutional landscape and the political expectations of Scotland. He saw in the government's phobia about Clydeside insurrection a valuable opportunity to wrest a measure of power back from Whitehall to Scotland. This was ever a priority for Johnston, founded both in his rational belief that the Scottish economy needed its decisions taken closer to home, and in a less rational, but no less powerful, lifelong hatred of London and all its works. Indeed, his given reason both for initially resisting Churchill's invitation to join the Cabinet in 1941 and for declining a peerage in 1945 was that he intended to waste no more of his days in travelling to London. One of his few failures, in fact, was a project to bring a slender measure of devolution to Scotland by having the Scottish MPs meet as a body in Scotland. They met, or some of them, once, but like the nomadic Scottish Grand Committee of the 1990s, soon discovered that the venue for a debate is of little consequence if the debaters lack the power to translate their conclusions into implementation. Still, it is a modest enough disappointment to set beside the achievement of giving Scotland, through the advocacy of its designated government department, unprecedented power within the machinery of government. Johnston was the first Scottish Secretary to measure the success of his tenure in forthright terms of what he had managed to secure for Scotland, and the tally is undoubtedly impressive: the Scottish Tourist Board, the North of Scotland Hydro-Electric Board (he would later chair both), accountability of the Forestry Commission to Scotland, an emergency hospital scheme which formed a template for the National Health Service, and the creation of Scotland's still admired economic development apparatus. In the douce history of the Scottish Office, Johnston stands out as a burst of creative energy never equalled before or since. In Elger and the STUC, he found doughty allies.

Johnston formulated the strategy, which is still the STUC's talisman, of assembling a Scottish consensus with which to confront Whitehall. The first instrument for achieving this was an odd one, and he insisted on it as a condition of office. It was a 'Council of State', consisting of Johnston and his five living predecessors as Scottish Secretary, and its nominal remit was to consider problems of post-war reconstruction in Scotland, which, in practice, meant economic development in its broadest sense. Since those who had escaped the Reaper conveniently included both Conservative and Liberal grandees, Churchill was persuaded by Johnston that it amounted to 'a sort of national government of all parties idea, just like our government here,' and promised to look favourably upon anything about which it achieved unanimity. The principle of paying heed to Scottish consensus was thus established.

Next, Johnston decided to give his baby-grand coalition a parliament. In 1942, he created the Scottish Industrial Council, later the Scottish Council on Industry, which drew its membership and its funding from the broadest possible spread of economic bodies: the local authorities, the chambers of commerce, the banks, Lithgow's Scottish Development Council; and the STUC, which had a four-strong presence, led by Elger. Agreement among such disparate forces was not to be lightly defied. The council swiftly became quite simply the most formidable lobby of its time, gleefully brandishing Churchill's blessing to overcome the irritation of a preoccupied Whitehall. On Scottish Office reckoning, in less than four years of wartime existence the council drew 700 industrial developments, underpinned by £12 million of Treasury subsidy, to Scotland. Many of these were minor but some were not. The arrival of Ferranti in Edinburgh in 1943 was followed by NCR to Dundee in 1946, Honeywell to Newhouse in 1948, and IBM to Greenock in 1951. The contours had been mapped for what would a generation later be designated, with rather grander fanfare, as Silicon Glen.

When in 1946, the Scottish Council on Industry and the Scottish Development Council were merged, the resulting Scottish Council (Development and Industry) suffered initially from the encouragement which both Johnston's departure and the onset of post-war austerity gave a vengeful Whitehall to reassert its authority over presumptuous Caledonia. But the council developed an enduring talent for adapting to changing circumstances, and over the next couple of decades it pioneered concepts like industrial estates, regional policy, exports promotion and inward investment. In so doing, it wrote the rubric for development agencies across the world.

The STUC was, and would remain, enthused by the new role it had found. From wartime onwards, it would be as a crusading evangelist for the economic and political advancement of Scotland, rather than purely of Scottish trade unionism, that the STUC would be of most significance. A cynic might cogently see these consular trappings, which were not without their populist side, as a most convenient distraction from the awkward fact that the STUC's industrial authority (always greater in aspiration than in realisation) had diminished steadily across the inter-war period and would continue to decline. One lasting consequence of the war, for example, was that most major industries were now covered by national UK agreements on pay and conditions, greatly diminishing the importance of the Scottish union officials who dominated the STUC. Union amalgamation had also by this time reduced Scottish-based unions to less than a fifth of the STUC's affiliated membership. From now on, the Scottish TUC would be rather more Scottish than TUC.

What should not be overlooked are the commitment and zeal with which the STUC embraced its mission. As the war came to its end, William Elger was offered an honour by a grateful state in recognition of the energies he had deployed so constructively during the years of conflict. He declined, accepting only the formal appointment of Deputy Lieutenant of the County of the City of Glasgow. Johnston, addressing the 1944 congress in Dunoon, applauded the STUC's 'prominent, noteworthy and most creditable part' in the drive to draw business north of the Tweed. Johnston at that time (he later reconsidered) believed that the best way to achieve this was through the extension of public ownership – nationalisation – which would enable industry to be planned and directed to a degree that the private sector could not. As we shall see, the reality of nationalisation was to prove him wrong, since it centralised decision-making power away from Scotland, and in so doing it would bring the industrial and the patriotic sides of the STUC's being into somewhat painful conflict.

Indeed, within six months of Johnston's speech there came the first sign of STUC unease on this issue. A government White Paper on employment policy, published in the autumn of 1944, suggested that the Board of Trade should take responsibility for supervising the distribution of industrial development. In a thoughtful response the general council identified distinct disadvantages in decisions about industrial location being the prerogative of 'centralised government departments having no real intimacy with Scotland.' Intriguingly, the answer it proposed was an idea first roughed out at the Berkeley Hall in 1897: the creation of a separate Scottish department within the Board of Trade, which would work closely with both sides of Scottish industry and with the Scottish Office. More important was the marker put down against the era of industrial direction and public ownership which lay ahead.

With the coming of peace in 1945, the magnitude of the reconstruction task became awesomely clear. The achievements of Johnston's popular coalitions, though significant in pointing the way ahead, ran against a tide of industrial decline which now flowed afresh. Scotland had been central to wartime production.

Its heavy industries had enjoyed a dramatic boom that was quite unsustainable as the demand of warfare subsided. Between 1939 and 1945 employment within them had grown from 16 to 25 per cent of the Scottish workforce. But six years of war, and ten before that of recession, had left them woefully underinvested, their processes and their plant increasingly archaic. Despite massive injections of public investment, the output of Scottish manufacturing increased across the 1950s by just 18 per cent, against a UK increase of 34 per cent, and in many of the old mainstay sectors it fell sharply: in mining, for example, it was down more than 21 per cent. The technological breakthroughs which a mechanised war had forced to fruition – in electronics, light engineering, aviation, radar, chemicals, and nuclear power – had brought little industrial benefit to Scotland. Even at its short-lived height the German bombing blitz had made only a minor impact on production and the government had consequently done little to disperse industrial targets, preferring instead the convenience of proximity. The two nights when Clydebank underwent aerial bombardment in March 1942 had cost 1,100 lives, yet an official report found that by 1 April production was virtually back to normal. There was some lasting damage at the Royal Ordnance Factory at Dalmuir and at the Singer plant, which had been partly converted to armaments, but little significant destruction at the bombers' prime target, John Brown's. In the decades to come, the Axis powers, their industrial capacity laid waste by defeat, would rebuild to a modern standard that would leave Britain's older industries lagging far behind.

Allied to these industrial concerns, were the social imperatives which the ending of conflict inevitably magnified: employment, welfare, above all housing. Official estimates put Scotland's housing need at half a million new dwellings. Anticipation of peacetime's challenges therefore dominated the 1945 general election, and was wisely exploited by Labour in a memorable poster campaign: Labour for the Future; Labour for Security; Let's Build the Houses – Quick. The STUC, relishing its new eminence in the Scottish body politic, pitched in with its own manifesto. This called for an end to the 'nineteenth century ideas of absolute capitalist control,' and argued that achievement of the welfare state advocated by the Beveridge Report of 1942 depended, for the good of the nation, in the sort of planned economic development which could only come through public ownership of strategic industries like coal, gas, electricity, water, steel, and transport. Against that, it weighed its nagging concern that Scotland maintain a say in determining industrial location. Labour's was a bold agenda, yet one which the people of Britain, wearied but also drawn together by the levelling adversity of war, seemed to share. In July of 1945, the first general election for ten years brought the result which had so long seemed impossible: the return of a Labour government, this time with a landslide majority.

So began the administration of Clement Attlee, now conventionally regarded, and with good reason, as the most effective and remarkable of the century. Yet, when Scotland looks back on those years, the nostalgia is prefaced by a moment's hesitation. For one thing, the impetus which, to Churchill's lasting bewilderment, carried his prosaic coalition deputy to Downing Street was not quite so potent in Scotland as elsewhere. Labour in Scotland won a bare majority of seats – 37 of the 71, plus three for the residue of the ILP – compared with the party's national showing of 393 out of 640 constituencies. It was the smallest swing to Labour anywhere in Britain, less than 10 per cent against a UK average of 12 per cent. Other forces were at work in Scotland. In April 1945, two by-elections on successive days had produced unpredicted outcomes. In the first, at Motherwell, Dr Robert MacIntyre had won the seat for the Scottish National Party, giving the SNP its first ever taste of parliamentary success. A day later, Sir John Boyd Orr swept to victory in a Scottish universities seat as an independent of pronounced nationalistic leanings. As a consequence, Attlee authorised Labour general election candidates in Scotland to make vaguely sympathetic noises towards some sort of home rule, though no such commitment infiltrated the party's manifesto. But there was a more general sense in which Scotland had its own agenda to follow in 1945. Johnston's wartime mobilisation of a 'Scotland versus the rest' philosophy had struck a chord, and even the Unionist candidates promoted the idea of a special and lasting partnership in Scotland between the two sides of industry. Johnston, anticipating the centralism which the Attlee government would need to impose in order to achieve its challenging objectives, declined to serve in it. It was a typically shrewd foresight. In order to drive through his colossal programme, Attlee maintained and augmented the heavily centralised Whitehall machine which Churchill had assembled to meet the contingencies of war. The power of the Cabinet, the Cabinet Office and the Treasury grew immensely. The weaker figures who followed Johnston into St Andrew's House – Joseph Westwood, Arthur Woodburn, and Hector McNeil – were small men in a Cabinet dominated by giants like Cripps, Bevin, Bevan and Morrison. They could do little to stop Whitehall reclaiming the territory Johnston had seized.

Some of these Scottish concerns were already evident when STUC delegates met at Dunoon in 1946 for their 49th congress. The debates rang with hope that the new government, dedicated to planning, to public ownership, and to involving workers in decision-making could bring about the productive growth that hardening economic conditions so evidently demanded. Yet there was a persistent cautionary note. Delegates from a range of traditional industries – heavy engineering, flax, linoleum – spoke of mounting lay-offs. There were numerous calls for investment in Scotland's ageing infrastructure, and in particular for special measures to stimulate development and stem population loss in the Highlands, a recurrent concern for the STUC in this period, and one in which it can justly claim to have been ahead of its time. George Middleton, who would be general secretary before the decade was out, seized on the previous spring's by-election upsets to predict that there would be a resurgence of nationalism unless Scotland's economic institutions were strengthened and afforded some autonomy. Middleton, much given in those days to speaking awkward truths, also pointed out the limitations inherent within the recent flagship developments that the STUC had played such a part in bringing about. At Hillington, where the Scottish Council had developed Europe's first purpose-built industrial estate, it might be possible to attract back the motor industry which had departed Scotland before the war, Middleton said (by this stage, Scotland's only vehicle-builder was the Albion trucks plant at Scotstoun). Yet the lack of ancillary industries meant that even a new assembly plant there could only hope to manufacture a fifth of the value of the car.

Not merely listening to, but periodically joining in with, these debates were a number of government ministers, notably the Minister for Labour and National Service, George Isaacs. At the following year's St Andrew's congress, marking the STUC's golden jubilee, Isaacs was joined by a still more senior colleague: Attlee himself. It was the first time a sitting Prime Minister had attended the STUC. He came accompanied by Sir Stafford Cripps, who seven months later would move (after an abortive attempt to oust Attlee) from the Board of Trade to become a famously austere Chancellor of the Exchequer. They both set out at length the importance of expanding output to sufficient levels to pay for the government's ambitious social and reconstruction programmes. The message, which Cripps's policies at the Treasury would soon confirm, was that planning would exact a heavy economic price. Delegates were courteous and attentive, but less than dazzled. Cripps, already associated with a tightening and unpopular regime of wage restraint, was treated to a detailed litany of complaints about job losses in Scotland's mainstay industries and the slow pace at which new development was being brought to Scotland. As if by illustration, Glasgow's docks were at that moment paralysed by a six-week strike by 3,000 dockers, called in protest at redundancies implemented as trade through the docks declined. Cripps watched with baleful interest as a row broke out over demands from the dockers for STUC intervention, which the general council insisted lay beyond its proper authority because the matter was before the industry's National Joint Council for adjudication. The vote went in the general council's favour, and the day after congress ended 2,000 London dockers came out in sympathy. As a vignette of the tensions and difficulties inherent in the close relationship between organised labour and the first majority Labour government, the STUC's fiftieth birthday congress served rather well.

Another associated difficulty impacted very inconveniently on the STUC. The government was determined to put at the centre of its industrial reforms structures whereby the concerns of the workforce could be directly represented in strategic decision-making. In some cases, this was to mean appointing workers' representatives on the boards of the nationalised industries, which in itself created tensions between those so elevated and the expectations generated among their peers. Several unions, including the miners, declined the offer of worker-directors, a decision which would come to look less than visionary. More generally, the search was on for experienced and competent union officials to help manage the restructured industries and services. In some cases, this provided unions with a little-regretted opportunity to wish a fond farewell to old stagers. But it also sapped a good deal of talent. As the complex new hierarchy of public boards and agencies spread, the upper ranks of the STUC were to prove a fertile recruitment ground. No fewer than four general council members departed in the space of two years, including the long-serving miners' delegate, Peter Henderson, who became a coal board personnel officer; and the 1948 STUC president, David Robertson of the railway clerks, who took up an administrative post in the newly-nationalised railways. Ending 'absolute capitalist control' was proving a complicated business.

Eventually, governmental poaching cost the STUC a general secretary. Elger's sudden death had left no heir apparent. His able deputy, James Jack, had only been in post for a few weeks, and so the STUC turned to a more experienced figure, the bakers' leader Charles Murdoch, who had put in a decade's service on the general council. Murdoch was a vigorous, handsome and highly articulate man, though with a strongly pragmatic outlook, which seemed to make him a natural enough successor to Elger, alongside whom he had served from the first on the Scottish Council for Industry. But these same qualifications appealed also to the government's talent scouts, and at the end of the 1948 congress in Perth, Murdoch departed for a post with the Gas Board.

Fifty is an age for taking stock. To mark the 1947 half-century, the general council published a pamphlet, *Fifty Years of Progress*, which conveyed a powerful sense of satisfaction at the distance travelled from the Berkeley Hall. Murdoch contributed an article which, as if in testament to Elger's memory, looked back to the founding purposes of the STUC and concluded that its objectives had always been to reflect Scotland's particular circumstances rather than to pitch itself against the TUC: 'The Scottish congress is not . . . a competitor of the British congress, nor does it justify its existence on orthodox nationalist lines,' he wrote. 'In fact, it has emphatically expressed the view that in any scheme for the government of Scotland, provision should be made for the same industrial legislation being applied throughout Great Britain.' They were words that would quickly tarnish. A rather more perceptive assessment was provided in Joseph Westwood's foreword: 'A great many of the aims which [the STUC] set itself have now been achieved, and the trade unions have come to be recognised as a vital factor in the industrial well-being of the country. From being distrusted as a threat to industrial peace, they have come to be respected as an agency with a great power for good in the orderly progress of industrial relations.' The STUC relished the compliment, and the pamphlet elsewhere noted proudly, if a little ambitiously: 'The congress is regarded by departments of state and local authorities as the industrial authority in Scotland upon matters arising from existing or contemplated industrial and social legislation, and the views of the general council are sought by these public bodies.'

The complacent tone was forgivable. Despite the drab austerity of the immediate post-war years, there was a sense of optimism in the country as a whole, a sense that the war had finally resolved history's central dilemmas. A future of orderly, consensual, progress towards a more just and compassionate society seemed to stretch endlessly ahead. The plans for the New Jerusalem had been agreed, even if it might be a while in construction. There was, as rarely since, a mood of confident hope. It was a mood that lasted a long time, certainly to the Suez fiasco of 1956 and arguably beyond. When, in 1951, Attlee's exhausted reforming government gave way to another long stretch of Conservative rule, there was little sense of ideological lurch. The new government, headed by a Churchill somewhat past his best, was largely in the business of consolidating rather than overturning what Attlee had wrought. It reversed one of the last Attlee nationalisations, steel, and partly denationalised road haulage, but otherwise left mostly alone. The era dawned of what would come to be called 'Butskellism', reflecting the virtually indistinguishable policies of the two front bench Treasury teams, headed by Rab Butler and Hugh Gaitskell. Political debate was about the pace of progress rather than its direction. The national agenda was mostly common ground. Health, education and housing provision would be steadily improved. Plans were in process for industrial renewal. The benign stability delivered by Keynesian economics and the Bretton Woods agreement would deliver gradually increased well-being, which would be shared equitably as it came. The journalist Neal Ascherson would later recall of the early Fifties: 'Sobered, we surveyed the cool, grey plateau on which mankind was to spend the rest of time.'

But agreement about a project need not make its accomplishment either simple or inevitable. The challenges of reconstruction and modernisation, in Scotland particularly, were all too evidently destined to be formidable. The STUC, determined to play its part in meeting them, needed a new general secretary for the new age, following Murdoch's ascent to the giddy heights of the Gas Board. Its choice was, at first sight, an incongruous one.

Almost everything about George Middleton's background seemed to run contrary to the imperatives of the moment. Seized with the potential for power-sharing which its wartime alliances had opened up, the general council settled upon a man who had condemned the 1939 manifesto as 'imperialist.' At a period when the STUC's priorities lay in establishing responsible common cause with a Labour government, it chose to be led by a man who was not only a long-standing member of the Communist Party but who had held the party post most commonly rumoured to be full of nefarious purpose, namely industrial organiser. At a time when the general council was locked in recurrent acrimony with the trades councils, it appointed as general secretary a delegate from the most persistently troublesome trades council, Glasgow. Having the previous year congratulated itself on the sophisticated role in Scottish society to which maturity had brought it, the STUC now seemed to be taking a step backwards towards the more confrontational style that it claimed to have left far behind.

Since the deliberations that surrounded the appointment were not recorded, they can only be approached by conjecture. One attraction of Middleton may have been his experience, given a general council which had lost several leading lights to public office. A bulky, vigorous man with a grin like a deflated football, he had been a kenspeckle figure around the movement for the best part of 20 years, and had served on the general council for five of them. It is also irresistible to wonder whether the general council wanted a general secretary who was rather less likely to be poached by government. More probably, there was a sense – which comes across in some debates of the period – that the STUC was conscious of being swept along by the reforming pace of the Attlee government, and felt some need to re-establish a distinctive voice for itself. Scottish industrial output and employment were already starting to lag behind the rest of the UK, and the closer relationship with the TUC which Elger had built no longer seemed wholly appropriate to the Scottish priorities that the STUC now presumed to embody. A proven organisational record may also exercise some appeal in a fast-changing age. But all of that is to focus, quite unfairly, on Middleton's background and to neglect his personal qualities, which were formidable. Whatever the reasons for it, the choice turned out to be an inspired one. George Middleton is remembered by many as the STUC's greatest general secretary, and the organisation approaches its second century housed in a headquarters building named in his honour.

Not uncommonly for one schooled in the Scottish Communist tradition, Middleton's idealism was underpinned by a robust practical belief in the need to focus on attainable rather than distant objectives. He proclaimed his pragmatism in a powerful, if unexpected, way as he took up office in May 1948: he applied, and was accepted, for membership of the Labour Party. Rather quaintly, the 1949 STUC president, William McGinniss of the general and municipal workers, suggested to that year's congress that this gesture would both 'dispel any doubts' in the movement about Middleton's politics and 'result in the continuance of the responsibility and dignity of the STUC.' Middleton's view of that assessment sadly went unchronicled. Yet his pragmatism had a more substantive side. Over the next few years, he would refocus the STUC's efforts into a series of campaigns on well-chosen and specific Scottish industrial objectives. Much of this was undertaken in close co-operation with the SCDI, on whose executive Middleton sat. Frequently, the two bodies jointly organised conferences or deputations, and in 1951 the general council issued the first of what were to become annual financial appeals to affiliates to help bankroll the work of an over-stretched SCDI. Indeed, it is often hard to disentangle the threads sufficiently to trace back the origins of campaigns to one or other body. What counted was that many of them, particularly in the later 1950s, were successful. An era was coming in which the STUC and its allies would mount highly publicised raiding parties on Whitehall in pursuit of industrial prizes for Scotland, and often return triumphant. Under George Middleton, the image of the STUC as a tribune for Scotland, rather than merely for Scottish organised labour, would be burnished as never before.

Middleton proved to possess a bankable talent which had seemed much less important for previous general secretaries but which would ever after be seen as central. He was a highly accomplished communicator. There were two dimensions to his presentational skills, and both were to stand him in excellent stead. First, abrasive past performances notwithstanding, he soon exhibited a rare talent for charming congress into voting in his and the general council's favour. It was not just a question of oratory, though he had that black art to maestro standard. Long years on innumerable fractious committees had also lent him a capacity for smoothing over confrontations and dressing up compromise in high principle. He was never slow to appeal to the bonds of friendship and understanding which, he insisted, united trades unionists, though he could be sharp enough in debate. As an anonymous wag (Jimmy Jack?) was to write in the *STUC Bulletin* at the end of his general secretaryship, 'He possessed to an extraordinary degree the "common touch" . . . although some might complain that he imparted it occasionally in a ferociously uncommon manner.' Not without irony, these skills served him well both in representing a right-wing general council to congress and in taking a harder line than Elger ever had against errant trades councils, Glasgow prominent among them.

More importantly, Middleton turned out to be a most effective performer in the mass media of radio and television which came into their own during the 1950s. He projected a bluff, rugged common sense to which a Scottish audience instinctively warmed. He was the first STUC general secretary to 'front' the organisation to the public at large, and he did it very well. But some of the credit for that must lie with his deputy, Jimmy Jack. The best communicator in the world needs something to communicate, and Jack founded the STUC tradition – which persists to this day – of generating informed, thoroughly researched papers on the Scottish economy. The STUC during this time was rarely found wanting on matters of fact, which lent great force to its authority as a lobby for investment in Scotland. The high point of such endeavours is often remembered as the period around 1960–61, when Middleton and Jack were joined in their sojourns south by another gritty Communist, a patternmaker from Aberdeen Trades Council called Jimmy Milne, who was that year's STUC president. All three would ultimately serve as general secretary, and in sum they spanned almost 40 years in the post.

Of all the Attlee reforms, none held greater significance for the labour movement than the nationalisation of the coal industry. Yet, none would come better to encapsulate the peculiar difficulties which nationalisation created for Scottish industries. Talking to older miners today, it sometimes seems that every one of them was taken by his father to the nearest pit-head on Vesting Day, 1 January 1947, to be shown the proud new lettering which proclaimed the ownership of the National Coal Board. As a symbol of hope, the moment bore a powerful potency. For the Scottish miners, and for the STUC, colliery nationalisation marked the final achievement of a policy aim which they had pursued without deviation for half a century. It had been achieved in the teeth of opposition from the coal owners, a body of dynastic scions which, in Scotland particularly, had managed the industry with a dismal blend of greed and ineptitude. Output from Scottish pits had declined from a peak of 42.5 million tons in 1913 to 21.4 million in 1945, the year Attlee came to power. Nationalisation, under principles of socialist planning, seemed to many to be just the radical step needed both to arrest this endemic decline and to improve the lot of those who worked in the industry. The Scottish Area of the National Union of Mineworkers, as the union had been known from 1945, had both welcomed the prospect of nationalisation and had contributed extensively to the 12–point Miners' Charter on pay and conditions which the NUM had agreed with Shinwell, the Minister of Fuel and Power (though it was ultimately only delivered in part). So, hopes were high in Scotland as elsewhere on 1 January 1947. That needs to be borne in mind, for it was not long before the hopes began to sour.

Most of what went wrong over the next 15 years proceeded from the best of intentions, though the results were no less dispiriting for it. The first source of dissatisfaction was the compensation paid to the coal-owners. Opinion among Scots miners on what was appropriate ranged from minimal compensation to outright confiscation. Many in the wider public had reason to share that view, since the owners had prepared for nationalisation by running down coal stocks, just in time for what turned out to be the coldest winter of the century. But the Government, drawing on the precedent created by Lloyd George when the early telephone networks were brought under state ownership, decided on 'reasonable' compensation paid, according to a complex calculation, in gilt-edged government stock and charged against the accounts of the newly-nationalised industry. There was widespread outrage when a sum of almost £165 million (nearly £22 million in Scotland) was announced. Not only did this place a huge debt burden upon the industry. It also seemed to many to underestimate the owners' responsibility for the derelict state of many of the assets, and overestimate the credence that could be attached to the owners' projections about the future performance of the industry. The owners, for example, blithely predicted that output from the 275 Scottish collieries in production at Vesting Day would defy every precedent by soaring from 22 million tons to 27 million by 1949, 34.6 million by 1955 and 37.4 million by 1961. The government itself, while never formally disbelieving these figures, had already settled on an informal target of reaching 30 million by the mid-1960s, which was ratified in the 1950 *Plan for Coal*. Some in Scotland thought this disappointingly unambitious, but the NCB itself acknowledged in the *Plan* that achieving the target would be 'no easy task.' It was right. By 1960, output had fallen to 17.6 million tons, and a decade later it was at 11.2 million. More worryingly, only in their first three years as a nationalised industry were the Scottish deep mines profitable. The next operating profit would come in 1991, and by then there was just one pit left.

Nevertheless, under both Attlee and the Conservative governments which followed him, the target was pursued with a will. The early progress was impressive, if measured by endeavour. The *Plan for Coal* and its 1955 refinement, *Scotland's Coal Plan*, envisaged closing more than 140 Scottish pits and replacing their output as follows: 40 remaining pits were to undergo development, and 39 to benefit from major reconstruction programmes; 60 surface drift mines were to be built or reconstructed; and 15 new deep mines – yielding 8.75 million tons a year – were to be sunk. Alongside this was set a no less ambitious investment programme in better welfare and housing provision. By 1955, 34 of the drift mines, nine of the reconstructions and one new sinking were complete, and work was underway on many of the others. There was certainly a rational case for the investment. The old coal owners had exhausted most of the reserves at 1,000 feet or less below the surface, and to access new seams would require sinkings to a depth of 2–3,000 feet. Like many of the Attlee nationalisations, the coal programme had an element of the rescue operation about it.

But problems were already becoming evident. Pits under reconstruction naturally lost output, which made the capital costs harder to justify against NCB targets and pushed up Scotland's average cost per ton. At the same time demand, and therefore price, was falling. Some of the new geology being broached was, inevitably, more difficult than anticipated. Scotland's losses, however they were calculated, were mounting. It was by now clear that many of the new projects would contribute less than expected towards the 30 million ton target. The response of the NCB's Scottish Divisional Board was to scale up the reconstruction, and the projections of the benefits to come from it. Eventually, 14 of the 15 planned new sinkings went ahead. The two smallest were successful. Of the 12 bigger projects, four were successful, two moderately worthwhile and six unqualified disasters. The Rothes, in Fife, is perhaps the epitome of this last group. Work started on it in 1947, using plans drawn up pre-nationalisation which put its life-span at a century. These contrasted with the warnings of local miners who knew the terrain and who predicted that the board would be lucky to get a pound of coal out of it. The sinking cost £9 million, against an initial estimate of £5 million. That is to discount the cost of building new housing to accommodate miners brought in from other coalfields to man the new wonder-pit. The Rothes opened in 1957 and closed in 1962 having produced less than 700,000 tons across its five-year lifespan. It was meant to produce 6,000 tons a day.

By then, London had lost patience with the Scottish reconstruction process. Demand across the UK had continued to fall – particularly as restrictions began to be applied on domestic coal-burning – and by the early 1960s no-one would have wanted Scotland's 30 million tons even had it been achievable. Not only was it not achievable, but the cost of mining what was being produced compared dimly with other coalfields. What had worked, after a fashion, in Scotland no longer made sense when placed upon the wider British canvas. Scotland's difficult geology had always made the cost structures of Scottish coal somewhat delicate. Prior to nationalisation Scots pits had managed to make a profit by having higher productivity, lower wages and poorer conditions (including more shifts) than those south of the border, and by tailoring what they did closely to the demands of the local marketplace. But marketing was now driven by UK-wide strategy. Nationalisation both harmonised pay and conditions, and required the economics of the coalfield to pass muster against a much broader range of comparitors. The government, meanwhile, was determined to hold down the price of industrial coals, in which Scotland specialised, to help recovery in the industries which used them. Certainly, Scotland's reconstruction programme, though one of the largest, was not the only one in which costs escalated. Overall, the *Plan for Coal* had been budgeted at an average of £38 million a year. By 1953, the average was running at £53 million. But the Scottish investment, judged against national criteria, became increasingly hard to justify against the returns available from elsewhere.

Nor had nationalisation produced the expected transformation in industrial relations. By 1947, the country was once more plunging into economic crisis. The costs of Britain's post-war military commitments rose rapidly to meet the new circumstances of a perceived Soviet threat (Attlee decided to build a British atom bomb, effectively without consulting his Cabinet). America had entered recession, dragging Europe after it more rapidly even than usual through Truman's cancellation of the Lend–Lease agreement. The massive structural trade deficit which Britain had allowed to develop in the war years weighed heavy on the post-war economy. Seven months into the life of the NCB, the government asked the miners to abandon the seven-hour shift agreed in the Charter and revert to eight hours. Another seven months on, Cripps announced a wage freeze. Abe Moffat – the Scottish miners' president, and one union official who had turned down the offer of a senior post in the new NCB – led a spirited resistance to the policy, but it was ultimately accepted both by the NUM and by the TUC. The TUC general secretary, Vincent Tewson, sold the policy to congress on a promise that wage restraint would result in prices coming down. But then Cripps devalued sterling from $4.03 to $2.80, which had the opposite effect. Across the Scottish coalfield, unofficial stoppages broke out, as branches demanded a pay rise for the lowest-waged workers. In October 1949, the NUM president, Sir William Lawther, came to Scotland to try to calm the defiance spreading through the Scottish pits, and was stiffly rebuffed. Eventually, Moffat won over the NUM to opposing wage restraint, and came close to winning over the TUC. The acrimony smouldered on for several years. Very quickly, the NCB had come to be seen by many Scottish miners as little different from any other employer. The old coal owners, avaricious but local, were at least susceptible sometimes to pressure. The new management, monolithic in distant London, was rarely much moved by Caledonian grievance.

It was a pattern which was to be repeated in many of the industries nationalised by Attlee: gas, electricity, the railways, steel. Nationalisation, an almost unqualified good as far as the labour movement south of the border was concerned, was a decidedly mixed blessing for Scottish trade unionists, and for the wider Scottish economy. It replaced the imperatives of mammon with those of the public interest, but at the heavy cost that Scotland lost strategic control over much of its industry and that Scottish trade unionism found its ability to influence the pay and conditions of its members still further diminished. Not only were most of these industries now regulated by 'national' agreements, but it soon became clear that the STUC's importance within Scottish society was sometimes less evident to Whitehall than to the STUC. In 1954, for example, when the Conservative government decided to establish 'regional' railway boards, the Scottish board was set up without trade union representation, unlike most of the English boards. In grand, if vain, dudgeon, Middleton wrote to the British Transport Commission: 'Why exclude the accents of trade unionism from the counsels of the body appointed to supervise the running of the railways in Scotland?' The compensation was that public ownership did often bring investment on a scale that the old industrial dynasties would never have contemplated, even if some of it did turn out to be misconceived. Besides, the changing structures of global capitalism might well have led in due course to much the same process of centralisation. Indeed, 30 years later, Scotland would suffer a much greater outflow of corporate control through the centralising impulse of market forces. Little of that perspective, of course, was evident at the time.

What was evident was that Scotland, despite the beneficial effects of governmental intervention and direction, was starting to trail behind the rest of the UK economically. A motion at the 1951 congress was moved to declare the STUC 'extremely gratified' at the improvements achieved in Scotland's economic position. It noted happily that the rate of factory build in Scotland since 1945 had been 12 times that of the period 1933–38; and that unemployment had stabilised at around 60,000, which happened to coincide with the number of jobs then notified as vacant plus the number due from new plants under construction. The following year, the *STUC Bulletin* contentedly reported a Lloyds survey of world shipping, which showed that while the UK was losing ground in the global shipbuilding market to Germany, Japan and the US, it remained the world's biggest shipbuilder, and Scotland's launch tonnage – now 39 per cent of the UK total – was rising in both absolute and proportional terms. But it was not long before the mood of celebration started to darken.

Middleton had taken to issuing in the press an annual New Year message, and the opening sentences of these missives provide a crude but striking sketch of how economic hope in Scotland slowly faded across the Fifties. Hence, we find him welcoming 1954 with the words: 'A rough assessment of the economic prospects for Scotland in 1954 suggests that there may be a decline of a minor character in the staple industries . . . [but] it should not be assumed that unemployment will increase as a consequence.' A year on, his confidence had proved justified: '1954 has been a remarkably good year for Scottish industry. Employment has remained at a high and stable level . . . industrial disturbances, except some of a very minor character, have been absent in Scotland and the workers, encouraged by the trade unions, have played a full part in raising output.' But by the onset of 1956, doubts had started to cloud this bright picture: '1955 has been a fairly good year in Scotland for work and wages with, of course, the qualification that we suffer still from a number of black patches in the employment picture.' A year later: '1956, and especially the latter part of it, has been a period of concern, fear and worry for all of us.' And finally, on the eve of 1958: 'Those who read this New Year message are, I regret, going to be disappointed if they expected it to begin on a light-hearted, cheerful note.'

The indicators matched Middleton's mood. The early Fifties brought a rapid recovery in world trade from the immediate post-war slump, and raw material costs fell. When the Tories returned to office in 1951, they inherited an economy which was much more buoyant than might have been expected given the costs of the Attlee reforms, and over much of the 1950s Britain as a whole enjoyed growing prosperity. But Scotland's reliance on declining heavy industries meant that its share of the national wellbeing was shrivelling. Scotland's unemployment rate in the latter two-thirds of the decade averaged over 3 per cent, against a UK average of 1.6 per cent. Compared with the levels of unemployment regarded as routine today, these were still modest enough totals, but it was the divergence which counted. During the Fifties, Scotland's share of UK gross domestic product dropped from 9.3 to 8.7 per cent, and its GDP-per-head – the best measure of relative prosperity – from 92 per cent of the UK level to 88 per cent. By 1955, Middleton was declaring gloomily that 'latest figures show unemployment in Scotland more than two and a half times what it is for the United Kingdom as a whole.' Such comparisons were to become a familiar motif of STUC rhetoric across the Fifties, and to remain one thereafter. Industrial deprivation caught on in those years as a totem for Scottish grievance and resentment. That too was to be a lasting legacy. Thirty years later, a pop song would depict industrial failure as a wrong perpetrated on Scotland, comparable to the Highland Clearances: Lochaber no more, Linwood no more. It was a metaphor which began with the STUC of the 1950s.

Yet it was also one whose political potency took time to develop. After the high of 1945, when Labour and ILP together captured just a shade under half the Scottish vote, support for Labour began slowly to ebb in Scotland, despite the reabsorption of the ILP. Labour's share of the Scottish vote fell to 46.2 per cent in 1950, was back up to 47.9 per cent in 1951, and down again to 46.7 in 1955. That year, the Tories managed to capture more than half the Scottish votes and seats, a moment on which today's shrunken rump of Scottish Conservatism can only look back with amazed longing. Thereafter a long trend of decline for the Tories, and of ascendancy for Labour, set in. At the 1959 general election, Labour actually captured fewer votes in Scotland than the Tories (46.7 per cent, against 47.2), but gained a majority of the Scottish seats (38 of the 71) thanks to the perversities of the electoral system. It was a majority Labour would maintain ever after, and its achievement in 1959 was due in some measure to Harold Macmillan's jaunty complacency about the country having 'never had it so good,' which played less well in Scotland than in a more vibrant south. Scotland's economic preoccupation, one in which the STUC was a prime mover, now lay mainly in trying to wrest industrial prizes from Whitehall. It was in the nature of that mission to portray London's benevolence, however generous, as grudging, and Scotland's gains as hard-won. Industrial and political aspirations were once more coming into alignment.

From 1945 onwards, the STUC openly endorsed Labour at each succeeding general election, and when Labour lost the 1951 election (despite its share of the UK popular vote reaching an all-time high), the STUC published a rather gracious message of 'profound thanks and gratitude to Mr Attlee and his ministers for the special consideration and attention given to Scottish problems.' But, away from the grand election stage, George Middleton had two other political dilemmas to wrestle. The first, and lesser, was nationalism. Robert McIntyre's win at Motherwell in 1945 had put the SNP on enough of a roll to discomfit a Labour Party which, particularly in the municipal context, had begun to take on rather drab establishment colours in Scotland. Under the charismatic influence of John MacCormick, then a Liberal, nationalism entered a period of folksy populism which briefly mobilised public imagination, though to only modest effect in the polling booth. In 1942, MacCormick set up the Scottish Convention, a consciously non-partisan movement which, a year later, Labour decided its own members could legitimately join. Both Neil Maclean and, from the Communists, Willie Gallacher were early adherents, as were some individual trade unionists, though the STUC was wary from the start. In 1946, the convention called together a representative national assembly, a civic facsimile of a Scottish parliament. It was a precursor of the Scottish Constitutional Convention of the 1980s and 1990s, and for a while a successful one. MPs from all the Scottish parties took part, as did local authorities, churches, voluntary groups, arts organisations, industrial bodies and trade unionists. Between its first and second meetings, it drafted a *Blueprint for Scotland* which advocated a parliament in Edinburgh.

But relations with Labour were already beginning to sour. It was, after all, a Labour administration which held stewardship of the 'Westminster government' whose inadequacies the convention deplored. In 1948, MacCormick stood at a by-election in Paisley. He had spent the previous few months trying unsuccessfully to forge the Scottish Liberals, Nationalists and Unionists into an anti-Labour home rule alliance, encouraged by the rhetoric of a Churchill who had taken to attacking the Attlee measures for their centralism. The Tories, extremely shrewdly, not only decided not to field a candidate against MacCormick but actively campaigned on his behalf. Labour won, but its tolerance of MacCormick and his movement was at an end. However, Labour could not yet quite afford to ignore him, because the 1948 convention launched a home rule petition, romantically known as the National Covenant, which gathered 1.25 million signatures in its first 18 months, and ultimately more than two million. By contrast, Labour's White Paper on Scottish Affairs, published in January 1948, looked like exactly what it was: a half-hearted and insipid response to a sudden nationalist upsurge. It proposed giving the Scottish Grand Committee powers to conduct second reading debates, setting up a periodic Scottish Economic Conference at which Scottish Office civil servants would meet the heads of nationalised industries, and mounting an inquiry into Scotland's economic position within the Union. It bore a close resemblance, in fact, to the 'Taking Stock' reforms which the Conservatives would implement after the 1992 general election, and was no more effective in firing public enthusiasm. After that gesture, Labour – though nominally still in favour of home rule – lost interest, and indeed the vogue of the convention soon began to dissipate. It had thrown a dash of primary colour against the dreich backdrop of post-war Scotland, but it had never come close to distracting serious attention from Westminster politics, where there was no shortage of big issues to be addressed.

Under Middleton, however, the STUC abandoned all pretence at endorsing the home rule cause. It is a period of its history which is today conveniently down-played. But the fact remains that for most the Fifties the STUC, which claims credit today for nudging Labour into support for home rule, was opposed to a Scottish parliament; while Labour was, however cursorily, in favour until a special conference in 1958. It was a position to which the STUC came by degrees and almost by neglect. As we have seen, its attention was very much focused on economic objectives, beside which political nationalism was seen as an indulgence. In 1947, a motion from the Scottish Horse and Motormen, calling on the government to consider 'a Scottish body with special powers in order that problems peculiar to Scotland . . . can be expedited' (intentionally transparent code for a Scottish parliament) was nodded through congress without dissent. The following year, despite vocal apprehension from some unions about resurgent nationalism, congress criticised

Labour's White Paper as falling short of the needs and expectations of the Scottish people. But the measures it proposed instead did not include a Scottish parliament. They focused on the STUC's industrial concerns by demanding a Scottish national planning commission, a Scottish department of trade and labour and, oddly, a 'cabinet' of Scottish ministers which would liaise with representatives from Whitehall departments. At that same congress, the Scottish Secretary, Arthur Woodburn, was also wise enough to put the anti-nationalist case in industrial terms, arguing that undermining UK-wide wage negotiations would result in Scottish workers being paid less than their English counterparts.

Such arguments were to dominate the STUC's view for many years to come. The modern researcher could be misled by the frequency with which approving references to 'devolution' crop up in STUC papers of the period, but at that time the word had a much more specific connotation than it later came to acquire, and meant strictly the repatriation of administrative, not legislative, authority. It was Abe Moffat who finally, if inadvertently, nailed the ambiguity. At the 1949 congress he had tried unsuccessfully to challenge the general council's report for its lack of commitment to a Scottish parliament, and the following year the general council itself moved to redefine the STUC's stance. Its motion, grandly headed 'The Future of Scotland', was to become the standard STUC text on matters devolutionary until the 1960s, and is worth quoting at some (though not full) length. It declared the STUC to be 'profoundly concerned with the economic and social welfare of Scotland,' but insisted that these concerns were best pursued through a labour movement dedicated to socialist planning. The key passage read: 'The trade union movement is not insensitive to the influences created by the cultural heritage and deep-seated traditions of Scotland, but submits that economic security remains the primary factor for the Scottish people and this cannot be divorced from the economic prospects of the country as a whole. Scotland's economic prosperity, it should be obvious, is inseparable from that of England and Wales and it cannot be imagined as a self-supporting entity.'

The motion, it may be noted, did not explicitly rule out the prospect of a Scottish parliament constituted within the United Kingdom. But Moffat's miners moved an amendment seeking to insert a positive commitment to a parliament, which was defeated by 243 votes to 78. Another amendment from

Glasgow Trades Council was also heavily defeated, even though its demands were more artfully restricted to 'a greater measure of self-government.' The 1950 decision would come to be seen, whether or not at the time it really was, as a definitive rejection of a Scottish parliament: an interpretation made specific in a general council motion at the 1955 congress in Rothesay, when an attempt by Greenock Trades Council to revive support for a Scottish parliament fell by 209 votes to 118. In 1951, the STUC's evidence to the Catto Commission, the first of two Fifties Royal Commissions on Scottish affairs, restricted itself to administrative devolution. In the event, both that report, and the findings of the Balfour Commission three years later, gave short shrift to the sort of administrative reforms which the STUC proposed. The STUC submission to Balfour urged resuscitation of the Scottish Economic Conference, which had met sporadically in the wake of Labour's 1948 measures; the setting up of Scottish trade, labour and supply departments; and the creation of an authority for the Highlands. The Commission rejected all three. The STUC would continue to press for these measures, implemented in large part by the Wilson governments of the 1960s, but it also accepted, as a motion at the 1954 congress put it, 'that the Catto Committee Report has established the validity of the argument that Scotland's economic prosperity is closely linked with the remainder of the United Kingdom.'

The main reason for the cooling of the STUC's fervour for home rule was that the Scottish agenda was felt, with the Attlee reforms, to have moved on, and the case for constitutional change to have dropped a very long way down it. A substantial minority continued to vote for the proposition whenever it arose at congress, but it was no-one's top priority. There was, though, a second factor at work, which was also the bigger of the political challenges Middleton faced. The home rule cause in the early Fifties was tainted by the support of the Communist Party, at a time when the labour movement was at particular pains to keep the Communists at arms length. There is rich irony in it having fallen to Middleton, the most recent of converts from the faith, to be the instrument of this ostracism; and there was richer irony still when the issue came to a head in confrontation with his old power base, Glasgow Trades Council.

Some of the edicts which the general council issued in the early

Fifties, above Middleton's signature, read now like excesses of McCarthyism – with which prejudice, of course, they shared the era. Middleton found himself servicing a distinctly right-wing general council, and a sometimes vindictive one at that. Perhaps the best that can now be said about the stance taken is that it was very much of its time, and needs to be understood within the context of that time. The early Fifties felt the Cold War at its coldest, and the depth of the frost denoted real fear. The division of Europe after 1945 had carved ideological differences into cruel and alarming geography, to which the atomic bomb added terrifying science. The STUC's actions against the Communist threat it perceived do not read attractively now, and were possibly unjustified then. But they were less exceptional than retrospection might make them seem. Several were enacted in tandem with Clement Attlee's Labour Party of such justly radical repute.

The general council's chosen disciplinary weapon was the 1941 handbook for trades councils, which had given it a right to determine which external bodies were suitable for trades council recognition. In the early Fifties, this power was used to place out of bounds organisations which the general council suspected to be connected to the Communist Party, and to apply sanctions – up to and including dissolution – to trades councils which consorted with the outlaws. The first years of the Fifties brought a string of prohibitions against groups like the British Peace Council, the Scottish Peace Committee, the Scottish Youth Peace Festival, the Edinburgh Labour Festival Committee. Events such as May Day rallies which had previously drawn together the labour movement's disparate forces became objects of suspicion and diminishing support. The normal formula for proscription orders was that, evidence having been adduced that a body was 'inspired by the Communist Party, association with it would be contrary to the terms of the *Handbook for the Guidance of Trades Councils.*' Among the trades councils which fell foul of these instructions were Dundee (officers replaced), Rutherglen (suspended, and reformed under new leadership), Airdrie and Kirkcaldy. Several Communists lost their seats on the general council, including Will Pearson, the Scottish miners' president, who was unprecedentedly voted off by the congress (1950) which he chaired as STUC president.

Peace, paradoxically enough, was the pretext for much of

this internecine warfare, particularly after the onset of the Korean War had demonstrated vividly just how easily the two super-power blocs of the post-war world could be brought into dangerous confrontation. No less paradoxically, it was Ernest Bevin as Foreign Secretary who emerged in the eyes of the Left as the villain of the piece, thanks to his increasingly hawkish pro-American foreign policy, and the costly rearmament programme which it entailed. The issue wrought divisions at all levels of the movement. Harold Wilson and Aneurin Bevan resigned from the Cabinet in protest at the consequential cuts in spending on social provisions (the STUC's contribution to that episode was to withdraw its invitation to Bevan to address its Dunoon congress a few days later, and replace him with Alf Robens, just appointed Minister of Labour and later to chair the Coal Board). With Moscow increasingly co-opting the language of peace to characterise its own foreign policy, the peace issue became the focus within the STUC for the acrimony between the general council and the Communists. Indeed, Pearson's sin seems to have been to make some mildly pro-Soviet remarks in support of a general council motion, unanimously adopted, on the 'Maintenance of Peace'!

Glasgow Trades Council's offence also involved peace. At the 1951 Dunoon congress, delegates had approved by 239 votes to 85 a general council motion on 'The United Nations and the Preservation of Peace' which welcomed proposed peace talks between the Western allies, endorsed the government's rearmament programme, and proclaimed the need for vigilance to 'contain' the Korean War. They had also rejected, by 215 votes to 114, an amendment from the miners which encapsulated the Communist agenda for peace: a Moscow-initiated proposal for a peace pact between the five major powers, including the Soviet Union; a ceasefire in Korea; admission of Communist China to the UN; and a halt to rearmament of Germany and Japan. It had been a fiery debate. John Brannigan, the Horse and Motormen's pugnacious leader, had done nothing to cool tempers by laying in to 'the Communists, the fellow-travellers and others in Britain who talk about peace . . . but who all the time submit to the dictates of the overlords of the Kremlin' (diplomacy was never high among Brannigan's aptitudes). It might, none the less, have seemed a somewhat remote issue to provoke what was arguably the STUC's most serious internal ruction. Such were the tensions of the times.

Shortly after congress, Glasgow Trades Council circulated an artfully edited account of the debate to its own affiliates. The document set out the terms of the amendment at length, and mentioned that it had fallen in favour of the general council motion, but omitted to report what the motion had said. Three months later, on 14 August 1951, the trades council approved a motion on 'The Preservation of Peace' which was, in all essentials, the defeated Dunoon amendment. Thoughtfully, it sent a copy to Attlee, informing him that it represented the views of the trade union movement in Glasgow. It also sent a statement of protest to Bevin about the actions of US soldiers at Innsbruck in attempting to prevent young British delegates from travelling to a youth rally in East Berlin. Middleton and the general council reacted swiftly, as they had previously done against Dundee and Rutherglen. Glasgow was reminded that the trades council handbook both forbade the adoption of motions which contravened STUC policy without unions having first had an opportunity to mandate their trades council delegates, and forbade trades councils from acting on these motions until they had been placed before the general council or congress for approval. There was a brief and vituperative correspondence. The general council then agreed to dissolve the trades council, and announced that Middleton and Jack would take over its offices in West Regent Street on 31 October until a new council was formed.

Glasgow, however, was of different mettle from other trades councils which had been disciplined, and promptly secured an interim interdict to prevent seizure of its premises. It also, to Middleton's lasting fury, began issuing circulars to unions, presenting its actions as a defence of the independence of an organisation formed in 1858 against a bullying congress half its age. When the matter finally came to full hearing on 8 January 1952, Glasgow Sheriff Court accepted a compromise worked out between the respective lawyers, which allowed the STUC to form a new council but prohibited it from taking control of the records, premises, funds or staff of the old council. Costs were split between the litigants. It was a moral victory for the leaders of the old trades council, but also a pyrrhic one. Three days later, the general council appealed to unions to withdraw affiliation from the old council and join the new. The overwhelming majority complied and on 5 March, the new council was inaugurated with 596 delegates representing 271 branches of 61 unions.

The affair provoked bitter exchanges at the 1952 congress in Perth. Some delegates, like David Currie of the clerical workers, spoke in favour of the general council's actions, accusing the trades council leaders of trying to set themselves above congress. Others reported that it had become increasingly difficult for non-Communists to gain a hearing in the old council. But two of the most notable speeches came from opponents of the general council's conduct. Abe Moffat teased Middleton, so long a Glasgow Trades Council Communist, for arguing that differing policies could not mix within the movement: 'If there is one authority at congress who knows about different policies,' Moffat remarked, 'it is Mr Middleton.' Jimmy Milne, on behalf of Aberdeen Trades Council, reminded congress that the STUC had been formed to uphold the rights of trades councils: 'The general council has no right whatsoever to interfere with the passing of any resolution by any trades council,' he insisted. Middleton told Milne he ought to know better: 'The present sect or rump who constitute themselves as the Glasgow Trades Council are not the legitimate banner-bearers of the rich and proud history of Glasgow Trades Council,' he thundered. Delegates agreed. The general council's actions were endorsed by 230 votes to 113.

It was the high point of the general council's Torquemada period. Edicts would continue to be issued against this body or that on grounds of Communist sympathies, but the party's biggest prize in the movement had been reclaimed. Even as the court action over the Glasgow disaffiliation was pending, Middleton launched an exhaustive programme of reconciliatory meetings between the general council and all the Scottish trades councils, many of which he attended personally. From September 1951, when the new Rutherglen council was set up, these meetings sometimes numbered three or four a week. In the last three months of the year alone, 32 were held.

The Communist Party did not vanish from the Scottish trades union scene, though it did lose many members after the Soviet invasion of Hungary in 1956. But after the catharsis of the Glasgow schism, the two sides managed to get each other into rather better proportion. Twenty years on, when Jimmy Milne became general secretary, no-one saw any need for him to renounce his membership of the Communist Party, and indeed his term brought relations between the STUC and the Scottish Council of the Labour Party closer than they had generally been before or have often been since. In the intervening years, the Communist Party had given the Scottish labour movement several of its most respected leaders, going some way to prove its contention that it had always been willing to work with the grain of the movement. When he retired in 1987, one of them, Mick McGahey, insisted in an interview with *Scottish Trade Union Review* that fears of CP 'domination' had always been false: 'The Communist Party in Scotland is a good proletarian-based party. From the days of Gallacher, the party in Scotland was always well established in industry and made a contribution to the trade union movement . . . there was always the amalgam, their political work associated with their trade union work. There was no question of one or the other. They were part of that broad Scottish people's movement . . . there is no such thing as Communist-dominated. We operate as Communists within our industry and our union. We work with our colleagues of the broad Left in the Labour Party, who are a unifying force after all.'

Fence-mending with the trades councils was not the only objective which took Middleton and the general council out on the road in those years. From 1952 onwards, a regular programme of regional economic conferences was sponsored by the STUC all over Scotland, often with former Attlee ministers like Hector McNeil as the guest speaker. The objective was both to gather local data and grievances for presentation to government, and to consolidate the notion of the STUC as champion of Scotland's economic interests. It did no harm, either, to the STUC's own housekeeping. Membership was by now on a steadily upward trend, rising from 613,177 in 1945 to 817,695 in 1965. It was a boom time for trade unionism in Britain, and no less so in Scotland: in January 1957, one of the oldest thorns in the STUC's side was finally removed when Scotsman Publications, now owned by the Canadian, Roy Thomson, finally agreed to recognise unions. Even though the number of purely Scottish unions continued to dwindle, and amalgamations took place, the numbers of unions affiliating to the STUC also rose across that period, from 79 to 91 (which would turn out to be the record high). Most English-based unions were by now seeing advantage in affiliating to the STUC. This is no doubt a tribute to the organisation's heightened relevance at the time, though the STUC has also always done rather well from holding its congress in spring, right at the start of the union conference season (which runs through to the TUC in September). This allows UK union leaders to use it to set the agenda, and sound out mood, for the months of debate that lie ahead. With the spread of the electronic mass media in the Fifties, the appeal of that platform to London-based general secretaries grew. Few of them have ever been conspicuously bashful about stepping out under the TV lights.

But it would be wrong to portray the STUC's economic mission in the Fifties and Sixties merely in terms of publicity-hungry lobbying. Middleton and Jack pursued the industrial prizes they sought with tenacity, resourcefulness and guile. One example will serve to demonstrate the time and effort that the STUC put into these campaigns.

On 9 July 1954, the general council issued a statement welcoming a decision by the steel company Colville to build a £20 million new plant at Motherwell. A few weeks earlier, on 24 June, an STUC deputation had been to London to see the Steel Board to insist 'that Scotland should receive special consideration in their capital allocations for new blast furnace capacity.' It was a typical STUC demand of the time, and seemed to have borne fruit. But the matter was not allowed to lie there, for the July statement went on to argue that Scotland needed a strip mill too: 'The production of this type of steel . . . would assist immeasurably in attracting a share of the motor car industry to this part of the country.'

Over the next few years, the STUC badgered away at this objective, adding it to the extensive shopping list which accompanied the general council on an ever-busier round of ministerial meetings. Early in 1957, it became known that the Steel Board was looking to build a fourth British strip mill, and the STUC and its SCDI allies moved rapidly into action to win the development for Scotland. That year's congress in Rothesay, attended by Labour leader Hugh Gaitskell, approved a motion arguing that the mill should be sited at Grangemouth. This was followed up by a concerted publicity drive, which sought and secured the backing of all the Scottish political parties. Jimmy Jack chipped in with an immensely detailed paper on the advantages of Grangemouth, pointing to its modern harbour facilities and to the presence of an estimated 300 million tons of coking coal under the Forth.

On 30 May, a deputation under the auspices of the SCDI took

the case to London for talks with the Scottish Secretary, John Maclay, and the President of the Board of Trade, Sir David Eccles. The breadth of opinion represented in the deputation – which included leading lights of the SCDI, Glasgow Chamber of Commerce, Sir John Toothill of Ferranti, plus Middleton and John Lang from the STUC general council – plainly impressed even sceptical Whitehall, for it provoked a Prime Ministerial statement in which Harold Macmillan promised that Scotland's claim 'would be fully investigated,' but warned that the scale of the investment made an early decision unlikely. In the event, the issue lay before Cabinet for 18 months. The STUC concluded that there was everything to play for, and immediately issued another hefty economic analysis of the case for Grangemouth.

For the next few months, the arguments raged back and forth. In August it emerged that Colville directors were arguing against the mill coming to Scotland, where they believed existing capacity to be sufficient. The STUC demanded a further meeting with Maclay, which took place on 14 October. The Scottish Secretary was presented, courtesy of Jack, with elaborate evidence to convey to his Cabinet colleagues about the new industries a strip mill could attract to Scotland. The following month, these arguments were endorsed by a special conference in Stirling, attended by local authorities, Chambers of Commerce, and unions. By February, the political impetus from Scotland had driven back both steel industry leaders and some English ministers to the assertion that Scotland lacked sufficient coking coal to make a strip mill viable. The STUC immediately responded with a closely-documented paper which mapped the precise position and extent of the coking coal deposits beneath the Forth, detailed the development programmes which would enable Forth Valley pits at Valleyfield, Airth and Kinneil to mine a projected 1.25 million tons of it a year, and finished up with a chemical analysis of the quality of other coking coal deposits beneath Milngavie, Lanarkshire and West Lothian. In case anyone was still minded to argue, the paper carried a written endorsement from HR King, production director of the NCB's Scottish division. Another motion at April's Aberdeen congress demanding a strip mill was underpinned by a further STUC analysis, this time of Scotland's relative employment disadvantage. Scotland, it said, had 10 per cent of Britain's population and 22 per cent of its unemployed population: whereas in Britain there was one job vacancy for every two jobless people, in Scotland the ratio was one to six. A strip mill at Grangemouth, concluded the paper, 'would be a major project much needed to replace many of the industries going out of production.' The same month, Middleton addressed a major SCDI conference on the strip mill at Glasgow City Chambers.

The pressure had become irresistible. On 18 November, Harold Macmillan announced that the government had decided to split the strip mill investment in two: one mill to South Wales, another to Colville's Ravenscraig works at Motherwell. The consequence of this decision was to create 500,000 tons of new strip capacity: more, Macmillan admitted, than current demand could sustain, and he expressed the hope that new industries could be attracted, to Scotland in particular, to absorb the extra sheet. He also acknowledged that the solution the Cabinet had reached was a political rather than an industrial one: the implication being that the lobbying had paid off. According to the *Financial Times*, Colville's reservations had been bought off by an early government promise of subsidy, whereas the Welsh firm involved, Richard Thomas & Baldwin, which had wanted a strip mill from the first, was still waiting to hear what aid would come its way when the decision was announced. The STUC general council, in a statement on 1 December, reinforced Macmillan's reservations about demand, warning that 'greater progress in industrial growth and the winning of new industries is needed if Scotland's army of almost 90,000 unemployed . . . and the widespread under-employment which exists are to be remedied.' The statement also pretended to chagrin at Scotland only landing half the investment, and at the rejection of Grangemouth as the site. But it could not resist a generous dose of self-congratulation: 'It represents a singular success for the efforts of this Scottish TUC to provide more industrial development north of the Border. We are convinced that without the effort which has been put in, the entire project would have gone to Wales. Scotland would have got nothing.'

There was truth in the boast, as there would be when other investment bounty was brought home, by similar dogged pleading, to Scotland: an atomic power station to Dounreay, announced in 1954; the long-cherished motor industries – BMC to Bathgate and Rootes Group to Linwood in 1961 and 1963 respectively; a pulp mill to Corpach in 1962 and an aluminium smelter to Invergordon in 1968; a steady build-up in petrochemical and container activity at Grangemouth, a Forth Road Bridge in 1964 (the STUC had been pursuing that project for so long that it had almost given up, offering to settle for a tunnel instead). Jerusalem, it seemed, could indeed be builded in Scotland, provided the blueprint for its construction was presented persistently and persuasively enough.

It is customary now for the role of the STUC in all this to be deprecated by some in the Labour movement. One front bencher to whom I spoke remarked sourly that issuing press statements about investments did not amount to a decisive role in bringing them about. Certainly, Middleton was to brag at the 1961 congress in Rothesay that the general council had 'issued more statements about the economy of Scotland than any other organisation.' Yet the evidence of the times argues powerfully that the influence of the STUC was indeed important, and seen to be so by others beyond itself. A series of 'Jobs for Scotland' conferences, organised by the STUC from 1960 onwards, attracted growing audiences of MPs, local authority leaders, industrialists and officials. Six months after the Ravenscraig announcement, on 2 May 1959, Harold Macmillan received a deputation to Downing Street led by Milne, Middleton and Jack. It was the first time the STUC had been granted audience by a sitting Prime Minister, and the general council was evidently determined not to waste the opportunity in pleasantries. Macmillan was presented with a full and cheerless analysis of Scotland's circumstances in relation to unemployment, dock traffic, shipbuilding (about which Jack had compiled some justifiably alarming projections), mining, steelmaking, and factory build. The case was put forcibly for further industrial diversification. Macmillan responded sympathetically to most of the points raised, promised to consider carefully the remedies proposed, and acknowledged that Scotland's unemployment did seem to be endemic. According to the deputation's report of the meeting, the Prime Minister recalled that 'he himself had at one time given up hope for the north-east coast area of England . . . now, however, it was very prosperous with many new industries.'

Macmillan does not seem to have been too intimidated by the length of the STUC's shopping list, for he was to receive them twice more in the remaining years of his premiership. In April 1960, Milne chaired an extraordinary conference on the Scottish economy convened by the general council at Glasgow City Chambers. It was attended by 49 of the 71 Scottish MPs, representing all the Scottish parties, and the following month a representative deputation of three Labour MPs, three Tories, one Liberal and the STUC high command met Macmillan in London to convey its conclusions. Middleton, never one for hyperbole, described the Prime Minister's response as 'fairly satisfactory' and 'fairly receptive.' This seems to have been something of an understatement, for very shortly afterwards the Scottish Board for Industry called together more than 300 firms to try to interest them in supplying components for the car industry that was shortly to begin production in Scotland. A further meeting with the Prime Minister took place at Admiralty House on 22 January 1963. Scottish unemployment had climbed above the 100,000 mark the previous month, and this time the STUC wish list was still longer. In addition to the usual pleas to help strategic industries and encourage new ones, the deputation wanted the upgrading of development districts under the Local Employment Act, higher benefits to the unemployed to stimulate demand, increased industrial direction, special measures to help the Highlands, and the creation of a Scottish Development Authority. According to the *Glasgow Herald*, Macmillan called the meeting 'very fair and friendly' and promised to examine closely the STUC's 'very practical suggestions.'

By then Macmillan's decaying government was nearing the end, and though his surprise resignation on health grounds that October gave way to a brief inter-regnum under Sir Alec Douglas-Home (with whom the STUC held one meeting), there was a sense that the past was making a vain last stand against an impatient future. Few in the trade union movement doubted that it would be a Labour government which would complete the construction of the New Jerusalem, nor that completed it would be. Yet already the signs were becoming increasingly compelling that it had been founded on shifting sand.

The evidence was there in a growing economic crisis, manifested in a quiet but steady governmental retreat from the goal of full employment; in demands for 'pay pauses' which generated a rash of disputes in numerous industries; and in curtailed spending on the nationalised industries, most notably the plan to close 16 Scottish pits deemed uneconomic, and the drastic cutbacks in Britain's rail network proposed in the 1963 report of ICI's Dr Richard Beeching. It was there, too, in the troubles which swiftly beset many of the new industries so recently erected in Scotland. What was happening to the coal reconstruction programme was also happening elsewhere. Both Rootes and BMC steered close to calamity in their early years, driven off the commercial straight and narrow by high costs and low productivity. Little of the hoped-for components industry around them materialised. Moreover, plants like Ravenscraig owed their existence to political rather than industrial logic and, being resented accordingly by industry leaders, were ever after condemned to fight tooth and nail for every penny of the investment they needed. When, 20 years later, a radical Tory government freed their managements to follow commercial imperatives, the pillars on which so many hopes had rested swiftly toppled.

By the early Sixties, the logic of industrial direction had begun to be increasingly questioned. Indeed, as early as August 1956, during a conference on automation, Middleton had raised one concern that was to become a staple of Scottish debate through to the present day. 'There is in Scotland,' he said, 'a considerable dependence on the branch factory, especially in the newer types of industry, the performance of which could be endangered if more centralisation should occur as a result of automation.' It was a remarkably far-sighted prediction. Besides which, the Eden and Macmillan governments, while accepting industrial subsidy and direction as political necessities, were unable to settle on any very coherent policy strategy to guide them. In January 1957, an STUC deputation, meeting Scottish Office and Board of Trade ministers to press for accelerated provision of advance factories to promote diversification, was greatly taken aback to be told that the newer industries were highly volatile and Scotland would do better to concentrate on its traditional heavy sectors, which were 'the most stable of all.' A month later, an SCDI analysis showed that of the £2 million recently brought to Scotland by US inward investors, £1.5 million was in heavy engineering. The £500,000 invested in light or precision engineering in Scotland was less than half the figure which US firms had spent on such work in England. The regional aid regime also kept changing. The 1945 Distribution of Industry Act had created development areas, which enjoyed special industrial incentives. The 1958 Distribution of Industry (Industrial Finance) Act focused both financial incentives and coercive planning provisions on areas where unemployment exceeded 4 per cent. In 1960, the development areas were replaced by a patchwork of smaller development districts, defined as locations in which unemployment averaged above 4.5 per cent. As the Sixties progressed, such districts began to join up until, ultimately, almost all of Scotland qualified for some sort of aid. In fairness, the supplicants were no more united on strategy than was government. The STUC was still by and large committed, through its 'Jobs for Scotland' and 'Quest for Jobs' campaigns, to locating the newer industries in areas of greatest deprivation. But the influential Toothill Report, published by the SCDI in 1961, suggested instead that investment be concentrated on 'growth points' like the New Towns, designation of which had begun with East Kilbride in 1947 and would continue through to Irvine in 1966. Rather more ominously, Toothill doubted that the new industries, however vigorously attracted, could ever replace the jobs destined to go from older mainstays like shipbuilding, mining and jute – all of which were now struggling.

In its dying days, the Conservative government discovered a new enthusiasm for planning. A Scottish Development Department was set up in the Scottish Office in 1962 to devise ways of bringing economic growth to Scotland, and the following year the first fruits appeared in a white paper, *The Central Scotland Plan*. Similar documents were promised for the rest of Scotland, a project which the STUC, not unjustly given the publicity fanfare which surrounded it, described as a pre-election stunt. The *Plan* lent heavily on Toothill (also on the voluntary National Plans pioneered in France), by discussing strategies for encouraging new – privately-owned – industrial concerns to cluster in designated growth areas, rather than sending state-owned, or subsidised, concerns to unemployment blackspots.

The *Plan* was never implemented, because it was overtaken by the defeat of the Conservative government in 1964. It is of interest mainly because of the shift in economic thinking it indicated, one which the new government of Harold Wilson partly endorsed when it published its own *Plan for Expansion* in January, 1966. The approach originated so boldly by the Attlee government, with its emphasis on state ownership and direction as the means to industrial renewal, had come full circle, and stopped. For the next three decades, the unions would be much pre-occupied with trying to stem the ebb of 1945's brave hopes. Yet that was not how things looked in 1964. A new era of hope, so long delayed, was at last at hand. The Conservatives who had squandered Attlee's legacy through thirteen long years were gone. A Labour government was back, a young and fiercely bright Labour government, committed to white hot technology and a new classlessness. Labour would put things right.

Of devolution and discontent: Willie Ross (top) and Harold Wilson with Jimmy Jack at STUC headquarters.

Of devolution and discontent: a long wait for a bus in Glasgow during the 'Winter of Discontent'.

Weathering the storm: the former British Leyland plant at Bathgate, 1989.
(Picture: Alan Wylie)

Weathering the storm: Felix Smith from Bilston Glen on the miners' picket line, 1985.

Weathering the storm: the miners' picket, Ravenscraig steelworks.

Weathering the storm: Jimmy Milne (right) with the Ravenscraig convener, Tommy Brennan.

Of devolution and discontent: home rule in the seventies – protesting against the '40 per cent rule'.

Weathering the storm: home rule in the nineties – Scottish Constitutional Convention joint chairmen Lord Ewing (left) and Sir David Steel.

Weathering the storm: the STUC's anti-poll tax campaign, 1988.

Weathering the storm: Bill Speirs at the launch of Scotland United.
Speakers include the SNP's Fiona Hyslop. (second from left)

Weathering the storm: Campbell Christie with South African President Nelson Mandela. (Picture: Alan Wylie)

Weathering the storm: entertainers, church leaders and others join forces with the 1994 general council to launch an STUC recruitment campaign.

CHAPTER SEVEN

FRIEND AND FOE

Just as true turning points are often unremarked when they happen, so the long-awaited transcendence usually disappoints. The election in 1964 of Harold Wilson's Labour government felt at the time like the coming of a dawn for which the country was not only awake and ready, but feverishly impatient. The last, long months of Conservative rule – scandal-ridden, other-worldly, hapless, risibly sanctimonious – had been a dam slowly, but inexorably, crumbling. Behind it lay a great weight of change, and of anticipation. In almost every area of national life, it seemed as though pace and perceptions had moved far ahead of government: in the arts and sciences, in moral and philosophical debate, in business practice, in that indefinable but unignorable abstraction, the popular mood. It was the hour of Lady Chatterley, of Christine Keeler, of Joe Orton, of Mary Quant, of David Bailey and David Hockney, of Peter Cook and David Frost, of Jim Slater and Peter Walker, of the Beatles. Beside such dazzling company, the ministers of Macmillan and Home looked like shambling mediaeval barons, vainly denying the renaissance. America's renaissance president had been cruelly gunned down the previous November. Now it was Britain's turn.

Harold Wilson and his fractious but talented team – Jenkins, Callaghan, Crossman, Brown – had succeeded in donning the mantle of the new tomorrow, of the people who could deliver a new Britain forged, as Wilson famously told his party conference on 2 October 1963, 'in the white heat of a technological revolution.' It was a conceit, like many of the period, which would become terribly easy to mock, and sooner rather than later. Weighed down by such a burden of expectation, and of hubris, much of what Wilson did over the ensuing six years inevitably seemed at the time superficial and disappointing. It looks less so from today's perspective. History, as James Callaghan predicted when he succeeded to the premiership in 1976, has been kinder to Wilson than were his contemporaries. The Wilson governments achieved a great deal, particularly in the field of social reform. But in the extraordinary times they governed, they could never run as fast as the pace demanded of them and they sometimes came badly adrift in trying.

Scotland played a key part in delivering Wilson his slender majority. For all the weight of expectation, Britain in 1964 was a more conservative country than was apparent from the eager young faces that filled its screens and prints, and Labour actually won fewer votes than at any election since 1945. Only the lottery of the electoral system translated this into an overall majority of three. While the Labour vote fell in England, it rose sharply in Scotland, from 46.7 to 48.7 per cent (against 44.1 UK-wide), yielding a net gain of five Scottish seats. This was the election in which Scotland definitively established its dependable capacity for manufacturing Labour MPs on an industrial basis, though the quality was not always as reliable as the quantity. But it is perhaps a reflection of that innate conservatism that Scotland in 1964 (and, to a lesser extent, in the ensuing 1966 election) seemed to be voting Labour for rather different reasons from the rest of the country. Little of the government's liberal reforming impulse, the accomplishment which history most honours, commanded much emphasis. Labour's appeal to Scottish voters was much more practical and prosaic: housing, education, planning, jobs. The party's public face north of the border accentuated the distinction. Scotland, arguably, delivered the election to Harold Wilson. Wilson, in turn, delivered the Rt Hon William Ross as Secretary of State for Scotland.

Ross was a grim-faced, gruff-spoken former dominie for whom the word dour might have been custom-built. Throughout the years of the sexual revolution, the pop culture, the permissive society, and psychedelia, Scotland was presided over by a man who looked, and was, the archetypal Presbyterian elder of the old school; severe on frippery and indulgence, and guided by a personal code that leavened the Old Testament with Burns rather than Bob Dylan. None of that greatly mattered to the STUC, which was not over-populated with flower children itself. But other aspects of the STUC style did notably grate on a man who, during eight unchallenged years in the job, became the closest approximation yet to a Prime Minister of Scotland (so much so that when the Scottish Office's hideous premises at New St Andrew's House were being fitted out in the early 1970s, the workmen daubed the walls of the biggest ministerial chamber 'Willie's room' – Labour was in opposition at the time).

Ross was prone to give the impression that he saw fighting Scotland's corner to be his job, and no-one else's. The multi-hued economic raiding parties in which the STUC had engaged so enthusiastically during the long years of Tory rule were no longer required now Labour was in office. Ross harboured a particular suspicion of the SCDI, refusing to believe that its largely managerial membership could bear anything but malice towards a Labour administration. The bigger point, though, was that the supplicancy of lobbying presumed a grudging government, and Ross was not remotely prepared to concede that a Labour administration was that. Instead, he pinned his faith publicly on the ability of central planning to deliver 'economic discrimination in Scotland's favour,' and less publicly on a close relationship with Wilson (who affectionately called him 'Old Basso Profundo') which would enable him to carry Scotland's case in Cabinet. In fairness to Ross, he often won, and his stewardship did bring Scotland some significant economic bounty, such as the choice of Dounreay in 1966 as the centre for Britain's fast breeder reactor programme, and the location of an aluminium smelter at Invergordon in 1968. But it also deprived the STUC of what had been a defining function, and as Labour's planning ambitions gave way to economic crisis management, trade union impatience in Scotland with Labour began to gather force.

Not much of that was evident at first, though. Indeed, the first Bill in the first Wilson Queen's Speech gave form to a long-standing STUC objective: the creation of a Highlands and Islands Development Board. Though the board lacked the compulsory purchase powers which the STUC thought were needed to break the chill grip of landlord neglect, it did valuably combine a social mission with the board's economic development remit. The HIDB could build schools and village halls as well as industrial premises, and was thus better equipped to address its over-riding objective of reversing a seepage of population which had been taking place almost without interruption since Culloden. By the time Wilson left office in 1970, the board was able to claim credit for bringing more than 5,000 jobs north of the Highland boundary fault. More importantly, it had brought about the beginnings of a lasting reversal in the trend to depopulation. When the board was created, the northern half of Scotland's land mass was home to just 300,000 people. By the early 1990s, the figure had climbed back to 370,000, the highest it had been since the Twenties.

Everywhere, in those first few years, there seemed ample grounds for optimism. Never had the physical face of Scotland undergone such ubiquitous and exciting change. At every turn slums were being torn down and their inhabitants decanted into thrilling tower blocks, housing estates and new towns. Shabby old town centres, grim Victorian schools and Gothic hospitals were being replaced with bold cubes of exquisitely poured concrete. Dusty corner shops were being submerged beneath the plate glass of bright new supermarkets. Raised motorways were marching triumphantly through grimy city centres like liberating battalions. In truth, much of the impetus for all this pre-dated Wilson, and much of it had very little to do with government policy at all. But it was Wilson's happy aptitude to assume credit by association for every manifestation of change, from footballing success to the Beatles' latest masterpiece, in a decade which had been made to wait so long for change that it assumed all transformation to be an absolute good. Happier still for Wilson, it was several years more before people began to realise that much of what had been replaced was superior to what had replaced it. The posthumous achievement of the Wilson era was to teach the British that change is quite often for the worse.

Some hopes soured more quickly. Wilson was creditably determined to loosen the Treasury's hold on economic policy and decided, bravely if over-ambitiously, to create a rival to it: the Department of Economic Affairs, headed by his volatile deputy, George Brown. The theory was simple. The DEA, armed with the instruments of economic planning, would hack a bold trail through the undergrowth of Treasury parsimony. It came swiftly to nothing. Wilson, demonstrating a characteristic tendency to explain away his policy flops by affecting to chastise himself for indulging his colleagues' inadequacy, later attributed the failure to having allowed Brown to take on extraneous responsibilities such as prices and incomes, and overseas economic policy. Certainly, that added the Board of Trade and the Foreign Office to the

DEA's formidable list of Whitehall enemies. Much the bigger reason though was that the Treasury, which knows more about the tactic of divide-and-rule than any government, did not wish the DEA to prosper. Therefore, it did not.

In 1969, with the economy still reeling from an unwisely postponed devaluation, Wilson wound up the DEA. Only one fragment of it survives today, a curio that no-one has got around to binning because it would not be worth the trouble of doing so. The DEA spawned a network of regional councils, which were to inform the regional plans that the DEA would put into force. The Scottish Economic Planning Council was chaired by Willie Ross, and peopled by the sort of great and good who had previously mounted offensives on London under the banner of the SCDI. The STUC had four seats on it, including George Middleton as vice-chairman. After the abolition of the DEA, the days of the councils were presumed numbered. But oddly, when Edward Heath came to get rid of them, his Scottish Secretary, Gordon Campbell, successfully argued for the Scottish Council to be retained, merely excising the unword 'planning' from its title. It survived, and survives, as an inexpensive, if little-noticed, sop to Scottish collectivist traditions, exercising an advisory influence on the Scottish Secretary of the day which corresponds exactly with the willingness of the Scottish Secretary to pay it any heed. Malcolm Rifkind, while admitting little of the council's input to his policies, reportedly enjoyed its thrice-yearly meetings. Ian Lang, never at his most comfortable with the Scottish consensus, was a less committed fan. Michael Forsyth, casting around in the mid-Nineties for political placebos to wean Scotland off the home rule narcotic, toyed with giving the council a higher public profile, though no measurably greater authority. The STUC would continue to value its seats, particularly after the onset of the Thatcher era, when it was eased remorselessly out of other public bodies. But the council after 1969 would forever bear the look of a maiden aunt consigned to a dark corner of an engagement party because nobody could think of an easy way not to invite her.

In its formative months, however, the DEA was a beast of awesome, if vague, potential, and George Brown as its Secretary of State seemed to represent a pole of economic power in Cabinet equal to the Chancellor, James Callaghan. There was, therefore, due dismay when Brown appeared at the 1965 STUC Congress in Rothesay, deputising for a Wilson absent for the first time in three years, and told delegates plainly that wages, no less than prices and taxes, must be levers in the hands of the department he now commanded. His speech, testing the ground for a government statement shortly afterwards, made the case for an encompassing policy that would tie wages to productivity in return for governmental constraints on price rises. Brown had already been pursuing these objectives on a piecemeal and exploratory basis, though not with the STUC. As Harold Wilson would later recall in his memoirs, 'Manufacturers collectively, and trade by trade, would receive from him a peremptory demand to justify the current wave of price increases. One moment he was banging the table at the bakers who were intent on raising bread prices; the next he was holding the baking unions in check on their wage demand.' It was a heroic, if largely futile, exertion for a deputy Prime Minister, and Brown had begun canvassing support for the creation of an independent mechanism to relieve him of such chores. Matters had got off to a promising enough start on 16 December 1964, when the TUC general secretary, George Woodcock, joined employers' leaders and senior ministers at Lancaster House to sign a tripartite Declaration of Intent on Productivity, Prices and Incomes. It was an early appearance of that legendary figure from the Wilson years, Solomon Binding, in that the Declaration was supposed to represent a solemn and binding agreement by the parties to abide by its high ideals. But, as everyone knew, the proof would come in implementation rather than declamation, and in particular would hang on the willingness of the unions to brook governmental interference in free collective bargaining. The STUC congress, once more setting the tone for the coming round of union conferences, gave Brown an early but clear indication of how tough a row he was going to have to hoe.

Its response fell short of defiance, but went no further than a distinctly conditional assent. Brown had spoken the day before the economic debate, which is usually the centrepiece of the STUC congress. On this occasion, given the acute sensitivities of the moment, prodigious effort went into rolling the numerous economic motions and amendments into a composite with which everyone – including the government – could live. It proved impossible, and the best that could be produced was a sort of tactful gripe. The composite paid dutiful tribute to the government's intentions on price controls and planning (Wilson's national plan was by then in the final stages of preparation), but made clear that there could be no acceptance of a policy which stabilised wages at their current level. There was little room to fudge the bite in that condition, which was why the TGWU, of which Brown happened to be a sponsored MP, moved that the composite be remitted – held in abeyance – for future consideration. The nominal rationale was that a conference of trade union executives was to take place in London a few weeks hence, and it was important that the movement spoke there with a single voice. The real reason, no-one doubted, was that the fragility of the government's majority could have made a divergence with the unions on such a central policy tenet well nigh fatal. It was a demanding test of STUC loyalty and responsibility, and delegates rose reluctantly to it. The motion was remitted with only the miners and the railwaymen dissenting. All the same, a marker had been put down. If the inevitable second election gave Labour a healthier working majority, the government need not expect carte blanche from the Scottish trade union movement for wage restraint.

The point from Rothesay was not lost on Wilson. By the time he reached his own party conference at Blackpool that autumn, he had concluded that a voluntary agreement on prices and incomes was untenable. Not only had the summer union conferences produced ample echoes of the STUC dissension, but a number of headline-grabbing pay settlements had since set a pace which the government could only regard with dismay. On 1 September, Callaghan and Brown persuaded the Cabinet that controls over prices and incomes must be made statutory. The Board for Prices and Incomes, previously restricted to issuing reports and recommendations, would in future be able to adjudicate on settlements or price rises referred to it by Brown. These would be deferred while inquiries took place, and the ensuing decisions could be enforced by ministerial order. Brown met the TUC general council for 12 tetchy hours, finally winning its agreement that the powers be put in place as an 'early warning system' for inflationary movements, but that statutory enforcement could be activated only with a vote of both Houses of Parliament. Wilson's memoirs portray this accommodation as a sensible way to give the voluntary regime a last chance to prove itself. Richard Crossman's diaries, however, suggest that the formula was a compromise between Callaghan's demands, pressed upon him by the US Treasury Secretary Henry Fowler, for fully statutory controls, and Brown's lingering respect for free collective bargaining (responsibility for making the legislation work was deftly shuffled from the DEA to the Ministry of Labour). Either way, the principle of statutory wage restraint had been established. When the legislation came to parliament the following year, it cost Wilson the resignation of his Technology Minister, Frank Cousins, the TGWU general secretary who had been brought into the government. It also meant that Labour ministers were obliged to stand up in the Commons on a regular basis to explain why groups of workers should be denied pay rises. The junior minister most directly responsible was Roy Hattersley, who would recall in his memoirs 30 years later that his first such outing required him to lead a debate on why the artificial limb fitters at Roehampton Orthopaedic Hospital should be refused an extra few pennies a week. Relations between the Wilson government and the unions would never be the same again.

The STUC was already at odds with the government over a scarcely less important, though slightly less sensitive, issue. In 1960, Macmillan had approved the establishment of a US submarine base at the Holy Loch for the Polaris nuclear system. A wave of public protests in Scotland ensued in which trade unionists played a leading part, often joining forces with folk singers and other arty protesters in what was to become a lasting alliance. In December 1960, the STUC co-organised in Glasgow one of the first major demonstrations against the decision, and the following year's congress in Rothesay approved a stringently-worded general council statement deploring the base. At that stage, the STUC's stance fell just short of unilateralism. Its principal objection to the Holy Loch was that the decision to deploy Polaris from the base lay solely with the US, even though the presence of the weapons enhanced Scotland's vulnerability as a nuclear target. But the very vehemence of its campaigning opened an uncomfortable gap with Labour. In 1957, Hugh Gaitskell had, with Aneurin Bevan's decisive help, dissuaded the party from embracing unilateralism, but public acrimony continued between the party leadership and supporters of the Campaign for Nuclear Disarmament, and reached a height at the 1960 party conference. The STUC, by contrast, had no difficulty in campaigning alongside

CND over the Holy Loch. In November 1960, the STUC brought a proposal before its liaison committee with the Scottish Council of the Labour Party for a joint campaign, but Labour's Scottish high command declined until such time as a clearer policy steer could be had from the London leadership. It was a long time coming, and the general council resolved that the STUC should meantime set its own course. Over the next couple of years, the annual peace motion at STUC congress edged ever closer to outright unilateralism, finally making the position explicit in 1963 at Dunoon. There, Michael McGahey successfully moved a composite which both deplored the Polaris programme and declared robustly against a British nuclear capability. At a push, that could almost be reconciled with Labour's policy which was then nominally against a British deterrent. But Wilson's defence spokesman, Denis Healey, was a scathing critic of CND, and was already building a close friendship with the US defence secretary, Robert McNamara, which would develop further after 1964 when Healey took over the Ministry of Defence. Over the next six years, he would draw Britain's defence policies into close alignment with the US's, becoming a principal architect of the West's multilateral strategy. The STUC was undeterred, and at Perth in 1964 – just months before the general election, and with Wilson in attendance – delegates unanimously approved a general council motion which demanded the removal of all nuclear capability from Scotland, the negotiation of a non-aggression treaty between NATO and the Warsaw Pact countries, a total ban on nuclear testing and the eventual establishment of a European nuclear-free zone. Shortly after the election, Healey accused the STUC of promoting a 'false sense of security.'

Rebellion on such issues was electorally containable. The STUC's declarations on global geo-politics have always formed an important part of congress for delegates, though one which attracts little outside attention. Even the Scottish press which, particularly since the 1950s, had followed STUC affairs closely, has rarely been much impressed by the STUC's locus for issuing withering rebukes to Washington, Moscow or the United Nations. At times, the foreign affairs session at congress has been significant mostly as an opportunity for harmlessly letting off steam, though the speeches can be erudite and passionate and the STUC is proud of its prodigious network of overseas contacts. During the 1960s, it struck an increasingly independent course over issues like Vietnam, Rhodesia, and East–West relations, refusing to be hidebound by the policies of the Labour government or the TUC. Having declined in the 1950s to follow the TUC into the NATO-orientated International Confederation of Free Trade Unions, the STUC instead built up bilateral relationships, including with Eastern bloc trade union movements and with revolutionary movements in South and Central America, South Africa and the Middle East. Many of these would come to prove valuable: the STUC, for example, had powerful links with black trade unionists in South Africa in a period when much of the movement was still inclined to regard Nelson Mandela as a terrorist. Others would prove contentious: a long association with the Palestinian cause jarred with the friendship the rest of the movement maintained towards the Israeli Labour Party and unions. This was psychologically important for the STUC in rediscovering a sense of its own policy independence, and thus shedding ambiguities which dated back to William Elger's time. In the longer term, some of these linkages would generate policies – not least on Palestine – that the rest of the movement would gradually adopt, thanks in no small measure to STUC input. In the 1980s and 1990s, the STUC's bilateral connections with regional trade union movements in Spain, Italy, France and Flanders would bring fresh thinking to debate about the role a devolved Scotland could play in a Europe of the Regions. But, more often, the immediate impact of STUC pronouncements on foreign affairs was, and remains, slight. At the 1966 congress, delegates boldly endorsed a motion which took issue with almost every aspect of Wilson's foreign policy: support for the US in Vietnam, maintaining a military presence east of Suez, a cautious pace of decolonialisation. Wilson, when he rose to speak, cheerfully ignored foreign affairs altogether.

It fell to a new general secretary to pilot the STUC into this new, and very different, era. George Middleton retired in 1963, though he would retain a busy portfolio of posts in public bodies, from the Scottish Economic Planning Council to fisheries regulation, until his death in 1971. The choice of Jimmy Jack to follow him into the general secretaryship was as close to an automatic succession as any in the STUC's history. Jack lacked Middleton's rumbustious manner and his winning way with a microphone, but he was a reliably cool and safe pair of hands at a time when that was probably the aptitude most needed. With almost 20 years as a full-time STUC official behind him, Jack knew better than anyone what was, and was not, deliverable. He was, though, more than just a conciliator or facilitator. There was a steely core to him. He was an unswerving enthusiast for the European Economic Community at a time when such a view was profoundly unfashionable in the movement, as it would remain long after Jack was gone. Campbell Christie remembers attending a summer school in about 1963, at which Jimmy Jack shared a pro-EEC platform with Bruce Millan, later Scottish Secretary and one of Britain's European Commissioners. In the course of the economic debate at Rothesay, too, when the STUC's relationship with the new government was under acute stress, Jack took the opportunity of replying forthrightly to commentators who had wondered aloud whether the STUC would give Labour as hard a time in office as it had the Tories. Jack's answer was that the STUC would certainly be 'as vigorous in its demands.' Coming when it did, the implication of the statement was that, should circumstances arise, the STUC might be even more demanding. After the 1966 election, which delivered Wilson the comfortable majority (97) he had sought, such circumstances began to arise with growing frequency. Scotland in general, and the Scottish labour movement in particular, was beginning to find its patience with the Wilson government growing increasingly thin.

Two months before the election of 1966, the Scottish Office published the Scottish version of the National Plan which the DEA had issued the previous year. *The Scottish Economy: A Plan For Expansion 1965–1970* was certainly ambitious. Perceiving, as the STUC and SCDI had earlier been forced to, that the decline in employment in Scotland's traditional industries was now both endemic and structural, it proposed bold remedies. The older industries would be pruned back, reorganised and modernised. Resources would be focused, meantime, on creating newer industries, like electronics, for which incentives would be provided and a skilled workforce nurtured. Special measures similar to those in the Highlands (but without an HIDB or its social remit) would be introduced to repair decaying regional economies elsewhere in Scotland. The diagnosis was faultless, and the prescription sounded wonderful. In place of the Toothill strategy of concentrating resources on growth points, all of Scotland bar the Edinburgh–Leith conurbation (an omission remembered yet in Leith) would now enjoy development area status, entitling incoming industries to Regional Development Grants of up to 40 per cent of project cost. The programme would create 130,000 jobs to replace those displaced from the older industries, and would reverse Scotland's increasingly alarming rate of economic emigration. The plan was costed at £2 billion. What was not explained was how it was to be afforded.

Within a very short time it became apparent that only fragments of the plans were destined ever to be put into force. By spring of 1967, the STUC president, Willie McLean of the miners, was appealing to the government in his congress address to recognise that its hopes of attracting private sector industry to Scotland had failed, and instead to direct public sector investment north of the border. The nationalist critique is that, having secured his landslide on 31 March 1966, Harold Wilson no longer needed to keep the Scots sweet. Scotland, having over-fulfilled its quota in 1964, contributed just three more Labour MPs to the 1966 majority, on a notably lesser swing than Labour achieved elsewhere. It was a critique that was to make a stunning impact on Scottish politics at the Hamilton by-election the following year. But it does not really hold water.

For one thing, the government did continue to deliver parcels of economic bounty to Scotland after 1966, even if they did fall woefully short of the scale envisaged in the plan: a major rescue package for the Fairfield shipyard at Govan just nine months after the election; a more radical restructuring of shipbuilding on the Clyde in the wake of the following year's Geddes Report; a Scottish Transport Group; a steel platemill at Motherwell. But the bigger truth about the Wilson government was that it inherited from Macmillan and Home an economy suffering from several chronic ailments, which duly worsened, absorbing ever more of the government's energy and sapping its reforming intent. One was an inbuilt propensity for inflationary expansionism in the public finances, and on that legacy the early Wilson remorselessly built. Another was a parlous trade balance, aggravated in large measure by an unrealistically over-valued pound which the Wilson administrations tried to prop up for three years longer than was prudent. All governments choose a key economic indicator on which to focus their policies and pin their reputations, and Wilson chose the balance of payments. It was a bet which could only be made to come good at the cost of damage to other economic measurements, some of which impacted rather more directly on the populace, like unemployment. The trouble with planning is that it presupposes not merely imagination but resources. The Wilson governments had imagination in spades, even if some of it was misguided. But resources were destined rapidly and drastically to tighten.

None the less, the 1966 election campaign, which Wilson launched with a speech in Glasgow, rang with economic optimism. Callaghan had set the tone on 1 March with a 'pre-Budget' speech in the Commons which painted a generally rosy economic picture. The balance of payments deficit was showing signs of subsiding, trade was on the up, and unemployment, particularly in Scotland and northern England, had fallen by nearly 30,000 the previous month. The Scottish total dipped below 60,000 for the first time since the mid-Fifties. One of Wilson's first engagements after polling day was to arrive, trailing clouds of glory, at the STUC congress in Aberdeen, where he spoke proudly of the government's initiatives to transform Scotland's economic fortunes – the HIDB, industrial incentives, extension of development areas – and implied that more of the same was to come. Up to a point, it was: the following year, the government would introduce the Regional Employment Premium, which subsidised employment in the development areas. Echoing an election slogan of Willie Ross's, Wilson told the STUC: 'This is your country, work for it.' Delegates responded warmly to that, if less so to his insistence that a prices and incomes policy remained essential to the restoration of full employment.

Yet, within weeks, the government found itself having to grapple with economic adversity in a way that was to poison its relations with the trade unions for the remainder of its time in office. First Callaghan, having planned and prefaced a neutral Budget, found himself confronted on returning to No. 11 with a grimmer set of Treasury projections, and in his delayed Budget in early May he announced a new fiscal measure, Selective Employment Tax. Promoted as a way to shift workers from the service sectors into manufacturing by imposing a payroll tax on services, its principal attraction to the government was that it could be quickly and cheaply collected. It was, at root, a tax on jobs. The STUC general council countered with a statement pointing out the importance of service employment to rural Scotland in particular and doubting, presciently, whether manufacturing employment would grow sufficiently to take up the services jobs lost. But worse was to follow.

On 16 May, a newly-radicalised National Union of Seamen – whose leaders were famously described by Wilson as 'a tightly-knit group of politically motivated men' – launched a national strike over pay and conditions which paralysed Britain's trade. It lasted seven weeks. Wilson intervened personally three days before it began to plead for the abandonment of the 17 per cent pay claim, but he was unable to prevail. An official report published just before his intervention, which recommended 30 per cent for doctors, did not help. Only with TUC support was the government able to talk the seamen out of a full-scale oil embargo. The strike had two long-reaching effects: it helped precipitate a run on the pound, which in turn drove the government into a set of harshly deflationary economic policies; and it cemented a growing resolve within the government to curb the power of the trade unions.

At first, the market reaction against sterling, prompted by the virtual suspension of British trade, was contained by intervention. But then senior sources in the French government, with which Wilson was holding exploratory talks about EEC entry, briefed journalists to the effect that a sterling devaluation was a likely precondition. Pressure became crisis. Wilson, continuing to insist that there would be no devaluation, forced through a bitterly divided Cabinet a drastic series of measures: a 2 per cent rise in interest rates; tighter credit controls; sharp rises in indirect taxation and in postal and telephone charges; a one-year surcharge on direct taxation; cuts of £150 million in domestic government spending and of £100 million in spending overseas, particularly on defence; tighter foreign exchange controls, including a £50 limit on sterling taken out of the country by British travellers; and, above all, a six month wage freeze with further constraint to follow. George Brown resigned in protest, but was persuaded by Wilson to stay (he would finally go, in the midst of another sterling crisis, two years later). The Parliamentary Labour Party, now chaired by Emanuel Shinwell, was also dissuaded from revolt by the need to unite against a censure motion tabled by the Conservatives.

Trade unionists were not so easily mollified. Frank Cousins, recently departed from government, announced that the TGWU would not observe the pay freeze, and other general secretaries followed suit. The support of the TUC, regarded as crucial, hung in the balance. Two days after the freeze was announced TUC leaders met Callaghan, Brown and the Minister of Labour, Ray Gunter, and further meetings took place in the ensuing days, some of them attended by Wilson. The unions protested that they had agreed to accept voluntary restraint on the condition, now breached, that mandatory restraint would not follow. Finally, the TUC general council agreed to 'acquiesce' in the pay freeze, provided the position of lower-paid workers was safeguarded. The STUC, while scarcely central to the debate, gave no such undertaking. The STUC general council spoke in stark terms of betrayal, declaring the announcement of the package a day that would never be forgotten. In the space of eight weeks from September 1966, Scottish unemployment rose by a third, to almost 80,000. Economic emigration over the next year would reach an unprecedented 50,000. There would be no more talk of the STUC waiting to take its policy lead from London.

That November, Harold Wilson received an STUC delegation at Downing Street to hear of their 'serious and continuing uneasiness' about the severity with which deflation was impacting on Scotland. Jack read Wilson a characteristically long and precise account of the 'rapidly deteriorating' circumstances in a wide range of industries, and argued that the good intentions of the government's regional policies were being undermined by economic stringency, which was further concentrating industry in southern England: 'anti-inflationary measures imposed rigidly on Great Britain as a whole always fall with unnecessary harshness on Scotland ... the period of the "squeeze" is now at a dangerous stage for Scotland.' The deputation asked for a string of specific measures to help Scottish industry, including intervention to bring proposed investment by Ford and Vauxhall to Scotland, and to help Linwood diversify beyond the Hillman Imp. Wilson responded with his usual courtesy, complimenting Jack's 'scrupulous fairness,' but had no more tangible response than a promise to consider what he had heard. The deputation came away empty-handed.

Five months later, when Jim Callaghan addressed the 1967 congress in Dunoon, he was accorded the roughest reception ever given to a Labour minister by STUC delegates. He put up a pugnacious performance, insisting (in the wake of a congress motion demanding urgent expansionist measures to curb unemployment) that he was not prepared to follow the Tory example of confecting a short-lived boom. If STUC delegates expected otherwise, they should not have voted Labour. Trade unionists were in the business of raising their members' living standards, he said, but governments had to pursue the same aim for all the people. Wages had been running ahead of output for three years: now they would be tied to productivity – 'there is no escape from this.' Then, to the fury of delegates, he urged the unions 'not to use the position of the lower-paid workers as an excuse to climb on their backs for larger increases for higher-paid workers too.' The Chancellor did not have to wait long for a reply. In one of the least gracious votes of thanks ever to issue from the chair at the STUC, Willie McLean stiffly reminded Callaghan, as a former union official himself, of the duties union delegates bore to their members and to their unions. That afternoon, congress approved by almost a two-thirds majority a grittily-worded composite demanding the repeal of the government's prices and incomes legislation. The debate was dominated by a new generation of bright left-wingers who had risen to prominence since the late Fifties. Lawrence Daly of the miners accused Callaghan of perpetrating a 'slander' on the NUM, which had seen its attempt to win better wages for lower-paid miners blocked by the government's own legislation. Alex Kitson, who had transformed the dwindling fortunes of the Scottish Horse and Motormen (by then renamed the Scottish Commercial Motormen's Union) since becoming its general secretary in 1959, said his union favoured a planned incomes policy but the government's legislation was 'being imposed upon workers to suit the government's purpose.' Also chipping in was one of the more colourful TUC figures, Clive Jenkins of the clerical workers, who claimed that the government's target of 3 per cent growth meant unemployment staying at its current 'totally unacceptable' level.

The government had been pondering industrial relations reform before the crisis broke. In the same month as his bullish address to the 1966 STUC congress, Wilson had earned himself a markedly frostier reception by telling the national committee (annual conference) of the engineering workers: 'The sooner your rulebook is consigned to the industrial museum, the more quickly the union will be geared to the challenge facing industry and the nation.' Two days later, he made a similar appeal to defence workers to abandon restrictive demarcation practices. The effect of such remarks, and of Wilson's belligerently anti-Communist assault on the seamen, was to focus concerns among trade unionists about what sort of reforms the government had in mind. The previous year, it had established a Royal Commission chaired by a law lord, Lord Donovan, to examine relations between unions and employers' organisations, and the role of the law in regulating these. What had seemed a reassuringly vague remit at the time suddenly looked ominously broad.

The STUC prepared its submission to Donovan in May 1966 with some care. The evidence was written by a young STUC researcher, Jim Craigen, who would later become MP for Maryhill and a member of Labour's front bench team on Scottish affairs. Its principal thrust was to portray the STUC as a vibrant, dynamic body occupying an indispensable place at the heart of Scottish life: 'Since its formation in 1897 Congress has provided a service to organised labour in Scotland which it is doubtful if the TUC could have performed so effectively. The texture of Scottish life with its separate traditions in law, church, education and government is such as would have compelled the establishment of a separate Congress .... Congress is consulted by the government on a wide range of subjects affecting workpeople in Scotland, from education, housing and health to legal aid. As the most representative organ of Scottish opinion it has assumed a growing role at a time when the tendency towards regionalism may well continue to develop.' The paper represented the STUC as an essential counter-weight to the centralisation of economic activity in south-east England and the Midlands, and stressed the STUC's perpetual readiness to adapt its procedures to changing circumstance. As an exercise in elegant self-justification it could not be faulted.

In one respect, the STUC need not have worried. When the Donovan Report was finally published in June 1968, its recommendations proved less than shattering. Though it declared its aim to be to further the effectiveness of pay policy, it rejected all the more draconian remedies that had been laid before the Commission, such as compulsory pre-strike ballots, a reduction in unions' legal immunities, and a mandatory 'cooling-off' period before industrial action. Instead, it concentrated on proposals to streamline collective bargaining by formalising agreements, encouraging single-table bargaining, and registering major settlements with government. It also proposed the establishment of an industrial relations commission to investigate issues arising from the bargaining process.

Though there was some union disgruntlement at the expansion of the government's locus in bargaining, reaction was fairly muted. The long-evaded devaluation of the pound, from $2.80 to $2.40, had finally been announced in November 1967, and the consequent inflationary effect on prices at a time of continuing wage restraint had produced an angry backlash in Britain's workplaces. Between 1967 and 1970 the annual number of working days lost to strike action would soar from 2.8 million to 11 million. A long dispute at Ford had provoked threatening noises from Wilson about union excesses. Given that climate, the general feeling was that the Donovan reforms could have been a great deal more intrusive.

But that, it transpired, was also the view of government. Wilson had promised to leave a gap in the legislative programme for whatever Donovan proposed. Immediately the report appeared, however, the Employment and Productivity Secretary, Barbara Castle, began an extensive round of talks with the TUC and the CBI with the evident aim of finding a means to bring a halt to the unofficial strikes which were becoming an increasing feature of workplace conflict. The discussions did nothing to earn her the affection of union leaders: the newly-elected TGWU general secretary, Jack Jones, called her 'the Queer One.' Then on 17 January 1969 her White Paper was published. Adapting the title of a tract written by her hero Aneurin Bevan, Mrs Castle named her document *In Place of Strife*.

Most of its 27 proposals merely gave form to the Donovan recommendations. But the sting lay in a handful of clauses which revived in amended form the ideas Donovan had rejected. The government was to have the power to requisition ballots ahead of any strike judged a serious threat to the economy or the national interest; to order a 28-day suspension of action where a strike was called unofficially in contravention of agreed procedures – so-called 'unconstitutional strikes'; and to punish transgressions by fines. The reaction of the labour movement, to the apparent surprise of ministers, was outraged defiance. Thousands of workers took instantly to the picket lines, including 40,000 in the shipyards and engineering plants of Clydeside. Willie McLean, vice-president of the Scottish miners, openly celebrated the spontaneous outbreak of 'what can be rightly described as political strikes.' The TUC summoned an emergency conference of union executives at Croydon, which declared outright opposition to the punitive clauses in the White Paper.

Once again, the poll position of the STUC in the union conference season made it the focus of attention. The day after the White Paper was published, the general council had begun a special weekend session at Culross which had culminated in a lengthy statement welcoming some parts of the paper but deploring others, including the omission of Donovan proposals like special training provision for women. The statement strove virtuously for a balanced tone, declaring: 'Criticisms of the government are intended to be constructive contributions . . . and should not be regarded as merely defensive postures in response to proposals for unpalatable legislation.' But by the time delegates gathered in Rothesay in mid-April, attitudes on all sides had hardened markedly. The day before delegates debated the White Paper, the Chancellor, Roy Jenkins, had confirmed that the government intended to enact it. Richard Crossman, among others, had been urging Castle to soften her approach, and to give her White Paper 'green edges' – in other words, to make the proposals more conditional. Jenkins's announcement made them sound like a draft Bill.

Perhaps mindful of Jim Callaghan's reception two years earlier, Barbara Castle did not arrive in Rothesay until the day after congress had debated her proposals. She grimly pronounced herself pleased to learn 'that I am responsible for the best debate this congress has had for years.' There had been very little else in the debate to please her. Congress had opened with a forthright warning to ministers from that year's president, the left-wing firefighters' leader Enoch Humphries, that 'a direct clash with the trade union movement grows more menacingly inevitable.' It had then gone on to approve, by a margin of almost two-to-one, two motions declaring unalloyed hostility to the key reforms. Ben Smith of the local government staff, on the general council's behalf, moved the principal composite which called the disciplinary proposals 'the most serious threat to British trade unions for many decades . . . which mean relinquishing the fundamental rights of trade unionists.' An emergency motion from the TGWU called them 'anti-democratic measures aimed at free trade unionism,' and argued that the package should be rejected in its entirety rather than, as the general council motion would imply, regarded as a curate's egg. The speeches were no gentler: nearly forty affiliates registered a wish to speak. Mick McGahey called the White Paper 'infamous' and urged unions to 'fight as they had never fought before' to defeat it. Raymond MacDonald of the TGWU accused the government of courting 'cheap popularity by knocking the unions.' Clive Jenkins, drawing characteristically extravagant parallels with Franco's Spain and Castro's Cuba, urged delegates to make plain that 'they were unwilling to be foot soldiers in Major Barbara's conscript army.' Alex Moffat said it was 'the most vicious attack on the trade union movement' since Baldwin's assault after the General Strike. Alex Kitson reported that opposition now extended to Labour's National Executive Committee, of which he was a member. Agnes McLean of Glasgow Trades Council said the White Paper was 'not the road to heavenly paradise, it [was] the road to Auschwitz and Buchenwald.' So it went on: the only real disagreement was over whether or not to trouble formally acknowledging the more acceptable clauses in the paper. Eventually it was rejected outright.

The next day, Barbara Castle mounted a spirited defence of her document, pointing out that the TUC had managed to welcome 24 of the 27 proposals. But there was no mistaking her resolve to stand by all of them. 'I have not come here this morning as a siren holding out a poison package but as a socialist arguing a coherent philosophy,' she said. 'The time has come for the trade union movement to drop defensive attitudes and to go into the attack, to claim a new status in society instead of being just tolerated as licensed conspirators, which has been the miasmic mistrust which has been hanging over trade union rights for the past half century.' It was a bravura performance, particularly when she took on directly the criticism of the package's compulsion clauses: 'Look, comrades, we are talking about collective bargaining. We are talking about your right to be free to negotiate a bargain, to strike a bargain. The question then that we have to face is whether that bargain, once struck, shall be kept.' By then though, the STUC, and the wider movement, was united beyond persuasion. Enoch Humphries, in his vote of thanks, supposed that Castle was required to take a message back from the congress to the government: 'The message is that there is something wrong with the lens of the projector.'

Within weeks, a quarter of a million union members were

mounting strike action against the Bill and the TUC had convened
its first special congress since the aftermath of the general strike.
In Scotland, the STUC general council found itself struggling to
contain a deluge of unofficial strikes, some staged to protest
against *In Place of Strife*, others to resist the mounting toll of
redundancies and plant closures. Wilson, by now, was looking
for a way out of the havoc Castle's plans had wrought. He had
begun suing for peace with the TUC and the major unions,
seeking a form of words which could give the impression that
the legislation had been deferred because the unions had agreed to
put their houses in order voluntarily. Eventually, in late June, an
agreement of sorts was spatchcocked together in which Solomon
Binding loomed large, and *In Place of Strife*, to Barbara Castle's
enduring wrath, was abandoned. Wilson would continue to
insist that the affair was something better than a climb-down,
though even his own account of it admitted that 'strikes did not
diminish in number, scale or duration following the agreement
of June 1969 . . . .' He might have been tempted to ride out the
tide of union fury, possibly gaining some electoral credit for his
resolve, had he been able to carry his party with him. But the
National Executive Committee had declared itself hostile to the
reforms. Cabinet support had ebbed away steadily. Eventually,
Douglas Houghton, chairman of the Parliamentary Labour Party,
conveyed the bleak news that a majority of Labour MPs were
inclined to vote against the Bill. Wilson thus faced the unattractive
prospect of the measure passing through the Commons with more
Tory than Labour MPs voting for it. He had little choice but to
retreat, greatly damaging the authority of his government. A
year later, having been poorly advised by Jenkins about an
anticipated batch of bright economic indicators, Wilson called a
general election and, to the surprise of most observers including
himself, lost. The Conservatives, now led by Edward Heath, were
back in power.

The more independent policy path struck by the STUC during the
Wilson years eventually led it to an old destination: home rule
for Scotland. The Communists and their broad-left allies, who
had grown in influence in the STUC over the Sixties, were the
guides for this journey, through the track was neither as swift nor
as smooth as retrospection has sometimes chosen to remember.
In the early years of the decade, the movement had not given

the matter much thought. The Communist Party, having blown hot and cold for some years, finally came down on the side of self-determination in 1964, but with no great opportunity to do much about it. The movement's mind was on other things. A Labour government was in office and the SNP, though managing the odd flurry at by-elections (notably at West Lothian in 1962, where Tam Dalyell and Billy Wolfe staged the first of their epic contests), was failing to make any real electoral impact on Scottish politics. Its vote was growing – up from 0.8 per cent in 1959, to 2.4 in 1964 and 5 per cent in 1966 – but scarcely to a degree that commanded much attention (Tony Benn's Diaries reveal that in the run-up to the 1964 election, James Callaghan suddenly awoke in the middle of the night and realised that the committee which had drafted the party's manifesto had forgotten to put in any mention of Scotland!). However, as Scotland began to feel the bite of Wilson's deflationary measures after July 1966, all that abruptly changed.

Three blows to Labour's equanimity fell in quick succession. First came the Glasgow Pollok by-election of March 1967 at which the likeable local vet George Leslie unexpectedly secured more than 28 per cent of the vote for the SNP, enabling the Tories to recapture a seat Labour had held since 1959. Eight months later, a still more unthinkable upset took place. The Hamilton by-election on 2 November saw a flamboyant lawyer, Winifred Ewing, overturn a Labour majority of 10,000 to sweep to victory with 46 per cent of the vote. It was a quite stunning result, and it suddenly established the SNP as a fashionable alternative for disaffected Labour voters (and tactically-voting Tories) in an era susceptible to fashionable alternatives. Labour Party leaders affected to dismiss it as a flash in the pan, but they knew better. At the following May's local elections, the SNP won more than a third of the popular vote and more than 100 council seats. Labour, to its bemusement, even found itself in opposition in Glasgow, where the Tories and SNP formed the administration.

The dowdy world of Scottish politics had suddenly come to life. Scotland's constitutional position had barely registered as an issue over the previous 30 years: for the next 30 it would be the dominant preoccupation of all the Scottish parties. Prior to Hamilton, debate on the governance of Scotland had concentrated on the structure of local authorities: the previous November, the STUC had proposed to the Wheatley Commission a two-tier system of regional and district councils which was closely mirrored in the Commission's eventual proposals. Now, however, it was the possibility of a Scottish parliament that suddenly commanded attention, and it was at this moment that the Communists in the person of Michael McGahey, ever a wise tactician, chose to make their move within their principal vehicle: the STUC. The belief has grown up in the years since then that the STUC threw itself heartily into the home rule cause while Labour, under Willie Ross's stern supervision, continued to cling to its old centralist dogma until the 1974 general elections brought a nationalist surge of such magnitude that it could no longer be ignored. The truth, however, was not quite so simple.

For one thing, Labour was every bit as impressed by the sudden rise in the SNP's fortunes as was the STUC, and many within its ranks were urging a devolutionary course. A whole clutch of pro-devolution motions were tabled for the party's 1968 Scottish conference, and there was also a debate on the issue at the UK conference, where a future Lord Advocate, Ronald King-Murray, proposed the creation of Scottish and Welsh assemblies. Prominent voices in favour included a long-time devolver of great persuasiveness, John P Mackintosh, MP for East Lothian. But Ross was immovable, delivering a thunderous assault on nationalism at the Scottish conference. There was a unity of concern about the SNP threat (though, in the event, the vogue faded somewhat over the next 18 months, and Mrs Ewing lost her seat in 1970), but no unity of response. Most inclined to the view – which was not without substance – that the real problem lay in the government's failure to make good its economic promises to Scotland, and they belaboured it accordingly. The party's Scottish executive set up a working group which, in an intriguing parallel to the Tories' approach in the Eighties and Nineties, beavered away at schemes for administrative devolution and for making Westminster more sensitive to Scottish concerns. The Scottish Select Committee came into being in consequence. Then, in late 1968, the government announced a Royal Commission on the Constitution. Royal commissions were a favourite Wilson device for putting awkward issues on the back-burner, and this one was a response both to nationalist sentiment in Scotland and to a growing band of ministers, led by Dick Crossman, who found an intellectual appeal in devolution. Policy-making in the Labour Party is not a conspicuously dynamic process, but there is no question that wheels did turn in the party's counsels after Hamilton.

The Tories too were watching the nationalist successes with interest. Their slide from favour in Scotland had been precipitous: down from 36 seats to 20 in little more than a decade. Suddenly the SNP had shown a capacity for damaging Labour which Scottish Conservatism seemed to have lost and, as Pollok had shown, it could work to the Tories' advantage. A band of young blades from the liberal wing of the party, where the romantic side to nationalism had periodically exercised a certain charm, formed themselves into something called the Thistle Group, and shortly afterwards came out in favour of a Scottish Parliament with significant powers. They seemed to make little immediate impact on their Scottish elders, who saw no need to deviate from the Unionism of the party's full title, least of all at the behest of unknown youths called Rifkind, Ancram and (Peter) Fraser. Edward Heath, on the other hand, was intrigued by what was going on in Scotland and summoned a member of the party's loyal beerage, Sir William McEwen Younger, to report. Younger recommended an indirectly-elected assembly and Heath startled his Scottish faithful by warmly endorsing the idea at the 1968 Scottish Tory Conference in a speech which afterwards became known, with sardonic intent, as the 'Declaration of Perth'. He announced that the ever-dependable Sir Alec Douglas-Home would draw up a scheme, and in March 1970 a blueprint for an elected, but largely toothless, 'Scottish Convention' was unveiled. This conceit survived as far as the manifesto on which Heath won the 1970 election, but was swiftly forgotten thereafter when it appeared that the nationalist bubble had burst.

So the STUC was not alone in turning its mind to matters constitutional after Mrs Ewing's coup. Neither was it immediately more resolute in seizing the moment. McGahey's motion at Aberdeen in April 1968 was drafted as non-prescriptively as possible to secure the widest possible support. Asserting 'the desire of the Scottish people for a Scottish parliament,' it sought legislation to establish a parliament 'the ultimate form and powers of which should be determined by the Scottish electorate.' McGahey's speech was also crafted to broaden the appeal of the proposition. He invoked the ghosts of sainted devolvers like Keir Hardie and Bob Smillie, drew a careful distinction between 'healthy' nationalism ('love of one's own country, love of one's own people, and pride in their traditional militancy and progressiveness') and chauvinism, and explained why nationalism and internationalism – always an STUC icon – were compatible. 'The best nationalists in Scotland are represented in the STUC and the Scottish Labour movement,' he said. Nor need devolution lead to separation: federalism was an established form of decentralisation perfectly congruous with socialism.

McGahey's motion won wide support on the floor, not least from another formidable left-winger, Hugh Wyper of Glasgow Trades Council, who said it would be folly to allow Scotland's desire for self-determination to be channelled into support for the SNP. But there was a second, very different, motion on home rule on the order paper. The foundry workers moved a some-what confused anti-devolutionary motion which, in extolling the benefits of national negotiation, concluded that 'any attempt to secure total devolution, ie complete separation, would lead directly to a lowering of the living standards of the Scottish people.' This found little favour, but the artful imprecision of McGahey's motion allowed the general council to argue that both be remitted for more detailed consideration. It fell to another Communist, Jimmy Milne, to convey this decision, which he did with little conspicuous enthusiasm. 'We feel that the resolution of the Scottish miners advocates in so general a form the argument for a Scottish parliament that we would have to oppose it,' he said. Significantly, though, the general council opposed the foundry workers' motion, not on the grounds that it too was vague – which it was – but because its wording was 'completely out of sympathy with the present trend of opinion in Scotland.' Moreover, Milne promised that the general council would actively investigate the devolutionary options, prepare a report ahead of the next congress and, if necessary, hold a special conference on the issue. McGahey agreed to remit: the foundry-workers pushed their case to a vote, and lost by a margin of almost seven-to-one. It meant that the STUC seemed to have left Aberdeen once more committed to some sort of home rule for Scotland.

Remitted motions can lead a somewhat ephemeral existence in the STUC. But such was the political turbulence created by Hamilton that letting the matter lie was plainly not an option for the general council. Neither was the STUC by then much disposed to cower before the reprimand Willie Ross had given it after the debate on the McGahey motion, the occasion on which he admonished it for a tendency to become the 'Scottish Trades Union Congrouse.' By the time delegates gathered in Rothesay a year later, the STUC was already preparing its evidence for the Royal Commission on the Constitution, then known as the Crowther Commission but eventually to report as the Kilbrandon Commission in 1973. The general council had also, as promised, produced an interim report. Perhaps surprisingly, given the unfocused nature of the debate at Aberdeen, the report came out forthrightly in favour of a devolved parliament with legislative powers. Even more surprisingly, it was adopted at Rothesay without a vote, and went on to form the core of the STUC's written evidence to Crowther. The contrast with the stolidly unionist evidence submitted by the Scottish Council of the Labour Party burnished the legend of a Labour Party nudged reluctantly towards devolution by the STUC.

In fact, by the time the STUC came to present its oral evidence to Crowther on 20 July 1970, its resolve had distinctly weakened. The legislative parliament of the written submission had become a 'deliberative' assembly of 142 elected members. It would enjoy neither legislative nor fiscal powers of its own, existing principally to supervise the allocation of the Scottish Office budget, and to guide the implementation of Scottish legislation passed by Westminster. An uninspiring analogy was drawn with the way the Scottish officers of UK unions operated. At every opportunity, the oral evidence stressed the STUC's fervent opposition to the break-up of the United Kingdom. The discomfort of the new position was captured in Jimmy Jack's somewhat tortured response on being asked by Crowther whether his starting point was the need to leave the unity of the UK undisturbed: 'For the time being, at any rate; because it is also explicit in our evidence that the basic argument which we advance is one which, when it is met, does imply there might well be a time when we were well off, generating our own new resources, standing on our own two legs and no longer appearing to be on public relief or "on the parish." This would be a different thing and we could, I might say personally and perhaps indiscreetly, at that particular point be hoist with our own petard.' Well, quite.

Two things had happened in the interim to cloud the STUC's constitutional vision. One was the election of a more traditionalist, and more right-wing, general council under the chairmanship of a devo-sceptic, Alex Donnet of the general and municipal workers. More importantly, the political climate had changed. The presentation took place a month after Labour's defeat at the general election. Winifred Ewing had lost Hamilton and, though her avuncular colleague Donald Stewart captured the Western Isles, the SNP momentum seemed to have faltered. At a key by-election in South Ayrshire three months before the general election, the SNP was driven into third place by the Labour candidate, Jim Sillars, who was head of the STUC's organisation and social services department, and destined to lead an unpredictable political career. There was also little doubt that the rift between Wilson and the unions, principally over *In Place of Strife*, had damaged Labour's election chances, and there was a perceived need to close ranks in the face of the new challenge of a Tory government pledged to economic and industrial austerity. For the STUC, the priority was to fight for Scotland's rightful share of a Treasury cake scheduled to shrivel. Constitutional reform therefore slipped a little down the STUC agenda over the next few years, though it would never again vanish entirely from view. For the time being, there were bigger battles to fight.

CHAPTER EIGHT

OF DEVOLUTION AND DISCONTENT

The Heath administration which took office in June 1970 was of rather different stamp from the baleful, cornered, compromising creature, mired in the trenches of class warfare, that it ultimately became. Heath, in those early days, was possessed by the spirit of Selsdon Man, the meritocratic, deregulatory, fiscally ascetic, entrepreneurial, subsidy-hating capitalist invented by a meeting of party panjandrums at the Selsdon Park Hotel, Croydon, early in 1970 (though the name was Harold Wilson's). History would award Margaret Thatcher the distinction, but it was Selsdon Man who led the first real assault on the post-war Butskellite consensus. Public spending would be curbed, taxes cut, and there would be, in the motif of the moment, no more lame duck industries. The kindest thing to say about this agenda is that oppositions often do set out with bold ambitions, most of which, probably fortunately, they fail to implement in government. Selsdon Heath was a creature of the same species as White-hot Technological Wilson. They both started out meaning it.

Selsdon Heath presented the STUC with three swift and monumental challenges. Two were built on familiar territory. The 1971 Industrial Relations Act took up where Barbara Castle had been forced to leave off, in introducing legislative restraints on union activities. It sought to establish the concept, later revived by Margaret Thatcher, of treating unions as corporate bodies which could be held responsible in law for the actions of their members, a principle last enshrined by the Taff Vale judgement. It would provide the STUC with its most distressing internal strife since the 1950s. Second, Heath was determined to curb inflation and public expenditure. But his deflationary strategy lacked both direction and consistency, particularly after the sudden death of his gifted first Chancellor, Iain Macleod. He toyed with free collective bargaining, with fiscal stringency, with tight monetary policy; and, as unemployment climbed from 600,000 to 750,000 during 1971 and inflation rose sharply in its wake, reversed all these approaches. Millions of pounds were pumped back rapidly into the economy by Macleod's successor, Anthony Barber, to create jobs. Statutory control of wages was introduced to curb inflation. The Industry Act of 1972 signalled a willingness to pour government money into industry. The government's evident pliancy gave the unions everything to play for, and would lead to its eventual destruction.

The third, and most direct, challenge for the STUC came to be seen as one of the most significant turns in the meandering strategy of the Heath government. Though the STUC shared in the shock of Labour's 1970 defeat, and in the apprehension about what was to follow, it was in far from despondent mood as Edward Heath took office. In 1971, union organisation exceeded 40 per cent of the Scottish workforce for the first time (it would peak, a decade later, at just over 48 per cent). STUC affiliated membership was fast approaching 900,000, and the 1971 general council report listed no fewer than 182 public bodies on which the STUC was represented. There was, too, a sincere belief afoot, now easily forgotten, that Labour had become what Wilson called the 'natural party of government,' and that Heath was a mere Gothic interlude. Therefore, there was little of the instinct which George Middleton had fostered in the Fifties to work with the prevailing political grain. But the bigger incentive in taking on the government was the perception that battles could be won. In early 1971, Rolls-Royce was bankrupted by its failure to control the development costs of the RB211 aero-engine. Heath, having firmly refused to prevent the insolvency, finally baulked at the threat to one of Britain's most illustrious industrial names. The aero-engine division was separated off from the car group, nationalised, and rescued at heavy cost to the public purse. When, in June 1971, the government refused a vital subsidy to Upper Clyde Shipbuilders and sanctioned the company's liquidation, there was no hesitation among workers at the threatened yards or in the STUC that the decision could and should be contested.

UCS had been born out of trouble, and was destined to be in trouble ever after. It was created in February 1968 in the wake of the Geddes Report, commissioned to see what could be done to halt the endemic decline of British shipbuilding. From building nearly half the ships launched in the world in 1950, British yards' market share had slumped to 6 per cent by the mid-Sixties, and the number of yards on the Clyde had fallen over the same period from 28 to seven. Brand new yards in countries like Germany and Japan outbid and outpaced the under-invested facilities owned by rarely-impressive dynastic families in Britain. There had been some stop-gap remedial measures: in 1965, when the Lithgow family lost patience with the loss-making Fairfield's at Govan, a new joint public-private company with some comparatively advanced ideas about production and industrial relations was created to rescue the yard. But Geddes, and Tony Benn's Shipbuilding Industry Act which flowed from it, brought much more radical reform. The Shipbuilding Industry Board was set up to promote modernisation, and equipped with a £200 million fund to subsidise orders for British yards. Its members included the feisty miners' official, Joe Gormley, and the cultured Anthony Hepper, head of the firm which made Pretty Polly hosiery, who would become chairman of UCS. Clydeside shipbuilding was reorganised into two consortia, based on the Upper and the Lower Clyde. The five yards of UCS – Yarrow's, Stephen's, Connell's, Brown's and Fairfield's – were merged with a £5.5 million government dowry. By the end of UCS's first year, the cash-flow problems that were forever to dog it had already reached the extent where a fresh government injection of £3 million in working capital was required. Further subsidies would follow.

The perpetual shortage of working capital was due both to under-estimation of the yards' needs at the outset of UCS, and to a three-year no lay-offs guarantee, unprecedented in the industry, which the redoubtable Dan McGarvey of the boilermakers had blasted past the inexperienced Hepper. The deal meant that order books had to be kept full at all times to occupy the workforce, with the result that orders were accepted at little or no profit margin and for every conceivable kind of vessel, thus impeding the processes of modernisation and standardisation which were supposed to be the logic of the merger. The yards' suppliers soon formed the habit of insisting on immediate payment for fear that insolvency loomed, which in turn further aggravated the UCS cash-flow difficulties.

By the time Hepper approached Heath's industry minister, John Davies, in June 1971 for a further £6 million grant to keep UCS going, the company had run as short of governmental goodwill as it had of funds. Even Tony Benn had rejected a plea in 1969 to bankroll a five-year guarantee for the yards, and had insisted on a rationalisation programme under new management which was accomplished with some success. But the new government took a chillier view. In its first cautious meeting with Heath's Scottish Secretary, Gordon Campbell, just weeks after the election, the STUC had been told that the new government had supported Labour's interventions to bolster UCS, though it was also unhappy about the 'blanket system' of state subsidy for industry. A year later, when Hepper petitioned Davies, it was the latter instinct which was prevalent. Davies, a former oil executive and director-general of the CBI, had already suspended credit guarantees to shipowners commissioning vessels from the UCS, which meant that shipowners stopped paying for their vessels by instalments as work progressed. Yarrow's had been hived off from the company, its UCS shares bought by Sir Eric Yarrow for £1, so depriving the consortium of its best-equipped yard and one which, though loss-making, occupied a reliable naval niche. Davies had pointedly refused to endorse a prediction from the UCS directors that the remaining yards could eventually become financially viable. He was much influenced by the junior minister responsible for shipbuilding, Nicholas Ridley, who while still in opposition had drawn up a secret plan for the dismemberment of UCS. Ridley's prescription was that Yarrow's be separated off and moved into the Lower Clyde group if it so desired; and that all subsidies to the rest of UCS be stopped. Exercising the talent for tactful language that was to distinguish his career, Ridley wrote: 'We could put in a government "butcher" to cut up UCS and to sell (cheaply) to Lower Clyde and others the assets . . . we should sell the government holding in UCS even for a pittance.'

Hepper's request was refused, and Davies and Heath agreed to put the company into liquidation. There was immediate uproar in the Commons, but the more dramatic intervention came from the 8,500 UCS workers themselves. At the end of July, they announced that they were occupying the yards, and that both the assets and the £90 million of work-in-progress were now under the control of their shop stewards. So began the trade union campaign which was to capture the imagination and sympathy of the public like none before it. It made celebrities of union conveners like Jimmy Reid, Jimmy Airlie and Sammy Barr (who had first suggested the occupation strategy). It turned Reid's gritty slogans – 'no bevvying,' 'the economics of Alice in Wonderland,' 'the right to work,' 'we don't only build ships on the Clyde, we build men' – into catchphrases of an era. Money and support flooded in from around the world: John and Yoko Lennon sent £1,000 and a quantity of roses. It contributed to the resignation of a junior minister – Teddy Taylor – and to a deepening electoral disdain for Edward Heath's government. It established the tactic, copied internationally, of the dignified, disciplined, publicly popular union work-in. Labour, Liberal and Nationalist spokesmen, and some Tories, rallied to the cause, as did performers, clergy and academics, undaunted by the fact that the protest's two best-known leaders, Reid and Airlie, were prominent Communists. And it worked: in February 1972, the government yielded. Ministers announced a £35 million grant to keep three of the yards operational, plus £12 million to ease the sale of the fourth, John Brown's at Clydebank, to the US rigbuilder Marathon. The political consequences were profound. Tessa Blackstone and William Plowden of Heath's think tank, the Central Policy Review Staff, were later to write: 'Ministers' decision, against the CPRS's advice, to save this lamest of lame ducks was the straw in the wind pointing to the gale which before long was to blow the government's industrial strategy entirely inside out.'

The STUC was intimately and enthusiastically involved from the outset. As Davies was being roasted in the Commons during an emergency debate on 15 June 1971, the day after the liquidation announcement, a special train was heading south from Glasgow packed to bursting with Clydeside shop stewards, councillors, union officials and reporters. It had been organised by the STUC, and when the lobby reached London, Heath refused to see the stewards (he later relented) but agreed to meet the STUC instead. That meeting took place the following Monday. The STUC deputation pressed Heath on the 'absolute essentiality' of preserving shipbuilding on the Upper Clyde, but emerged to describe the meeting as fruitless. On the same day, 100,000 workers across Clydeside were voting to down tools in 48 hours' time to support the biggest demonstration seen in Glasgow since the General Strike. Tony Benn, Willie Ross and Vic Feather, the TUC general secretary, joined Jimmy Jack, Jimmy Milne (now Jack's deputy) and the UCS stewards in leading the 40,000-strong march to Glasgow Green. By then, the STUC general council was in continuous session, and maintaining close liaison with Airlie and the other stewards. One of its first decisions was to convene a special recall congress to be held on 16 August at Partick Burgh Hall. The STUC swiftly became the recognised touchstone for politicians wanting to test out possible initiatives. It was among the first ports of call for both John Davies and Harold Wilson when they paid visits to Clydeside in early August, though Heath during an embattled sojourn to Glasgow rather unwisely refused to meet Kitson, who duly took up position with a coterie of gleeful reporters and nervous Downing Street aides outside the Prime Minister's hotel suite and roared his resentment at the slight to the STUC.

The recall conference was the first in the STUC's history, as Jack remarked in a speech that rang with portent. Normal standing orders were waived to permit participation by interested parties who were not delegates, including Jimmy Reid. But its significance ran deeper than that. First, it was used as a testing ground for putative solutions to the UCS crisis. The Government had set up a committee of industrialists – the 'Four Wise Men' – after the liquidation announcement to report on what might be salvaged: the STUC was among those which gave evidence to it. The committee's recommendations, accepted by Davies, were that Brown's and Connell's close, while an attempt, no more, be made to save Fairfield's and Stephen's through manning reductions, new productivity agreements, a reformed management structure and more 'realistic' wage rates. That formula was plainly unacceptable to the Labour movement, and even the liquidator disagreed with the committee's gloomy assessment of the yards' prospects. But no agreed alternative was on offer. Benn, having been the architect of the post-Geddes structure, was now arguing that the entire shipbuilding industry should be fully nationalised. Wilson proposed that the Government take over financial responsibility for the yards and pay them to build ships for it 'on spec' which the government would then sell on profitably when – if – demand rose. A widely-circulated plan from a management consultant for

Brown's and Connell's to be phased out over five years while their workers underwent retraining and redeployment aroused cautious interest from the stewards. Now Feather, whose support for the UCS campaign had gone far beyond the TUC's normal level of interest in Scottish issues, turned up at Partick with another proposal: the creation of a government-funded Clydeside Development Authority, which would both take over ownership of the UCS and develop alternative industry into which shipyard workers could be transferred. This plan won broad support from both delegates and stewards, and became a focus of the campaign. But the government rejected it.

The Partick congress provided an valuable service to the UCS campaign. Coming at the end of the first euphoric fortnight of occupation, two weeks in which all those involved had been astonished by the breadth of public support, the congress afforded the first opportunity to sit down together and take calm stock of where the high-octane vehicle in which they had suddenly found themselves was heading. But it also, rather more enduringly, performed the same function for the STUC itself. The Wilson years had, as we have seen, devalued the STUC's role as a pillar of the all-purpose Scottish lobby, and the STUC had been unable to adapt its style in any very convincing way to changed circumstance. The UCS campaign, and its coalescence at the special congress, pointed the way to a new method of operating, and one that would sustain the STUC through the next quarter century. An industrial issue had been translated from a sectional to a Scottish grievance. What it showed was that the broad consensus which it had been possible to assemble in pursuit of investment could also be mobilised in as broad, and often a broader, form as an instrument of protest.

In the wake of Partick, the general council set in motion two initiatives that firmly consolidated this role. From today's perspective, it is hard not to gape at the presumptuousness. First, it established a Committee of Inquiry into the UCS affair, empowered to summon witnesses and take evidence, like a cross between a Royal Commission and a parliamentary select committee. The committee was composed with ostentatious balance: an academic, Professor Raymond Illsley of Aberdeen; a distinguished trade unionist, Frank Cousins; and an industrialist, General Motors' Scottish managing director, George Perry. Among the witnesses who gave evidence were leading figures of UCS management like

Sir Iain Stewart and Kenneth Douglas, politicians like Tony Benn, and sundry economists, community workers and trade unionists. It was, as ever, Jimmy Reid who provided the *coup de théâtre*, presenting the committee with leaked documentary evidence of how the liquidation had begun with the Ridley Plan. The essence of the plan had already been published by the *Guardian*, but Reid's documents added a pungent whiff of treachery by revealing the secret discussions Ridley had held with shipyard managers in preparing his paper. This disclosure had a bigger impact than the committee's report itself, which predictably came out against the yard closures. But the report did lend valuable empirical ammunition to the campaign, for example by analysing the true cost to the public purse of making a worker redundant in an area of high unemployment like Clydebank.

The second initiative was, if anything, still more audacious. Debate at Partick had waged far beyond the immediate threat to the UCS, and had linked that highly visible campaign to the difficulties facing a whole range of Scottish industries, and to concurrent economic issues like the demand for an ore terminal at Hunterston. It was a linkage which broadened still further the consensus behind the stewards' campaign. UCS became the metaphor for a more general industrial and economic jeopardy, which would in turn become the favourite metaphor for the assertion of Scottish political grievance. To its credit, the general council seems to have grasped immediately the potential this created for the STUC to become, if not quite the 'spokesman for Scotland' it had claimed to be in its evidence to Donovan, at least the mechanism that enabled Scotland to speak for itself with a coherent voice. Meeting in October 1971, just after publication of the Committee of Inquiry report, the general council decided to convene a 'Scottish Assembly' the following February at which the widest achievable representative gathering of opinion would debate Scottish unemployment and explore the scope for a common economic strategy.

It was a quite remarkable event. The general council, having prepared the ground carefully, sent out some 700 invitations, and more than 1,500 people gathered in Edinburgh's Usher Hall on St Valentine's Day, 1972. They represented as broad a spectrum of Scottish civic life as had ever been assembled: all the political parties took part, as did the SCDI, the churches, the universities (staff and students), the local authorities, CBI

Scotland, the Chambers of Commerce and, of course, trade union and trades council delegates. An 18–strong commission, representing the spread of participating bodies, was elected to take forward the process through an agreed charter of broad economic principles, and to make direct representations on Scotland's behalf to Whitehall. It was chaired by the STUC president, Raymond MacDonald. But the aspect of the day to linger longest in most minds was the strength of feeling which emerged from the floor in favour of vesting greater control over Scottish affairs in Scotland. Though the STUC itself still lacked any very precise policy on home rule, Jimmy Jack spoke out strongly in favour of what he predicted would be 'a workers' parliament.' Still more surprisingly, reluctant devolvers like John Boyd, the engineering workers' general secretary, and Hamish Grant of CBI Scotland declared themselves moved by the intensity of the sentiments expressed, and resolved to look afresh at the case for self-determination.

In one sense, the assembly turned out to be anti-climactic. A further gathering the following year, convened by the commission rather than by the STUC, drew a far smaller and narrower attendance, and the initiative petered out. A number of the participating bodies had begun to take cold feet. Prominent among them was the Labour Party, which had by now set up a sub-committee of its own on home rule that would shortly produce a report rejecting a Scottish parliament in favour of greater administrative devolution. Labour was watching horrified as the polls reported an unmistakable revival in support for the SNP, buoyed both by laying populist claim to the vast reserves of oil now being proven off Scotland's shores, and by exploiting the ambiguities that EEC entry, to which Heath was devoting concentrated attention (and over which Labour was hopelessly split), would create in the relationship between Scotland and Westminster. During the course of 1973 Labour's worst fears began to be realised. First, the SNP came close to winning a by-election in March in Dundee East; then, in November, Margo MacDonald overturned Labour's 16,000 majority to take Govan. Some of the same unease was surfacing in the STUC itself. The self-congratulatory mood at the 1972 congress in Dunoon in the wake of the Government's retreat on the UCS was slightly soured by complaints from the Left, led by the draughtsmen, that the STUC's heady indulgence in national politics was leading it to neglect grassroots activism of just the sort that had won a future for the UCS yards. A year later, at Aberdeen, delegates passed a motion, on Jimmy Jack's prompting, expressing concern that the assembly project was being hi-jacked by the SNP.

Yet the UCS campaign and the assembly had, in another sense, pre-empted the SNP upsurge by putting 'the Scottish issue' back at the top of the agenda and in a way which ensured that it was not the sole preserve of the Nationalists. The STUC's own dedication to the cause of a Scottish Parliament was now irrevocable, and it provoked a growing estrangement with Labour's Scottish Council. The belief grew up, or was affected, within Labour's Scottish high command that the STUC had been bounced into its inconvenient devolutionary fervour by the undue influence of Communists and fellow-travellers. In due course, the finger of suspicion stretched as far as people like Alex Kitson, a key figure certainly in developing home rule enthusiasm within the Union movement, but one who also happened to be a member of Labour's National Executive Committee and would later become party chairman.

After July 1971, Labour allowed its liaison committee with the STUC to fall into disuse, and when the STUC tried to revive it the party insisted on the condition that all those taking part on behalf of the general council must be eligible for Labour Party membership. The general council refused, and for several years the two bodies communicated only on an informal and ad hoc basis. Relations did begin to thaw somewhat after Labour converted to the devolutionary cause, and a looser liaison mechanism was established in 1975, in which the STUC, Scottish Labour Executive and the party's Scottish MPs met quarterly. It became the still more broadly-based Campaign Co-ordinating Committee after the 1983 general election, though its status fluctuates – or so STUC critics claim – according to the enthusiasm of successive Labour Scottish leaders for consultation with the STUC or anybody else. Ironically enough, much of the credit for the thaw went, by common accord, to a Communist, Jimmy Milne, who succeeded as STUC general secretary when Jimmy Jack retired in December 1975.

The divisions reached their height in October 1973 when the Kilbrandon Commission, established all those years before by Harold Wilson to stifle the home rule flame, re-ignited it by coming out in favour of a legislative Scottish parliament to take over the work of the Scottish Office. The STUC welcomed Kilbrandon, with minor reservations: it disagreed with the proposed downgrading of the Scottish Secretary's Cabinet rank, the suggested reduction in Scotland's Westminster representation, and the feasibility of electing the parliament by proportional representation while Westminster and council elections remained unreformed. By contrast, Labour's Scottish council, having issued its own anti-devolutionary paper one day ahead of the report, fastened balefully on the potential loss of Westminster influence. Ross joked rashly that Kilbrandon meant 'kill-devolution,' and told the 1974 STUC congress: 'It offers no solution. There was no authoritative, decisive suggestion coming from this body. Far from it.' But, by then, Labour was poised between two 1974 general elections in which the SNP vote would rise from 22 to over 30 per cent. Harold Wilson and his colleagues at Westminster had come to realise the electoral price the party as a whole was paying for its Scottish council's devolutionary obduracy, and within weeks Ross had been compelled into a grudging change of tack. It was a coercive process in which the STUC was to play an important part.

If the STUC had become preoccupied with the mischief of politics, it was not for want of industrial issues. The week that opened with the occupation of John Brown's at Clydebank ended with the Industrial Relations Act receiving the Royal Assent. The demonstrations in support of the UCS in Scotland had been matched elsewhere in the country by crowds of even greater proportions – an estimated 200,000, the biggest protest since the Chartists, and until the poll tax, paralysed central London on 21 February 1971 – chanting 'Kill the Bill.' But they had not killed it, and it was now law.

It was law of a form that would simultaneously unite trade unionists against the government and turn them against each other as few statutes had previously done. In some respects, it started from the same premise as *In Place of Strife*, by seeking to eradicate the unofficial action which, on Heath's calculation, by now constituted 90 per cent of the strikes that took place. Like *In Place of Strife*, it almost certainly caused more unofficial – and official – disruption than it curbed, with much of the unofficial action being organised through a Communist-inspired network of shop stewards, the Liaison Committee for the Defence of Trade

Unions. Harold Wilson was pleased to tell the 1973 STUC congress in Aberdeen that the 24 million working days lost to strikes in 1972 alone were roughly equivalent to the total number lost in five years and eight months of his Labour governments, and that in two and a half years of the Heath administration nearly 46 million days had been lost.

The legislation made the legal immunities protecting trade union action conditional on unions registering under the Act, which required them to submit their rulebooks for official approval. It introduced a rigorous disciplinary code, enforced through penalties applied by a new Industrial Relations Court on activities which fell outwith its prescriptions. The notions of a cooling-off period and compulsory strike ballots were revived, both of them enforceable on government application to the court. Unions were to be held accountable nationally for the actions of their local representatives, on pain of heavy fines and sequestration of assets.

Though much preoccupied with UCS, the STUC had played an energetic part in the campaign against the reforms. On the day the initial White Paper was published, Jack declared it 'even more obnoxious than trade unionists had expected' and predicted that it was 'likely to lead to even more bitterness and strife than was experienced over the Labour government's proposals two years ago.' That winter the STUC organised 'Stop the Bill' rallies in all the Scottish cities, culminating in a 15,000-strong rally at Green's Playhouse in Glasgow addressed by Vic Feather. Jack organised briefings for union officials throughout Scotland on the implications of the measures. The general council wrote in protest to the Employment Secretary, Robert Carr, eliciting the deliciously unctuous response that 'the government believes the requirements to be perfectly reasonable and no more than a reflection of standards already set by the best unions and the STUC . . . .'

But, for all that endeavour, the policy lead came from London. The TUC, after some hesitation, decided at a special congress in Croydon in March 1971 not to authorise a campaign of industrial action against the legislation, though it would later bring out 1.6 million workers for a one-day protest strike on 1 May 1973, supported by the STUC. Instead, Croydon adopted the twin-pronged strategy of a nationwide publicity campaign and a policy of non-registration. It also decided that trade union representatives should withdraw from the industrial relations commission and the industrial tribunals system, and refuse to nominate members to serve on the new court. The following month, the STUC in Aberdeen, though going further than the TUC by approving the principle of workplace action against the legislation, essentially replicated these decisions, with the implication – formalised a year later in Dunoon – that it would enforce them through its own disciplinary procedures. Both congresses thereby created several years of internal acrimony for themselves.

The union campaign found unlikely allies in many employers who, not for the last time, resented having placid relations with their workforces undermined by populist legislation, and readily agreed to the insertion in agreements of what became known as the TINA LEA clause (standing for, This Is Not A Legally Enforceable Agreement). Later, in 1973, a group of anonymous employers even paid a £47,000 fine imposed on the engineering union by the Industrial Relations Court so as to purge the union's contempt, prevent sequestration of its assets, and avoid a national stoppage.

But though the unions were as one in thinking the legislation deplorable, the strategy of defiance was much less conducive to unity. Non-registration was not as simple a recourse as it sounded. For one thing, it exposed individual unions to potential insolvency: the TGWU, for one, put its £22 million assets at risk by refusing to pay a £55,000 Industrial Relations Court fine. Many unions were also already registered under earlier legislation, the Friendly Societies Act, which bestowed various rights. Unless they actively deregistered from that, their registration was automatically transferred under the new legislation. It was a problem that was to cost both the TUC and the STUC, temporarily but traumatically, a number of affiliations. When the Industrial Relations Act became law, the TUC calculated that 72 of its affiliates were committed to non-registration, 24 still thinking about it and 22 resolved to register: which put the affiliation of nearly three million members in jeopardy. For the STUC the problem was on a smaller scale, but in some respects more distressing. There were endless negotiations to persuade affiliates against registration, but by March 1973, when the general council concluded that the prevarication must stop, 12 STUC affiliates were registered and another, the National Graphical Association, had already disaffiliated after its members balloted for registration.

The miscreants included a couple of big unions, the health service employees and the seamen, and also Scotland's biggest teaching union, the Educational Institute of Scotland, which had only recently voted to affiliate to the STUC after years of internal argument. EIS delegates patiently explained their dilemma in a pained debate at Dunoon. The union had decided to register before it decided to affiliate. At that point, the TUC had adopted a non-registration policy, but the STUC had not, and the EIS was not affiliating to the TUC. STUC affiliation had divided the union, and a deregistration instruction now might reverse the decision. The teachers appealed for 'a little tolerance and understanding.'

The general council did its best. But finally it felt obliged to set a deadline of 31 July for compliance with non-registration. Only one union, the power engineers, backed down. Six – the EIS, the Co-operative officials, the bakers, the actors' union Equity, the Scottish Further Education Association and the seamen – were disaffiliated. The bank employees, the health service workers, the scalemakers, the Forfar Factory Workers' Union, and the power-loom overlookers all followed the example of the NGA and decided not to affiliate for 1973–74. STUC affiliation in 1974 was, in consequence, more than 60,000 down on the previous year's figure. In due course, a couple of unions changed policy and reaffiliated, but most stayed out until the return of a Labour government brought the repeal of the Act.

Edward Heath's relationship with the unions started calamitously and got worse. Jack Jones's memoirs unexpectedly portray a Prime Minister who seems to have treated union leaders with somewhat greater courtesy than he was always able to muster towards his Cabinet colleagues, yet personal civility did nothing to retrieve his policy from abject failure. By the time the Industrial Relations Bill came before the Commons, Heath had already twice declared a state of emergency in response to strikes by the dockers and the power engineers, as well as ordering troops to clear refuse left uncollected in a string of disputes involving local government workers. Power cuts were fast becoming established in the public's mind as the distinctive motif of his administration. More importantly, the outcomes of the disputes were variable enough to make strike action well worth a try: the postal workers, out for seven weeks, gained very little, while the power engineers secured a much better settlement than had been on offer.

Two disputes in early 1972 exemplified the critical weakness of both the government and its policy. The first began in January, when the miners launched their first national strike since 1926. It was a testing time for the union as well as for the government. Joe Gormley had just been elected national president, beating Mick McGahey, the Scottish miners' president, by a hefty 25,000 votes. Gormley had won in part because of a superior election machine, in part because the miners, who had a tradition of political balance at the top of their union, already had a left-wing Scot, Lawrence Daly, as general secretary. In an era of growing union assertiveness, everyone had something to prove. The government, having set a pay rise 'guideline' of 8 per cent, started out determined to resist the miners' wage claim of between 35 and 47 per cent, to which the Coal Board had responded by offering 7.9. Gormley, despite his unease at the narrow ballot margin for the strike (58.8 per cent), was determined to establish his authority by winning, and had wooed the left by declaring during his presidency campaign that miners deserved to be the best-paid workers in the country. The pay claim, incidentally, had started life in a motion from the branch at Woolley colliery in Yorkshire, which was led by a little-known militant called Arthur Scargill. It had become national policy at the union's 1971 conference in Aberdeen.

Both the STUC and the TUC urged the government to look on the miners as a special case, whose dirty and dangerous job merited a substantive advance in real pay levels. The strike was solid: all 280,000 miners were out, and the union was thus able to direct its pickets away from the pit gates to prevent coal movements elsewhere. A two-month overtime ban had already helped run down coal stocks over a notably cold winter. The government responded with the now familiar state of emergency and interruptions to the electricity supply. The miners struck back with a stunningly effective tactic: the flying mass picket. It took a thousand miners less than an hour to close Ipswich docks, and a token presence thereafter to keep them closed. The turning point came in early February when a mass picket led by Scargill closed Britain's biggest coke stockpile, the Gas Board's Saltley depot in Birmingham, from which up to a thousand lorries a day ferried supplies to all corners of the country. By now, the miners had the active support of other unions, and on the day Saltley was closed local strikes by the TGWU and AUEW swelled the ranks of picketing miners to over 10,000. Scargill was later to call it the happiest day of his life. Heath was less happy, and a few days later he caved in by agreeing to an inquiry under Lord Wilberforce into the miners' case. Wilberforce's formula, hurried into print on 18 February, gave the miners an average 18.5 per cent, and that same day the government accepted it. By the time Heath left office, the miners had climbed from 13th place to first in the league table of manual workers' wages. For the moment, what counted was that they had humiliated the government and holed its pay policy.

A few weeks later, a work-to-rule by the railway workers inflicted similar damage on one of the founding theories of the Industrial Relations Act. Ministers were convinced that the penal powers in the legislation would be needed only as an initial deterrent, and that the real restraint on militancy would come from empowering grassroots union members by enforcing cooling-off periods and pre-strike ballots. So, as conflict grew on the railways, the government applied successfully to the Industrial Relations Court for a 14-day cooling-off period, and the union complied. Then the government applied to the court, again successfully, for an order that the union ballot its members before continuing the action. The union did, and the work-to-rule secured a majority of more than 80 per cent. Once again, a pay rise well above the government's guidelines was agreed.

Despite the difficulties which non-registration was causing the unions, it was plain that Heath's industrial policy, and the authority of his government, were by now in shards. The Rolls-Royce and UCS rescues had demolished the government's will to let market forces take care of inefficient capacity. The miners and others had confounded its promise to control wage inflation by voluntary restraint. Mass unemployment had forced it to abandon its belief in tight money, and price inflation was soaring. The Industrial Relations Act had proved neither salutary nor pacific. In the spring of 1972, Heath launched a last-ditch attempt to persuade the unions, on threat of statutory restraint, to adopt a structured voluntary incomes policy. It failed. The STUC's congress, held in April in Dunoon, once again set the tone for the movement's response when it unanimously adopted a motion rejecting any form of incomes policy. The resolution was propelled by a burst of vintage McGahey, which included the tart recollection that the STUC had been just as forthright in rejecting a Labour incomes policy as advocated at the 1965 congress by George Brown, 'now belatedly left us for another place' (Brown, having lost his Belper seat in 1970, had been ennobled as Lord George-Brown). Delegates followed up with a warning to the Labour Party not to imagine, if and when it returned to office, that it could cosily agree an incomes policy with the TUC and expect it to be obeyed. The general council persuaded congress to remit that motion, but the point had been made.

There was no option left for Heath but to try to win the confrontation he had failed to prevent. On 6 November 1972 he announced that he would be enforcing a statutory incomes policy by way of a Counter Inflation Act, which became law early in 1973. The Act set up a new pay board and a price commission, empowered to control wage and price rises over a three-year period. There was an immediate reaction from the unions. The civil servants embarked on their first ever national strike, and there were stoppages in the hospitals and elsewhere. The flames were fanned by jail sentences of two and three years imposed on building workers in Shrewsbury who had been convicted of picket offences under the conspiracy laws. The STUC general council condemned the severity of the sentences and offered financial support, though the pickets' union, UCATT, replied that there were legal barriers to accepting it. John Henry of Edinburgh Trades Council, who later became STUC deputy general secretary, remarked however that the courts' recourse to a century-old statute to convict the pickets had confirmed the ineffectiveness of the Industrial Relations Act.

By now an atmosphere of almost permanent adversity had settled on the country, which was deepened by external stimuli. The outbreak of the Yom Kippur War on 6 October was followed by a 200 per cent increase in the price of crude oil imposed by the Organisation of Petroleum Exporting Countries, OPEC. Oil was suddenly both in short supply and prohibitively expensive: Britain's trade deficit rocketed from £909 million in 1973 to £3.54 billion in 1974. The government, denied even sufficient respite to savour the fulfilment of Heath's personal ambition to take Britain into the EEC, was forced to institute fuel efficiency measures, knowing full well that the conditions strengthened the hands of the energy unions. A strike by the power engineers set the now familiar round of power cuts in motion, and the government hastened to settle the dispute. But the miners were another matter. Heath's pay policy was by now into its third phase, a 7 per cent norm. The miners were committed to a claim of 35 per cent. The government authorised the Coal Board to offer slightly over the norm, in fictitious deference to the miners' 'unsocial hours', but was unwilling to meet the union's ambition to achieve real advances in its members' living standards. William Whitelaw, the government's affable troubleshooter, began a series of informal meetings with Gormley, Daly and McGahey, but was unable to mediate. On 8 November, the NUM executive sanctioned an overtime ban, to begin four days later. The day after it started, Heath declared a state of emergency designed, it seemed at the time, to heighten the public's sense of crisis: street lights were switched off, and television went off the air at 10.30pm. A month later, he raised the stakes dramatically by announcing in a memorably grim broadcast that the country was to be put on to a three-day working week to conserve energy.

If the aim was to browbeat other unions to talk the miners into surrender, it had negligible effect. Both sides, government and unions, by now saw themselves lined up in a historic confrontation and there was little disunity. The STUC general council organised protest meetings in 18 Scottish cities against the pay policy and in support of both the miners and the power workers. At the biggest demonstration. 7,000 trade unionists marched through Edinburgh on 27 January 1974, and 2,300 crammed the Usher Hall to hear defiant speeches from Jack, McGahey and Daly. The general council distributed 700,000 leaflets throughout Scotland in the course of the meetings, and after the three-day week was announced, produced a further half million leaflets under the headline: 'Don't Blame the Miners.' Trade unionists, said the leaflet, 'must appreciate that a defeat for the miners is a defeat for every working man and woman in Britain.' The TUC offered early in January to ensure that other unions would not try to match any exceptional increase awarded to the miners, though it was never clear how this undertaking would have been delivered. In any event, the miners balloted their members on a strike. The result, announced on 4 February, was an 81 per cent majority for action. Three days later, Heath called a general election: the theme – who governs?

The February 1974 election was an unpleasant affair, with an ambiguous outcome. The Tories won the largest share of the popular vote, but five seats fewer than Labour. To the question 'who governs?' the country had not answered 'the trade unions.' But neither had it answered 'Edward Heath.' The biggest beneficiaries were actually the Liberals whose vote rose to 20 per cent, though the electoral system translated that into just 14 seats. Heath spent a miserable weekend trying to talk them into coalition, and then resigned. Harold Wilson was back in Number 10, though at the head of a minority government. When the inevitable second general election followed in October, he managed to increase that to a working majority of just four. The natural party of government was destined to cling to office by the skin of its teeth.

The STUC had played its full part in the blasting of Heath but, UCS aside, it was not a leading part. The physics of the corporate state operated on the reverse principle to centrifugal force: government, labour and capital were drawn together in London. The influence which unions now exercised on public policy worked by centralised negotiation. That trend might have been expected to intensify under a Labour government dedicated to partnership with the unions; and, indeed, as Wilson and Callaghan were forced to edge steadily into their own version of prices and incomes policy, so it did. But the electoral arithmetic which had given Wilson his tenuous grasp on office had also given him a mighty Scottish problem; and one consequence of that was to push the STUC into the limelight.

By October 1974, the one seat which the SNP had won in 1970 had become 11; the much-hyped football team. The team had been borne to victory on a slogan whose simple emotional appeal would have been a credit to any football terracing: 'It's Scotland's Oil.' The STUC's campaign literature for the elections was focused on trying to persuade working class electors that voting SNP was a 'wasted vote' which could only help the Tories, but its impact was limited. Most of the SNP seats, certainly, had been won from the Tories (including Gordon Campbell's, which had fallen to Winnie Ewing) but a 30 per cent share of the vote in Labour's Scottish heartland was a phenomenon that Wilson could not afford to ignore. Preoccupied as he was by the tribulations of minority government (it took several attempts to rub the Industrial Relations Act off the statute book), Scotland preyed heavily on his mind during those spring and summer months of 1974. The SNP advance had demonstrated both the vulnerability of Labour's vote in Scotland to the lure of home rule (private polling for the National Executive Committee reckoned 13 Scottish Labour seats to be at risk), and the symbolic potency of the oil which would start to flow ashore the following year.

Wilson needed to get Scotland right, and quickly. He needed to get the party's devolution policy fixed, whatever Willie Ross might say, and he needed to convince Scotland that its economic welfare would be well looked after even as the oil revenues were pumped purposefully into the Treasury. 'Oil is no panacea for Scotland's industrial and economic problems,' Ross had told the STUC at Rothesay weeks after the first 1974 election. But that was not what Scotland wanted to hear as it watched the rigs being towed into place off the Grampian coast. Two years earlier, the STUC congress had unanimously approved a motion from Aberdeen Trades Council demanding that a hefty share of the revenues be directed to 'financing substantial new government investment in Scottish industry,' an objective it would pursue doggedly with the new Labour government, and the STUC's election literature in 1974 called for oil to be nationalised. Calculatedly and swiftly, Wilson moved to realign his party with the mood that the SNP had so deftly caught.

With his Scottish colleagues still unhappy and divided about devolution, it was the STUC, staunch in the cause, which seemed more closely attuned to what Wilson believed needed to be done. During the course of the February election campaign, he had privately suggested to Jack that the STUC should come and see him once he was back in power to discuss a range of Scottish issues. It is far from clear that the STUC realised quite what was afoot. When a general council deputation went to see Wilson on 21 March 1974, less than three weeks after he had taken office, its principal objective was to plead for government help to save jobs following the closure of the *Scottish Daily Express* operation in Glasgow (both Jack and Milne would have a close involvement in the doomed campaign to raise a viable co-operative, the *Scottish Daily News*, from the ashes). But Wilson swiftly turned the discussion to devolution. Pointedly, he told them that the door to Number 10 was always open to them: any time they had something to suggest, they were welcome. He also proclaimed, a tad extravagantly, that 'the Labour Party could not have even formed a minority government had it not been for the activities of such as the Scottish TUC.'

Knowing time was not on his side, Wilson had begun the policy shift. Undeterred by an acrimonious debate, culminating in an awkward fudge, at Labour's Scottish conference a month after the February election, and by Ross's 'kill-devolution' speech at Rothesay the month after that, Wilson had promised a consultative paper on devolution by the time of the Queen's Speech. It appeared in May, and took the form of a non-committal list of sundry options for reform. It was, to all purposes, a blank page and the STUC, along with Labour devolvers like Harry Ewing, hastened to fill it. The general council submitted a detailed paper which enthusiastically backed Kilbrandon's advocacy of a legislative assembly. It came out against significant revenue-raising powers, though saw some scope for varying minor taxes like motor licence fees; it endorsed Kilbrandon's idea of an Exchequer Board independent of Whitehall to decide Scotland and Wales's fair share of resources; it opposed the Kilbrandon proposals for a Westminster veto on assembly legislation, for proportional representation, and for a reduction in Scotland's Westminster representation; it sought assurances (to quell persistent disquiet in the civil service unions) that pay and conditions for public servants would remain uniform throughout the UK; and, more daringly, it demanded a 'sizeable' share of the oil revenues to be used by a Scottish Development Agency, chiefly responsible to the assembly, to restructure the Scottish economy.

There followed a richly comic interlude, which can have done the STUC's relative credibility no harm in Wilson's eyes. In June the Scottish Labour Executive met, supposedly to endorse the pro-devolution policy which a sceptical Cabinet had now been persuaded to support. But most of the executive played truant to watch Scotland draw with Yugoslavia in the soccer World Cup. The few who showed up turned out to have an anti-devolutionary majority, and the rump executive duly voted down every option in the consultative paper. When the STUC general council bowled along to St Andrew's House a month later, on 19 July, to expand on its proposals, it found Willie Ross is less than rosy humour. Eight days earlier, the government had announced that it would create a Scottish Development Agency, and the STUC plainly saw the tide running its way. Earnestly, Jimmy Jack explained the importance of the assembly being able to determine its own budget priorities and to guide Scotland's economic destiny. Ross, however, was interested primarily in talking about the bits of

Kilbrandon the STUC had rejected, tossing in for good measure some reservations about the Exchequer Board idea and about the post-devolutionary voting rights of Scottish MPs at Westminster – the issue which Tam Dalyell would later patent as the 'West Lothian Question'. Wilson, on the other hand, was not to be deterred.

Willie Ross never lacked in party loyalty nor in his appreciation of the principle of collective ministerial responsibility. Wilson knew that Ross would toe the line, solidly if not quite graciously, once the Cabinet was persuaded to the cause. But the Scottish party was plainly another matter. Wilson, intent on calling another election at the earliest opportunity, now moved shrewdly to bring Labour's Scots to heel. He ordered a special Scottish conference to be held in August at the Co-operative Hall in Glasgow's Dalintober Street and quietly enlisted Alex Kitson, whose motion had won over the UK executive to devolution in July, to see to the vote. Kitson, fixer *par excellence*, did the business. Come the day, the key union votes stacked up neatly in favour of an elected legislative assembly. Even Alex Donnet had been cajoled into casting the General and Municipal's vote on the side of constitutional change, which he did with a rueful speech about the need to pay whatever the price was of ensuring Labour's re-election. It was enough to swamp the party's anti-devolvers though not, as would come back to haunt the devolution trail, to quell their hostility. Labour could now go into the forthcoming general election committed, body if not soul, to home rule for Scotland. It had been quite a summer.

Barely had the dust settled before Wilson published a Green Paper, *Democracy and Devolution – Proposals for Scotland and Wales*, which broadly endorsed the Kilbrandon scheme, though with a conspicuous lack of detail. The STUC general council warmly welcomed it, as well it might, and followed up with a leaflet at the October election which said: 'We still believe that it is essential, if we in Scotland are to shape our future and create the kind of Scotland we desire, that an elected Scottish legislative assembly is backed by the Labour Party and [that], if elected, they are committed to bring this about.' As soon as the election was over, Wilson appointed Harry Ewing as a Scottish Office minister with special responsibility for devolution (an appointment about which Ross was reportedly informed rather late in the day), and set up a devolution unit in the Cabinet Office, headed by the Lord

President, Ted Short. Short's task was to supply the detail which haste and election circumspection had omitted.

By now the STUC saw itself, with every governmental encouragement, as a full partner in the great endeavour. It was to be a brief but exhilarating partnership. Wilson, Michael Foot and Tony Benn had all taken time off from election campaigning in Glasgow to meet the STUC general council. In January 1975 the general council set up an industrious sub-committee to work on the small print of the scheme. By the end of the following month, it had amassed enough material to use the open door at Number 10, and two days of meetings took place with Wilson and the ministerial devolution team. It was at this meeting that Wilson made the astonishing proposal that there should be an annual 'summit' between the Prime Minister and the STUC to review the state of Scotland. In the event, he was to resign a year later and his successor, Jim Callaghan, dropped the idea after one, much postponed, meeting in December 1976. Meanwhile, the sub-committee's labours had nudged STUC policy further down the road of decentralisation, particularly in relation to economic powers. In part this reflected the troubles besetting a number of important Scottish employers at the time: Hoover at Cambuslang, Chrysler at Linwood, the British Steel Corporation, Ferranti. The STUC was now insistent that, in order to focus on these sorts of problems, both the SDA and the HIDB must be made fully responsible to the assembly, rather than to Westminster. Control over the Scottish universities should likewise pass from the Department of Education to the assembly. The first assembly elections should be held in early 1977.

This was an ambitious agenda, but the degree of fine detail which accompanied it plainly impressed Wilson, because less than three weeks later, on 17 and 18 March, an extraordinary, and wholly unique, event took place. The Prime Minister brought no fewer than seven senior ministers to Scotland for two days of consultation with the STUC. Borne along by their leader's new enthusiasm for the wisdom of Scottish trade unionism, the likes of Eric Varley, Michael Foot, Ted Short and Willie Ross sat dutifully through a programme of STUC tutorials on the state of the Scottish coal and steel industries, the onshore jobs potential of North Sea oil, the parameters of the SDA and the impact on Scotland's poorer regions of stringency in social spending. But the main item on the menu was devolution, and Wilson took his leave promising that a legislative assembly would be delivered at the earliest possible moment. In his retirement speech to congress the following month, Jimmy Jack declared: 'The glory of the Scottish TUC lies much more ahead of it than behind it.' His optimism was understandable. But Wilson's visit turned out to be the high water mark of STUC influence on government.

What neither Wilson nor the STUC could overcome was the residual hostility to home rule within the Labour Party. The synthesis of nationalism and collectivism which the STUC embodied, and which is now the dominant strain in Scottish politics, was certainly a venerable and a sturdy creed. But there was, and to an extent remains, within the Labour Party an equally powerful belief that collective provision is best delivered through centralism. This was, after all, the guiding philosophy of the Attlee government and of Wilson's own earlier administrations, with their emphasis on planning and nationalisation. Many in the Labour Party, in Scotland and elsewhere, saw no good reason to abandon it just because of Scotland's passing peccadillo with the SNP. Opposition was growing, particularly among northern English MPs jealous of the indulgence being lavished on their uppity neighbour, and among prickly left-wingers like Neil Kinnock and Eric Heffer. An eccentric but deadly band of constitutional particularists like Tam Dalyell and George Cunningham were also beginning to make their presence felt. There were doubters in Cabinet too, with Callaghan the most important, whose patience was stretched by a succession of special Cabinet meetings convened by Wilson to talk about Scotland. At the same time, some of the more boisterous devolvers like Sillars were venturing ever further out on a proto-nationalist limb, prodded by a deeply excited Scottish press which had bought the devolution dream wholesale and, in the process, by and large abandoned for good its traditional rightward leanings. As 1975 wore on and Short's White Paper drew closer, the tensions between these two divergent forces within the party heightened. In such circumstances the movement's invariable instinct is to fudge.

It was not the only armed truce within the party. Wilson and several of his most senior colleagues, notably Roy Jenkins, had become convinced that, two years on from Britain's entry to the EEC, withdrawal had become implausible. The problem was that most of the rest of the labour movement remained virulently anti-EEC. It included the STUC, which regarded the Community as a capitalists' club and passed regular motions saying so. It also included many of the keenest devolvers, who saw Brussels at that time as an even less palatable source of subjugation than Westminster. Wilson's solution, a rare example of an audacious fudge, was to conduct a showy renegotiation of Britain's terms of membership, and then put the matter to a referendum, at which both collective responsibility and the whips' office would be stood down to allow MPs and ministers to campaign for their preferred cause. The 'yes' campaign, awash with business money, won. A split in the Labour Party had thus been avoided, but at a lasting cost to personal relationships and to party morale.

While all that was still simmering away, the devolution White Paper was published in November 1975. Rarely can have a government publication have tried so hard to please so many and ended up pleasing so few. *Our Changing Democracy* sought a middle path between those who devotedly supported devolution and those who, just as devotedly, opposed it. There was, of course, no middle path. The latter group was dismayed at the elaborate and constitutionally contrived machinery that was to be wheeled into place to placate cantankerous Scotland (and, to a lesser extent, Wales). The former group was still more incensed at the way in which the powers of the proposed assembly had shrivelled away from the initial promise. Full authority over the SDA and HIDB had disappeared: so too had clear responsibility for agriculture, forestry and fisheries. The Scottish legal system, whose distinctiveness was a core argument for an assembly, would also remain a UK responsibility. Worse still, Westminster was to have a right of veto over all legislative and executive decisions of the assembly, exercised through the Scottish Secretary. The STUC general council, having sensed a faltering government resolve, had met Short two months earlier to plead for a scheme at least as robust as Kilbrandon. Now it felt that its long months of patient co-operation had been betrayed, and its frustrations boiled over in a scathing response to the paper. The STUC, it said, had consistently argued that the assembly must have powers to deal decisively with Scotland's economic and social problems: 'the proposals in the White Paper fall far short of these objectives.' In a phrase that was to enter the lexicon of the devolution debate, the statement also poured scorn on the notion of the Scottish Secretary 'as a Governor General-type figure with sweeping power.'

Three months later, the general council met Short and Ross to see what scope there was to repair the fractured consensus. It did its best to sound reasonable. Splitting control over the development agencies was messy, and the assembly should be in charge, albeit within a broad framework of UK policy. The same went for farming and fishing, the universities, the legal system. Ministers had only minimal hope to offer. Ross said he felt the SDA would 'in time' devolve to the assembly. Otherwise, there was no more than an undertaking to think about what had been said. The general council followed up the meeting with a detailed paper to ministers, and was able to draw modest encouragement when, on 25 May, the government announced that the SDA would after all fall within the assembly's ambit. But that was all.

The White Paper generated ructions across the political spectrum. The SNP, having decided in a tense debate at its May 1975 conference to go along with devolution as a half-way house to independence, now suffered a backlash from the purists that would reverberate for years. Margaret Thatcher, who had succeeded Heath as Tory leader in February 1975, took it as her cue to begin the retreat from her predecessor's uncertain dalliance with devolution, a journey that would ultimately cost her the resignations of the Shadow Scottish Secretary, Alick Buchanan-Smith, and his promising junior, Malcolm Rifkind. But the biggest upheaval was within Labour itself. Sillars, the Paisley MP John Robertson, and Labour's Scottish research officer, Alex Neil, promptly resigned to form a new party. It was called the Scottish Labour Party in fond emulation of Keir Hardie's proletarian 1888 vehicle, though its membership came to be dominated by far-left students and a number of distinguished Scottish political journalists who had played a more than observational role in its creation. In 1979 both Sillars and Robertson would lose their seats, and their party collapse. But for the moment it was the talk of the steamie. Aside from anything else, at around the same time the maverick Labour MP John Stonehouse announced that he would sit as an independent. Not long after, the former Education Secretary, Reg Prentice, defected to the Tories. The government had lost its Commons majority.

In March 1976 a much greater sensation shook the political firmament. For reasons which still arouse lively speculation,

Harold Wilson resigned. Jim Callaghan, who succeeded him, brought in new faces to most of the key posts concerned with devolution. Bruce Millan replaced Ross, Michael Foot replaced Short and the trenchant advocate, John Smith, was installed as Minister of State at the Privy Council Office, with day-to-day responsibility for piloting devolution on to the statute book. The STUC, which was also under new leadership in the crusty form of Jimmy Milne, decided to launch a renewed attempt at getting the devolution scheme beefed up before the Scotland and Wales Bill began its Commons passage in the autumn. On 18 June, the general council met Foot and Smith to press the familiar case against a Westminster veto and for devolved control over the universities, the legal system, the economic powers associated with regional aid, the primary industries and the rest. It was a case that had gained weight shortly before when Labour's Scottish executive, now more solidly enthused by devolution, had steered a motion in similar terms through the party's Scottish conference. Foot was long on fraternity – stressing the government's wish to maintain STUC co-operation – but short on specifics. Matters like the universities, he said, were still under consideration. A final decision on agriculture, fisheries and the legal system would be announced by the end of the Parliamentary session, Smith said, but the government feared 'an English backlash' if the assembly took control of regional aid. Foot added that there were legal problems in earmarking oil revenues for pre-ordained purposes. The better approach was to strengthen the SDA.

The STUC now felt able to make common cause with the Scottish Labour Executive, or most of it, on devolution. For a few brief months, a new optimism reigned. Helen Liddell, former head of the STUC's economic department and now Labour's general secretary in Scotland, told the 1977 congress: 'In the space of the past year there has been a historic drawing together of the Labour Party in Scotland and the STUC . . . we have come closer together than we have ever been before.' A slight exaggeration, but certainly relations were more congenial than they had been for some years. A joint meeting between the executive and the general council was held, from which flowed a July conference on devolution at Westminster, attended by more than 60 Labour MPs. Callaghan meanwhile put the Scottish party to work drafting an agenda for the assembly and beginning the process of candidate selection. The former Royal High School building on Edinburgh's

Calton Hill was being prepared for the legislative majesty that was coming. A 'supplementary statement' to the White Paper was published in August which confirmed the devolution of the SDA and abandoned much of the gubernatorial grandeur which was to have attached to the Scottish Secretary: such was the form of the Bill when it finally appeared a few weeks later. But the opponents of devolution had not gone away. As would happen again in later years, the business community suddenly discovered sufficient interest in Scottish politics to mount a campaign against home rule. Ironically enough, the 'Scotland is British' campaign was fronted by none other than Sir John Toothill, whose reflections on the Scottish economy had once held such sway with the STUC. In October 1976, Labour's UK conference held what was, astonishingly, its first devolution debate of the Seventies. The government's plans were approved, but only after resentment at the concessions being made to obstreperous Scottish opinion had been exposed in its full virulence. One Tyneside delegate accused the party leadership of paying more attention to 11 Scottish Nationalists than to its own northern England MPs.

Any lingering doubts ministers might have had about the resilience of such hostility evaporated as the Bill began its Commons passage. A Second Reading was secured only after the government had conceded the principle of referenda in Scotland and Wales to bring the assemblies into being. The Committee Stage found the measure besieged, not least by the indefatigable Tam Dalyell and his celebrated West Lothian Question about the entitlement of Scottish MPs to vote in the Commons on English issues when devolution denied them a vote on the same issues applied to Scotland. It became clear that the Bill would only pass if debate on it was guillotined. But Margaret Thatcher now completed her retreat from home rule by whipping her party against the guillotine. More seriously, 22 Labour MPs – including two from Scottish constituencies, Dalyell and Willie Hamilton – rebelled, and others abstained. The guillotine was lost, and the Scotland and Wales Bill was effectively dead. 'The tragedy of the situation,' said a typically gritty statement from Jimmy Milne, 'is that of those government backbenchers who either voted against or abstained on it, most did so from a misguided belief that the Bill could lead to separation. The reality is that the failure of the Bill could have the most divisive effects on the British working people . . . the only beneficiaries of the situation are the SNP.'

If Scottish trade unionists had grown exasperated with the government over devolution, the wider movement had more familiar grounds for grievance. Labour's 1974 manifestos had enlivened political discourse with an old phrase of Jean-Jacques Rousseau's adapted to a new meaning: the social contract. It was a grand label for an ambitious accord. The origins lay in a speech by Jack Jones at the 1971 Labour conference, in which he floated the idea of 'a joint policy' agreed between Labour and the unions, on which both could campaign come a general election and to which both would be tied once Labour was in office. It was an attempt to get around the need for a formal incomes policy, though it was portrayed in more expansive terms. The TUC–Labour Liaison Committee, a more effective channel than its Scottish counterpart, got down to business, and had the bones of a deal by February 1973. Two months later, Harold Wilson was at the STUC congress in Aberdeen, appealing to delegates to support a deal based on 'free consent, a free compact between a Labour government and the trade union movement' (the Aberdeen congress is otherwise memorable for an earnest speech from a fresh-faced young General and Municipal official, urging delegates to boycott the men-only bar across the road from the hall. His name was George Robertson, and he later went into politics).

The essence of the deal was that the government would deliver an agreed programme of measures – repeal of the Industrial Relations Act, a substantial increase in pensions, an arbitration service, a range of workplace legislation – in return for 'responsible' co-operation from the unions. Given an election fought on the issue of whether union muscle had made the country ungovernable, the appeal was obvious. Duly elected, the Labour government went diligently about keeping its side of the bargain. In quick succession, the Trade Union and Labour Relations Act restored the immunities withdrawn by the Industrial Relations Act, the Employment Protection Act offered new job security, the Health and Safety at Work Act improved conditions, and the Sex Discrimination Act established the principle if not the practice of equal employment rights for women. State pensions were raised by more than 20 per cent, and there were substantial increases in the whole range of benefits and subsidies known, in the jargon of the day, as the 'social wage'. The Advisory, Conciliation and Arbitration Service (ACAS) was created. Yet the unions' part of the deal, much less clearly defined, was much less clearly delivered. The understanding, necessarily loose because of abiding hostility to anything that smacked of wages policy, was that pay rises should roughly match inflation. In 1974, inflation rose by 17 per cent and wages by 25 per cent. The gap had begun to narrow in the second half of the year, though less because of moderating pay claims than of accelerating inflation (it would peak in mid-1975 at nearly 27 per cent, by which time wage rises were running at 32 per cent). Wages were far from the only source of inflation – rising oil and commodity prices, coupled with the cost of the government's social spending played a large part – and Denis Healey's later claim that he would have had inflation in single figures by autumn 1975 had the unions met their obligations on wages must be viewed sceptically. But they had not met them, and despite Wilson's attempts to insist that the union side of the social contract was also about things like productivity, everybody knew it. In any case, that level of inflation was plainly unsustainable, and was worsening an already alarming trade deficit. Something would have to be done.

Healey wanted a pay policy, the one instrument that Wilson had forbidden him. Michael Foot, the Employment Secretary, had threatened to resign if the Government adopted statutory wage restraint. The social contract had been accepted by the 1974 TUC only after powerful warnings from the Left that it must not lead to wage restraint. In Scotland, the warnings were starker, and echoed beyond the Left. The STUC's April 1975 congress in Aberdeen approved by large majorities two motions which left little room for ambiguity. The first, moved by McGahey, declared: 'The Scottish trade union movement will oppose a wage freeze no matter what form it may take.' The second, from the civil service unions, vowed to oppose 'any form of restriction on or interference with free collective wage and salary bargaining.' It was moved by a ruddy-complexioned man by the name of Campbell Christie. There was swift reassurance the following day from Foot, who told delegates: 'The statutory control of wages, a wage freeze, or any other form of statutory control of wages is doomed.' Prophetic words.

The STUC, however proud of its new intimacy with government over devolution, was scarcely a player in this sort of game. In those days, the Budget usually coincided with the STUC congress, and the STUC's most visible contribution to

UK economic debate took the form of an annual emergency motion deploring the Chancellor's speech; there was unanimous approval, for example, for a general council motion describing the 1975 Budget as 'a serious attack on the standard of living of working people.' Meanwhile, UK union leaders would parade before the cameras outside the congress hall to give their reactions to the latest dispensations from Denis Healey, who was fast acquiring a demonic reputation among the unions. But the manoeuvres which took the government down the road of pay policy happened a long way from Scotland. Jack Jones, who had pleaded with delegates in Aberdeen to 'respect the social contract and support it,' was once again architect of an ingenious deal between ministers and the TUC. The formula was for a flat-rate limit on pay rises of £6 per week. Crucially, it would be employers rather than unions who would be penalised for any breaches of the policy, and there would be controls on price rises. It was, as even Jones would later admit, 'near to statutory policy,' and it offended the craft unions whose members' pay differentials were bound to be eroded. None the less, Jones and Len Murray, the TUC general secretary, got it through the TUC congress by a larger margin than it had secured on the TUC general council, and with less hostility than it would attract a few weeks later at the Labour Conference. More importantly, in the year that followed the trade union movement proved that it could after all deliver voluntary restraint: there were some breaches of the £6 figure, but more than three million workers settled within the limit, and inflation duly fell from 25 to 12 per cent.

The following year, the policy was slightly more coercive (Healey was threatening to withdraw tax cuts for lower-paid workers unless the deal was agreed), and slightly less successful. There were more breaches, and a thriving cottage industry grew up in devising artful ways of measuring improved productivity so as to justify settlements above the limit. The Treasury had wanted a percentage rather than flat-rate norm, as had unions whose members had been disadvantaged by the squeeze on differentials. In the event a complex mix of the two was agreed, in which the format varied with the wage level. The union reaction was also mixed. At the STUC congress in Rothesay, a McGahey composite attacking the formula and demanding a return to free collective bargaining was narrowly defeated by 1,017 to 967 after an intense debate. The previous day, Bruce Millan had argued forcibly that Britain must not throw away the competitive advantage it had gained for the sake of a 'general free for all.' Now Albert Spanswick, UK general secretary of the health workers, argued that without a social contract there could be no guarantee of the social wage, while Campbell Christie attacked the TUC for endorsing the previous year's formula. Delegates gave the government the benefit of that doubt, but went on to carry overwhelmingly a motion deploring the stringencies that had followed Denis Healey's settlement the previous December with the International Monetary Fund. Beating up Healey was a pastime in which everyone could join.

A year later, the norm was set at 10 per cent: this time without formal TUC consent and at a cost to Jack Jones, the social contract's most faithful apologist, of being shouted down at his valedictory TGWU conference. There was little ambivalence when the STUC came to consider it at their 1978 congress in Aberdeen in a debate dominated by union leaders from south of the border. Both Sid Weighell of the railwaymen and Tom Jackson of the postal workers argued for keeping the door open to some form of flexible or voluntary incomes policy, with Weighell arguing that real collective bargaining was to be found in 11.5 million trade unionists negotiating with government. But the mood had swung. Alistair Graham of the Civil and Public Services Association opened the debate with the words: 'I hope that today this congress is going to put paid to the talk of a fourth stage of incomes policy.'

What was becoming apparent was that successive years of constraint had created immense pressures within the trade union movement. However the policy was cast, it was bound to create anomalies and jealousies between different groups of workers. There is no shop steward in the land who cannot point to circumstances that make his or her members exceptional, and distant understandings reached between general secretaries and ministers on the lawn at Chequers are not an infallibly compelling reason to let the members down. An under-remarked aspect of the industrial conflict for which the Seventies are remembered was to expose the limits in the control which the much-reviled 'barons' of the TUC and the national union leaderships had over their grassroots memberships. Besides, it was far from clear that self-discipline was buying much of a return. Certainly, the pay policies were having an impact on inflation, which in early

1978 dipped into single figures for the first time since 1973. But inflation was not the only indicator to affect workers' living standards. Persistent pressure on Britain's reserves took Healey to the IMF in the winter of 1976 (Britain, he reportedly joked, seemed to be about to join the Third World and OPEC at the same time). The consequence was to enforce swingeing cuts in public spending, and tight limits on borrowing. In July 1976 Healey cut public spending by £1 billion, and the following December, after the IMF deal, announced measures to take a further £3 billion out over two years. In the event, the flight to the IMF turned out to have been prompted by a Treasury over-estimate of the Public Sector Borrowing Requirement, and in spring 1978 Healey found room for a reflationary Budget. By then, though, unemployment had been rising for three years. Sky-high interest rates had frozen industrial investment. Doubts had also arisen about the worth of the legislative reforms the Government had provided as its side of the social contract. A bitter year-long dispute at the Grunwick film laboratory in north-west London, where management refused to recognise the workforce's chosen union, brought both the Employment Protection Act and ACAS into play – to no avail. The company ignored an ACAS finding against it, and refused to be budged by either mass picketing or a government inquiry. Meanwhile, it gained a court order to stop postal workers blacking its mail. Neither the government nor its laws seemed proof against the malice of a determined employer. The presence of embarrassed-looking ministers on the picket line did little to dispel the impression of impotence.

For all these reasons, the spring and summer of 1978 found a host of union voices warning ministers, publicly and privately, from Right and Left, that a fourth year of restraint could not be delivered. But Callaghan, with an election imminent and the economic runes brighter than they had been since the previous election, wanted to show the government economically resolute and politically in command. In July a White Paper, *Winning the Battle Against Inflation*, peremptorily announced a 5 per cent pay ceiling for the year ahead. This time there was no negotiation. The TUC rejected the policy, decisively yet less vehemently than it might have done because it believed, as did most commentators, that the election would come before the pay round began. But Callaghan turned up at the TUC congress in Brighton in September to convey, via a tuneless rendition of

Waiting at the Church, that the election would not come until the following year.

Before the end of that month, Ford workers launched the first major assault on the 5 per cent norm. After nine weeks on strike they settled for 17 per cent and, adding to the government's humiliation, the Commons motion punishing the company for the transgression was defeated with the help of rebel left-wing MPs. By then, the policy was in tatters and the country in the grip of the worst industrial conflict since Heath. Strikes broke out throughout the public sector, most famously among grave-diggers, school cleaners, dustmen and hospital porters. Pay claims began to leapfrog one another: the water workers rejected 14 per cent, the teachers claimed 35, the miners and power-workers 40. It provided irresistible political capital for the Conservatives who, having been held level in the polls by Labour for several months, now pulled strongly ahead. 'Our citizens expect and are not getting an ordered or orderly society,' Margaret Thatcher told the Commons. 'They expect the rubbish to be cleared, the schools to be open and the hospitals to be functioning.' Clive Jenkins claims the credit, if that is the word, for labelling a grim few months the 'Winter of Discontent'. Towards its end, the TUC and a beleaguered government reached an accord, roundly condemned by several speakers at April's STUC congress in Inverness, under which wage bargaining would in future be informed by an economic assessment agreed between the government and the TUC (an idea Labour would revive in adapted form a decade later). But by then, more than 13.5 million working days had been lost to industrial action. And so had Labour's prospects of winning the general election of May 1979.

The 'Winter of Discontent,' was not the actual instrument of the government's downfall. There is little doubt that the temptation was strong among ministers to abandon devolution after the fall of the Scotland and Wales Bill. But there were compelling reasons to soldier on. For one thing, Jimmy Milne's bleak forecast proved prescient: at the district council elections in May 1977 the SNP took more than 130 seats from Labour, which lost control of every major district it had held. For another, the government was by now in a minority, and had been dependent in the Commons since 23 March 1977 on the Lib–Lab Pact, which was conditional on the devolution proposals being resurrected in more acceptable form. Indeed, the Liberals' devolution negotiating team, led by Russell Johnston, would later claim credit for many of the changes evident when the new legislation, announced by Foot in July, emerged. The STUC general council had also been lobbying hard after the demise of the first Bill to maintain momentum, and had even suggested that the government call a snap referendum. At meetings with Foot and Smith on 11 March and 12 July, it continued to press – vainly – for more muscular economic powers and for a tax-varying mechanism. It also now proposed a free vote on proportional representation (the April congress had been narrowly persuaded to remit a motion demanding PR in the assembly), and suggested a way around the West Lothian Question by specifying matters on which Scottish MPs would be barred from voting. Unsurprisingly, given the government's diminished voting strength, this latter idea was dismissed by Foot as impractical. He also admitted that the new Bill would contain 'nothing of any major importance' in terms of additional economic powers.

The principal difference was that the Bill had been split into two, the Scotland Bill and the Wales Bill. Much of the impetus for that had come from Labour's Scottish executive, and the STUC had backed the idea. The Liberals had failed to win three key demands – proportional representation, a right for the assembly to vary income tax by 1p in the pound, and the replacement of its prescribed list of powers with a list of the specific matters on which it could *not* legislate. But they had secured a number of changes, including a block grant revised on a set formula every four years, a right for the assembly to choose the timing of its own elections, and a diminution of Westminster's veto on assembly legislation. It was a tidier, less convoluted package. The Scotland Bill could be plausibly presented as an improvement on its predecessor and the SNP, without much enthusiasm, agreed to support it.

The Bill struggled through its Second Reading on 14 November 1977, little helped by a lacklustre performance from Bruce Millan and an eloquent one from Tam Dalyell. Required, by its constitutional nature, to undergo its Committee Stage on the floor of the House, it faced as rough a ride as any legislation in recent memory. Labour's divisions were now out in the open, and it was a Labour MP, and a Scot, who struck the most grievous blow. George Cunningham, Dunfermline-born but representing Islington, successfully moved an amendment requiring that at least 40 per cent of the electorate (not merely of those who turned out) must vote in favour of the assembly at the forthcoming referendum for the legislation to take effect. It was an awesome hurdle, not least because it meant that the non-votes of the apathetic, absent, ill or, in a few cases, dead, would count against the assembly.

Both the Scotland and Wales Bills gained the Royal Assent on 31 July 1978, and the focus switched to the referendum. The STUC sought to muster non-Scottish support within the labour movement by organising a round of meetings with the TUC regional councils in north-east and north-west England, and with the Wales TUC. It also met the SNP leadership, at the SNP's request, and was taken aback by the party's confidence that devolution would prove a stepping stone to independence. Still, at first the omens for devolution looked bright. Labour bested the SNP at three key by-elections: Donald Dewar, the lean and talented Glasgow lawyer, won Garscadden in an acrimonious contest; then George Robertson, erstwhile scourge of sexist drinking in Aberdeen, saw off Margo MacDonald in Winnie Ewing's old seat of Hamilton; and finally John Home Robertson held Berwick and East Lothian, left vacant by the death of the most able devolver of all, John P Mackintosh. But the intensity of the hatred left seething between the two parties foreshadowed a debilitating feature of the referendum campaign which would take place the following February: the 'yes' camp was destined to be fatally divided.

There turned out to be three 'yes' campaigns, each of which viewed the others with some distaste. Labour's Scottish high command had decided early in 1978 to resist any attempts 'to lure the Labour Party into all-party alliances' and had announced that its campaign would be restricted to its own members, the Co-operative Party and the STUC. This rather neglected the fact that not all STUC affiliates were pro-devolution, and that many individuals who were, including the general secretary, were members of parties other than Labour. But the decision was confirmed as the campaign began by Liddell, who said: 'We will not be soiling our hands by joining any umbrella "yes" group.' The SNP, meanwhile, were told by their leader, Gordon Wilson, not to share platforms with 'people who are normally our opponents.' And so the 'yes' campaign paraded as follows: the broadest grouping was 'Yes for Scotland', which embraced most of the

SNP, most of the Liberals, the SLP, some Communists, a diverse selection of academics, clergy and celebrities, and quite a few trade unionists, like Alex Kitson, who held true to the principle of the broad-based campaign; then there was 'Labour Says Yes', swiftly renamed 'the Labour Movement Yes Campaign' in the hope of attracting more trade unionists, which was by and large confined to the Labour Party; finally, there was 'the Alliance', a rather select body set up mainly to provide a platform for Buchanan-Smith, in which he was joined by Russell Johnston and Jimmy Milne. A few pro-devolution Tories ventured out on their own.

It was a shambles. The 'no' campaign was also divided between 'Labour Vote No' (which included future front-benchers like Brian Wilson and Malcolm Chisholm) and the business/Tory-led grouping, 'Scotland says No'. But these bodies were more given to co-operation than were their pro-devolution counterparts: Danny Crawford of the building workers cheerfully admitted at the 1978 STUC congress that he was active in both. Besides, incoherence mattered less to them, since they were not the ones proposing major constitutional change. They had little difficulty in conveying the impression that those who wished this upheaval on Scotland were incapable of organising a whelk stall. And, thanks to the 40 per cent rule, the public apathy engendered by the disorder among the devolvers was almost as valuable as a 'no' vote. Anything which played on the public's unease about devolution suited the 'no' campaigners just fine – even the mendacious suggestion by Lord (formerly Sir Alec Douglas-) Home that voting 'no' would be rewarded by a better devolution bill from Margaret Thatcher. The Labour 'yes' campaign, despite some union financial backing, found it hard to rise above the splits in many constituency parties, some of which decided to avoid trouble by abstaining from both campaigns. It also insisted on making its publicity material as party-specific as possible, which was of questionable tactical advantage given the government's unpopularity in the throes of the 'Winter of Discontent'. Bringing the Prime Minister north to speak had, at that juncture, no more positive an effect. It was not the movement's finest hour, though the dislocation had its comic aspects. The present writer, for example, was a member of the Edinburgh committee of 'Yes for Scotland', which rented its splendid meeting rooms from the building union, UCATT. UCATT was anti-devolution.

By March 1, the day of the vote, the referendum campaign

had become a metaphor for the terminal crisis that gripped the government. The Welsh, obligingly, voted against devolution by a simple majority. The Scots managed a slender majority in favour, 1,230,937 votes to 1,153,502, but it only amounted to 32.9 per cent of the electorate. With the Scotland Act now moribund (and the Lib–Lab Pact ended) the SNP decided to force a vote of no confidence in the government, a tactic which split its own ranks. Thatcher, suffering no such inhibitions, followed suit. The government lost by one vote, and Callaghan announced an immediate election. At the STUC congress in Inverness, cut back to three days because of the election campaign, Jimmy Milne remarked gloomily that 'coming events cast their shadow . . . .'

Charitably, Scottish voters did not punish Labour too severely for the devolution debacle; it was the SNP that suffered most from the melancholy public feeling, which would last half a decade, that the nation had shot its bolt. All but two of the SNP seats fell, mostly to Labour, which ended up with 42 per cent of the Scottish vote and 44 out of 71 seats. But the rest of Britain had had enough of botched devolution, uncollected bin bags and Jim Callaghan. The Conservatives swept into government with an overall majority of 43. Thatcherism had begun. Things might have been rough for the STUC and its affiliates during these past few years, but they were about to get immeasurably worse.

CHAPTER NINE

WEATHERING THE STORM

The world changed on 4 May 1979. A new Prime Minister stood on the steps of Downing Street and invoked, with the aid of a small piece of card, St Francis of Assisi about bringing harmony, truth, faith and hope. The Labour movement looked on sourly, but without any real premonition of the tempest that was to follow. They had endured Tory governments before. Margaret Thatcher's ministerial team included many who had toiled alongside Edward Heath: indeed, it was later said that only two of her initial Cabinet had voted for her as leader. Some ministers, like Sir Keith Joseph and Sir Geoffrey Howe, had certainly been airing some pretty gaunt theories about the money supply in the learned prints, but everyone remembered what had befallen Selsdon Man. The unions still had around 12 million members, and were little inclined to notice that a third of them (and more than half the manual workforce) had voted for Margaret Thatcher. After all, they had just demonstrated both the means and the will to defy governmental intransigence. The STUC was no less complacent. Its membership, having topped the million mark in 1977, was still rising (it would peak, at 1,090,839 in 1980). Its recognition and stature as an independent trade union centre seemed to be growing in due proportion: in July 1979, the Soviet trade union movement laid on a massive study tour of the USSR for the STUC, and no fewer than 324 Scottish trade unionists set off in two specially chartered airliners. Besides, Scotland had held true to Labour despite the demoralising debacle of devolution. No doubt the electoral pendulum in the south would swing back in due course, as it had done before. The STUC needed only to bide its time. There had been a temporary setback. A testing period lay ahead. But few doubted that the movement could meet whatever challenges it would face.

A small vignette demonstrates how quickly these perceptions changed. At the 1979 congress, held between the devolution referendum and the general election, Labour's Scottish chairman, Sam Gooding, had reassured a worried STUC that home rule 'remains a live issue in our manifesto . . . you must look forward to an early implementation of the devolution measures when we return a Labour government.' A robust demand for a powerful assembly was stoutly passed, with successive speakers insisting that this most vital of issues must not be allowed to wither. A year later, in Perth, devolution was almost completely overlooked. Bruce Millan mentioned it not at all in his speech. The last day of congress, distracted by the breaking story of Jimmy Carter's disastrous raid on Teheran, was winding down and delegates were getting ready for home when Andrew Forman of the shopworkers, a former president, rose to object to the home rule motion being abandoned along with other minor business which had fallen off the end of the timetable. 'I think we must give an expression of opinion of that issue,' he said. Dutifully, delegates sat through a brisk speech from George Bolton, the Scottish miners' vice-president ('Those who are trying to argue that devolution is a dead duck will find themselves in the same position as King Canute and will get very wet feet indeed'). Then they went home.

A cynic, particularly one who had been talking to the Labour Party leadership, might have been tempted to the view that the apparent loss of interest in devolution in 1980 coincided altogether too neatly with the collapse of the SNP threat. But STUC delegates simply had more urgent matters to occupy their minds. 'We meet in an extremely different atmosphere and circumstances,' that year's president, Willie Dougan of the Boilermakers, had said at the start of the week. He was right. A three-month strike by steelworkers had just ended, unsuccessfully, and 70,000 British Steel jobs were disappearing as prelude to a decade-long contraction of the industry. Howe had just presented what seemed an unthinkably harsh Budget (it was nothing compared to the next year's). VAT had been doubled. Notice had been given that pensions and benefits would no longer be linked to average earnings. There had been tax rebates for the wealthy, and the beginnings of a traumatic recession – unchecked by intervention – in manufacturing industry. Finally, an Employment Bill was before the Commons, described by Dougan as 'the most serious attack on fundamental trade union rights since the last Tory government introduced its Industrial Relations Act.' It would, he predicted confidently, meet the same response from organised labour. So it did, but the outcome was very different.

Also on view at that congress was a glimpse of a very different agenda, one that would destabilise the labour movement more than anything Mrs Thatcher could contrive. Tony Benn told delegates: 'We have some very practical work to do and that is to rebuild the party by recreating the alliance which underpins the foundation of the party, between the trade union movement and the Labour Party.' Benn went on to explain what he meant: 'All those who are privileged to represent the party at any level – be they Labour councillors, be they MPs, be they ministers – all should be accountable to those who elected them . . . we cannot accept that people climb on the back of the labour movement and then, when they are elevated to top positions, they are entitled to undo what has been done.'

Benn, like many on the Left, had concluded that the sorry end of the Callaghan government had arisen not from electoral disaffection with socialism, but from the government's failure to offer a distinctively socialist vision. Intent on moving the party leftwards, he proposed a transfer of sovereignty away from the leadership in Parliament into the constituency parties, which would hold powers of life and death over errant parliamentarians. The unstated, but universally recognised, subtext to this drive for party 'democracy' was that Labour's constituency machinery was in a dismally poor state of repair. It meant that handfuls of determined zealots could often capture control of local parties in very short order. The battle lines were being drawn for a period of civil war that would play at least as big a part as Margaret Thatcher in keeping Labour out of office for a generation.

Benn's speech at Perth came at a pivotal moment in his offensive. In the wake of the election defeat the 1979 Labour conference took two important decisions. One was to approve mandatory reselection of MPs; the other was to set up a commission of inquiry, under David Basnett of the General and Municipal Workers, into the causes of the defeat and the lessons to be learned. Basnett, who fancied himself as a fixer in the Jack Jones mould, found himself fronting a committee dominated by the impatient Left. Two months after the Perth congress, the committee reported to a conference in Bishop's Stortford which, to Callaghan's dismay, approved plans to elect the leader by electoral college (composition to be decided), transfer the job of writing the manifesto from the Shadow Cabinet to the National Executive Committee, and mandatorily reselect MPs. Callaghan opposed the report unsuccessfully at the party's anarchic Blackpool conference that autumn, which also committed the party to unilateral nuclear disarmament. He resigned shortly afterwards. The late Peter Jenkins, political columnist on the *Guardian*, wrote: 'At Blackpool in October 1980 the Labour Party, in the name of Democracy, finally parted company with the people.'

The party was openly fragmenting. On the Left, numerous fringe factions, of whom the best organised was the Trotskyite Militant Tendency, were gearing up to grab a piece of the action in Britain's erstwhile natural party of government. On the Right, David Owen, Shirley Williams and Bill Rodgers were beginning the journey into a party of their own, the Social Democratic Party, which would fail as an enduring political force but succeed in dividing the opposition to Margaret Thatcher for most of her 11-year term. Among those who remained, the battle was on for the leadership. Callaghan had timed his departure so that the contest took place under the old rules, a move widely seen as intended to secure the succession for Denis Healey. But Healey had made too many enemies as Chancellor and, besides, many MPs were worried that they would now face deselection if caught voting for the titan of the Right. Benn had refused to stand under the old 'undemocratic' rules, and the 'stop Healey' movement coalesced instead around Michael Foot. Foot, a patently deep and decent man, but one now out of his time and his depth, became leader in November 1980. Two months later, at a special conference in Wembley, the party completed its dive into electoral aversion by agreeing a composition for the electoral college which gave the unions, fresh from the 'Winter of Discontent', the largest say in electing the leader: 40 per cent, against 30 each for the parliamentary party and the constituencies. The next day, Owen, Williams and Rodgers – now joined by Roy Jenkins – issued the Limehouse Declaration, the founding creed of the SDP.

Scotland was generally resistant to these machinations, but not to their consequences. Scottish constituency parties proved, with few exceptions, much less prone than their English counterparts to penetration by the unsmiling cadres of the far Left. Labour in Scotland was too worldly, too closely interlocked with its communities, and very possibly too embedded an establishment for upstart theorists to make much of an impact. Its left, though influential, was not the left of the bearded polytechnic lecturers, but of the Communist tradition: practical, solidly based in the workplace and in the trade union movement, and actually rather than aspirationally working class. Scotland was also still, despite the fiasco of the devolution referendum, much more interested in its own affairs than in the cosmic abstractions peddled by the entryists. Even in the dog-days for home rule that followed the referendum, it made sense to plot Scottish politicians not merely on a Right–Left axis, but also on a Nationalist–Unionist scale, to which incantations from Trotsky's Transitional Demands bore no very obvious relevance. Scots, it was often said, were too sensible for such indulgences: and while 'sensible' sometimes meant stodgy, there was also a new generation coming to the fore in Scottish Labour after 1979 who were level-headed, tough, articulate and hugely able. A decade later, they had risen to occupy many of the key posts in a Labour Party at last starting to win its long battle against unfitness for office.

Nor did the SDP make much headway in Scotland. There were a couple of defections from Labour – Robert Maclennan in the Highlands, Dickson Mabon on the lower Clyde – and a couple of gains from the Conservatives, in the persons of Charles Kennedy in Ross and Cromarty (reactivating the Highland Liberal tradition) and Roy Jenkins, no less, who won the hearts of Hillhead's disaffected Tories at a memorable by-election in early 1982. But the SDP gathered relatively few members in Scotland, where its air of cool suburban rationalism seemed somehow terribly English. Parties which 'seem' English generally have a hard row to hoe in Scotland. The biggest loser of all from that was Margaret Thatcher whose hectoring Home Counties bray, to her lasting mystification, grated as savagely on Scottish voters' ears as on their traditions of collectivism. While their southern neighbours fell heart and soul for the saloon-bar swagger of Thatcherism or the suave reason of the SDP, Scots continued doggedly voting Labour, turning to the Liberals or the SNP when moved to express exasperation. Conservatism in Scotland, as the decade wore on, took on the trappings of an alien occupying force.

But Scotland's festering contempt offered no protection from the iconoclasm of Thatcherism, nor from the impunity which a fissured opposition lent it. Neither did the STUC have any better idea than English trade unionists what to do about it. During the new government's first year, general council deputations trailed their displeasure round the familiar circuit of ministerial meetings: five with the Scottish Secretary, George Younger; two with the Industry Secretary, Sir Keith Joseph; one with the Employment Secretary, Jim Prior. But they achieved little beyond a curt hearing, and in the years that followed their access would be increasingly restricted to Scottish Office ministers, and often junior ones at that. For the first time since the First World War, the STUC found most of the ministerial suites in Whitehall closed to it. It was scant consolation that the employers' organisations were faring little better from the government's abandonment of the old tripartite ways. Nor did more populist forms of protest dent the government's determination. The STUC threw itself forcefully into organising demonstrations to coincide with a TUC-ordained day of action against Prior's Employment Bill on 14 May 1980, bringing 20,000 on to the streets of Glasgow and 12,000 out to march through Edinburgh. It was followed up by a week of action, which included protest stoppages, but the response was disappointing. More to the point, the government simply declined to take any notice.

Prior's Act was the first of eight major tranches of legislation which drastically confined the scope of union activity, and as this book goes to press a ninth is under consideration. The Prior measure removed legal immunities from most secondary action and all secondary picketing, banned some forms of closed shop, and offered unions state funding for ballots; the 1982 Act outlawed political or sympathy strikes, further restricted the closed shop, and made unions legally liable for unlawful acts by their officials; in 1984 ballots were made obligatory to authorise industrial action, elect union executives, and approve the operation of political funds; 1986 saw workers below the age of 21 lose the protection of wages councils; the 1988 legislation gave strike breakers the right to sue their unions for taking disciplinary action against them, outlawed more aspects of the closed shop and tightened up ballot procedures; in 1989 paid time off for union officials was restricted to specified activities; the 1990 Act ended the closed shop in any form, held unions liable for unofficial action conducted by their members, authorised selective dismissal of workers taking unofficial action, and made all secondary action unlawful; and the 1993 legislation allowed workers to join or transfer to the union of their choice, required all ballots to be postal, introduced a 'cooling off period' between ballots and strikes, obliged union members to agree periodically in writing to deduction of union subscriptions, and abolished the wages councils. The government had sowed a legal minefield around almost every facet of union activity.

But the bigger deterrent to industrial action was an economic one. As unemployment soared, workers were often too frightened for their jobs to risk taking industrial action – particularly as it was made relentlessly easier for employers to fire them. The pattern of employment also changed steadily over the Thatcher–Major years: mighty public sector concerns were broken up and sold into private ownership; managerial vogues like down-sizing and outsourcing created ever smaller core workforces, and a growing reliance on a peripheral workforce of part-timers, short-term contract workers, sub-contractors, and casual labour – all hard to organise. Workplaces became smaller, and corporations were subdivided into discrete operating companies, whose workers were legally prohibited from taking action in each others' support. At Wapping in 1986, and at Timex in Dundee in 1993, entire workforces were dismissed for taking industrial action, and their jobs given to others prepared to accept harsh management terms. Most importantly of all, there was a rundown in the traditional manufacturing which had been the unions' most fertile recruiting grounds. When new jobs came they were often in service sectors notoriously resistant to union organisation, or in high-technology manufacturing, usually foreign-owned and often non-union. It was a process that struck Scotland, particularly during the recession of the early 1980s, in a particularly grievous manner.

Between 1979 and 1981, Scottish manufacturing lost 11 per cent of its output and 20 per cent of its jobs. 'The past year,' said the General and Municipal's Jimmy Morrell in his STUC presidential address at Rothesay in April 1981, 'will go down as one of the worst years in the history of the trade union movement in Scotland.' Scottish unemployment had risen during the year by almost 100,000 and the STUC's affiliated membership, having climbed steadily since the 1930s, had suffered a fall of 18,000 which, everyone knew, was only the beginning. Some closures now coming on an almost weekly basis were, as Morrell pointed out, 'factories which were once household names.' The Singer plant at Clydebank, which in its heyday had employed 23,000 people, closed. The Carron iron works at Falkirk, Scotland's oldest company, was gone. But the names which caused the greatest anguish were of more recent provenance. One by one, the pillars of post-war hope for which the STUC and its allies had lobbied so determinedly in the Fifties and Sixties were allowed to topple: British Leyland at Bathgate, the Corpach paper mill, the Invergordon smelter, the Linwood car factory. The STUC burned with fury. Jimmy Milne, introducing the 1981 annual report, impatiently brushed aside comparisons of the recession with the depression of the 1930s: 'The Thirties happened after the severe defeat of the 1926 General Strike. Today the movement is largely undefeated and is still unbroken.' Morrell had a message for George Younger: 'If you want a fight, you've got one. For while it is true that the past year has been in some respects a depressing one it has also been in other ways inspiring. Working people up and down Scotland have refused to go down on their knees and the general council has sought to play its part in that process.' They were brave, truculent words, but they were also hollow.

One of the defining moments of Thatcherism had taken place shortly before the congress: the 1981 Budget. The government had reached exactly the stage at which Selsdon Heath had turned and retraced his steps. Recession had caught industry in a lethal pincer movement: domestic demand had collapsed, and exports were being crippled by a pound held high, ironically enough, by sales of North Sea oil. Unemployment was at 2.7 million and projected – accurately – to exceed three million the following year. The government's opinion poll rating was plummeting. The Cabinet was still diluted with what had come to be known as 'wets', who had successfully seen off attempts to slash departmental spending the previous year, and who were now arguing forcefully for a measure of reflation. If ever there was a moment for a U-turn, this was it. But at her party conference the previous October, Thatcher had uttered a phrase written for her by the playwright Ronald Miller: 'You turn if you want to. The lady's not for turning.' So it proved. With his leader's backing, Howe announced both significant tax rises and a £3.5 billion cut in public spending. TINA ('There Is No Alternative') joined the lexicon of Thatcher slogans. A lot more industry, and a lot more jobs, were destined to be laid waste.

The STUC general council had certainly fought the onslaught, every way it knew how, but it had lost. As the storm clouds gathered over Linwood, the STUC already had a campaign in motion to save the 4,800 jobs, half the original workforce, which remained at the plant. The closure was announced on 11 February 1981, and two days later, the STUC held a meeting with shop stewards, union officials and the local MPs and agreed a plan from Milne for a broad-based campaign. That same afternoon talks, chaired by the Strathclyde Regional Council convener, Charles O'Halloran, took place with an eclectic group of concerned parties: the CBI, the SCDI, the SDA, Renfrew District Council, Paisley Chamber of Commerce and even representatives of the Scottish Office's economic planning department. A telex was sent to Jean-Paul Parayre, president of the plant's owners, Peugeot-Citroen, requesting a meeting, and the Foreign Office was asked to lend its weight to the demand. Milne, setting out what was to become a familiar approach, explained to the press that the union campaign to save the plant would run in parallel with representations on behalf of 'the whole community.' A week later, a deputation met Younger, who was fast developing a delicate skill in appearing willing, within the bounds of collective responsibility, to mitigate in Scotland the harsher effects of the government's economic stringencies. Younger said he felt he had already brought as much pressure to bear on the French management as he could, but agreed to try once more. Jimmy Milne left the meeting fuming at the Secretary of State's 'feebleness.' The unions, meanwhile, were compiling evidence that the company had ordered its accounts in such a way as to make the performance of the doomed plant look much worse than it was. But when a deputation from the campaign met management in Paris a week after the Younger talks it was plain that the decision was final.

An unspoken, but significant, problem was that it was often not just ministers who were unresponsive to union protests against these closures of the early 1980s. Union officials were often privately dismayed at the lack of fight evident among their members. Such was the ferocity of the recession that workers seemed oddly fatalistic about redundancy, as though they believed the government's message that the surgery was traumatic simply because it had been too long postponed. TINA persuaded more than just the supporters of Margaret Thatcher. On the day the Linwood closure was announced, I was sent along as a young reporter to write a 'colour' piece about local reaction. In the shops and the small supply businesses around the huge plant there was plenty of raw anger. Yet the reaction among the workers themselves, clutching their redundancy letters, was eerily taciturn: 'phlegmatic' was the word I wrote that afternoon. Lunchtime football games went on as usual around the factory buildings, to the accompaniment of Radio One on the tannoy. I asked one young lineworker if I could see his letter, and he just shrugged. 'Keep it if you want,' he said. I have kept it.

There were some chinks of light in this dark period for the STUC, but they were few. On 1 March 1980, a year after the referendum, more than 400 people packed the Edinburgh Trades Council Hall to inaugurate a body that seemed too unlikely to merit serious consideration: and, indeed, was to potter away in near obscurity for more than half a decade before receiving it. It announced itself as the Campaign for a Scottish Assembly. No-one disagreed when Jimmy Milne, who had played a leading part along with Labour devolvers like George Foulkes and the SNP's Keith Bovey in getting the initiative started, declared that a year of Margaret Thatcher had strengthened rather than diminished the case for home rule. Not that this brought the prospect any closer. All the CSA really had going for it was the breadth of its support. In the hall were Labour MPs, trade unionists, nationalists, Liberals, Communists, clergy, academics (Dr Jack Brand of Strathclyde University, was elected CSA chairman), and even a Tory, Helen Millar, who won one of the biggest cheers of the day by asking (an absent) Lord Home how his improved assembly was coming along. The favourite theme was unity, and the need to heal the divisions that had levied such a grievous price the previous year. When the Labour MP Dennis Canavan attacked government spending cuts, he was shouted down by demands that he stop making 'political' speeches and stick to devolution. Isobel Lindsay, then of the SNP, roundly rebuked colleagues for jeering Mrs Millar's presence. Ray Michie, later a Liberal Democrat MP, told the meeting: 'We have to throw away the flags, stop the shouting, and divest ourselves of our gullibility and naiveté.' They were stirring words, though a year later they would be answered ominously when the SNP decided to boycott a CSA rally to mark the second anniversary of the referendum. Many of the nationalists active in CSA were members of the '79 Group', a faction formed to shunt the SNP leftwards, which was already in trouble with the party leadership and would be purged a year later. But the bigger problem was that the referendum debacle had hardened opinion within the SNP against having anything to do with measures short of independence. Still, the CSA beavered away drafting policy papers on this and that, and generally doing no great harm. It was a very small acorn, but it would eventually produce a sprightly oak.

Another chink of light, and ultimate false dawn, came in the spring of 1981. That February, the National Coal Board chairman, Sir Derek Ezra, had told leaders of the mining unions that he needed to reduce capacity by 10 million tonnes. The miners claimed that up to 50 pits and 30,000 jobs would have to go in consequence. Before full details could be announced by NCB area directors, the NUM executive declared that it would ballot on strike action unless the government intervened to prevent the cutbacks. Several NUM areas jumped the gun and began unofficial stoppages without awaiting a response. A reincarnation of that old grouping the 'Triple Alliance' was formed, with the steelworkers and the railwaymen promising to support a national miners' strike. The government took a quick survey of coal stocks, and decided that it was not the moment for a fight. Talks were hurriedly arranged between Ezra, NUM president Joe Gormley, and Energy Secretary David Howell, from which Gormley emerged to announce that the government had agreed to increase subsidies and the action could be suspended. A few people recalled an article in the *Economist* three years earlier, which had disclosed details of another 'Ridley Plan', this time on the contingency arrangements needed to defeat a miners' strike. These arrangements, which included high coal stocks, non-union labour to truck supplies, and ready recourse to coal imports, were not in place in 1981, but they soon would be. Soon, too, there would be different faces on the scene: Gormley (having lingered long enough to disqualify McGahey on age grounds as a successor), would retire, to be replaced by Arthur Scargill; Ezra would make way for Sir Ian MacGregor, well-established as a diminutive hard man at BSC; and Howell would be replaced by Peter Walker. Confrontation had been postponed, not abandoned. But, for the moment, it seemed like another encouraging parallel with the humbling of Heath: the Tory government had backed away from taking on the miners.

The other fleeting source of cheer available to the labour movement was that the government was becoming spectacularly unpopular. By the end of 1981, the polls were showing Margaret Thatcher to be the least admired Prime Minister since records began. Even with the apparently irresistible rise of the SDP, and Labour's equally precipitous slide into internecine carnage, electoral nemesis seemed only a matter of waiting. But then something at once ludicrous and cathartic happened. Argentina invaded the Falkland Islands and Margaret Thatcher went to war. The bravery of the armed forces who recaptured, at a heavy cost, the dreich South Atlantic colony outshone both the government's culpability in encouraging the Argentine *junta* to regard the islands as up for grabs, and the distinctly Ruritanian air which surrounded the whole episode. Thatcher's faintly absurd tendency to turn up the Elgar and wave the Union flag suddenly seemed vindicated, and much of Middle England persuaded itself that a great war leader had won a great war. Even the subsequent humiliation of Grenada, when her loyal ally Ronald Reagan invaded a Commonwealth country without telling her, failed to dull the sheen. A year later, and with more than three million people still out of work, Britannia stormed to the polls and won an overall majority of 141. Though her vote actually fell from its 1979 level, she was able to open up a commanding lead thanks to a strong showing by the SDP–Liberal Alliance, and a heroically discordant campaign by Labour, performed to the libretto of a manifesto which Gerald Kaufman called 'the longest suicide note in history.' It was Labour's worst defeat since 1935, and would have been much worse but for the eccentricities of the electoral system. Four years of anarchy had cost the party three million votes since 1979: its share of the popular vote was 27.6 per cent, just two points ahead of the Alliance. Only in ever-perverse Scotland did Labour show at all strongly, largely because the SNP, having indulged in its own fraternal strife, polled less than 12 per cent. In nearly 300 constituencies across Britain Labour was in third place or worse. As Denis Healey would later write, 'that Tony Benn lost his seat in Bristol was small compensation.' Indeed it was. With that size of a majority, Margaret Thatcher could do almost anything she wanted. The night returned, blacker than ever.

In the period following the 1983 general election, there was a recognition at the top of the labour movement that the arithmetic had changed, and that tactics had to follow suit. The Labour Party replaced Michael Foot with Neil Kinnock, who embarked on a long and bruising campaign to rid the party of its more voter-unfriendly elements and policies. The government, meanwhile, seemed well versed in what Shakespeare calls the insolence of office. Norman Tebbit introduced by far the most predatory of its Industrial Relations Bills, which mounted an assault on Labour Party finances that fell a long way short of being subtle. It was a rare moment of triumph for the labour movement when all 37 unions with political funds voted to retain them, and several others voted for the first time to create them. But it was not enough to forestall the grudging realisation that the clock which had stopped in 1979 would never again be restarted.

At the September 1983 TUC, Len Murray signalled a shift in strategy into what became known as the 'New Realism', a recognition that the unions needed to adapt their policies and approach to circumstances that had changed, not just radically, but permanently. Before the election, at special conferences in Wembley and at the Kelvin Hall in Glasgow, the unions had committed one another to mutual support in defying the Tory laws. But the election had dispelled hopes that the laws, and the government which begat them, would be a fleeting aberration: Mrs Thatcher, plainly, was there to stay, and a way would have to be found of enduring her. It would not be a smooth route for the TUC – thirteen years later, its congress could still argue fiercely over which, if any, of the Tory laws a Labour government should repeal – nor would Murray's be the only such initiative. In 1987, his successor, Norman Willis, unveiled his own ambitious collage of proposals for realigning unions to a changed environment; and in 1996, Willis's successor, John Monks, unwrapped yet another package, this time called the 'New Unionism'. Yet Murray's was the decisive shift of course. 'We cannot talk as if the trade union movement is some sort of alternative government, Bonnie Prince Charlie waiting to be summoned back from exile,' he said. 'We cannot just say that our policies are fine and that it is our members who are all wrong.' He won his vote, narrowly, and commentators began to talk cautiously about a new style of trade unionism, constructive rather than confrontational, running with the political grain. Yet, there was to be one last, mighty throw for the old style of industrial confrontation, and it was to come just six months later with the miners' strike of 1984–85.

The STUC was not much impressed by the new realism. Its principal activity in the period immediately prior to the election had been to organise the Scottish end of the 'People's March for Jobs', a conscious echo of the NUWM marches. Sixty marchers left Glasgow's Queen's Park on 23 April 1983, forming the vanguard of the 600 who would arrive in London six weeks later, and six days before polling day. Its first congress after the election, at Aberdeen in April 1984, offered few concessions to Murray's conciliatory approach. A pugnacious composite declaring outright opposition to the Tory laws was successfully moved by the print union leader Tony Dubbins, battlescarred from months of picket line attrition outside the non-union Warrington works which printed Eddy Shah's Messenger Group newspapers. The TUC general council had told Dubbins during that dispute that it would support him only within the bounds of the law, which he claimed was a breach of the Wembley accord. He readily acknowledged that his STUC motion did commit unions to go beyond the law: 'The movement does not need any "New Realism", or modern principles of trade unionism. The only realism and principles we need are the old, tried and tested ones which form the cornerstone of our movement – unity and solidarity. If we have those, no Tory legislation can destroy us.' Two years later, Dubbins would have his answer in the cold wind that whistles down Wapping Highway.

But that debate was indicative of the mood as Mick McGahey rose to move an emergency motion calling on the movement to rally round the miners with both financial support and 'various forms of action' as they embarked on their epic battle for mining jobs and communities. It was the speech in which McGahey, scornful of criticism over the lack of a national ballot, famously diagnosed the condition of 'ballotitis', rightful action smothered by an excess of balloting. The Scottish miners, protesting at the threat to Polmaise Colliery, had set in motion with their Yorkshire colleagues the rolling programme of area action which Scargill would seek to translate into a national strike mandate under the NUM's Rule 41. While there could be no question of the Scottish movement turning its back on the miners, there were many who felt privately unhappy about the lack of a national ballot, the issue that was to dog the strike. Alex Kitson, seconding, struck a note which, while fully supportive, was just slightly more circumspect legally: 'We won't instruct anybody. We will leave it to the conscience of our members to support the miners. We have always done that and when we have appealed to them, they have fallen in behind us.' One by one, the big unions trooped to the rostrum to promise their support: Jimmy Morrell of the General and Municipal Workers, Johnny Walker of the train drivers, Ken Cameron of the firefighters, Ron Curran of the Public Employees, Andy Barr of the railwaymen. Barr had a message for the Prime Minister: 'I can tell her that if she attempts to move the coal by rail she will be moving it herself. There will be no railwaymen.'

It was not quite that simple. At that same congress, Clive Lewis of the steelworkers moved what was fast becoming an annual motion on the precarious prospects of the Scottish steel industry. The steelworkers knew that British Steel's ambitions to be rid of most of its Scottish capacity had been frustrated only by political pressure, not least the implicit readiness of George Younger to resign as Scottish Secretary. Political pressure had brought integrated steelmaking to Motherwell, and only political pressure was keeping it there. Therefore, anything which afforded a politically tenable excuse to close Ravenscraig would be fatal. Furnaces and coke ovens allowed to crumble for lack of fuel would be just such an excuse. Yet the steelworkers were bound to the miners in the Triple Alliance. Moreover, no-one outside the steel union itself had expended more energy in fighting to save the Scottish steel industry than Mick McGahey. Miners at Polkemmet knew, too, that their pit's future was entirely dependent on the survival of Ravenscraig. It was an acute dilemma.

Scargill asked the steelworkers' leader, Bill Sirs, on 29 March 1984 to block all movements of coal into the steelworks. Sirs replied firmly that he was not prepared to see his members' jobs 'sacrificed on someone else's altar,' a position that prompted scathing references to the 'Cripple Alliance' in mining communities. It fell to the STUC to try to broker a compromise in Scotland. Milne and Douglas Harrison, STUC assistant secretary responsible for economic matters, embarked on a series of tense and occasionally vituperative negotiations. The key players were McGahey and his deputy, George Bolton; Lewis and the Ravenscraig union convener, Tommy Brennan; and Johnny Walker, whose members drove the coal trains from

Hunterston to Motherwell. On 6 April, McGahey agreed to allow two trainloads of coal a day into Ravenscraig to keep the fabric of the plant intact. In the days that followed, similar deals were reached in the steel towns of northern England and Wales. But British Steel management was not prepared passively to accept the unions' dispensations. Over the next few weeks, the trains from Hunterston grew steadily longer, until each required two locomotives to haul it. Further talks were held, which resulted in the allowance being cut to one train a day; whereupon British Steel switched to road haulage. An appeal went out for volunteer drivers to truck the coal in at £50 a trip and dozens, for whom 'cowboys' was the kindest union epithet, accepted. This sudden influx of non-union truckers in turn enraged the TGWU. Mass picketing in the early part of May at both Ravenscraig and Hunterston saw some of the most volatile confrontations of the strike in Scotland, as police horses cleared the way for the lorries, and numerous pickets were arrested. Finally, Milne managed to broker a deal whereby TGWU drivers would bring 18,000 tonnes a week into the plant. It avoided the sort of running battles which were already starting to escalate over the same issue at Scunthorpe and Orgreave, but it was also much more coal than Ravenscraig needed merely to keep its furnaces fired. Ill-feeling was destined to smoulder on between the erstwhile Triple Alliance partners for many years to come. It was finally put to rest in June 1990 when the Scottish miners, at their conference in Perth, voted to throw their weight behind the campaign to save Ravenscraig, and Tommy Brennan, fighting the last battle for his plant, was invited to speak at the miners' gala.

Mediators in such charged circumstances rarely win friends. South of the border, relations between the NUM and the TUC deteriorated rapidly. Arthur Scargill, not a man given to collegiate decision-making, believed that allowing the TUC to become involved in influencing the strategy of the strike would result in a sell-out: memories of 1926 were repeatedly invoked. 'The TUC can give us support, providing they want to give that support as individual unions,' Scargill said in June 1984. Shortly afterwards, he made it clear that he saw the role of the TUC in simple, supportive terms: instructing workers not to cross picket lines or handle 'scab' supplies (which was now unlawful), and raising money for the miners. He had already signalled his contempt for the TUC by coming off its general council in favour of McGahey after the NUM's seat entitlement fell from two to one. When Labour MPs complained privately to Len Murray at the outset of the strike about the lack of a ballot, Murray replied bleakly that the TUC had been asked to keep its distance. But as the strike wore on, the TUC was becoming increasingly appalled at the violence taking place, and at the lack of any evident way out of a conflict in which the two most determined class warriors of the age, Arthur Scargill and Margaret Thatcher, were plainly intent on throwing every available weapon at each other. Six months into the strike, the TUC and NUM top leaderships met for the first time since the dispute had begun, and as a result the TUC promised at its September 1984 congress to mount a blockade on fuel supplies. But the statement was swiftly disowned by several of the union leaders, notably Eric Hammond of the electricians, whose support it presumed. The TUC, however, had decided that it must now carve a role for itself in resolving a dispute that was damaging the standing of the wider movement, particularly after it emerged in October that the NUM had been seeking support from the Gaddafi regime in Libya, which not long before had gunned down a policewoman in central London. Therefore, the new TUC general secretary, Norman Willis, took on an increasingly forlorn role in trying to coax to life a peace talks process in which Scargill was disinterested, and in deploring the violence on the picket lines: for which trouble, he was rewarded by having a noose dangled before him as he addressed miners in Aberavon in November. As winter descended, and a steady trickle of miners began to rejoin those who had stayed at work, the TUC grappled with the thankless task of liaising between an equally obdurate Scargill and MacGregor. Long before the strike had limped to its brave, but ignoble, end, the TUC had been awarded a prominent place in Scargill's extensive demonology.

No-one shook a noose at Jimmy Milne. The centre of political gravity was certainly closer to the NUM's in the STUC than in the TUC, and closer still to that of the Scottish miners, in whom the conduct and aftermath of the strike wrought a growing estrangement from the Scargill general command in Sheffield. Milne, McGahey and Bolton, Scottish Communists all, were tied by bonds of mutual understanding and loyalty that contrasted starkly with the rancid relationship between Scargill, Willis and Neil Kinnock. An important part of that understanding was the need to maintain common purpose with the widest possible spread of support. In his introduction to the STUC's 1985 report, penned in the last demoralising days of the strike, Milne felt moved to write: 'The magnificent sacrifice, dedication and loyalty displayed by the membership of the NUM and their families has inspired the movement. By their own exertions to save the mining industry in Scotland, by their example, they have paved the way for the salvation of the entire trade union movement.' It was hard to imagine Len Murray or Norman Willis wanting to write that.

But the bigger, if less romantic, truth is that in a UK confrontation the STUC never could be, and never was, tested in the way that the TUC was. It was not at the centre of the action, and its opportunities and responsibilities were consequently lesser. It could, and did, lobby in general terms for reason to prevail, and went so far as to write to Thatcher in November 1984 requesting a meeting at which the general council would put the case for reopening negotiations between the NUM and the NCB. Thatcher responded dismissively that Younger was the appropriate minister for the STUC to meet, and on 25 January the STUC led one of its familiar ensemble deputations to the Scottish Office's Alhambra House premises in Glasgow: the churches were there, as was an impressive array of Lord Provosts and regional conveners, and the SCDI. The deputation told Younger that the strike was causing immense hardship and economic damage, and that the only way to settle it was by negotiation. Younger agreed. It was scarcely a breakthrough.

For the most part, the STUC's role was that to which Scargill wanted to confine the TUC: support, rather than interference. The STUC went about it with dedication and gusto. John Henry, the deputy general secretary, took charge of a tireless fundraising effort, much of it conducted through trades councils and unemployed workers' centres, with the proceeds being kept in a special account out of the reach of the sequestrator. Almost £2 million in cash was raised, and huge quantities of foodstuffs were donated at weekly street collections. Funds were also raised through a December benefit concert, a Scotland-wide prize draw, and a Christmas financial appeal. Just as importantly, the STUC maintained rhetorical support. It organised a Scottish Day of Action on 9 May 1984, in which leaders of the STUC's extensive civic militia joined thousands of workers at seven demonstrations in Scotland's major cities and towns. There were further demonstrations right through the summer, organised jointly by the STUC and the Scottish miners, culminating in a further all-Scotland march and rally in Glasgow on 15 September. At all these occasions, STUC speakers enthusiastically endorsed the miners' cause, if not the tactics by which Scargill was waging the dispute. In the autumn, the STUC convened a joint meeting with Labour's Scottish executive, the Scottish Labour MPs and the Scottish miners' leadership, from which flowed a broad-based conference, reminiscent of the 1972 'Scottish Assembly', on the carefully-worded theme of 'the Scottish economy with particular reference to the mining industry.' Symbolically, it was held in Partick Burgh Hall where, 15 years earlier, a conference had debated the Scottish economy with particular reference to Upper Clyde Shipbuilders. Come the New Year, the round of collections and demonstrations began anew.

The most important effect of the STUC's involvement was to broaden the issue, and thus the base of support on which it could draw. As far as the government was concerned, the point at issue was the rule of law, the primacy of democratic government over syndicalist coercion, as summed up in Margaret Thatcher's long-resented reference to 'the enemy within.' In Scotland, Jimmy Milne would later write, the cause 'developed beyond the primary issue of opposing pit closures, to the need for a broad defence of the right to work and maintain the economic viability of Scotland.' It is Milne's legacy to have fostered in the STUC a lasting aptitude for finding the common ground in any given issue on which civic Scotland can stand together, the approach that would drive STUC strategy throughout the Thatcher and Major era. It could not always succeed, yet it could usually impress; and it was to give the STUC a relevance across those unforgiving years which no other part of the British trade union movement could rival. Rarely was it accomplished with greater finesse than during the miners' strike, despite the potential for division in which that brave but vainglorious affair abounded. Eric Clarke, the Scottish miners' secretary (and later a Labour MP) told the 1985 STUC congress in Inverness: 'The constructive role of the STUC during the strike . . . was more, and far more, than was achieved by the whole of the TUC, and is a foundation to start off the very hard fight back.'

It was indeed a hard fight. Albert Wheeler, the NCB's unyielding Scottish area director, had enforced more ruthlessly than in any other coalfield a policy of dismissing miners for misdemeanours, great or trivial, committed during the strike. By the time of the return to work in March 1987, more than 200 of the 700 'victimised' miners were from Scotland; many would stay sacked, and none would be reinstated until long after Wheeler had been promoted out of Scotland. McGahey, barely recovered from a beating he had suffered in the closing weeks of the strike, issued an emotional appeal on their behalf at Inverness: 'Do not tell me about the Tolpuddle Martyrs. I got that from my mother's milk, but there are Tolpuddle Martyrs of 1985.' The Scottish movement did stand by them, then and later (McGahey acknowledged a £1,000 cheque from the steelworkers). But for the NCB, victory had established what the fast talk of the day called 'management's right to manage.' The old co-operation between management and union in the day-to-day running of the pits was, for the moment, gone.

So too, in a very short space of years, were most of the pits. Wheeler's zeal had extended beyond dismissals. During the strike, the Bogside pit in Fife and Polkemmet in West Lothian had been allowed to flood as a result, the miners claimed, of deliberate management sabotage. The Frances colliery near Kirkcaldy, once scheduled to become Scotland's showcase pit, had been badly damaged by fire. None re-opened, and in the next few years, most of Scotland's deep mines followed them into oblivion: Bilston Glen, Seafield, Polmaise, Killoch, Barony. Wheeler is said to have told colleagues soon after the strike that the Scottish coalfield was to reduce to just one pit, the Longannet complex near Kincardine. By decade's end, it had just about come to pass: only Monktonhall, rescued from mothballs by a miners' co-operative, and Longannet survived, the latter taken over on privatisation by a consortium in which the Scottish miners were partners. George Bolton and Campbell Christie, successors respectively to McGahey and Milne, were among its directors.

Even these pits teetered on the brink. In late 1987, it emerged that the coalfield's mainstay customer, the South of Scotland Electricity Board, had secretly explored the prospect of importing its coal requirements because of dissatisfaction at the cost of Scottish coal, for which the purchase contract was due for renewal. A two-year campaign ensued in which the STUC and the Scottish miners fought shoulder-to-shoulder with their former protagonists in management to save the remaining fragments of the Scottish mining industry. At one meeting, the British Coal (as the NCB was now known) chairman, Sir Robert Haslam, warmly thanked the STUC for its 'helpfulness,' and asked that it keep its talent for publicity at his disposal. The SSEB, trying to get itself trim for privatisation, swiftly learned what life was like on the wrong end of the Scottish consensus. It found itself publicly indicted on a charge of sabotaging Scottish interests – even though it, not British Coal, was the Scottish protagonist. Eric Clarke opened an emergency debate on the matter at the 1988 STUC congress in Ayr by offering 'a vote of thanks to the STUC and especially Campbell Christie, and his officers and staff, to the local authorities, the Parliamentary Labour Party and many other people in other parties, our academic friends and church members and many other people' who had actively supported the campaign. He might have added to this extensive cast list Malcolm Rifkind, Younger's successor as Scottish Secretary, who roused himself to 'bang heads together' in pursuit of a deal. Eventually one was secured, thanks to a combination of public pressure, legal action by British Coal, and a marked improvement in productivity at Longannet. The industry, not just the miners, had this time fought for a future.

By then, Arthur Scargill and the NUM were a shrivelled relic of the might they had once been. The Nottinghamshire miners, most of whom had worked through the strike, had split away to form the Union of Democratic Mineworkers. Of the 800 pits nationalised in 1947, only fifty remained. Nearly 140 had closed since the strike, and 100,000 jobs had gone from the industry. Because Scargill refused to negotiate alongside the UDM, his members had had successive meagre pay deals imposed upon them. Scargill was isolated within the Labour movement, held in contempt by much of what remained of his union, and facing allegations of personal financial impropriety. And yet, more than seven years after the great defeat, there was to be one small, but sweet, consolation. The Government was by now embarked on what the Energy Secretary, Cecil Parkinson, had called 'the ultimate privatisation.' In October 1992, Michael Heseltine, President of the Board of Trade, announced in the Commons that 31 of the remaining pits were to close in readiness for the sell-off, at a cost of 30,000 mining jobs and up to 70,000 in other industries. The usual belligerent noises from Sheffield, calmly anticipated by ministers, were duly made. But then something astonishing happened. The Shires of England rose in revolt. Tens of thousands of people marched in protest in leafy suburbs a hundred miles from the nearest pit village. In London, 100,000 massed to hear Scargill speak in Hyde Park. More importantly, enough Tory MPs threatened to rebel to force Heseltine to retreat, and trim his hit list to 10 pits, with the rest being placed under review. It was a brief reprieve. In due course, most of the condemned pits did close, and the industry reverted to private ownership. Yet to those who had sacrificed so much in 1984–85 there was a sort of vindication. The government had made the mistake of equating public derision for Scargill with indifference towards an industry which, it now transpired, people still held integral to the character of Britain. The miners, if not their leader, were still loved.

Scottish miners knew that. Each June, they formed up in dwindling numbers with a diminishing array of bands, and marched proudly to their gala, waved on their way by friendly applause and good wishes from the people in the Edinburgh streets. In 1991, the STUC took over the running of the gala from a Scottish NUM reduced to fewer than 2,000 members, and it became an annual celebration of the Scottish labour movement, though with the miners still to the fore; just as they had been when Bob Smillie counted his membership in six figures. Yet if the Scottish miners remained the talisman of the movement's best traditions, the strike symbolised something very different. As was reinforced at Wapping the year after the miners' defeat, the odds had shifted completely, and irrevocably, from the days of Edward Heath. In any trial of strength now between unions and government, between industrial action and industrial law, there could only be one outcome.

Coming just weeks after the return to work, the Inverness congress was never going to be a joyous occasion, but neither was it the embittered and fractious gathering that it might well have been in the circumstances: or that the TUC congress was in Blackpool five months later. Proceedings at Blackpool, both before and behind the cameras, blazed with post-strike recriminations and with an acrimonious row, which took most of the week to fudge, over whether or not the engineering union should be expelled for accepting government funding for ballots in defiance of TUC policy. Had not the general council backed down, several right-wing unions would almost certainly have joined the engineers in a rival TUC. Then, on the day Neil Kinnock arrived in Blackpool, Arthur Scargill managed to persuade delegates to reject general council pleas and call on a future Labour government to repay the money confiscated from the NUM in fines and sequestration: Kinnock, visibly furious, described that prospect as 'very, very remote.'

The contrast between the two congresses stood greatly to the credit of Jimmy Milne, who had announced ahead of Inverness that he planned to retire the following year. His successor had been named as Campbell Christie, deputy general secretary of the Society of Civil and Public Servants. Among many at Inverness recording their appreciation of Milne's work was Labour's Shadow Scottish Secretary, Donald Dewar, who said: 'I would certainly want to pay tribute to Jimmy Milne . . . I am sure that we will have an equally happy relationship with Campbell Christie when he comes in.' In the event, relations with Christie would not always be quite so happy; but the compliment to Milne from a Labour right-winger bore handsome testament to the effectiveness with which an old Aberdeen Communist had maintained unity within the Scottish movement.

Christie came with an impressive pedigree. Born in 1937 in Carsluith, he was raised in Glasgow and joined the civil service at 17, drifting into what was then the rather soporific world of the civil service unions. By the early Sixties, he had become secretary of the National Assistance Board section in the Civil Service Clerical Association, where he developed a reputation for provocative oratory that unsettled the right-wing Catholic grouping which dominated civil service trade unionism at the time. As the Sixties wore on, Christie and his younger brother Leslie became leading lights in a left-wing caucus, known disparagingly as the 'Sauchiehall Street Mafia', which steadily transformed the SCPS from a 40,000-strong apolitical staff association into a disciplined broad-left TUC union with a six-figure membership. By 1976, he was deputy general secretary of his union, and rapidly becoming the Left's best strategist within the TUC. His departure for the STUC mystified and dismayed many of his southern colleagues. The SCPS was scheduled to merge with the larger, but woefully undisciplined, clerical grades' union, and Christie was to become its general secretary. Beyond that, many saw him as the likely Left candidate to succeed Willis. In an interview with the *Scotsman* at the time of his appointment

Christie said he was chiefly motivated by the wish to help shape a Scottish parliament. He also undoubtedly knew that the Left could no longer capture the TUC general secretaryship though, somewhat recklessly, he admitted in 1990 that he would still take the job if offered. Meanwhile, the union merger was called off, and Leslie Christie became SCPS general secretary.

Campbell Christie took over the STUC leadership at the 1986 congress. The venue was Jimmy Milne's home town of Aberdeen, chosen with the intention of saying a grateful farewell to an outstandingly effective general secretary. But it was not to be. A week before congress, Milne collapsed and died. The celebration became a wake, with the movement's elders queuing at the rostrum to add their laments to the mourning that overhung the entire congress. Hugh Wyper, that year's president: 'His capacity for work was generated by his convictions, and alongside that his love for his fellow human being.' Alex Kitson: 'Jimmy Milne has been a great leader. Thanks to him there is more solidarity in this congress than there is in any other part of the trade union movement in the UK.' Mick McGahey: 'He was not one who ever forgot the need for social change, but he was most careful in how he arrived [at] and achieved that social change.' Neil Kinnock: 'We should remember him not just as a man of causes and commitment but as a man of culture too, who believed that the freedom of the mind should be employed for the great purpose of freeing men and women throughout the world.'

The next year would also bring the death of Jimmy Jack, and the retirements of Johnny Walker, Hugh Wyper, Alex Kitson and Mick McGahey. South of the border, too, a new generation was taking the place of those who had piloted the trade union movement through its days of power and influence in the 1960s and 1970s. In the space of a year, the leaderships of the three biggest TUC unions – the transport workers, the engineers, and the General and Municipal – changed hands. What was less clear was what sort of a movement was going to be there for them to lead.

In the foreword to his last annual report, Jimmy Milne had written: 'It has been a depressing year. All our worst fears have been realised.' He was referring particularly to the closure of the Gartcosh cold rolling mill, a key element in Scotland's steadily *dis*integrating integrated steel industry. But the comment bore wider interpretation. Under-remarked at the time, a collapse in oil prices was dragging the Scottish economy down into a second recession in five years, just as the rest of the UK was recovering its growth momentum. In July 1986, Scottish unemployment recorded its biggest rise in nearly three years, with oil-rich Grampian contributing a sixth of the increase. By the time of the 1987 general election, eight of the ten British constituencies with the worst unemployment increases over the preceding two years, and half of the worst 50, were in Scotland. The contrast between Scotland's economic doldrums and the burgeoning wealth in the south-east of the country, coupled with a relentless government drive to free up market forces by deregulation, had also exposed Scottish companies to an unprecedented onslaught of predators. According to research commissioned for an erudite 1989 STUC publication, *Scotland's Economy: Claiming the Future*, the capital value of Scottish-owned industry fell by more than half in the two-year period 1985–86, from £4.7 billion to £2.3 billion. The most notorious of the takeovers was Guinness's unprincipled acquisition of Distillers, but that same period saw Arthur Bell, House of Fraser, and Coats Paton pass out of Scottish ownership. It was an exceptional, but far from isolated, burst of activity: in 1988 even the rump of UCS, Govan Shipbuilders, would pass into Norwegian ownership. In that case and some others, takeover improved the prospects of struggling industries, yet the pattern was one which greatly worried the STUC because it drained the higher corporate functions, wherein strategic authority lay, away from Scotland. Not only had many of Scotland's economic mainstays collapsed, but much of what remained was passing out of Scottish control.

There were new jobs coming on stream, but they were stubbornly resistant to union organisation. 1983 was the seventh, and last, year in which the STUC recorded an affiliated membership of over a million. Thereafter, the picture was one of unrelieved decline, and by the STUC's 99th year affiliations were down to 670,632, below the level of its golden jubilee year in 1947. Jobs growth was in the services sector, particularly financial services which – buoyed first by the investment opportunities of North Sea oil, and latterly by deregulation – increased employment by an annual average of 3.25 per cent in the late 1970s and 4 per cent in the 1980s. But while the white collar unions gained some success in building membership within the back office workforces of the financial institutions, much of the growth took place in small fragmented workplaces, always stony ground for union recruitment, and many of the more routine jobs fell victim to new technology.

Manufacturing was recording some successes, but few that offered much scope to the unions. The advent of desktop computers created an immense boom in the electronics industry and the SDA's inward investment operation, given a ministerial byline in 1981 with the creation of Locate in Scotland (LiS), proved highly successful at attracting growth companies to what had become known as Silicon Glen. By decade's end, Scotland was assembling a third of Europe's personal computers and the industry's output was averaging an annual growth rate of 14 per cent. Yet it was, by nature, a capital-intensive sector, and its workforce grew by just 5,000 jobs in the 1980s, while the rest of Scottish manufacturing shed 200,000. It also, of course, accelerated the trend towards external ownership. Most frustratingly of all for the STUC, much of the Glen, particularly the US companies which dominated it, was non-union. The STUC suspected LiS of deliberately marketing non-unionism as part of its sales pitch to inward investors, something LiS has always denied. Christie chafed at the contrast with the Wales TUC, which was conventionally given advance notice of forthcoming investments by the Welsh Development Agency and thus afforded an opportunity to negotiate for union recognition. The STUC lobbied LiS for a similar facility, but got nowhere.

The more the unions' scope for action was legally constrained, the less incentive there was for people to join them. A combination of punitive legislation and enduringly high unemployment made workers ever more reluctant to cause trouble, and employers ever less inclined to pay any attention to union representations. Even in the offshore industries, which had absorbed workers displaced from traditional manufacturing, many of the biggest employers refused to recognise the unions to which their workers belonged. An unofficial grouping, the Offshore Industry Liaison Committee (later to form itself, none too successfully, into a union), mounted a series of protest actions on offshore installations against difficult odds, but still made little headway in securing union recognition. The STUC and its affiliates seemed to be shut out of most of the Scottish economy's growth sectors, and worryingly reliant for its membership on declining traditional industries.

These cheerless factors would dominate the industrial agenda for Campbell Christie and the STUC into the 1990s, throwing up a succession of difficulties. The dangers of a branch plant economy, identified all those years before by George Middleton, were vividly demonstrated in January 1987 when the US vehicle builder Caterpillar, having suffered incursions on its global market share, abruptly announced that it was going to close the Uddingston plant where, 16 weeks earlier, it had rewarded productivity by bestowing a £62.5 million investment package called 'Plant With a Future'. It was a chilling reminder that in multinational companies, as in forestry, remote branches are always the first thing to prune. The workforce, led by the charismatic John Brannan (and with Jimmy Airlie as their national officer) mounted a UCS-style occupation of the plant. Christie immediately sent them a message of support: 'The whole of Scotland is on your side, and we will help in every possible way to turn that goodwill into financial and industrial support.' Both halves of the statement were true, but it did little good. Malcolm Rifkind, whose department had poured millions into the plant over the years in regional aid, tore strips off Caterpillar's president, Peter Donis, at a meeting in London. Demonstrations were mounted in Scotland and Westminster. The STUC summoned its usual all-singing, all-dancing coalition to build public pressure on the company, and backed up the lobbying with more substantive work. It commissioned a report from Strathclyde University's highly-regarded economics unit, the Fraser of Allander Institute, on potential market opportunities for the plant, researched regulations whereby the government might prevent Caterpillar from stripping the premises bare, and helped assemble a working group – which included local authorities, civil servants, clergy and the SCDI – to pursue alternative buyers. But Caterpillar was having none of it, and after 103 days the occupation was ended and redundancy terms agreed. Writing in the 1988 STUC report, Christie called the episode 'one of the most organised and effective campaigns in defence of the right to retain employment in Scotland in recent years.' Yes, and it failed.

As competition for members intensified, some unions – particularly but not exclusively on the Right – began offering employers terms and conditions that a few years earlier would have been unthinkable. Inward investors, if they recognised unions at all, wanted single-union deals, and they began to find themselves confronted with beauty contests between unions, each trying to outdo the other in offering a package that would win the employer's favour. These 'sweetheart' deals, some of which included no-strike clauses, were to plumb a deep well of trouble for both the TUC and the STUC. The more aggressively unions pursued them, the closer they sailed to the TUC's 'Bridlington Rules', which the STUC also enforced, against poaching other people's members. One of the landmark single-union deals was reached by the engineers with Nissan in Sunderland, but it was Eric Hammond's electricians' union (later to amalgamate with the engineers) which played the game most voraciously. The Wapping dispute, in which Rupert Murdoch dismissed his 4,500-strong print workforce in favour of a single-union deal with Hammond, created years of resentment and endless demands for the abrasive Hammond to be cast from the movement. In the event, it was the electricians' refusal to obey instructions to pull out of three other deals that brought their suspension, and later expulsion, from the TUC.

It also brought a wealth of embarrassment to the STUC. The STUC had long maintained a reciprocal arrangement with the TUC, whereby it would replicate any disciplinary sanction imposed for breaches of Bridlington. So, when the TUC suspended the electricians in spring 1988, the STUC general council, despite misgivings on Christie's part, moved to do likewise; even though the electricians' offences had no bearing on Scotland, and their Scottish officer, Alf McLuckie, was about to become STUC president. The general council, having neglected to take legal advice before announcing the suspension, hastily took it now as the electricians applied for a court interdict. The advice was that the general council had better back down, and fast, which it did. It was a less than dazzling performance. There was a postscript, too, which did nothing to repair the STUC's authority.

Because most STUC affiliates were English-based, they had a choice when inter-union disputes arose in Scotland of taking their grievance through either TUC or STUC procedures. More often than not, to the STUC's chagrin, they chose the TUC route. Such a dispute had arisen in early 1987 over the Finnish-owned Caledonian paper mill in Irvine, where the electricians had signed a single-union deal in an industry traditionally organised by the print union, SOGAT. SOGAT had laid its complaint before the TUC rather than the STUC but, once the electricians were suspended from the TUC, it transferred the matter to the STUC in the hope this time of nailing them. For the next two years the STUC stalled. Even though it had amended its rules, it knew to expect a legal challenge if it moved against the electricians. Eventually, its disputes committee found against SOGAT – only to be told by the 1990 congress in Glasgow to think again. It took to late 1990 to find a fudge.

This hapless episode was overshadowed by a much greater fiasco which, though it reflected rather better on the STUC, was to cast a longer shadow over the Scottish union movement. In autumn 1987, the SDA announced that 18 months of secret negotiations had persuaded Ford to build a £40 million components plant in Dundee, employing up to 950 people. It was an exceptional investment both in strategic terms and in the benefits it would bring to a city of high unemployment. But there was a catch. The engineers, it emerged, had agreed a single-union deal with Ford, a piece of fast footwork which some suspicious minds correlated with the presence of their general secretary, Gavin Laird, on the SDA board. The engineers argued that, since it was a greenfield development, the deal could not infringe Bridlington. But the other Ford unions, led by the TGWU, pointed out that Ford had a national agreement, the 'Blue Book', which governed both recognition and wage rates, which the Dundee plant would undercut. They feared, cogently, that the company planned to use Dundee as a Trojan horse to undermine pay and conditions at its 22 other UK sites. Unfortunately, they elected to pursue their grievance through the TUC rather than the STUC, disputes procedure.

Five months of vitriolic exchanges erupted between the AEU and the other Ford unions, as the TUC's investigative machinery, which began with an eight-week hiatus for conciliation, ground into motion. Sweet reason was little encouraged by the fact that the Bridlington rules were already under review with respect to single-union deals, which give all sides in the conflict everything to play for. In the midst of it, manual workers at the other Ford plants went on strike over pay, reinforcing threats of widespread disruption if the Dundee deal was allowed to stand. Not without a measure of courage, the STUC general council declared at its first meeting after the row broke: 'The STUC unreservedly welcomes the Ford Motor Company to Dundee. They are absolutely clear that nothing should be done that would prevent the creation of the new plant in Dundee with the resultant jobs gain.' The trouble was that the STUC could do nothing about it, though it repeatedly offered its help. Norman Willis plodded thanklessly round the combatants, but was unable to soften attitudes. Finally, he led a last-ditch mission in March 1988 to Ford's HQ in Detroit. Only then did he invite the STUC to become involved. Next day, the company announced that it was abandoning the Dundee project. There were powerful grounds to wonder about the sincerity of its intentions in the first place, and plausible reasons to suspect that its doubts about the project were aggravated, if no more, by currency fluctuations and a government review of regional aid provision. But opinion in Scotland was not much interested in nuance. Rifkind blamed 'trade union Neanderthal attitudes,' while his deputy, Ian Lang, offered an alternative archaeological reference to 'bone-headed prehistoric monsters.' The word from the SDA to anyone who would listen was that the STUC's chances of getting near any future potential inward investment were precisely nil. Five months later, Willis told the TUC congress: 'The lesson of Dundee for all of us, certainly for me, is never, never, never, never, never again.' The STUC agreed with that much, at least. The episode had brought relations with the TUC to their lowest point in decades, and Christie crisply proposed a new arrangement whereby inter-union disputes affecting Scotland would be automatically referred to the STUC. The TUC said no.

Single-union 'sweetheart' deals did look convincingly like the way of the future. Few incoming employers, given the degree of choice the legislation afforded, would willingly opt for the sort of multi-union structures that history had bequeathed the older industries. Yet such deals have done little to halt declining unionisation or membership. Nor have they noticeably enhanced union influence. The unions who played the game most aggressively merely won a bigger share of a shrinking cake. With the closed shop outlawed, sole recognition was no guarantee of recruitment, and in many cases the emasculated role which single-union deals provided offered a poor return for a membership subscription. The engineers' deal at Nissan was not technically no-strike, but it did leave little part for the union to play in bargaining or the pursuit of grievances. An elected company council, not a shop stewards' committee, settled pay. Workers discussed problems not in union branches but in work teams. Five years after the plant opened, union membership stood at roughly a third of those eligible, and when the engineers mounted a successful campaign of selective action for a shorter working week in their industry, their great prize of Nissan was left untouched.

What these experiences, no less than the miners' strike and Wapping, did teach unions was that tactics in the new era counted for more than muscle. The fabric of the movement remained remarkably intact, despite the atrophy of membership. The STUC and TUC devoted less of their energy to composing draft Budgets and would-be legislation for the government to ignore, and more to pursuing attainable objectives. Small struggling unions did not vanish, but merged into bigger amalgamated groupings which had the financial and organisational resources to survive a hostile environment. The big unions of the 1990s are very different from those of the 1960s, and organise different workforces. The biggest now is not the TGWU, the engineers or the miners, but Unison, a 1.4 million-strong amalgam of the public employees, health workers and local government officers with a presence across most of what remains of the public sector payroll. The railway staff and the seamen are merged, as are the clerks and the draughtsmen. Unions have learned to offer members an expanding portfolio of services, to make up for the protection they can no longer guarantee; and to broaden their bargaining agenda to appeal to a wider range of workers, for example by pursuing childcare provision and flexible hours to suit working mothers. They have also learned to adapt their objectives and their strategies to changed circumstance. The big setpiece confrontations of the Thatcher age were nearly all about saving jobs, not advancing pay and conditions. For those sorts of issues, the unions have adopted more subtle forms of campaign, often with surprising success. Multi-year pay deals have been agreed, in return for job security. The Scargill legacy taught that the best kinds of industrial action hurt the employers more than the members. Unions have learned the effectiveness of rolling programmes of action, rather than the all-out strike. The obligation to ballot has impelled them to develop techniques of persuasion in place of coercion, both with their members and with the public. A long overdue professionalisation of their public relations has taken place, so that groups like the ambulance staff, the railway workers and the nurses have embarked on action with the public inconvenienced but on their side. Sometimes, too, the ballot habit can work to their advantage more directly. Postal balloting and the increased complexity of collecting subscriptions has required them to keep their membership lists in better order, and so to develop more direct contacts with their members. A large ballot majority for action can convince an employer that the workforce is serious in its intent, and thus prompt an improved offer without action having to be taken. Ballots, once an imposition, have become an integral part of the industrial relations toolkit. It is not the way of life the unions might choose, but it is life none the less, and as such infinitely preferable to the alternative.

One of the elements missing from it, though, is influence on national policy-making, the purpose for which the TUC and STUC were set up in the first place. Yet somehow, the STUC of the Eighties seemed to rise above the evaporation of that influence, and consistently to appear much bigger than the sum of its dwindling parts. The 'somehow' was politics, but not of the governmental type. The STUC was shut out of the processes of governance just as thoroughly as its English counterpart – the number of STUC nominees on Scotland's 15 health boards, for example, fell from 32 in 1979 to none in 1991. In 1988, the government decided to replace the SDA and HIDB with new structures, Scottish/Highlands and Islands Enterprise, which merged the old development agencies with the Scottish end of the Training Agency (provider of state training for the unemployed) and delivered the bulk of their work through a decentralised network of local enterprise companies (LECs). The reforms placed the STUC in something of a dilemma. It suspected, justly, that a prime motivation of the reform was to nobble the development agencies, in deference to the long-held malevolence of some Tories towards their 'interventionist' ways. But the STUC was itself given to advocating decentralisation in economic decision-making and, more particularly, it had argued the previous year, in a manifesto called *Scotland – A Land Fit for People*, for merger between the Training Agency and the SDA. Therefore, it responded much more positively than did the Labour Party to the Enterprise reforms. But its constructiveness went unrewarded. Both the central boards and their self-appointed LEC counterparts were required by the legislation to draw two-thirds of their membership from private business. Only a couple of the lowland LEC boards and none of the Highland ones included trade unionists. The 1990 STUC congress in Glasgow threatened to withdraw STUC support for the reforms. It did not budge ministers an inch.

But government was not the whole of Scottish politics in the 1980s and 1990s. As the Conservatives' electoral mandate in Scotland shrivelled, a new form of civic politics began to gather force, one which contrived both to assert and to embody Scotland's collectivist traditions in conscious defiance of the cult of individualism that underpinned the new Conservative thinking. It worked at two levels. First, when the government insisted that there was no such thing as society, Scottish issue coalitions replied by saying, in effect, yes there is and we are it, here sharing the same banners: trade unionists, clergymen, artists, politicians of various hue, thinkers, councillors, professionals and the rest. Second, as the 1987 general election approached, at which the Conservatives gained a third term on a reduced majority, the Scottish political lexicon began to throw up new phrases: the 'doomsday scenario' (whereby the Conservatives continued to impose their policies on Scotland, though with no electoral mandate north of the border) and the democratic deficit (meaning Scotland's inability to determine the manner of its government at the ballot box). The issue coalitions provided a potent symbol of these arguments, in that what they presented themselves as was Scotland against Thatcherism. Such power as they had was symbolic, not executive. It lay purely in the consensus they represented: by accentuating the majority, they further isolated the minority. The STUC was the principal catalyst which drew these coalitions together, and found the areas of common policy on which they could, usually, stay together. It became the normal and the natural convener of the assembly-in-waiting.

There were two shortcomings to this strategy, and they were important ones. The first was that the Conservatives proved rather hard to shame, even after the 1987 election reduced them to just 10 of the 72 Scottish MPs and less than a quarter of the vote. The second was that non-Tory Scotland was not as united as the STUC wanted to believe. In particular, Labour and the SNP increasingly regarded each other with a deeper loathing than they could muster against the Tories. They were, aside from anything else, keen rivals for the same vote. After the 1987 election delivered

Labour 50 seats, the SNP progressively targeted its strategy against Labour rather than the Tories, jeering that Labour's 'feeble fifty' MPs could do nothing to shield Scotland from Thatcherism. It suited this strategy to stand aside from the issue coalitions, which had a natural Labour preponderance, and to scorn their failures. The tactic was seen at its starkest in the long campaign to save the Scottish steel industry.

Ravenscraig was virtually the last survivor of the great industries brought to Scotland by consensual Fifties industrial direction, and had taken on a symbolism as a totem of national defiance which did nothing to mitigate its jeopardy once British Steel had been privatised in 1988. Detractors called it, not inaccurately, an industrial virility symbol, though it retained a real importance to the Scottish economic base even after the decline of industries, like car-making and shipbuilding, which it had been built to supply. It was Scotland's, and the STUC's, dominant industrial issue of the latter 1980s and the belief grew up, including among Scottish Office ministers, that its closure would be punished by the swift extermination of the Scottish Conservatives. Ian Lang used to chide the Scottish press for their steel fixation, pointing out that there were 30 industries in Scotland which employed more people, but the rebuke never carried much conviction. And so, when the Gartcosh closure was announced in August 1985, all the opposition parties – and some Tories – lamented in unison. One Tory, Iain Lawson, was moved to defect to the SNP and join steelworkers in a march to London. Younger was sufficiently unnerved to arrange the first ever formal meeting between the STUC and Margaret Thatcher, which took place at Prestwick Airport on 5 September 1985. Thatcher said she was 'a great fan of Ravenscraig,' a remark commonly supposed to refer to its resistance to the miners' blockade rather than to its steelmaking capabilities, of which, the STUC commented afterwards, she 'did not have a firm factual grasp.' The STUC, having held a recall congress on the issue, threw itself into organising a cacophony of marches, conferences and lobbies, some of which Tory MPs attended.

But after Gartcosh, the same consensus could never quite be assembled: not least because, as the SNP took to pointing out, it had not worked. Once steel was privatised, the Scottish plants were progressively starved of investment, and the high volume work was loaded elsewhere. In November 1987, ahead of privatisation, Rifkind sought a fresh guarantee of the plant's future from BS's irascible chairman, Sir Robert Scholey, to replace the three-year lifelines secured by Younger in 1982 and 1985. He was told that Ravenscraig would remain in production until at least 1994, 'subject to market conditions.' With less than his usual perspicacity, Rifkind called this meaningless assurance 'superb news for Ravenscraig.' Two-and-a-half years later, the final assault on the Scottish operations began. First the Clydesdale seamless tubes mill at Bellshill was closed, then the hot strip mill at Ravenscraig. The Dalzell platemill next to Ravenscraig was earmarked for rundown (it would eventually survive).

The mighty coalition was once again mobilised, as the Standing Committee for the Defence of the Scottish Steel Industry, and the STUC and its allies worked tirelessly to build resistance. But this time the SNP, while attending some meetings, insisted on playing its own game. Part of that game was to embarrass Labour with 'the Scottish card', by challenging it to support the Scottish plants' case for investment against those of the English and Welsh plants, something it knew Labour could not (as a UK party) afford to do, but which the SNP could do perfectly happily. Lawson, a raucous voice on the issue, was joined in the campaign by Jim Sillars who, having joined the SNP at the beginning of the decade, had won a sensational by-election from Labour at Govan, his wife Margo MacDonald's former seat, in November 1988. Their involvement in the campaign became increasingly energetic, publicity-driven (a three-day fast outside St Andrew's House was one stunt among many), and divisive. There were occasions when they co-operated with the broad campaign – for example, in an abortive 1990 attempt to win a place on the British Steel board for the multi-purpose Scottish left-wing academic and industrialist, Sir Kenneth Alexander (shareholders were unimpressed at being handed an STUC leaflet, *Motherwell Works*, as they took their seats) – but it was always on their own terms. There was, too, a more serious point of division: namely, within government. The Scottish Office still felt politically obliged to pitch its weight behind what it had begun to realise was a forlorn endeavour, but it was increasingly fighting a lone battle in Whitehall, where the prevailing view was that BS, having been privatised, was no longer the government's concern. The STUC found a sympathetic ear in its innumerable meetings with Scottish ministers, but the ear that counted was now beyond its, and their, reach. Fully alive to these forces, Scholey felt empowered to treat the Scottish Office with lofty disdain. Ministerial demands for detailed justification of his decisions were met with the brusque reply that commercial information of this sort was none of the government's business.

Probably, it would have made no difference anyway. Ravens-craig had been put in Motherwell against managerial wishes, and kept there against managerial wishes. Once BS had been cut loose from political control, the plant's fate was irrevocably sealed. Aside from anything else, one of BS's first acts on privatisation was to buy up a substantial share in the steel distribution industry, which meant that it could often achieve a more appetising return from importing products – like welded pipe for the oil industry – than it could from making them in Scotland, and with a fraction of the overheads. In January 1992, just weeks before a general election, the company demonstrated its final disregard for Scottish ministers by announcing Ravenscraig's closure. The Scottish Conservatives prepared for the long-promised nemesis; yet to their astonishment, and everyone else's, it did not come. Other forces, political rather than industrial, kept vengeance at bay.

Retrospection yields the dispiriting, and somehow surprising, realisation that almost none of the Eighties issue coalitions achieved their primary objectives. They did not save Caterpillar or Ravenscraig. They did not change government policy on health, devolution or the economy. Yet, in a broader sense, the coalitions were remarkably successful in distilling and sustaining the extraordinary mood that settled in Scotland against the Thatcher upheaval. The electorally deadly impression of Conservatism as an alien malevolence, suppressing Scotland's will, stemmed in large measure from the consensus that the STUC and its allies were able to portray.

The strategy was adaptable to many levels of agitation. It had its solemn and scholarly side. In July 1986, for example, the general council and Strathclyde Region jointly convened an Economic Summit, which numbered employers' bodies among its partici-pants. The summit decided to set up a broadly-based Standing Commission on the Scottish Economy, chaired by the redoubtable Sir Kenneth Alexander. Members included local authorities, aca-demics, journalists, the voluntary sector, the SCDI, industrialists, the clergy and others. The Standing Commission held seminars, took evidence, commissioned research, and finally produced two reports containing more than 200 recommendations. The material in the reports constituted some of the best modern analysis of Scotland's economic structures, though attention became rather unfairly focused on one of the less practical proposals, namely the creation of a 'white knight' agency to protect Scottish companies from hostile takeover. The interventionist flavour of the recommendations was never, in any event, going to carry much weight with ministers. What counted more was the fact of such work being conducted. It bore the trappings of an alternative government; or, rather, an alternative way of government.

The coalitions could also convey their message by the no less powerful medium of communal fun, a commodity in short supply in those years. As is often the case, adversity in Scotland produced an cultural upsurge during the 1980s, and rarely had Scottish writing, theatre or music seemed more vibrant. The STUC, with Scottish Arts Council backing, had appointed an arts officer for the first time in 1985, and in the years that followed would become an enthusiastic supporter of theatre productions, exhibitions, music festivals, and young talent. In return, it was able to call on the services of sympathetic performers to enliven many of its demonstrations. The high point of these activities was the 'Day For Scotland', a summer festival of music and family entertainments held against the stunning backdrop of Stirling Castle on 14 July 1990. More than 30,000 people flocked to hear the music of Runrig, Hue and Cry, and Dick Gaughan, but also to celebrate their nation's hopes for itself. That they should do so at the invitation of organised labour, and in the eleventh year of Margaret Thatcher's rule, was its own powerful symbolism. It was the STUC at its best: promoting an occasion which, by being ostentatiously non-political, made a powerful political point. Though it cost the STUC a small fortune, it was a memorable and moving event; never more so than when Clive Lewis, that year's STUC president, stepped on to the spotlit stage in his son's leather jacket and set up a chant of 'Ravenscraig, Ravenscraig' in which the crowd thunderously joined. Not many rock festivals cheer for steelmills.

The prototype for that event had come during one of the STUC's biggest campaigns of the late 1980s. In moments of grandiloquence, STUC officials are occasionally prone to claim credit for removing Margaret Thatcher from office. It is a wild exaggeration, as they well know, though it contains a tiny germ of truth. The perverse misjudgement of the poll tax was one factor (Europe was a much bigger one) in persuading the Conservative Party that their leader had lost her grip both on public affection and on reality; the poll tax was implemented first in Scotland, largely at the prompting of a Scottish Tory party aghast at the impact of a rates revaluation; and the STUC played a decisive role in mobilising public defiance of it. It welded together one of its grandest coalitions: the All Scotland Anti-Poll Tax Campaign, and took on volunteer staff at Middleton House to mount a huge programme of events, one of them a 'Rock Against the Poll Tax' concert in Edinburgh's Usher Hall which drew the template for the 'Day for Scotland'. There were petitions, pamphlets, lobbies, and a witty poster campaign featuring a splendid image of Rifkind as a Gilbert & Sullivan governor-general with a paper hat and a wooden sword. A hot-line was set up in the STUC office to advise people on how to foul up the registration process for the tax. There was also an '11th hour protest' in September 1988, at which Scotland was supposed to stop whatever it was doing at 11am and make known its resentment by sounding car horns, ringing church bells and other like gestures; that one fizzled badly. Otherwise, though, the campaign succeeded in generating copious noise and fury, and in alerting the Scottish public to the enormity of what was coming. It involved almost everybody in Scottish civic life: the STUC, Labour, the Liberal Democrats, the Greens, youth groups and pensioners, tenants and civil libertarians, ethnic communities and charities, students and women's groups. But 'almost' was the key word. Missing was the SNP which, together with Scottish Militant Labour (born out of the Militant Tendency), cut a buccaneering dash by campaigning for non-payment. The STUC and the Labour Party decided not to do so.

It was a messy decision. Labour leaders worried, decently enough, about the morality of exposing vulnerable people to the cruelty of benefit arrestments and warrant sales; and not quite so altruistically about the impact on the finances of the local authorities, most of which Labour ran. 'The danger,' Donald Dewar told the 1990 STUC in Glasgow, 'is that you hit those who are innocent and vulnerable, that you make the target your own friends, and let the target you should be firing at – the government

– off the hook.' A mixed metaphor, but an honest enough sentiment. Yet a substantial minority in both the party and the STUC felt differently. A left-wing, nationalistically inclined group, Scottish Labour Action, was among those campaigning for non-payment. It had developed from the Labour Co-ordinating Committee, whose leading lights included Bill Speirs, appointed as Christie's deputy in 1988. Christie and Speirs both refused to pay, as did many senior STUC figures (Christie made a cabaret of dithering about whether to sign the authorisation form, as STUC chief official, to stop the money from his and Speirs's wages). But some in the STUC, particularly among the trades councils, wanted a non-payment campaign, obstructive industrial action by local authority staff and, once non-payment had begun to snowball, union pickets of poindings. Christie and the general council, having initially left open the possibility of a non-payment campaign, ultimately resisted such demands, though at times their tone conveyed duty more than enthusiasm. Certainly, they knew that advocating non-payment would have fragmented the coalition, and that the local government unions were properly worried about their members' jobs. Yet there seems little doubt that Dewar was also applying powerful pressure behind the scenes. In any case, the Scottish public reached its own decision on non-payment. By the third year of the tax, Scottish councils were reporting a staggering £312 million in outstanding arrears. It was civil disobedience on an unprecedented scale, and when the tax was subsequently introduced in England it provoked serious rioting in central London. The poll tax was dead in the water, and Thatcher badly damaged. The STUC could convincingly claim to have done more than most to fuel public awareness and resentment of the tax, even if ultimately it relinquished the limelight to others.

Broad-based campaigning was the STUC's principal means of exerting influence from the early Eighties onwards, but two other channels merit brief mention. The first is the European Union. Ever since the 1960s, the STUC had passed virtually an annual congress motion deploring the EEC (as it then was) and demanding Britain's withdrawal. Typical was the motion from Clydebank Trades Council, carried overwhelmingly at Aberdeen in 1984, which committed congress to a policy of working for withdrawal, seeking immediate suspension of British payments pending a more equitable budget settlement, and 'uphold[ing] the sovereignty of the British parliament.' Yet, shortly before that motion was nodded through, the economic debate had brought hints from two UK union leaders, Terry Duffy of the engineers and David Basnett of the general and municipal workers, of a shift in attitudes which was just starting to take place within the movement. Duffy had attended a demonstration against Europe-wide unemployment in Paris earlier in the year and had found the experience inspiring. Basnett put a blunter case: 'Having lost influence at home we must seek it abroad. Whatever our attitude, the EEC summits, the OECD summits have more influence on this government than we have ourselves.' Margaret Thatcher was by then locked into unceasing attrition with the perfidious foreigners of the Community, and not always winning. Perhaps, union leaders began to reason, the Community could secure improvements in the lot of working people that the unions could no longer achieve.

The turning point was 1988, the aftermath of Thatcher's third election victory. The previous year, she had signed the Single European Act, which committed the EU to become a single, common marketplace in 1992. It was just starting to dawn on the unions (and, it would later seem, on Thatcher herself) just all that market harmonisation might imply. Might it mean, for example, employment regulations becoming standardised at continental levels which were, by then, generally more benign than in Britain? The agenda for the STUC's congress in Ayr in April 1988 contained the usual anti-European motion, moved by the furniture-makers' union. This time, though, Christie stood up on the general council's behalf and asked that it be remitted because, as he acknowledged, the STUC did not yet know enough about the implications of the Single European Act and had commissioned some research on it. The movers, however, refused to remit and the motion was defeated by 1,163 votes to 509.

Five months later, the TUC invited Jacques Delors, president of the European Commission, to address their congress in Bournemouth. The wily French socialist put in a dazzling performance: 'While we are trying to pool our efforts, it would be unacceptable for unfair practices to distort the interplay of economic forces. It would be unacceptable for Europe to become a source of social regression,' he told a spellbound congress. Therefore, he intended to see to it that the integration project took on a 'social dimension,' which he defined as 'a platform of guaranteed social rights, containing general principles such as every worker's right to be covered by a collective agreement . . . social dialogue and collective bargaining are essential pillars of our democratic society and social progress.' For most trade unionists, it was the first glimpse of the agenda that would become the Social Chapter of the Maastricht Treaty, and they loved every syllable. Ron Todd of the TGWU remarked afterwards: 'The only card game in town at the moment is in a town called Brussels and it is a game of poker where we have got to learn the rules and learn them fast.'

Since then, the positive possibilities of the European Union have become a near fixation with British trade unions. Thatcher's isolation within the Community filled them with hope, and not merely because it imperilled her hold on the premiership. At last, it seemed, she had taken on a foe bigger than herself ('I fought Delors, and Delors won,' ran a joke of the time). Unions began to forge new links with their continental counterparts, and to back legal challenges to British employment laws through the European courts, sometimes successfully. Several posted officials to Brussels. The STUC subscribed to Scotland Europa, the Scottish Enterprise-run unofficial legation in Brussels. Campbell Christie, who had been appointed (as a TUC nominee) to the EU's Economic and Social Committee, devoted increasing time to his European activities. Even when John Major opted out of the Social Chapter, unions consoled themselves that the bigger British firms, those with continental operations, would have to adopt its practices, and that the rest would in time follow suit. At time of writing, Tony Blair's Labour Party, for all its showy aloofness from the unions, remains committed to adopting the Maastricht Social Chapter.

The other new channel for STUC influence was more personal to Christie, and more problematical for him. Thatcherism's purging of the old tripartite consensus in public policy-making, and of trade unionists from public office, did not mean that the role of non-governmental bodies had declined. On the contrary, Thatcher and her successor shifted a growing measure of public policy-making out of municipal or governmental control and into the hands of quangos, usually dominated by businesspeople and often got up as analogues for company boards. In Scotland, the shortage of elected Conservatives made this a particularly convenient recourse for ministers, who fished devotedly in the small pool of sympathetic business executives. It became a major criticism among the forces of opposition in Scotland, including the STUC, that a growing proportion of public policy-making was being moved beyond the reach of democratic accountability and turned into merely a matter of management.

Christie shared these concerns, yet he also realised that the old outlets for influence were unlikely to return. Even within the Labour Party, Neil Kinnock, John Smith and Tony Blair had systematically reduced the unions' policy role, and were hardly to be relied upon to afford much greater prominence in the event of a Labour government. Therefore, Christie reasoned, the STUC must find new forums in which to make its voice heard, even if it would be a minority voice and the forums far from the unions' beaten track. He began to seek representation on a widening range of bodies, some of which the movement held in modest esteem. Progressively, he acquired a bulging portfolio of seats on bodies of such questionable trade union political correctness as the Glasgow LEC, the CBI Scottish Manufacturing Group, Scottish Business in the Community, Scottish Coal (owners of the privatised pits) and Falkirk Hospitals Trust.

Some of these appointments drew criticism. In 1995, the general council instructed Christie to decline an invitation from the Scottish Secretary, Michael Forsyth, to join the board of Highlands and Islands Enterprise on the grounds that the STUC should nominate its own representatives, and that two STUC nominees for Highland LECs had been rejected. But it was an even less orthodox appointment which brought Christie the most serious challenge of his general secretaryship. In October 1990 he provisionally accepted an invitation to join the board of Guinness, whose 1986 takeover of Distillers on a combination of City sharp practice and broken commitments to Scotland had been so roundly condemned by the STUC. Christie defended the offer on the grounds that it would strengthen Scottish input to Guinness's corporate decision-making, enhance STUC influence in an impor- tant sector of the Scottish economy, and mesh well with revived trade union interest, reinforced from Brussels, in the concept of worker-directors. All the same, he recognised the sensitivity of the matter. But the company had left him in something of a fix, by insisting on complete secrecy until the appointment had been approved by its board in mid-October, and very limited circulation for several weeks thereafter. Christie, however, needed to get the decision approved by the STUC general council on 7 November, and knew that he would have to smooth some feathers first. So he embarked on a limited consultation with union officials in the drinks industry, and concluded that the reactions were mixed enough to let him proceed. He was wrong. The general council came close to ordering him to refuse the appointment, and passed a compromise motion 'noting' rather than approving it. In particular, the general and municipal workers, with 2,270 members in the company, were incensed. At the next general council, on 5 December, a motion to strip him of the general secretaryship was tabled by the general and municipal. It only gained two votes, but criticism of the way the matter had been handled was more widespread. Christie decided that he had to decline the Guinness offer. At the Dundee congress the following April, a move to authorise STUC officers to accept directorships had to be dropped in the face of objections from a number of unions. It was a chastening experience for Christie who, perhaps more than any of his predecessors, had become the public face of the STUC. The general council had taken the opportunity to remind him that the general secretary was a functionary of congress, and not the other way around.

But the widening of the STUC's political horizons was to continue, particularly after Tony Blair became Labour leader following the death of John Smith in May 1994. Blair greatly accelerated Labour's march, which had begun under Kinnock, into the political centreground and away from its trade union roots. The STUC, though as eager as the rest of the movement to see Labour elected, felt a particular resentment at what it regarded as its increasingly arms-length treatment by the party. Scots, Christie believed, did not harbour the same distaste for trade unionism that Labour's target voters in Middle England did, and he bristled at what he saw to be an unnecessarily slavish pursuit by Labour's Scottish high command of the line set by London. It led to a deteriorating relationship with George Robertson, now Shadow Scottish Secretary, and to a growing enthusiasm for dialogue with other parties. The new Labour creed was that the unions could expect 'fairness, not favours.' Increasingly, the message from the STUC leadership was that this arrangement cut both ways: that the unions too were not, as Christie put it in a radio interview in August 1996, 'in anybody's pockets.'

Christie and Speirs were roundly criticised by some general council members, particularly on the left, for their active involvement after the 1992 general election in the Scotland United group, dedicated to bridging the differences between the devolvers and the nationalists. That led to an organisation called the Coalition for Scottish Democracy, chaired by Christie, which in 1995 convened a Scottish civic assembly, conceived as an alternative to the party structures as a way of giving voice to Scottish society at its broadest. Shortly after the election, the general council blocked a proposal from Christie to invite the SNP leader, Alex Salmond, to congress. In 1994, Christie accepted an invitation from the Scottish Tory president, David McLetchie, to address the party's Scottish council, and in 1996 the Scottish agriculture minister, Lord Lindsay, became the first Conservative minister in 99 years to speak at the STUC congress. Also in 1994, the STUC published a paper on internal restructuring, *Towards the Next Century*, and took the opportunity to observe that in a Scottish parliament elected by proportional representation it might need to work with parties other than Labour, and to indicate a second preference in elections. This was arithmetically undeniable, though some observers detected a tentative overture towards an SNP which had moved leftwards as Labour had edged Right.

Of all the issue coalitions, the best-known, and the one to command the biggest share of STUC attention in the 1990s, was the Scottish Constitutional Convention. It had grown from an initiative of the Campaign for a Scottish Assembly (since renamed the Campaign for a Scottish Parliament: 'assembly' had become a derogatory term, used only by critics of devolution). In 1988, a steering committee set up by the CSA had published a rather grand document, *A Claim of Right for Scotland*. Mostly written by a former Scottish Office civil servant, Jim Ross, the *Claim* deployed a stirring prose style to assert the ancient Scottish principle that sovereignty lay not (as in the British constitution) with the Crown-in-Parliament, but with the people of Scotland. The idea was to create a rubric for the formation of a Scottish Constitutional Convention which, it was hoped, could be broad-based enough to simulate the common will of the people of Scotland; and which could draw up an agreed scheme for a Scottish parliament. The central principle was established from the outset that there would be no votes taken in the Convention, and that it could proceed only by negotiation and agreement. This was, of course, the sort of project which fitted the STUC's style like a glove, and it was a predictably enthusiastic participant from the first, as were the Liberal Democrats. Equally predictably, the Conservative Party decided immediately to have nothing to do with the exercise. The bigger uncertainty concerned Labour and the SNP. Both harboured deep suspicions that they were at risk of being bounced into something politically unacceptable. Eventually Donald Dewar, to the surprise of many, led Labour into the Convention. But the SNP, calculating that the Convention had a built-in bias against independence, decided to stay out, a decision which divided the party deeply, and exposed it to some of the most hostile media criticism in its history.

Undeterred, the Convention held its inaugural meeting on 30 March 1989 in the Church of Scotland's General Assembly hall. It was an impressive, if incomplete, miniature of Scottish civic society, and Christie queued in distinguished company to sign a declaration based on the *Claim of Right*. There were 58 of Scotland's 72 MPs; seven of the eight Euro-MPs; councillors from 59 of the 65 local authorities; seven political parties, including the Greens, the Communists, the Orkney and Shetland Movement and the remnant of the SDP; plus representatives of Scotland's ethnic communities, churches, educators, lawyers, women's movement, Gaels, and even some of its business groups. The STUC had three members: the general secretary, the general council chair, and the women's committee chair, and a number of unions took part as affiliate members. The Convention was to be jointly chaired by two grandee devolvers, Harry (now Lord) Ewing and the former Liberal leader, Sir David Steel. But it was the chair of its executive committee, Canon Kenyon Wright of the Scottish churches' umbrella council, who proved the most talented soundbite-monger. Mocking Thatcher's tendency to the regal pronoun, he warned her not to say no, because: 'We say yes, and we are the people.'

The people got down to business. Working groups were set up and, in November 1990, a first report, *Towards Scotland's Parliament*, was unveiled amid great fanfare in the Glasgow Royal Concert Hall. A fair degree of consensus had been reached about the powers of the parliament – broadly, it would take over the Scottish Office's huge remit – and its character, which would be as unlike Westminster as possible. But there were conspicuous gaps in several of the most difficult and sensitive areas. In several of these, the STUC had been pushing its own policies hard, and would continue to do so.

One was women's representation. The STUC women's committee had pioneered what became known as the '50–50 Principle', the idea that women, being more than half the Scottish population, should be guaranteed at least half the seats in the Parliament. A consultation exercise by the committee over the winter months of 1989–90 found widespread support among women's groups, and in January 1990 the committee published a pamphlet, *Equal Voice for Women*, setting out its case. Intensive lobbying followed. Finally, *Towards Scotland's Parliament* accepted the principle. It was a signal victory for the STUC, and particularly for its women's committee, which had promoted the idea tirelessly in alliance with other women's organisations. But the method of delivering it was left open to future determination, and was problematical. The Liberal Democrats and the Greens were strongly opposed to any legislative mechanism for ensuring gender balance. The STUC's preferred option, which had some support within the Labour Party, was for twin-member (one male, one female) constituencies. The problem was that this would require either very big constituencies or a very big parliament.

That led on to another acutely delicate area, the electoral system for the parliament. Christie and that year's STUC president, George Bolton of the miners, were both long-time supporters of proportional representation, and had begun to lobby hard for the general council to throw its weight behind the idea, on which the STUC had been canvassing affiliates for 18 months. They were helped by two factors, one well-known and the other unexpected. The well-known one was that PR was a fundamental requirement for the Liberal Democrats, and that continued Liberal Democrat involvement was a fundamental requirement of the Convention's consensual credentials. The unexpected one was that Labour's Scottish leadership had begun to edge towards an acceptance of PR for the Scottish parliament, nudged along by Liberal Democrat impatience. First the Scottish executive and then, in March, the party's Scottish conference, came out in favour of the principle of proportionality. The conference vote was close, but went in favour after Speirs talked the electricians' union into switching sides. That just left the STUC itself. The general council repeatedly postponed taking a decision through the spring of 1990, and the matter went to congress in April too close to call. In the event, the motion was amended, replacing 'proportional representation' with the vaguer 'electoral reform,' but went through by a healthy margin. It was enough to allow the Convention to promise that the existing voting system would be dumped for a Scottish parliament; and enough to keep the Lib-Dems aboard.

The Convention had travelled quite a long way in a short time. But, as it swiftly discovered, the unresolved issues were open to the ridicule of its opponents, who picked mercilessly at the obvious patches in the scheme. The Tories in particular had begun to play what seemed like a desperate game, by insisting that the Convention scheme was inherently unstable and that the fundamental choice came down to the Unionist status quo or outright independence, with nothing in between the two tenable. Still, as the 1992 election drew closer, it hardly seemed to matter. Thatcher was gone and her successor, John Major, seemed a man exquisitely fitted to the role of caretaker. The economy was back in recession, and this time it was the Tories' southern heartlands which were hurting most. Every rune in Scotland read Tory wipeout. They had lost a key by-election, in Kincardine and Deeside, to the Liberal Democrats. Ravenscraig had received its death sentence. The only questions seemed to be how well the Nationalists would do (in January 1992, a *Scotsman* poll rather startlingly found half Scotland's voters declaring themselves for independence), and whether Labour's UK lead, which was narrowing, would hold. No-one was prepared for what happened. The Tories not only won in the UK, but gained two more seats and 1.7 more percentage points of the vote in Scotland. It was only a marginal advance but, in the circumstances, it looked a lot like a triumph.

There was an air of stunned disbelief across Scotland, not least among Tory MPs who had been gloomily scanning job advertisements in the press just days before. Only as the dust cleared did it start to become evident what had happened. First, the chattering classes, beginning with the Convention and the press, had mistaken their own excited babble for the voice of the people. Second, the steady fall in Tory support across the preceding dozen years had reflected abstention as well as defection, and now the abstainers had been frightened back to the booths by the belief that the Union was in peril. Third, an advance in the SNP vote, though not translated into seats (Sillars lost Govan), had diluted the challenge to the Tories. Fourth, the holes in the Convention proposals had yawned wider than it had suited the scheme's sponsors to notice. Finally, a last-minute scare campaign by some of the government's allies in the business community, particularly the life assurers, had convinced some voters of the unlikely proposition that major employers would decamp at the first sniff of a devolved parliament.

The first reaction was anger, some of it directed at the fatal disunity among the parties representing the three-quarters of Scots who had voted for some form of home rule. Both the STUC and, fleetingly, Donald Dewar proposed a multi-option referendum. But there was no prospect of the Tories accepting that (their response was the 'taking stock' package of minor administrative devolution and largely cosmetic reforms in Westminster's procedures for handling Scottish business). Nor, it soon became clear, had the election disappointment remotely persuaded the SNP to play the devolutionary game. The only consolation was that the Major government, now with a threadbare majority in Parliament, began to unravel almost immediately after the election, damaged by a long succession of scandals and by deep divisions over Europe. All the same, the road back for the home rulers was going to be a long one. The Convention got down to the slow and glamourless business of filling in the gaps in its scheme. A constitutional commission was appointed, and its report in December 1994 launched a long process of negotiation between the Convention partners. Eventually, on St Andrew's Day 1995, the Convention published its agreed scheme, *Scotland's Parliament, Scotland's Right.*

It was a platform with which everyone involved could agree, if few enthuse. Revenue-raising powers had come down to a right to vary the basic rate of income tax by up to 3p in the pound, a proposal which the Tories lambasted, illogically but effectively, as a 'tartan tax.' Pure proportional representation had given way to an additional member system, based on a parliament of 129 members. Consensus had proved elusive on enforcing the 50–50 principle, and instead Labour and the Liberal Democrats signed an electoral agreement to use their best endeavours to secure gender balance, a pledge made harder to deliver when Labour's system of all-women shortlists fell victim to a legal challenge (the STUC, incidentally, had gone to some lengths to enforce gender balance within its own structures: the two general council seats reserved for women in 1981 had become three in 1986 and 12 in 1990, while new rules agreed in 1995 provided that all general council committees must have either a woman chair or vice-chair, and that the STUC president would be a woman every other year. Other changes in the period included renaming the trades councils 'trades union councils').

At last, there seemed cautious grounds once more for devolutionary optimism. The scheme might be no-one's dream package, but it had been achieved by a consensual form of cross-party policy making which was quite foreign to Westminster's adversarial traditions, and which owed a good deal to the STUC's pioneering work in teasing out the strands in any issue which could bind disparate opinion together rather than cordon it off. Many drew encouragement from the way the Convention had done its work, and hoped that the parliament could, some of the time at least, work in similar fashion. The Convention, too, was resolved that the parliament would be much more accessible, much less executive-dominated, and much less in thrall to cobwebbed ritual, than Westminster. Meanwhile, the polls were running strongly Labour's way, and Labour was committed to enact the scheme in its first year in office.

Yet in summer 1996 the confidence and the consensus shattered. The Labour Party, intent that nothing must undermine its prospects of election victory, and concerned that voters still doubted its capacity for fiscal discipline, had grown alarmed at the 'tartan tax' bombardment from the Tories. The other Convention partners, by contrast, regarded the revenue-varying powers as modest, and were becoming dismayed at Labour's defensiveness and its inability to shift the argument on to more positive ground. Then, abruptly in June, Robertson announced that Labour would hold a referendum before legislating, and that the referendum would contain a separate question on the revenue-varying powers. Across the Convention partnership, and much of the Labour Party in Scotland, the cry was of betrayal. Robertson's junior spokesman on devolution, John McAllion, resigned, as did Harry Ewing from the Convention chair. A pamphlet, co-written by Speirs, called the two-question referendum the worst wrecking device since the 40 per cent rule in 1979. Opposition within the party was led by Bob Thomson of Unison, Labour's Scottish treasurer, and there was an extraordinary week in early September when the Scottish executive, desperately seeking a fudge, found itself committed to the bizarre notion of a second referendum, before public and media derision forced a beleaguered Robertson to dump the idea. The STUC, meanwhile, distanced itself from Labour's insistence that it would not raise taxes even if the power was approved, by publishing figures suggesting that a 3p rise could create 19,000 new jobs in Scotland. 'The STUC cannot speak on behalf of the Labour Party. What we can do is speak up for the jobless, the homeless and all those crying out for more public-sector investment,' said Speirs, a revealing remark from a former chair of Labour's Scottish executive. Christie, around the same time, likened Labour's economic policies to 'tired old monetarist orthodoxy,' and suggested that without higher capital spending there could be no economic dynamism. The STUC approached its centenary with relations at a very low ebb with the party it had helped set up.

In a way, it was oddly apposite. This narrative comes to its close with a general election just months away, and the crystal ball even foggier than usual. There might be a Tory Britain again, or indeed an independent Scotland; in either event the STUC would have every incentive to continue seeking new channels and new alliances to promote its views. Yet the same would surely apply, for different reasons, if Labour won. A Scottish parliament has lain at the centre of Campbell Christie's ambitions for the STUC since the day he took over from Jimmy Milne. If it came into being as the accessible legislature envisaged by the Convention – and the dimensions of that 'if' seem to expand all the time – then the STUC could expect to be to the fore among the civic institutions petitioning the parliament's dispensations. Such a role would flow naturally enough from its vocation in the Thatcher years as the choirmaster of Scottish discontent. The song would not need to be so strident, but it would need to be capable of being sung with equal conviction regardless of who was running the Scottish administration. Its force would not come from being in harmony with the party system, but from being distinct from it: albeit, within the social proximities of a small country. It would be, in other words, a role that placed the STUC's independence of mind and voice at a premium.

The events of its hundredth summer encourage every confidence that the STUC is the equal of that challenge. But then it probably always was. Jimmy Jack's promise that the STUC would be as demanding of Harold Wilson as it had been of Harold Macmillan came, after all, at a time when relations with Labour were at their warmest. The subsequent estrangement between the labour movement's political and industrial wings was not of the unions' choosing, yet it has confounded the STUC much less than the TUC. A thrawn confidence in its own liberty and licence is scarcely a new characteristic of the STUC. It was that same confidence that led a ragbag of tiny unions and cantankerous trades councils a century ago to step aside from the mighty TUC, and make their own way. Of course, much has changed. Many of the doors which the STUC set out to open for Scottish working people are now sealed shut, and others lead into abandoned rooms. But that is the stuff of means, not ends; of strategy, not purpose. The idea that became the STUC is the same at the outset of its second century as it was at the start of its first. The active ingredient, now as then, is Scotland. If Margaret Harding Irwin had been sitting in Campbell Christie's chair in the summer of 1996, it is hard to imagine that she would have done things any differently.

CHRONOLOGY OF KEY
EVENTS

1895: TUC votes to expel trades councils
1896: Provisional scheme for an STUC drafted
1897: Founding congress of STUC, Glasgow
1898: Second STUC congress agrees need for political party to represent working class
1900: Margaret Irwin succeeded as STUC secretary by George Carson; Scottish Workers' Parliamentary Elections Committee formed; disturbances as Scottish socialists oppose Boer War
1901: SWPEC fights first election, coming third in NE Lanark by-election
1902: Taff Vale ruling outlaws most forms of industrial action; SWPEC relaunched as Scottish Workers' Representation Committee
1906: MacDonald pact gives Labour 53 Commons seats in Liberal landslide
1907: Scottish Workers' Representation Committee becomes Labour Party's Scottish Section
1908: STUC votes narrowly to retain its lobbying role
1909: 'People's Budget'
1910: Election sees Labour representation in Scotland rise from 2 to 3 MPs
1912: National miners' strike costs record 40 million working days
1914: Labour movement splits over war; STUC backs Scottish parliament for first time
1915: STUC congress cancelled to limit splits over war; engineering and rent strikes on Clydeside; Keir Hardie dies; Munitions Minister Lloyd George jeered in Glasgow
1916: Clydeside socialist publications suppressed, and leaders jailed; conscription introduced; Lloyd George becomes Prime Minister
1917: Glasgow 'soviet' formed after Russian revolution; government takes over coal mines
1918: War ends; Robert Allan succeeds George Carson as STUC secretary; tension mounts over working hours

1919: George Square 'riot' brings jailing of leaders and government contingency plans to break strikes

1920: British Communist Party formed; government legislates for state of emergency

1921: STUC agrees sweeping reforms of its structures; miners' lock-out undermines Triple Alliance

1922: Red Clydesiders among victors in Labour's electoral breakthrough

1923: William Elger becomes STUC general secretary; STUC divided over affiliation of National Unemployed Workers' Movement

1924: Ramsay MacDonald forms first Labour government

1925: STUC survey reveals organisational disarray; government retreats from conflict with miners after threat of general strike

1926: General strike called – STUC cedes control of strike to TUC; STUC women's committee formed

1927: STUC opposes James Barr's home rule Bill, which fails; government outlaws 'political' strikes

1928: Mond–Turner talks usher in era of industrial co-operation

1929: Stock market crash brings depression; Labour wins general election; Scottish miners disaffiliate from STUC after split

1931: Ramsay MacDonald resigns, returning at head of Tory-dominated coalition; Labour decimated at election; Scottish Development Council set up

1932: STUC affiliations at lowest for a decade; ILP leaves Labour Party

1934: STUC founds weekend schools for women trade unionists

1935: STUC general council orders non-co-operation with broad left alliance

1936: Spanish Civil War creates fresh tensions in labour movement; STUC opposes rearmament; Scottish Economic Committee formed

1937: Bell Jobson first woman president of STUC; Scottish apprentices strike; STUC backs International Brigade in Spain, against labour movement policy

1938: STUC forms youth committee; joint Labour and Trades councils demerged

1939: STUC pledges support for war effort; new constraints imposed on trades councils

1940: STUC welcomes Churchill as PM; Scotland welcomes Munitions Minister Bevin

1941: STUC handbook restricts trades council associations; Scottish shop stewards accept joint production committees

1942: STUC affiliations top half million mark; Tom Johnston forms Scottish Industrial Council; Clydebank bombed

1944: Elger backs industrial conscription

1945: Peace brings first majority Labour government; SNP wins Motherwell by-election
1946: William Elger dies; Charles Murdoch succeeds
1947: Attlee and Cripps attend 50th STUC congress; coal industry nationalised
1948: Murdoch resigns, succeeded by George Middleton; National Covenant for home rule attracts 1.25 million signatures
1950: *Plan for Coal* published; STUC drops support for home rule; STUC begins outlawing Communist-backed groups
1951: Tories returned to power; Glasgow Trades Council disbanded
1952: Glasgow Trades Council wins court case over dissolution, but unions back new council
1954: STUC launches campaign for new steelworks at Motherwell
1955: *Scotland's Coal Plan* published; general election sees Tories take half Scottish seats
1956: Britain humiliated over Suez; Soviets invade Hungary
1958: Macmillan announces Ravenscraig investment, after intensive STUC lobbying
1959: Labour gains in Scotland fail to win election; Macmillan meets STUC general council
1960: STUC launches 'Jobs for Scotland' campaign; second meeting with Macmillan; STUC opposes Polaris base at Holy Loch
1961: BMC builds Bathgate car plant; Toothill Report changes regional policy thinking
1962: Scotland wins Corpach pulp mill investment; Scottish Development Department formed
1963: Rootes Group builds Linwood car plant; third STUC meeting with Macmillan; Beeching Report presages widespread rail closures; Jimmy Jack succeeds Middleton as STUC general secretary
1964: STUC meets Douglas-Home; Labour wins election; STUC congress backs nuclear-free Scotland
1965: STUC mauls George Brown over incomes policy; HIDB established
1966: STUC meets Wilson; Labour election triumph followed by wages squeeze; seamen strike
1967: Freeze earns Callaghan rough ride at STUC congress; Geddes Report on shipbuilding; pound devalued; SNP wins Hamilton by-election
1968: Donovan Report on industrial relations, Crowther (later Kilbrandon) Commission on constitution set up; STUC rediscovers home rule; Heath makes 'Declaration of Perth'
1969: STUC sets pace in union resistance to *In Place of Strife*
1970: Tories under Heath win general election
1971: UCS work-in; Industrial Relations Act

1972: Government backs down over UCS and miners; STUC convenes first 'Scottish Assembly'

1973: Second 'Scottish Assembly'; STUC backs Kilbrandon Report; STUC disaffiliates unions for registering under Industrial Relations Act

1974: Wilson returns to power, despite SNP upsurge; Wilson enlists STUC to help win over Scottish labour to devolution

1975: Wilson brings senior ministers to Glasgow to meet STUC; Scottish Development Agency set up; devolution White Paper disappoints STUC; Scottish Labour Party breaks away

1976: Wilson resigns; Social Contract starts to crumble under IMF deal

1977: Pay norm imposed; Scotland and Wales Bill founders; STUC affliations top 1 million members

1978: Scotland Act gains Royal Assent, but with referendum hurdle; collapse of pay policy sparks 'Winter of Discontent'

1979: Referendum fails to deliver devolution; Tories under Margaret Thatcher win general election

1980: Peak year for STUC affiliations; steel strike; Campaign for a Scottish Assembly launched

1981: Linwood car plant closes; Government retreats from confrontation with miners

1982: Political and sympathy strikes outlawed

1983: Len Murray unveils 'new realism' after Labour election disaster; STUC affiliations fall below 1 million

1984: Miners' strike starts; union ballots made compulsory

1985: Miners' strike ends; Gartcosh closes

1986: Jimmy Milne dies, and is succeeded by Campbell Christie; Standing Commission on the Scottish Economy set up

1987: Thatcher wins third term; Caterpillar closes; campaign to save Scottish coalfield launched

1988: STUC backs down from expelling electricians; Ford abandons Dundee project; poll tax campaign launched; STUC won over to European Union

1989: Standing Commission final report; Scottish Constitutional Convention launched

1990: Ravenscraig strip mill closes; Christie forced to renounce Guinness directorship; STUC 'Day for Scotland'

1992: Ravenscraig closes; Tories win fourth term

1993: Timex dispute

1994: General council blocks congress invitation to SNP leader

1995: Scottish Constitutional Convention launches devolution scheme

1996: Labour plan for two-question devolution referendum splits Convention partners

1997: STUC centenary congress, Glasgow

BIBLIOGRAPHY

The account in this book of events that took place within the STUC has been drawn largely from primary sources: minutes, reports, recollections, correspondence and STUC publications. But a principal objective has been to set the STUC story within the broader context of a century of Scottish and British history, and I have lent heavily on secondary sources for that context. I have also turned to other writers for additional or supplementary information on the STUC itself, particularly where they could offer a contemporary account of events unavailable in the memories of the living. Back files of newspapers were also a help in this regard. It was salutary to learn that editorialising is not the recent innovation we tend to imagine.

Sometimes, substantial information came from such sources. Sometimes I turned to them in simple despair at the enduring tradition among trade unionists, conceived solely to waste the chronicler's time, of using initials in preference to given names in official documents. Inevitably, some sources have been of greater help than others, and the following list of the books consulted makes no attempt to distinguish between them, for the good reason that I could think of no satisfactory way of doing it. What I can say, however, is that all the volumes listed below have been useful to some extent in the writing of this book, and that all are commended, with varying degrees of enthusiasm, to the student who wants to know more.

Allen, V. L., *The Militancy of British Miners* (Moor Press, 1981)
Allison, Jimmy with Conroy, Harry, *Guilty by Suspicion* (Argyll, 1995)
Arnot, R. Page, *A History of the Scottish Miners* (Allen & Unwin, 1955)
Arnot, R. Page, *The General Strike* (Labour Research Dept., 1926)
Ascherson, Neal, *Games with Shadows* (Radius, 1988)
Ashcroft, Brian and Love, James H., *Takeovers, Mergers and the Regional Economy* (EUP, 1993)

Bailey, Victor (ed.), *Forged in Fire – The History of the Fire Brigades Union* (Lawrence & Wishart, 1992)

Baldwin, Stanley, *This Torch of Freedom* (Hodder & Stoughton, 1935)

Benn, Tony, *Arguments for Democracy* (Jonathan Cape, 1981)

Benn, Tony, *Out of the Wilderness – Diaries 1963–67* (Hutchinson, 1987)

Blackstone, Tessa and Plowden, William, *Inside the Think Tank – Advising the Cabinet, 1971–1983* (William Heinemann, 1988)

Bowen, David, *Shaking the Iron Universe – British Industry in the 1980s* (Hodder & Stoughton, 1990)

Boyle, Stephen et al., *Scotland's Economy – Claiming the Future* (Verso/ STUC, 1989)

Breitenbach, Esther and Gordon, Eleanor (eds), *Out of Bounds: Women in Scottish Society 1800–1945* (Edinburgh University Press, 1992)

Broad, Lewis, *Sir Anthony Eden* (Panther, 1956)

Brown, Gordon (ed.), *The Red Paper on Scotland* (EUSPB, 1975)

Brown, Gordon and Cook, Robin (eds), *Scotland – The Real Divide* (Mainstream, 1983)

Buchan, Alasdair, *The Right to Work – The Story of the Upper Clyde Confrontation* (Calder & Boyars, 1972)

Campbell, John, *Lloyd George – The Goat in the Wilderness* (Jonathan Cape, 1977)

Carrington, Lord, *Reflect on Things Past* (Collins, 1985)

Charmley, John, *Chamberlain and the Lost Peace* (Hodder & Stoughton, 1989)

Clegg, H. A., *General Union in a Changing Society* (Blackwell, 1964)

Coates, Ken, *Work-ins, Sit-ins and Industrial Democracy* (Spokesman, 1981)

Cole, G. D. H., *An Introduction to Trade Unionism* (Allen & Unwin, 1955)

Cook, A. J., *The Nine Days* (Cooperative Printing Society, 1927)

Cooper, Duff, *Old Men Forget* (Rupert Hart-Davis, 1953)

Craig, F. W. S., *British Parliamentary Election Statistics 1918–1968* (Political Reference Publications, 1968)

Crick, Michael, *Scargill and the Miners* (Penguin, 1985)

Crosland, Susan, *Tony Crosland* (Jonathan Cape, 1982)

Diack, William, *History of the Trades Council and the Trade Union Movement in Aberdeen* (Aberdeen Trades Council, 1939)

Dickson, Tony (ed.), *Scottish Capitalism* (Lawrence & Wishart, 1980)

Dix, Bernard and Williams, Stephen, *Serving the Public – the History of NUPE* (Lawrence & Wishart, 1987)

Donnachie, Ian, Harvie, Christopher and Wood, Ian S. (eds), *Forward! – Labour Politics in Scotland 1888–1988* (Polygon, 1989)

Drucker, H. M., *Breakaway: The Scottish Labour Party* (EUSPB, 1977)

Drucker, H. M., et al., *The Scottish Government Yearbook* (various editions) (EUSPB, from 1976)

Duncan, Robert and McIvor, Arthur (eds), *Militant Workers – Labour and Class Conflict on the Clyde, 1900–1950* (John Donald, 1992)

Feather, Victor, *The Essence of Trade Unionism* (Bodley Head, 1963)

Flanders, Allan, *Trade Unions* (Hutchinson, 1952)

Foot, Michael, *Aneurin Bevan 1897–1945/1945–1960* (Davis-Poynter,

1973)

Foot, Michael, *Loyalists and Loners* (Collins, 1986)

Freeman, Alan, *The Benn Heresy* (Pluto Press, 1982)

Fyrth, Jim, *The Signal Was Spain* (Lawrence & Wishart, 1986)

Galbraith, John Kenneth, *A History of Economics* (Hamish Hamilton, 1987)

Gibb, Andrew, *Glasgow – The Making of a City* (Croom Helm, 1983)

Gilbert, Bentley, *David Lloyd George – a Political Life* (Batsford, 1992)

Gordon, Eleanor, *Women in the Labour Movement in Scotland 1850–1914* (Clarendon Press, 1992)

Grant, John, *Blood Brothers – The Division and Decline of Britain's Trade Unions* (Weidenfeld & Nicolson, 1992)

Hain, Peter, *Political Strikes* (Viking, 1986)

Haines, Joe, *The Politics of Power* (Jonathan Cape, 1977)

Halliday, Robert S., *The Disappearing Scottish Colliery* (Scottish Academic Press, 1991)

Hammond, Eric, *Maverick – The Life of a Union Rebel* (Weidenfeld & Nicolson, 1992)

Hargrave, Andrew, *Silicon Glen: Reality or Illusion* (Mainstream, 1985)

Harvie, Christopher, *Fool's Gold* (Hamish Hamilton, 1994)

Harvie, Christopher, *Scotland & Nationalism* (Allen & Unwin, 1977)

Hattersley, Roy, *Who Goes Home?* (Little, Brown, 1995)

Healey, Denis, *The Time of My Life* (Michael Joseph, 1989)

Howerd, Anthony (ed.), *The Crossman Diaries* (Condensed version, Magnum, 1979)

Hutchinson, George, *The Last Edwardian at No. 10* (Quartet, 1980)

Hyde, E. D., *Coal Mining in Scotland* (Scottish Mining Museum, 1987)

James, Robert Rhodes, *Bob Boothby: a Portrait* (Hodder & Stoughton, 1991)

Jenkins, Clive, *All Against the Collar – Struggles of a White-Collar Union Leader* (Methuen, 1990)

Jenkins, Peter, *Mrs Thatcher's Revolution* (Jonathan Cape, 1987)

Jenkins, Roy, *Mr Balfour's Poodle* (Heineman, 1954)

Johnston, Thomas, *Memories* (Collins, 1952)

Johnston, Thomas, *The History of the Working Classes in Scotland* (Unity, 1946)

Jones, Jack, *Union Man* (Collins, 1986)

Jones, Jack and Morris, Max, *A-Z of Trade Unionism and Industrial Relations* (Heinemann, 1982)

Keating, Michael and Bleiman, David, *Labour & Scottish Nationalism* (Macmillan, 1979)

Keegan, William, *Mr Lawson's Gamble* (Hodder & Stoughton, 1989)

Keegan, William, *Mrs Thatcher's Economic Experiment* (Allen Lane, 1984)

Kellas, James G., *The Scottish Political System* (Cambridge University Press, 1975)

Kennedy, Gavin (ed.), *The Radical Approach* (Palingenesis Press, 1976)

Knox, William, *James Maxton* (Manchester University Press, 1987)

Knox, William (ed.), *Scottish Labour Leaders 1918–1939* (Mainstream, 1984)

Kogan, David and Kogan, Maurice, *The Battle for the Labour Party* (Fontana, 1982)

Lawton, John, *1963, Five Hundred Days* (Hodder & Stoughton, 1992)

Lee, Jennie, *My Life with Nye* (Jonathan Cape, 1980)

Lenman, Bruce, *An Economic History of Modern Scotland 1660–1976* (Batsford, 1977)

Levy, Roger, *Scottish Nationalism at the Crossroads* (Scottish Academic Press, 1990)

Lewis, Jon E. (ed.), *The 20th Century* (Robinson, 1994)

Lewis, Roy (ed.), *Labour Law in Britain* (Basil Blackwell, 1986)

Linklater, Magnus and Denniston, Robin (eds), *Anatomy of Scotland* (Chambers, 1992)

Lloyd, John, *Understanding the Miners' Strike* (Fabian Society, 1985)

Lorenz, Andrew, *A Fighting Chance – The Revival and Future of British Manufacturing Industry* (Century Hutchinson, 1989)

McCormack, John, *Polmaise: The Fight for a Pit* (Index, 1989)

MacCormick, Neil (ed.), *The Scottish Debate* (OUP, 1970)

McCrone, Gavin, *Scotland's Economic Progress, 1951–1960* (Allen & Unwin, 1965)

McCrone, Gavin, *Scotland's Future – the Economics of Nationalism* (Blackwell, 1969)

MacDiarmid, Hugh, *The Company I've Kept* (Hutchinson, 1966)

MacDonald, Ramsay, *Wanderings & Excursions* (Jonathan Cape, 1925)

MacDougall, Ian, *A Catalogue of Some Labour Records in Scotland* (Scottish Labour History Society, 1978)

MacDougall, Ian (ed.), *Essays in Scottish Labour History* (John Donald, 1978)

MacDougall, Ian (ed.), *Labour in Scotland – A Pictorial History* (Mainstream, 1985)

MacDougall, Ian (ed.), *Militant Miners* (Polygon, 1981)

MacGregor, Ian, *The Enemies Within – The Story of the Miners' Strike 1984–5* (Collins, 1986)

McKay, Ron and Barr, Brian, *The Story of the Scottish Daily News* (Canongate, 1976)

McLean, Iain, *The Legend of Red Clydeside* (John Donald, 1983)

MacPhail, I. M. M., *The Clydebank Blitz* (Wm Hodge, 1974)

Magnusson, Magnus *et al.*, *The Glorious Privilege – The History of the Scotsman* (Nelson, 1967)

Marr, Andrew, *The Battle for Scotland* (Penguin, 1992)

Marwick, W. H., *A Short History of Labour in Scotland* (W & R Chambers, 1967)

Melvern, Linda, *The End of the Street* (Methuen, 1986)

Michie, Alistair and Hoggart, Simon, *The Pact – The Inside Story of the Lib–Lab Government, 1977–8* (Quartet, 1978)

Morgan, Kenneth O., *Labour People* (OUP, 1987)

Morris, Margaret, *The General Strike* (Pelican, 1976)

Muir, Ramsay, *Liberalism & Industry* (Constable, 1920)

Nettl, J. P., *The Soviet Achievement* (Thames & Hudson, 1967)

Newman, George, *Path to Maturity – NALGO 1965–1980* (Co-operative Press, 1982)

Oakley, C. A. (ed.), *Scottish Industry* (SCDI, 1953)

Peebles, Hugh B., *Warship Building in the Clyde* (John Donald, 1987)
Pottinger, George, *The Secretaries of State for Scotland, 1926–76* (Scottish Academic Press, 1979)
Powell, David, *The Power Game – The Struggle for Coal* (Duckworth, 1993)
Richardson, Ranald and Turok, Ivan, *Scotland for Sale?* (Strathclyde University, 1990)
Rose, Michael, *Industrial Behaviour* (Penguin, 1988)
Ross, Ian Simpson, *The Life of Adam Smith* (Oxford University Press, 1995)
Routledge, Paul, *Scargill – The Unauthorised Biography* (HarperCollins, 1993)
Sampson, Anthony, *Anatomy of Britain* (Hodder & Stoughton, 1962 & subsequent editions)
Samuel, Viscount, *Memoirs* (Cresset Press, 1945)
Saville, Richard (ed.), *The Economic Development of Modern Scotland* (John Donald, 1985)
Scott, John and Hughes, Michael, *The Anatomy of Scottish Capital* (Croom Helm, 1980)
Short, Edward, *Whip to Wilson* (Macdonald, 1989)
Skelley, Jeffrey (ed.), *1926 – The General Strike* (Lawrence & Wishart, 1976)
Skidelskey, Robert, *John Maynard Keynes – The Economist as Saviour, 1920–1937* (Macmillan, 1992)
Smillie, Robert, *My Life for Labour* (Mills & Boon, 1924)
Smith, Maurice, *Paper Lions, The Scottish Press and National Identity* (Polygon, 1994)
Smout, T. C., *A Century of the Scottish People 1830–1950* (Collins, 1986)
Steel, David, *Against Goliath* (Weidenfeld & Nicolson, 1989)
Steel, Tom, *Scotland's Story* (Collins, 1984)
Stewart, William, *J Keir Hardie – a Biography* (ILP, 1921)
Taylor, Robert, *The Future of the Trade Unions* (Deutsch, 1994)
Taylor, Robert, *Workers and the New Depression* (Macmillan, 1982)
Thomson, George Malcolm, *The Prime Ministers* (Secker & Warburg, 1980)
Tuckett, Angela, *The Scottish Carter* (Allen & Unwin, 1967)
Tuckett, Angela, *The Scottish Trades Union Congress – The First 80 Years, 1897–1977* (Mainstream, 1986)
Webb, Keith, *The Growth of Nationalism in Scotland* (Molendinar Press, 1977)
Wheen, Francis, *The Sixties* (Century, 1982)
Whitelaw, William, *The Whitelaw Memoirs* (Aurum, 1989)
Wilson, Derek, *The Astors* (Weidenfield & Nicolson, 1993)
Wilson, Harold, *Final Term – The Labour Government, 1974–76* (Weidenfeld & Nicolson, 1979)
Wilson, Harold, *The Governance of Britain* (Weidenfeld & Nicolson, 1976)
Wilson, Harold, *The Labour Government, 1964–70* (Pelican, 1974)
Woolfson, Charles and Foster, John, *Track Record – The Story of the Caterpillar Occupation* (Verso, 1988)
Young, Hugo, *One of Us* (Macmillan 1989)
Young, Hugo and Sloman, Anne, *The Thatcher Phenomenon* (BBC, 1986)

INDEX

INDEX